THE
CLERK'S
TALE

THE
CLERK'S
TALE

Young Men and Moral Life
in Nineteenth-Century America

Thomas Augst

The University of Chicago Press   Chicago and London

Thomas Augst is assistant professor of English at the University of Minnesota.

The University of Chicago Press, Chicago 60637
The University of Chicago Press, Ltd., London
© 2003 by The University of Chicago
All rights reserved. Published 2003
Printed in the United States of America
12 11 10 09 08 07 06 05 04 03   5 4 3 2 1

ISBN (cloth): 0-226-03219-1
ISBN (paper): 0-226-03220-5

Library of Congress Cataloging-in-Publication Data

Augst, Thomas.
    The clerk's tale : young men and moral life in nineteenth-century
America / Thomas Augst.
        p.   cm.
    Includes bibliographical references (p.) and index.
    ISBN 0-226-03219-1 (alk. paper) — ISBN 0-226-03220-5 (pbk. : alk.
    paper)
        1. Young men—United States—Social conditions—19th century.
    2. Young men—United States—Social life and customs—19th century.
    3. Young men—United States—Intellectual life—History—19th century.
    4. Self-culture—United States—History—19th century.   5. Literacy—
    Social aspects—United States—History—19th century.   6. United
    States—Social conditions—19th century.   7. Middle class—United
    States—History—19th century.   I. Title.
    HQ799.7 .A9   2003
    305.242′0973′09034—dc21

                                                                    2003007218

⊗ The paper used in this publication meets the minimum requirements of
the American National Standard for Information Sciences—Permanence of
Paper for Printed Library Materials, ANSI Z39.48-1992.

To my mother and father,
and to Muisi Krosi

Contents

Chapter Five   The Melancholy of White-Collar Work: Professional Ethos and the Modern Literary Sphere

Epilogue: Debris from the Business of Living

Illustrations

Acknowledgments

This book was made possible the remarkable staffs and collections of the American Antiquarian Society, the Massachusetts Historical Society, the New York Historical Society, the New York Public Library, and Winterthur Library. I thank Harold Augenbraum in particular for opening the doors of the New York Mercantile Library to me. I was able to undertake time-consuming study of manuscript diaries because of a Jacob Javits Fellowship from the United States Department of Education, a Charlotte Newcombe Fellowship from the Woodrow Wilson Foundation, and other support from Harvard University. The American Antiquarian Society and Winterthur Library provided me with short-term research fellowships. At the University of Minnesota, this book benefited from generous support of the Department of English and the College of Liberal Arts.

Many people helped me to write this book. Among my teachers and colleagues, I want first to thank Philip Fisher and David D. Hall for their encouragement and guidance since the inception of this project. I also thank Lawrence Buell, Tom Clayton, Robert Dawidoff, Amy Greenberg, Edward Griffen, Robert Gross, Jay Grossman, David Henkin, Amy Mae King, Trish Loughran, Bruce Mazlish, John McGreevy, Jeff Melnick, Joan Menefee, Daniel Miller, Rita Raley, Donald Ross, Jani Scandura, Donald Scott, Lyde Sizer, and Lynn Wardley for their assistance and support with various parts of this book. I am particularly grateful to Greg Jackson, Juliette Cherbulliez, Patricia Crain, Martin Roth, and Alexis McCrossen for their detailed, thoughtful engagement with the entire manuscript. In 2002, I presented chapters to the Southern California Americanist Group, the Early American Research Seminar at the University of California, Santa Barbara, and the Southern Minnesota Americanist Group, and I thank the members of these groups for their comments and challenging questions. I owe a special debt to Laura Davis, whose extraordinary research assistance and acute reading helped me to see more fully what this book was about.

At the University of Chicago Press, Douglas Mitchell provided endless enthusiasm for this project and shepherded it through the editorial process, and John Raymond and Claudia Rex carefully and patiently prepared the manuscript for publication. Early versions of parts of chapters 3 and 4 were published in (respectively) "Composing the Moral Senses: Emerson and the Politics of Character in Nineteenth-Century America," *Political Theory* 27, no. 1 (February 1999): 85–120; and "The Business of Reading in Nineteenth-Century America: The New York Mercantile Library," *American Quarterly* 50, no. 2 (June 1998): 267–305. I thank the anonymous readers at both journals and the University of Chicago Press for their excellent suggestions.

At crucial moments over the last several years, I was harbored or waylaid by many friends, including Bryan Reynolds, Hugh Kennedy, Jay Carney, John Morley, Jed Wyrick, Ross Munro, Dyan Solomon, Chi Long, Donald Weikert, Germán Esparza, Mathew Grant, Emily Rubin, John Petrini, Cal and Lewis. I especially thank Bettina Peters and Lee Woodyear, for helping me to escape the prisoner's dilemma some time ago, and Brian Walker, whose conversation and music continually renewed me in the otherwise quiet and solitary work of the scholar. For paying some of the cost of my solitude, I thank Christina Creveling, my brothers Paul and Alan, my sister Caryn, and other members of my family who accepted and, I hope, understood my physical absence. Most of all, I thank my parents Bertrand Augst and Jeanine Augst for teaching me by their example to value the intellectual life. Finally, I count myself very lucky that in both writing this book and learning to leave it, I have been humbled and sustained by the wisdom and grace of Muisi Krosi.

Introduction: The Moral Economy of Literacy

Charles French (1834–1904) was a clerk in a Boston dry goods store who, like so many young men, hoped to become a partner or open his own firm. One day in 1858, on the last page of a journal he was keeping, he wrote:

> The past is behind me, the future before, + with my past experience, I may perhaps hope that my future journals will contain more fortunate records, than those gone by. The past has been a statement of fact happening while I was a dependent. Shortly I expect to be able to chronicle the commencement of a life of Comparative Independence. May my motto be Trust in God, + Keep my Conscience Clear, and do my best to win.[1]

In anticipation of his twenty-first birthday, Charles French declares his independence by writing in a diary. With this simple gesture, he marked the threshold at which some boys in the mid-nineteenth century United States entered into their legal rights as citizens to vote, own property, and make contracts. His words represent as well a passage into adult freedom, the long-awaited moment when he would cease to be "dependent" on his family. Both senses of freedom suggest the continuing vitality of eighteenth-century political and moral philosophy, which linked civic ideals to gendered norms of autonomy. In the era of the American Revolution, "manly" and "manhood" denoted freedom from myriad forms of dependence, whether economic, social, or cultural, that would compromise the citizen's self-sufficient competence, his capacity to act on behalf of the public good. Likewise, the "comparative independence" that Charles French anticipated had to be earned by cultivating the moral virtues of manhood— industry, piety, temperance, and other traits that defined character in his time. As even his phrasing suggests, French seizes this moment as a rite of transformation, when he will cease to be a passive witness to a "past [that] has been a statement of fact" and become an agent and actor "able to chronicle the commencement of a life." To be free in this sense is to become the author of one's life, writing in a journal with "the future before."

Charles French's diary, which is stored at the Massachusetts Historical Society, is an artifact from the history of moral life—a history I seek to tell in this book. What did ideals such as independence entail for ordinary men entering the volatile world of business in nineteenth-century America? Why did so many young men like French write in diaries, as though this act might help them to succeed? My purpose is to explore the particular world in which young businessmen came of age in nineteenth-century America. I follow a few clerks as they moved, in the course of a day no less than a life, from the boardinghouse to the library, the lecture hall, the parlor, and the white-collar office. In these spaces they wrote in diaries, joined literary societies where they staged debates and delivered orations, and compared the styles of speakers in lyceums and churches. They wrote letters to distant family members, recited poetry in parlors, and sought out conversation with friends and strangers. They practiced penmanship and cultivated a taste for composition as writers, for fiction and nonfiction prose as readers. In these and many other ways, young men learned to pursue independence within a dense landscape of literacy, a habitus that knit together formal educational institutions, ethical training for respectable citizens and professionals, and informal habits of sociability both inside and outside the home. In a world in which basic literacy skills were becoming both standard and widespread, and where men and women alike were socialized into a mass print culture, how did the writing of diaries and other literary practices acquire social authority as what was ubiquitously described as the "capital of character"? How did clerks seek to make once-elite forms of literary culture compatible with the practical circumstances of business?

By exploring this landscape, this book has a second, less simple purpose: to interpret the meaning and form of moral life for an emerging middle class. The following chapters tell a few stories about the practice of moral life from the perspective of particular individuals as they confronted the ordinary business of living. These stories—what French calls his "chronicle"—have remained largely invisible because of the anonymity of the lives they concern and the obscurity of the handwritten manuscripts from which I have taken them. Unpublished diaries and other artifacts from the nineteenth century allow us to see how young men mapped their uncertain and anonymous world and created identities for themselves within it: as boys becoming men, as clerks becoming businessmen, as youths entering into domesticity. Through acts of reading, writing, and speaking, they committed themselves to values such as independence and sincerity, located themselves within the social spaces of family and work, and invested their free time in earnest programs of self-improvement. Through literary practices of character, young men navigated the boundaries between self and community, private and public, that even to our day shape middle-class identity. From several different perspectives on the literary world they inhabited, this book demonstrates how the moral ambitions of ordinary people were both fostered and frustrated at the onset of the modern era of American capitalism.

The world in which Charles French came of age in the three decades before the Civil War was very different from the world of his parents. Along with urbanization, population growth, and the transportation revolution, nationhood facilitated the expansion and articulation of commercial market relations; by 1860, the United States had become the second-largest industrial producer and the largest agricultural producer in the world. This expansion of capitalism in the nineteenth century resulted in the dissolution of traditional, "organic" forms of social organization represented by the ideal of the covenanted community. As rural communities became increasingly dependent on regional networks of trade, farmers produced cash crops for distant markets and commercial considerations replaced regard for kin in family members' decisions to move. With urbanization and industrialization, homes were separated from workplaces, and families were dispersed among a variety of jobs and economic roles. The master artisan's paternal regard for and intimacy with his apprentices gave way to wage relations and polarized class interests. The home decreased in significance as a site of economic production shared by women and men, becoming a "separate sphere" governed by domestic ideology where mothers raised smaller numbers of children. Towns and villages that were once informally bound together through face-to-face interaction and civic obligations were fragmented by social stratification and a new orientation to private life.[2] The experience of gender and class took new forms as work and leisure came to be organized primarily around an impersonal cash nexus of wage earners, employers, and consumers. The lives of ordinary people became more vulnerable to economic crises such as the depression of 1837.

For European observers such as Alexis de Tocqueville, what made American democracy so compelling was not only the historical novelty of its political institutions but the moral drama of rootless and restless young men becoming civilized while pursuing democratic freedoms in the midst of the "market revolution."[3] The young men and women who flooded into New York, Boston, Philadelphia, and other growing cities in antebellum America confronted social and psychological conditions that have been particularly associated with the emergence of liberal capitalism in the nineteenth century. "Market culture," Jean-Christophe Agnew argues, had "disruptive implications . . . for the cognitive and affective structures within which societies value their cultural goods," ushering in a "newly discovered protean social world" that blurred conventional signs of social and individual identity.[4] How did the expansion of personal autonomy in this world, the new possibilities for ordinary individuals to choose their fates in the free market, rebound to the collective good of society? In a world where "cash payment has become the sole nexus of man to man," as Thomas Carlyle lamented in the 1830s, where "all that is solid melts into air," as Karl Marx put it in the 1840s, young men increasingly looked beyond traditional moral norms and institutions for guidance in their values and conduct.

In nineteenth-century America, people talked about character in order to describe and respond to this crisis of moral authority. The term encompassed forms of self-representation and social identity, norms and conduct by which people recognize one another as sharing values such as independence. "Character" provided both a method for development of the self and a standard for social presentation. In the hundreds of conduct books published in the nineteenth century, character was most frequently linked to words such as citizenship, duty, democracy, work, building, conquest, honor, reputation, morals, manners, integrity, and "especially manhood," as historian Warren Susman has pointed out. Ralph Waldo Emerson's definition of character became a popular citation: "Moral order through the medium of individual nature."[5] As a glance at any of these how-to books will confirm, this moral order was understood in terms of middle-class Protestant virtues of hard work, self-control, internalized discipline, and "bourgeois" domesticity that modern scholars have associated with the development of liberal individualism and evangelical Christianity.[6] For nineteenth-century Americans to cultivate character meant mastering forms of self-control for which Victorian manhood has become notorious. As they took advantage of opportunities for social and geographic mobility, young men such as Charles French learned to assume new kinds of moral obligation for their own development. They identified these obligations with character: the duty to "self-culture" that William Ellery Channing described in his 1838 volume of lectures to young men, the duty to "self-reliance" that Emerson would promote in his own advice to young men.

On both sides of the Atlantic, liberal reformers responded to the profound changes wrought by the market revolution by locating moral authority in the individual's capacity for self-government. With the young people who were the intensive focus of their moral concern, ministers, educators, and parents developed a complex array of institutions that had as their primary end the cultivation of character. In the course of the century, the independence of young men became the central object of state-sponsored systems of compulsory education that taught increasingly standardized skills of reading and writing to an exploding population of school children. The new landscape included private and philanthropic institutions devoted to adult education: libraries such as the New York Mercantile Library, lyceums and lecture halls, and countless voluntary associations devoted to mutual aid and self-improvement. The private sphere also emerged as a crucial site for the cultivation of character, as mothers assumed new responsibility for early childhood education. Like the conduct books that flooded the book market throughout the nineteenth century, these new institutions of moral education instilled in future citizens what sociologist David Riesman described in 1961 as an "internal gyroscope"— a heightened sense of "inner-directed" obligations and internalized duties.[7] Especially among a Protestant middle class, this gyroscope enabled young adults to maintain a sense of moral equilibrium, direction, and gravity in the relative absence of compelled obedience.

The thousands of people who left rural communities to search for work in the bustling cities of antebellum America confronted the moral crisis of market culture every day, in practical struggles to realize character. With the expansion of political rights and economic opportunities that came with the market revolution, independence and other ideals of character became newly available to ordinary men like Charles French. Where eighteenth-century gentlemen had sought to claim moral status in public by subordinating private, material interests to the performance of civic duty, young men in the nineteenth century regarded economic life as the proving ground for moral distinction as members of the middle class.[8] The struggle for economic and social status in a competitive marketplace was the primary way in which ordinary young men sought the standing that had previously been identified with the hereditary prerogatives and civic duties of an aristocratic elite. The moral identity of manhood was something to be acquired *within* the marketplace, rather than apart from it in ascetic denial or aristocratic ease. In this sense, French's declaration evokes the myth of the self-made man that would be celebrated after the Civil War in autobiographies, success manuals, and the fiction of Horatio Alger, a myth that still has currency in the popular imagination. By the twentieth century, Americans increasingly found exemplars of character in the lives of businessmen, taking from their stories and homilies the wishful lesson that character was the only capital one needed to get ahead.[9]

From the broad perspective of history, we might say that Charles French's claim to independence replaces the classically inspired, humanist ideals of republican virtue with the bourgeois values of liberal individualism. "Virtue" in the nineteenth century became associated with privatized morality in the domestic sphere, and public life became an arena for the assertive pursuit of self-interest. Rather than addressing a public good, French's vow "to do my best to win" appears to be primarily concerned with success in business. Like his fellow clerks, he pays particular attention throughout his diary to the scale of his salary rather than the state of his soul, and makes economic mobility the specific measure of what it means to "win." Because his annual wage of $400 is stagnant while others receive raises, French suspects his employer is taking advantage of him. He dreams about going west and opening his own store. In these and many other ways, a clerk's claim to "comparative independence" seems motivated by the desire to extricate himself from the coils of wage slavery. Within this framework, morality assumes a casual, if not token, significance as a means to achieve self-sufficiency. French's vows to "trust in God" and "keep my conscience" are so casually aligned with worldly desire as to become a sort of mantra, a token "motto" that bolsters his self-confidence and hardens his resolve to conquer the field.

In this moment of a clerk's writing, we see a style of manhood for which Benjamin Franklin would become our most enduring model. In *The Protestant Ethic and the Spirit of Capitalism* (1903), Max Weber used Franklin as an exemplar of what he variously termed that "state of mind," "social ethic," and "philosophy of avarice" so typical of modern culture. "One need only reread" Franklin's *Autobiography,* Weber noted, to see how "the tremendous cosmos of the modern economic order" had transformed a spiritual ideal of vocation into a "worldly morality" of rational conduct.[10] With their equation of moral autonomy and the determination to "win" at the game of capitalism, French's words seem at first to illustrate a banality of moral imagination that Franklin bequeathed to generations of American men. In the United States, as Weber observed, "the field of its highest development . . . the pursuit of wealth, stripped of its religious and ethical meanings, tends to become associated with purely mundane passions, which often actually give it the character of sport."[11] The mundane passions and profane sport of ordinary people have been enduring sites of melancholy and critique in the modern academy, serving as exhibit one in the pathos of decline (secularization, the loss of community, and so forth) by which the social sciences have so often narrated the advent of "modernity." Since Weber, many scholars have often argued that concepts of self-culture and character were key terms in the formation of middle-class hegemony, lending moral justification to patterns of social inequality and acquisitive individualism.

From this perspective, antebellum clerks speak of independence from a script of ideology that has become all too familiar. Defining freedom as a game of competitive advantage, liberal individualism explains the inequities and pathologies produced by capitalist societies as wins or losses earned by individuals. Accordingly, when people invoked values such as "independence," it was to justify new kinds of social and economic behavior to themselves and to others. They sought to dignify the acquisition of wealth and the pursuit of social status as expressions of an intrinsic moral nature and individual exertions of character.[12] In this way, the competition for wealth and distinction becomes a measure of the man—of French's capacities for determination and prudence—rather than of his privileges and opportunities as a social type, a member of a particular class. Individualism indexed interior moral qualities to outward signs of social mobility, to winning and losing at the pitiless games of market culture.

There is much that is persuasive about this scenario, but I wish to reconsider its moral dimensions. However fully we describe ideas about character and the large social changes in which they were enmeshed, we have yet to understand how ordinary young men sought to practice a moral life for themselves, in the context of individual lives and choices. As historian Joyce Appleby has pointed out, our histories of American economic progress emphasize the dissolution of traditional forms of community but seldom encourage us to "wonder about the personal qualities and practical arrangements that made possible the fashioning of a new social order." How were young men equipped to "perform in a society of mobility, novelty, and individualized outcomes?"[13] The personal qualities and practical arrangements by which they did so not only contributed to what Appleby calls a "new cultural hero" for the entrepreneurial middle class—the self-made man—but a new sort of moral personality. The chapters that follow explore how young men entering business sought to "create a life" amid the social upheavals of the nineteenth century. My particular emphasis is less on the disruption of older patterns of community or the persistence and vitality of religious devotion than it is on the literary institutions, values, and practices with which members of an emerging middle class made the new world of modernity their own. When their real prospects in the "game" of urban capitalism were so dim, how did young clerks understand moral life? What form did autonomy take, given the complexity of the economic and social world in which they found themselves?

Different cultures invest tokens of adult maturity with symbolic importance, signs that separate men from boys: the age at which the law defines responsibility, religious rites of passage, or graduation from the age-graded course of study required by the state.[14] As Charles French's diary suggests, in the nineteenth century the initiation into manhood was accomplished partly through the simple act of writing. As French writes his declaration, his handwriting becomes large, as if testing his new independence with an assertive script: he commands its curves with fluid confidence, physically impressing a moral determination onto the page (fig. 1). To write with such

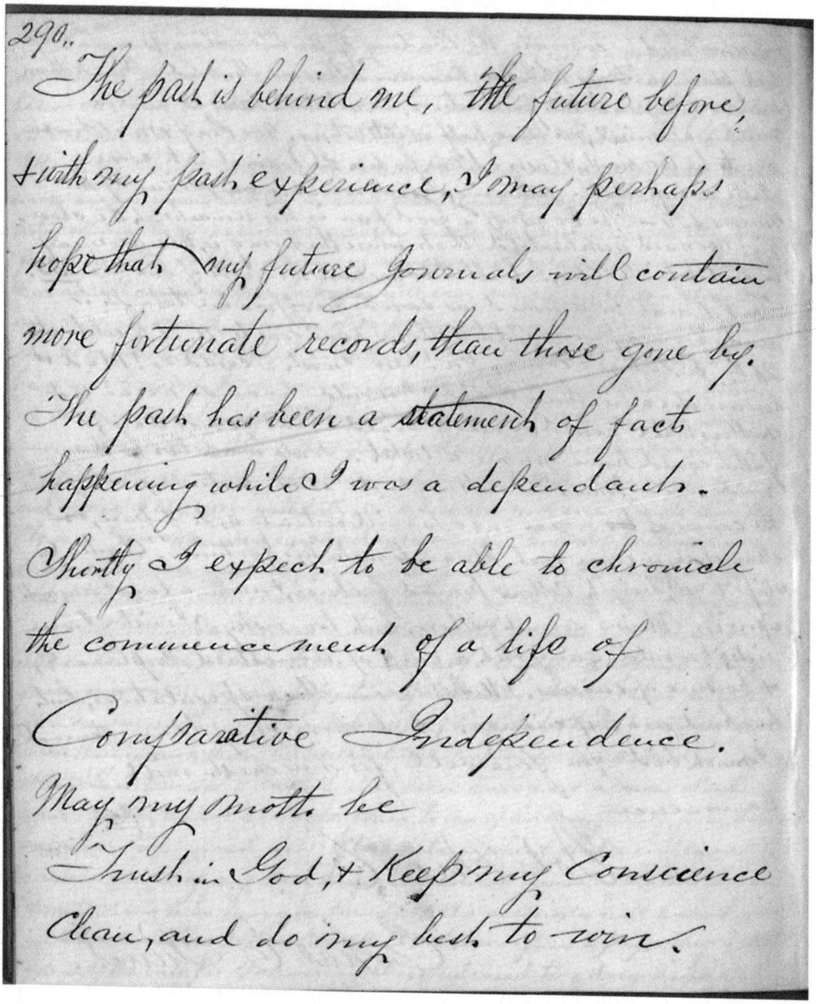

> 290.
>
> "The past is behind me, the future before, with my past experience, I may perhaps hope that my future Journals will contain more fortunate records, than those gone by. The past has been a statement of fact happening while I was a defendant. Shortly I expect to be able to chronicle the commencement of a life of Comparative Independence. May my motto be
>
> Trust in God, & Keep my Conscience Clean, and do my best to win.

Figure 1   Diary of Charles French, 1859, vol. 5, entry on page 290. As a clerk writes in his diary, civic ideals of political autonomy become personal traits: the confidence and self-assertion through which boys learn to claim their independence as men. Courtesy of the Massachusetts Historical Society.

apparent ease, with no ink spots or streaks to blur one's words, was learned only through arduous practice. Precisely because penmanship had not yet become a standardized, universal aspect of every child's early literacy training, a young man's "hand" in the mid-nineteenth century retains power as a moral gesture—an expression of one's difference from others, a means of claiming those qualities of character that distinguish men from boys.[15] Rather than expressing a unique or spontaneous individuality, a good script evinced character because it could only be acquired through self-control and rational habits. Any scholar who has spent months transcribing handwriting in manuscripts readily admires these hands now for the same reasons they were valued then—absolute consistency in lettering, even spacing of words, straightness of lines. One achieves freedom in the moral sense in the same way that one learns the difficult technical skill of penmanship, through a victory of the will over the vagaries of the body.

In its physical difficulty and ritual formality, writing in a diary was charged with both functional and symbolic importance as a rite of passage to moral maturity. In this sense, French's act of writing suggests how manhood continued to be defined by an ancient vocabulary of moral psychology. Aristotle's division of the self into higher faculties of reason and lower instincts or passions provided the basic foundation for seventeenth- and eighteenth-century faculty psychology, which through Locke, Watts, Hume, Hutcheson, and others would profoundly shape educational theory in modern Europe and America. Within this tradition, morality has always been identified with exercises of reason in which impulsive boys and weaker-willed women were thought to be deficient. In the late nineteenth century, William James continued to equate character with a gendered capacity for rational agency, as when he exclaimed in his "Talks to Teachers on Psychology" (1899): "There is no more contemptible type of human character than that of the nerveless sentimentalist and dreamer, who spends his life in a weltering sea of sensibility, but never does a concrete manly deed."[16] In French's declaration of independence, the act of writing becomes a "concrete manly deed," a resolve to make his future count for something besides "nerveless" dreaming, which James feminized as a "weltering sea of sensibility." Nineteenth-century Americans cultivated literary practices to give objective form to the moral will, to invest their autonomy as men in rational habits of literary practice.

The way that French claims his independence depends on his familiarity with the values of individualism that defined the meaning of character for a Protestant middle class. It depends as well, however, on his access to material objects and practices of literacy. Independence for French is not only an economic goal or political right but a self-conscious performance of will. With his command of a pen, French exercises habits of character that, for nineteenth-century Americans, defined manhood as a moral enterprise. Writing in a blank book enables him to rectify past mistakes, to trust in God, to form the determination to "win" on which his success and freedom as a man depends. With his cursive "hand" an ambitious clerk invests his diary with moral utility, the power to shape the outcome of one's struggles in the protean world of market culture. Through such gestures, young men vested writing with magical, if not mythical, powers of freedom. This clerk's diary, then, offers us historical evidence about how individuals used literacy to inscribe the moral will in their lives.

The diary of Charles French echoes another major lesson of Franklin's *Autobiography,* about the role of writing in self-creation. The story that Franklin told of his transformation from humble artisan to prominent citizen would become an important model for a secular tradition of autobiography that flourished throughout the nineteenth century. Like Franklin, the narratives of ex- or fugitive slaves such as Frederick Douglass dramatized the process of social formation as an assertion of literary authority: to be free is to write one's own story. Like Franklin and Douglass in their autobiographies, Charles French makes pen and paper tools of "advancement"; they are material and symbolic means of freeing himself from the accident of birth and asserting his identity as an individual. With their diaries, the young men in this book accounted for their personal experience as a kind of capital, a means of owning the self in a fluid social world. Through the act of writing, traits as ineffable as habits of thought, social graces, personal appearance, disposition, humor, and autonomy—or their lack—are transformed into means of self-possession, assets no less conducive to personal autonomy than the nickel and the loaf of bread with which the young Franklin first arrived on the streets of eighteenth-century Philadelphia. Although not rising to the personal triumph of emancipation—and certainly lacking the deep pathos of the slave narrative—the diaries of these young men are no less an act of an individual "writing himself into being," to borrow Henry Louis Gates's apt phrase.

Franklin's *Autobiography* would become a celebrated text in the canon of American literature as well as an archetypal story in the myth of American individualism. The diaries examined in this book, by contrast, record the mundane lives of ordinary young men who would not achieve lasting fame in the annals of American literature or history. The following chapters develop an alternative literary history, concerned not with the printed texts we now call literature but with how French and his peers used their modest skills as writers, speakers, and readers as they came of age in a market culture.[17] By situating these skills in the context of leisure and work, society and solitude, this book offers a historical perspective on how particular institutions and practices of mass literacy became integral to the moral aspirations and collective identity of ordinary people. And in doing so, it perhaps helps us to explain a species of moral utilitarianism that not only excused the vow to win made by Franklin and countless young men who followed his example, but made it the very mark of manhood. Precisely because the clerks in this book were not, like Ben Franklin, published authors, their diaries allow us to understand the democratization of literature—to see how the diffusion of literary authority in the nineteenth century became instrumental to the moral practice of everyday life.

As it follows young men through urban spaces of leisure, family, and work, this book develops two propositions about the practice of moral life. First, moral philosophy is not academic but rather a set of problems we face in striving to answer the question, "How should I live?"[18] To navigate the fluctuations of happiness requires mapping a topography of private and public, establishing values and boundaries that orient one's relations with others and with one's self. It requires that we learn to acquire those convictions on which the practice of moral life depends: convictions about the kinds of work for which we are suited, the kinds of social bonds to which we will commit ourselves, the kinds of stories we want to tell about our lives. Young aristocrats and elite members of the college-trained professions had for centuries sought to cultivate character through their exclusive education in classical languages, rhetoric, theology, and philosophy. Charles French and his peers gained access to the classical art of living in the nineteenth century as it became the object of mass media, universal education, and popular leisure. Their example suggests this book's second proposition: Ordinary people seek to answer the question of how to live by turning to cultural practices and objects available to them in a particular historical and social moment. No less than the ubiquitous quest for "self-help" in contemporary America, the antebellum devotion to "improvement" of character relied on knowledge that was increasingly available to mass audiences in the democratic marketplace. For even the most conventional and didactic insights, nineteenth-century organs of mass media such as the popular lecture, printed books, and periodicals and newspapers catered to a constituency of would-be citizens with unequal opportunities as readers and writers and unequal skills as moral philosophers.

The young men who populate this book cultivated character through forms of advanced literacy that became newly available to members of the middle class. Examining the primary ways in which clerks used diaries, chapter 1 suggests how mass literacy helped to both democratize and standardize ethical practices that for centuries had belonged largely to aristocratic elites. In Western philosophy, character has always represented a claim to moral distinction that depended on access to special forms of self-knowledge. In the nineteenth century, large numbers of ordinary young men used their diaries to analyze and interpret their lives as living ledgers. Making character a material object of rational management and temporal discipline, clerks were influenced both by older traditions of humanist education and Protestant piety and by newer values of liberal individualism. As they brought diaries along with them in their search for work, French and his peers made the common act of writing a ritual of ethical practice, a means of initiation into the "comparative independence" of manhood. As larger numbers of people picked up pens to account for their days, however, moral authority was personalized and individualized, loosened from the social roles and religious duties to which it had traditionally been tied. Like Franklin in his *Autobiography,* countless clerks acquired by writing a complex subjectivity suited to their social and geographic movement. In humble objects such as the diary, character became portable: an obligation to one's moral Other that idealized freedom as an exercise of self-making.

In beginning with the writing of lives, this book emphasizes the role *practices* played in the development of middle-class culture. In the increasingly common sites and rituals of mass literacy, ordinary people learned to make the business of living an individual exercise in literary taste. In chapter 2, I examine how young men came to organize their social and emotional lives around the literary skills they acquired at home and school. As young men came of age, they were socialized into forms of literacy that they shared with young women: the writing of journals and letters, the criticism of reading, conversation with friends and lovers. At each stage in their development to adulthood, young men acquired not only a technical facility that we commonly define as basic literacy but self-conscious habits of aesthetic taste—a literary sensibility that was formed under the discipline of teachers and parents, but was naturalized outside the classroom in linked contexts of leisure and sociability. Through the habitual exercise of literary taste, particular gender norms and social proprieties became what William James called "second nature" to middle class men and women. Shaped by sentimental conventions of intimacy, character became a domestic performance, increasingly identified with private feeling and less with public action, where manhood had traditionally acquired its moral standing. In the chapters that follow, I look at how moral life was transformed by new institutions and contexts of recreation and work.

In a culture preoccupied with business success, where did people look for moral guidance? As what one historian has called a "spokesman" for "an emerging middle class in the North," Ralph Waldo Emerson did as much as any intellectual to shape the way nineteenth-century Americans understood the challenges of market culture.[19] Chapter 3 considers Emerson's writing about character in the context of a particular venue of literary practice, the lecture hall, where Emerson achieved his greatest popularity among young men in his own time, and where spoken eloquence acquired its unique authority among his contemporaries. Seen within the ordinary contexts in which it was popularized for a middle-class audience, character encompassed a popular philosophy of moral life that defies many of the distinctions—between form and content, speech and print, production and consumption, aesthetics and utility—by which modern scholars and critics have typically defined literary value. Like other forms of reading and writing that became newly available in the nineteenth century, the lecture was a medium of spiritual exercise, a philosophical practice that potentially extended convictions about truth and the purpose of life to a mass democratic audience.

Although clerks typically had some formal education, they remained acutely aware of their exclusion from the social status and cultural privileges conferred by college education. A variety of philanthropic institutions sprang up in the nineteenth century that gave youth greater access to the liberal education that had previously been the preserve of aristocratic gentlemen. Chapter 4 looks at one of these institutions, a popular private subscription library that opened in New York City in 1820, in order to assess the ways that successive generations of clerks understood the uses of reading. Drawing on more than fifty years of annual reports that were compiled by its young directors, I demonstrate how the New York Mercantile Library Association managed its collection of books within an expanding marketplace of leisure. In the process of aggressively building its membership, the library promoted styles of learning and leisure that justified the moral value of reading fiction for young men entering business. The thousands of clerks who joined the Mercantile Library claimed a moral authority that prior to the nineteenth century had belonged primarily to learned professions such as the ministry and the law. As they turned to the mercantile libraries, lecture halls, and other institutions of urban culture, middle-class people increasingly sought character through "middlebrow" habits of recreation and consumption.[20]

The habits of character that young men learned during their leisure would be increasingly at odds with the forms that advanced literacy took in the white-collar workplace. Situating Herman Melville's well-known story, "Bartleby, the Scrivener" within the world of clerical work, chapter 5 examines the role that modern literary values came to play in the professional aspirations of middle-class men. Dramatizing the ethical dilemmas of managing a small law firm, Melville's story offers an important commentary about contests for moral authority that arose with a mass culture of print, and details some of the assumptions and strategies that guided the accounting of character in antebellum offices. When "Bartleby" is read in the lived context in which upwardly mobile young men staked their futures, it is, like the diaries of ordinary clerks, an artifact of historical changes in the economic value and social status of writing. Later in the nineteenth century, the penmanship that French and other clerks worked so hard to learn became the increasingly marginalized, manual work of scriveners and secretaries. At the same time, particular kinds of reading and writing were institutionalized in new hierarchies of educational achievement and specialized expertise. When seen together within a historical context of professional advancement, Melville's story, the diaries of clerks, and literary criticism in the twentieth-century academy demonstrate how the development of literature as an autonomous realm of aesthetic value altered the ways that middle-class men asserted moral responsibility. Within the increasingly specialized world of white-collar work, character became merely literary, divorced from the web of local knowledge and obligations that had governed a man's public identity.

This book follows a few clerks through the urban world of nineteenth-century America, then, to understand how individuals used literary practices to fashion a complex sense of self that was suited to the dislocations of modern capitalism. One might argue that there is nothing remarkable about the lives of the twenty or so clerks who inhabit the following pages. Why should we care about how these people saw their world and claimed a place for themselves within it? Some would eventually achieve modest success in business or other fields, while others would vanish more completely into the anonymity of history. At the time they wrote in their diaries, however, none of these men had good reasons to take their success for granted: with no large inheritance to look forward to, no plot of land to call their own, no college education to secure their status as gentlemen, they felt the weight of the future in their own hands. And yet it is the ordinary quality of these young men's lives that makes them significant. In the kind of work they did, for example, they were typical of increasing numbers of men in urban America who wished to be seen as working with their heads rather than their hands. The work subsumed under the title of "clerk" could include anything from running errands and taking stock to keeping books and answering correspondence. To be a clerk in nineteenth-century America was to occupy an amorphous, burgeoning category of white-collar work that became one of the urban vocations common among men of the middling ranks; indeed, after "farmer," "clerk" was the occupation most commonly listed on the rolls of passenger ships leaving for California from New York in the late 1840s.[21] In their free time, they became involved with widely shared leisure activities, using their skills with advanced literacy to shape norms of gender and class with which we continue to live.[22]

Over the course of the nineteenth century, millions of people in the United States would be socialized into forms of mass literacy that the clerks in this book helped to pioneer, and that in important ways continue to define social mobility in our own day. As instruction in basic literacy spread, literary taste acquired new kinds of value for economic and social advancement. In this sense, I do not use the term "literary" in its present disciplinary sense, to refer to a set of printed texts that, after years of schooling, students learn to interpret and appreciate according to particular norms of aesthetic or political taste. I use it to refer to forms of cultural capital, the display of which "entitles its possessor to the cultural and material rewards of the well-educated person," as John Guillory has noted.[23] To possess that "respectable" or "creditable" character valued by potential spouses and employers required that one cultivate a progressive facility for literacy inside and outside of school. It required that as an adult one exercise active critical judgment in multiple contexts of literary recreation, from the supposed privacy of the diary or the parlor to the public worlds of the library, lecture hall, and office. In the diaries they left behind, Charles French and his peers guide us to some of the sites where literature acquired its modern value as cultural capital—not only symbolic power in the competition for social status but functional power in shaping modern patterns of thought and feeling. Moving through the boardinghouse, the parlor, the school, the lecture hall, the library, and the office, the following chapters demonstrate how literary practices helped to effect the segregation and insulation from the rest of society that would become a distinguishing feature of middle-class identity.

The lives of these young men matter in part, then, because they represent larger historical trends in the standardization of moral knowledge and the spread of advanced literacy. But they are important for another reason as well, which remains in tension, if not at odds, with my efforts to place them in a social context: they are representative of the ways that people claim a moral standing for themselves as individuals, as having lives that matter. This book seeks to move our thinking about moral life toward practical techniques and material contexts of conduct—to pre-Enlightenment ethical traditions concerned with the social virtues—and away from the abstractions in which it has been mired since Kant. As a scholarly subject, moral inquiry has suffered from what Jean Bethke Elshtain calls an "overly grand tradition of political and ethical theorizing," which has prevented scholars from engaging with "the vitality and importance of everyday life."[24] It has been mystified by the social sciences because of such works as Max Weber's *The Protestant Ethic and the Spirit of Capitalism,* and gotten lost more generally in the specialization of knowledge in the modern university. Outside the academy as well, the dilemmas of moral practice have been obscured by myths of self-made men popularized by prophets of individualism and by generations of business gurus, from Samuel Smiles and Booker T. Washington to Dale Carnegie and Stephen Covey. Both modern social theories and the populist myths of liberal individualism have prevented us from seeing the means with which people give their own lives moral consequence. As the flourish of Charles French's pen only begins to suggest, young men gave the quotidian and ephemeral routines of everyday life aesthetic shape and direction.

In the diary, the home, the lecture hall, the library, and the office: in each of these spaces, young men cultivated character by learning to take a specifically literary interest in the moral value of their lives. The ease with which they did so, assuming happiness and independence to be tangible goods that they had the right and capacity to possess as their own, suggests how fully they benefited from the accident of their birth. They were not born into slavery, nor did they face the barriers and proscriptions imposed on women; they enjoyed economic and political rights that were still denied to most Americans. They entertained ambitions about their futures, as well as possibilities for geographical and social mobility, that only members of the Protestant middle class could take for granted in this particular way. Most importantly, they possessed skills in advanced literacy from which many people would remain excluded for decades. These skills enabled the emerging middle class to see its experiences as normative—as the seemingly ordinary expression of nature rather than the particular result of social and racial privilege. As they appropriated the sentimental language of democracy for their personal stories, young men such as French defined civic ideals as a matter of individual psychology and responsibility, an exercise in self-discipline and cultural ownership for which many of them thought they were uniquely qualified. By analyzing the material dimensions of literary practices in a very limited social milieu, I seek to demystify that larger process by which white manhood became the unmarked sign for seemingly universal moral values such as independence.[25]

It is these very differences, which set these clerks apart from most of their contemporaries, that makes their experiences particularly resonant for us now, at the beginning of the twenty-first century. Indeed, they have more in common with young adults in the modern high school or college than they shared with many of their contemporaries, and their experiences have become only more relevant to the ethical dilemmas and possibilities we all face in struggling to exercise our liberty. The people who first confronted the "protean social world" of market culture faced dilemmas of perception, value, and identity that have become endemic to the business of living in modern America.[26]

No less than for men and women coming of age today, nineteenth-century clerks gave their aspirations for freedom meaning in everyday life through practices of character. Freedom is a philosophical commitment realized by citizens in the lives they make for themselves, and not merely the product of the abstract rights conferred by laws and institutions. As Emerson declared in his essay "Fate," the Declaration of Independence is a mere "paper preamble" to the practical challenge of realizing a true freedom, which he and so many other nineteenth-century men and women understood as a specifically *moral* autonomy, exercised amid the social and economic conditions of modernity that would enslave us all. In trying to spell out the possibilities for emancipation in a democratic culture, Emerson sought to develop a philosophy suited to the needs of such a culture, a creed and ethos easily (if inadequately) summarized as "self reliance." This reliance on the self entails not a withdrawal from social commitments but rather a commitment to the "power every human being possesses in representing its next stage, its onwardness," as Stanley Cavell has described it.[27] As Cavell has noted in his meditations on Emerson and Thoreau, the project of self-realization that is at the heart of American philosophy proceeds in the absence of stable, hierarchical foundations of value. It is a philosophy of "the common, the low, the familiar, which is to say, among other things, of the here, in our poverty, rather than the there, in their pomp of emperors." How we constitute this onwardness, alone and together, is the primary dilemma for a democratic philosophy. It is not merely a spiritual dilemma for private conscience or a grand theme for scholarly theories, but a practical dilemma about how a society makes freedom tangible and meaningful in the lives of citizens. As Emerson says in his essay "Self-Reliance," "This one fact the world hates—the soul becomes."[28] But through what means, what exercises of freedom, does the soul become? I suggest that we understand "self-reliance," this power of realizing an ideal of one's self, as a drama of individual character.

We find democratic philosophy not in the paper preambles of our political liberties but in homely practices of self-founding. Our everyday lives take their onward shape from moral aspiration, in the values to which we commit ourselves, the choices we make about what it means to "win." However banal the results often look to others, we struggle to become authors of our lives, seeking to secure a space of freedom, to claim a moral authority that, prior to the twentieth century, was most often described as character. Throughout this book, ordinary young men practice self-reliance through diverse kinds of literary experience. Like Charles French's diary, the remnants of their experience make palpable the seeming poverty of moral life in America, its romance with egalitarianism, and its relentless materialism. It is to the poverty of such artifacts that this book looks with questions about the moral aspiration of everyday life. What gives a person's life worth when we account its value from the standpoint of the "the common, the low, the familiar"? What gives an ordinary life its moral interest and democratic dignity as a practice of individuality? Every diary begins from this poverty of condition: a person and a blank page before them.

Chapter One
Accounting for Character: Diaries and the Moral Practice of Everyday Life

The diaries that have ended up in archives frequently begin as travel journals, recording a first voyage from home in search of work. E. E. Belding memorialized his first trip away from home by writing a "Memorandum of journey to Buffalo and back" in 1834. He described the difficulty of the journey by carriage, noting that his fellow passengers were a mixture "of English Irish and New England, all very agreeable and sociable." After arriving in Buffalo on 21 May, he wrote on 24 May that there was "Nothing worth noticing this day only not finding business to suit us." On 25 May, he decided to return home because of a cholera epidemic in Cincinnati. Belding does not pick up his pen again until a year later, when he again ventured out into the world. There was "nothing worth noticing" in a young man's life, evidently, until he had left behind the predictable routines of childhood, broken away from defined roles and familiar comforts to face risk and uncertainty. Like Benjamin Franklin arriving in Philadelphia for the first time, Belding finds himself in a strange place with neither friends nor money to pave the way: "May 31 arrived at Troy this morning with but twenty cents left + don't know what to do nor where to lay my head yet I still trust in Divine Providence knowing that he will take care of me."[1] Like Charles French's declaration of "comparative independence," Belding's diary makes the very question of his fate the condition of hope—the preface to moral venture.

Young men entered the alien terrain of independence by writing in diaries. With their many arrivals and departures, nineteenth-century Americans had no simple standard for marking adulthood. "Full attainment of manhood," as Joseph Kett observes, might be tied to "the age of leaving home for the final time, the age of marriage or joining a church, or perhaps the age of entering a profession."[2] Prior to their legal emancipation at the age of twenty-one, young man would typically move through states of semi-dependence, leaving home several times for apprenticeships or to live with relatives, attending schools and academies seasonally. The first entries in the diary of Enos White (1803–ca. 1852) from 1821 record a struggle to leave his father's home in Weymouth, Massachusetts, to make a life for himself: "This Day I leave my Father after having got him to consent to my being Free. I leave in good spirits, although my prospects are very small, and the opinion of my friends is that I shall soon wish myself back again. I am now eighteen years and five months old with one decent suit of clothes and fifteen dollars in change to commence my career with." White's life as a man only begins, it seems, once he has secured his father's consent to "being free," and it is at that point when writing in a journal begins to matter—a gesture of defiance against the law of majority. In a second entry, from May 1821, he notes that he has moved back home. In the third entry, dated two years later on 24 March 1823, he declares: "I am now again free and 21 years of age."[3] In these long lapses between entries, we can perhaps imagine White's demoralization on reentering parental wardship, the frustration of his struggle to claim a life worthy of respect.

In the midst of the social and geographic displacements that increasingly defined manhood, young men used their diaries as totems and allies of moral aspiration. Take, for instance, the choice that William Hoffman (b. 1829) made about the kind of journal to keep. Beginning at the age of seventeen, Hoffman wrote from 1847 to 1850 in a heavy, leather-bound folio volume, some eight by twelve inches, with his name embossed on the cover. Obviously, this was not one of the "pocket diaries" that so many clerks carried casually as they went about their errands but a cumbersome physical object demanding its owner's solicitude. Hoffman carried this tome with him through the late 1840s as perhaps the most precious of his meager belongings as he moved by foot, carriage, and ferry from upstate New York to Albany to Manhattan in search of a retail post. For Hoffman, the record of a life—at least, the life to which he aspired—was worthy of a big, substantial book. For this reason, he had to leave it at his boardinghouse, writing in it only after he returned in the evenings, after working long hours as a clerk in various dry goods stores. Once back in his room, however, Hoffman found both the time and privacy he needed for writing to be in short supply. In 1849, while working in Albany, for example, Hoffman writes: "April 27 I do not know how much I did sell as I am so wearied when night comes & also my roommates are so sensitive on many things & especially on my sitting up after they have retired that I am obliged to defer writing till the lapse of several days: sometimes a whole week. Consequently do not get the occurrences of each day correctly registered." Why was it important for a clerk to "correctly register" the occurrences of each day, despite his exhaustion from work and the presence of sensitive roommates?

As these young men found jobs as clerks, working twelve to fourteen hours a day, independence became a matter of quotidian accounting, the struggle to find and value time apart from the pressures and exhaustion of making a living. Hoffman repeatedly expresses frustration about his failure to "register occurrences": "Monday Tuesday Wednesday & Thursday I have not time to note down the occurrences I do not have time."[4] The following year, when he was working in New York City, lost days had become months: "1850 March April May & June Here again I have neglected to record the proceedings of each day + as will be noticed have suspended such for quite a length of time."[5] Hoffman attributed these gaps in his diary to his own neglect, as though *having time* depended less on circumstances, which left very little room for self-reflection, than on his own perseverance: "I am recording the proceedings of the weeks as they have been neglected till this hour. The Boys are dozing on their beds etc."[6] As he stays up to write, Hoffman not only records the "proceedings of the weeks" but equates writing itself with moral responsibility. So it went for others: as clerks accounted for time in their diaries, they became accountable to themselves, blaming lapses of writing on their own "neglect" and perhaps judging other boys in the boardinghouse for their laziness or poor discipline.

Young men such as Hoffman, Belding, and White used their diaries to give their movements in market culture moral shape and direction. Across gaps of days, months, and years, each of these diaries tells a personal history, narrating a struggle for autonomy that was only fitfully achieved and impossible to take for granted. For Belding and White, writing was a ritual act that self-consciously transformed their separation from family, whether from necessity or inclination, into a rite of passage, a movement toward the elusive threshold of becoming responsible for one's self. In Hoffman's diary, this moral accounting becomes more perfunctory and particular, measured by a routine of daily observation performed with diligence or neglect. Individuals brought different degrees of intention and responsibility to the process of writing, and it is in a diary's particular use by young men where we find evidence of ethical practice. Whether someone writes in a diary at all, the sort of diary being used, the patterns of reflection staged within it, the conventions followed—these literary and material qualities testify to the ways that the act of writing inscribes an individual claim to moral distinction. In the silence of missed days, months, and years, these personal histories document the ephemeral process by which individuals acquire and regulate a moral consciousness about the meaning and drift of their choices. From self-conscious declarations of "comparative independence" to the record of months and years that have slipped away, young men sought in their diaries to make their tentative movements add up to something, to account for the value of their ordinary lives. Too often, as clerks became absorbed with the struggle of finding and keeping work, their diaries could seem like "nothing but an almanac," as one disappointed reader complained in 1810, recording the passing of time but not its value.[7]

When they are recovered from unpublished, fragmentary, and fragile papers stored in archives and libraries throughout the United States, these personal histories do not unfold as autobiographies typically do, from the certitude of age as a retrospective of one's life. Rather, they evolve in haphazard and tentative fashion, depending on the resources of time, education, inspiration, and energy that individuals were willing or able to devote to them. As a result, the literary content of diaries has often been minimized in comparison with the journals and life stories of more educated, expert, or historically prominent authors. Taken up with the banality of living—monotonous references to the weather, repetitive accounts of chores performed, spare notations of illness and death, and the like—diaries often submerge signs of individuality in the relentless tedium of everyday routines and unremarkable lives. It is precisely this "exhaustive, repetitious dailiness," as Laurel Thatcher Ulrich described the writing of the midwife Martha Ballard, that in recent decades has given the diary new importance as a window into micro-histories of ordinary people.[8] In the particular ways they accounted for their days, young men in the nineteenth century managed their personal transitions from agricultural to urban time, from farms to boardinghouses, and developed modern strategies of self-making that were distinct from eighteenth-century patterns of gender and identity.[9]

Rather than assessing the evidence that diaries seem to offer about a historical mentalité or worldview, or judging their quality as literary texts, this chapter analyzes the diary as a material artifact of moral life. It considers both the conventions of its form as they have been shaped by historical norms of ethical judgment and the singularity of its practice—as a performance of individual habits and motives. Every diary narrates an uneven and hesitant path of self-realization that, like Enos White's becoming "now again free," undergoes revision even as it aspires to coherence and wholeness. For this reason, we should value the diaries of ordinary people not for the way they resemble the finished, self-conscious achievement of literary texts but for the ways they remain ephemeral and incomplete, artifacts from the messy business of living. Every diary testifies to a material *process* of moral formation that takes place between individuals and the resources of literacy available to them in their social moment. In this sense, diaries dramatize the epistemological and narrative strategies by which ordinary people give form to their moral identities. Young men wrote to take an objective view of their own actions and motives, to make ethical judgments about the value of their perceptions, thoughts, and actions. As they compiled what Hoffman calls a "record" and Charles French calls a "chronicle" of events and observations, they also sought to compare and interpret their standing against a linear scale of progress spanning days, months, and years. In both of these ways, nineteenth-century clerks used their diaries like the faithful servants in the biblical parable of the talents, calculating the "interest" their lives accrue over time. As they did so, they wrote not in the confessional tones of modern privacy but with the omniscient clarity and formal detachment of a moral persona: "As will be noticed," Hoffman writes, as though his writing will be judged for its accuracy and quality. Treating their diaries as wise friends or companions, clerks entered a dialogue with their own future selves, the mature men who would look back on their younger selves for signs portending, justifying, or excusing what they had become. By writing in diaries, young men sought to acquire the moral authority that they hoped would follow from a judicious accounting of their lives.

In the duty to write and its neglect, we begin to see how character takes aesthetic form, in the ephemeral rhythms and quotidian rituals of literary practice. This chapter describes the longstanding relation between moral life and literacy, suggesting how the rhythms and rituals of ethical practice were shaped by secular and religious traditions of life-writing. Recording entries that ranged from the spare to the prolix, from meditations on the soul to inventories of the weather, young men sought to acquire knowledge about themselves and to govern their own conduct. They did so through daily repetitions of writing which, like the weather, gave their lives a temporal index that was at once spiritual and material—a constant reminder that life is comprised by a finite number of tomorrow, and tomorrow, and tomorrows. Just as Puritans sought to discern the design of providence in their meticulous records of daily life, so young men engaged in a moral accounting that, like fiscal accounting, had a general reckoning as its terminus. But as they used their diaries to navigate the alien climates of market culture, they attached moral value to the self as an end, accumulating experience as the capital out of which character is made.

Young men used their diaries to create moral identities for themselves in the context of ordinary life. Their writing was shaped by three distinct traditions of ethical practice: a classical tradition of humanist pedagogy, a Christian tradition of self-examination, and a utilitarian tradition of bookkeeping. Each of these traditions invested life writing with particular ethical functions, allowing individuals to achieve what the historian Michel Foucault termed "an intensity of relation with the self" concerned with the purpose and quality of one's life.[10] As they wrote in their diaries, young men drew in hybrid ways on the narrative and epistemological strategies of these moral traditions—strategies of memory, attention, and calculation—in order to cultivate character as a material object of rational habits and practical intention. I have exaggerated the separateness of these traditions in order to delineate the distinctive forms of moral accounting they made available to nineteenth-century Americans, and also to suggest a broad genealogy for the evolution of the diary as a site of ethical practice. These ethical frameworks supplied young men with rhythms and rituals of moral accounting, distinct ways of knowing and governing the self against a linear standard of progress. The values of humanist education, Protestant devotion, and liberal individualism all motivated young men to keep diaries. As this chapter demonstrates, however, young men in the nineteenth century drew on these values in competing and contradictory ways that located moral life not in obligations outside the self but in the temporal form and aesthetic shape of writing.

The expansion of literacy in the nineteenth century did more than create readers for books; it altered the very form of moral authority in a democratic culture. Within the objects and habits of mass literacy, the practices of character became more democratic and more personal. In the chronicles ordinary people made of their uncertain paths to freedom, moral life became both more interior and more individual, in ways that were better suited to social and geographic mobility in this protean world than religious duty and caste discipline. Although young middle-class men continued to look for guidance from Protestant piety and civic humanism, they altered their narratives and values as they brought diaries along with them into adulthood, into the boardinghouses and other temporary locations of market culture. The very looseness of these clerks' attachment to traditional motives of life writing—the diverse methods and moods that they brought to their personal histories—suggests how the nature and scale of ethical practice evolved with the expansion of liberal capitalism. Within the standardized objects and practices of mass literacy, young men acquired a consciousness of their own individuality.[11] By inscribing character in humble objects such as the diary, they increasingly identified social mobility and moral responsibility alike with material devotions of the will. As Hoffman's furtive record of his lost days suggests, character came to be rationalized as an obligation to the self, the duty owed to one's unrealized promise, to the blank slate of an unwritten future.

The Coin of Character

The concept of character, poised between descriptive accounts of human nature and normative ideals for the shaping of values and conduct, has always been identified with literacy. The word originally referred to the impress or stamp used in the minting of coins, where malleable material acquires its distinctive features. When John Locke used the term in *Essay Concerning Human Understanding* (1690), it still retained its association with the process of imprinting, writing, and engraving: "Let us suppose the mind to be, as we say, white paper void of characters."[12] Locke's theories of education and psychological development would develop the figurative implications of this metaphor. As the mind is shaped by experience, so too more generally would the "metal" of human nature acquire, through the impress of education, its distinctive type as the "coin" of character. This etymology of character may explain the repeated allusions to the printing process in Benjamin Franklin's *Autobiography* when he discusses the acquisition of "credit and character." Franklin describes various regrets as "errata," which, like the careless mistakes of a typesetter, deviate from the uniform and reproducible standard of the virtuous life. Like Locke's metaphor of the tabula rasa, Franklin's metaphor suggests that we understand character in normative terms, as a master text we seek to reproduce in our own lives, and against which we correct our errors and revise our habits. Like Locke's image of characters on paper, it also suggests how the modern psychology of introspection required a more discursive medium than the wax tablet Aristotle first used as an emblem for the imprinting of information on the mind.

With the revival of civic humanism and the development of romantic individualism, character acquired its modern importance as a term of moral distinction, referring less to a standardized type of nature than to a special sum of moral habits and qualities that singles out an individual for esteem and emulation. By the eighteenth and nineteenth centuries, character had come to mean "moral qualities strongly developed or strikingly displayed" (OED), those qualities that through some combination of heredity and influence marked a person as individual and unique.[13] In this sense, character became linked with the ancient rhetorical concept of *ethos,* which described a person's structure of motives, feelings, and thoughts that cause action and to which we impute moral responsibility.[14] It was in this sense that John Stuart Mill saw character as the very end of human liberty, the expression of one's moral autonomy as an individual: "A person whose desires and impulses are his own—are the expression of his own nature, as it has been developed and modified by his own culture, is said to have a character," Mill wrote in *On Liberty* (1859). "One whose desires and impulses are not his own, has no character, no more than a steam-engine has a character."[15] For Mill and other liberal thinkers in the nineteenth century, character represented an achievement of individuality, a moral standing that the inhuman world of industrial capitalism, symbolized by the steam engine, seemed to undermine.[16]

The power to actively shape and perfect one's nature as an individual—to have desires and impulses that are one's "own," as Mill puts it—has always been the practical goal of liberal humanist education in the West. In this tradition, individuals acquire a character through active development of the rational and moral faculties, in becoming capable of knowing and governing their own conduct. Rooted in the natural law tradition of Aristotle, liberal or humane education prepared young men for their future lives as citizens by making an "ideal wholeness of the individual" a practical object of comprehensive training in self-government. As an outgrowth of Hellenic cosmology, the purpose of liberal education has always been "to form a character or type, all of whose parts are in harmonious agreement, no one part of the character (or personality) being overdeveloped at the expense of another."[17] Liberal education equipped elite males in early modern Europe with secular arts of "self-fashioning," giving them access to what Stephen Greenblatt has termed "a distinctive personality, a characteristic address to the world, a consistent mode of perceiving and behaving."[18] Motivated by ends that were at once spiritual and material, their acquisition of character claimed moral authority through the educational privileges of gender and class.

The power to control one's identity has been a source of moral distinction, *of one's difference as an individual,* because it has always circulated in hierarchical economies of cultural capital—exercised through practical skills of speaking, writing, and reading that most people did not possess. As a schoolboy, for instance, George Washington wrote into one of his composition books a series of maxims under the heading, "Rules of Civility & Decent Behavior in Company and Conversation." By so doing, he practiced the obligations that came with his inherited social position. The rules resemble the didactic precepts by which educators since Plutarch linked civic education to refinement, preparing gentlemen's sons for their future duties by training them to be "virtuous, useful, and able in their distinct callings," as Locke would put it in his popular conduct book, *Some Thoughts Concerning Education* (1693).[19] As Jared Sparks described the rules in his *Life of George Washington* (1844), "Some of these are unimportant, suited only to form the habits of a child; others are of a higher import, fitted to soften and polish the manners, to keep alive the best affections of the heart, to teach what is due to others in social relations, and above all to inculcate the practice of a perfect self-control." This lay catechism had its origin in a treatise written by a French Jesuit in 1595, which over the seventeenth century appeared in print in Latin, Spanish, French, Bohemian, and several English editions.[20] As he copied these maxims by hand, the young Washington learned to identify the cultivation of character not only with the cosmopolitan values that circulated in aristocratic circles in Europe and the

American colonies but also with progressive training in advanced literacy. From rules of bodily deportment and polite conduct practiced by children, to readings of rhetoric and philosophy and mastery of ancient languages in the classical curriculum of the academy or the eighteenth-century college, this training fostered among elite men such as Washington "acceptance of personal autonomy, the deliberate construction of a personal identity, and the pursuit of a balanced character."[21] Through privileged access to advanced literacy, Washington accumulated moral knowledge and habits of civility that would make him a favorite exemplar of character in the nineteenth century.

Identified with the restricted practices of advanced literacy, the liberal humanist ethos of character throughout the early modern period remained—like the privileges of citizenship to which it was tied—largely the province of gentlemen. At the same time, developments in religious education and culture that began with the Protestant Reformation helped to institutionalize a more egalitarian relationship between literacy and moral authority. Training in self-government was extended to new populations that were previously unaccustomed to it. As a consequence, new sources of moral authority emerged that furnished modern identity with a distinctive sense of interiority.[22] The most important was a "caste discipline" of Christian pastoral guidance devoted to "the self-realizing personality," as Ian Hunter puts it. As Hunter has argued, the first public school systems in Europe were established by the churches as "instruments for the intensification and dissemination of Christian spiritual discipline and pastoral guidance." Post-Reformation Protestantism and Catholicism brought about the reform of popular culture by which large sectors of the European population acquired "capacities required for individuals to comport themselves as self-reflective and self-governing persons." *In The Protestant Ethic and the Spirit of Capitalism,* for example, Max Weber described early modern Protestantism as a massive campaign in spiritual training, which transferred ethical disciplines from the priesthood to the lay population. As distinctive literary genres of this period such as spiritual autobiography demonstrate, this ethical labor consisted primarily of "practices of self-watchfulness and self-control, special forms of devotional reading and writing," through which the faithful monitored their ethical standing and became personally responsible for their salvation.[23] The Christian pedagogy that twentieth-century critics have so often dismissed as religious brainwashing contributed, Hunter argues, to the "organizing routines, pedagogical practices, personal disciplines, and interpersonal relationships that came to form the core of the modern school" under the secular systems of mass education in the liberal state.[24]

With the expansion of citizenship and schooling in the nineteenth century, once elite forms of moral authority became available to ordinary people. On both sides of the Atlantic, reformers and educators drew on the pedagogical traditions of civic humanism and evangelical Protestantism to make arguments about the qualities that were requisite to the citizens of a modern democratic state. Like John Stuart Mill, they idealized the self-realizing moral personality, or character, as the purpose of education, and increasingly viewed institutions of secular "culture" as vital foundations to the expansion of liberal democracy and market capitalism.[25] In this regard, Stefan Collini has noticed that the idea of character became central to Anglo-Victorian politics during the debates over the franchise. Discussion of the Second Reform Bill in Britain in 1867 was not focused on a working man's rights but on whether his moral qualities allowed him to be trusted with the vote.[26] Similarly, the prevalence of the concept of character in nineteenth-century America should be seen as a consequence of the expansion of citizenship. Although it does not discuss the vote, for example, William Alcott's *Young Man's Guide* (1833; revised 1849) includes a copy of the United States Constitution in an appendix as though to consummate the book's purpose of "forming the character of young men." Alcott, the first cousin of another educational reformer, Bronson Alcott, invests the "weighty responsibilities" of character with a patriotic appeal to his young readers: "It is for you to decide whether this greatest of free nations shall, at the same time, be the best."[27] In seeking to win support for state-supported common schools, Horace Mann also argued that nothing was more crucial to the fate of the republic than educating the moral character of its future citizens, which the new state-supported common schools would take as their primary mission.[28]

With the expansion of education in the liberal state, character was democratized in the objects and practices of mass literacy. One of the best-selling commodities in the nineteenth-century publishing trade was the blank book. Throughout the early modern period, printers had made blank books, ledgers, and legal and business forms a staple in their inventory, counting on steady sales year after year. A profound consequence of the industrial revolution that, in the nineteenth century, helped to transform printed books into mass-market commodities was that paper became cheaper and writing implements more convenient to use. As a result, diaries acquired prominence as a consumer item. In an 1855 broadside, the New York firm of Kiggins & Kellogg announced the publication of diaries in eleven different sizes, ranging from small 2.5 × 5-inch Pocket Diaries to large octavo volume Daily Journals as well as a Counting House Diary and Workmen's and Employers' Time Books (fig. 2). As many such advertisements of printers and booksellers reveal, diaries occupied a broad spectrum

KIGGINS & KELLOGG,

PUBLISHERS, BOOKSELLERS, & BLANK BOOK MANUFACTURERS,

88 JOHN STREET, N.Y.

HAVING JUST PUBLISHED THEIR SERIES OF

DIARIES FOR 1855,

Comprising ELEVEN DIFFERENT SIZES, each in various styles of binding, would invite an examination of them by the Trade, before making their orders for others, feeling well assured that when seen, they will receive the preference over all others published. One peculiar feature possessed by our Diaries, which will, we think, be a strong recommendation to the user, is their having twelve pages devoted to "Cash Account," (one page to each month) one page for "Annual Summary of Cash Account," and twelve pages (one for each month) for "Bills Payable and Receivable," thus combining with a Diary, a Cash and Bill Book.

The following description will, to some extent, indicate their peculiar merits :

Pocket Diary.—Cap 18mo. Containing almanac, calendar, time table, a blank space for every day in the year, memorandum, cash account for each month, and annual summary of cash account. Tuck, gilt edge.

Pocket Diary for 1855.—Cap 12mo. Containing almanac, calendar, time table, list of Sundays, population of the United States, population of the principal cities and towns in the United States, present rate of postage, legal Interest laws in the different States, distance from New-York to the principal places in the United States, Presidents of the United States, a blank space for every day in the year, memorandum, cash account for each month, annual summary of cash account, and bills payable and receivable for each month. Tuck, gilt and plain edge, and cloth.

Pocket Diary for 1855.—Cap 8vo. Containing calendar, time table, a blank space for every day in the year, memorandum, cash account, annual summary of cash account, and bills payable and receivable. Gilt and plain edge. Tuck and cloth.

Pocket Diary for 1855.—Cap 8vo. long. Containing the same as the next preceding. Gilt and plain. Tuck and Cloth.

On all the above Diaries there are three days to a page.

Pocket Diary for 1855.—Cap 18mo. *One day to a page.* Containing almanac, banking table, counting-house calendar, and a blank page for every day in the year. Tuck, gilt edge.

Pocket Diary for 1855.—Cap 12mo. *One day to a page.* Containing the same as the above. Tuck, gilt edge.

Pocket Diary for 1855.—Cap 8vo. *One day to a page.* Contents and Binding the same as the preceding.

Daily Journal for 1855.—Demy 4to, half-bound. Containing calendar, time table, a blank space for every day in the year. *Two days to a page.*

Counting House Diary for 1855.—Long Cap 4to. Half-bound, paper and cloth sides.

Daily Journal for 1855.—Square cap 4to. " " " "

Daily Journal for 1855.—Cap folio. " " " "

Three days to a page, containing in addition, 12 pages for Cash Account and Bills payable and receivable.

THEY WOULD ALSO INVITE ATTENTION TO THEIR LARGE STOCK OF

Workmen's Pocket Time Book.—Crown 8vo. Weekly and Monthly. Three sheets and seven sheets. Full and Half-bound.

Employer's Time Book.—Cap folio. Weekly and Monthly. Twelve, eighteen, and twenty-four sheets.

Books of Blank Notes, Drafts, Shipping Receipts, and Bills of Lading.

Bill Books, payable and receivable, various sizes and different bindings.

EVERY DESCRIPTION OF

𝔄ccount 𝔅ooks, 𝔐emorandums, 𝔓ass 𝔅ooks, 𝔖crap 𝔅ooks, 𝔥erbariums, &c.

A Liberal Discount made to the Trade.

JULY 1, 1854.

Figure 2 Broadside, Kiggins and Kellogg Stationers, 1855. In the nineteenth century, blank books became diverse and abundant commodities in the mass market for printed goods. Courtesy of the American Antiquarian Society.

of paper goods. They were sold as expensive objects of fashion that appealed to the discriminating eye of the genteel classes, to people conditioned by best-selling sentimental fiction to the romantic cultivation of individual feeling. They were also sold as functional objects of commerce and education: diaries "in eleven different sizes," memorandums and "daily journals," or the cheap composition books used in the classroom for reading and writing drills by an expanding population of school children.

What is most striking about the nineteenth-century diaries that survive in libraries and archives is not their uniformity as a genre of consumer good but the diversity of their physical nature and uses. In the front of The Merchants' Desk Diary ("A great aid to a slippery memory, and a shield against forgetfulness") the stationer Henry Anstince reminds readers of Locke's commonplace that "a daily notebook, well kept, was a good evidence of a correct man of business."[29] It further notes that "a Record at the time of transaction is safer as a reference, than the best memory," and that "a good memory, like a good servant, should not be over-taxed because of its faithfulness." The writing in all diaries is pulled in two directions, between regularity and consistency and a more detailed, and complete, record that might "overtax" the space of reference. In meeting these competing aims, clerks could purchase small volumes that accompanied them on their various movements during the day. Or they might purchase diaries designed for one, two, or three "days to a page." These books were often ruled and sized in ways that encouraged writers to treat their experiences as brief "transactions," precluding any but the briefest of notations (fig. 3). James Cunningham (1825–1891), for instance, who had just opened a dry goods store with another merchant, writes for 27 September 1849: "Warm day—at business all day, introduced to several more merchants, assisting Father, + c [etc.]. Evening went to hear Christy's minstrels very much entertained—hard rain in the night."[30] Especially in stationary identified with white-collar work, diaries promoted brevity and efficiency as traits of a "correct man of business" or "Professional Men."[31] With their pages ruled and dated for brief entries, memorandum books and pocket diaries made the record of a life more strictly regular, a ledger of activity ruled by the epistemological values and writing practices of bookkeeping. They also made the process of self-accounting perfunctory, potentially indifferent to the ethical motives that, as we shall see, had motivated the writing of diaries for hundreds of years.

The ubiquity of the diary as a consumer object and the diversity of its uses each attest to the new centrality that the habit of writing came to have in the lives of ordinary people. Before the nineteenth century, relatively few people learned to write, and when they did it was typically years after they had learned to read. Young men who went on to write did so as a requirement

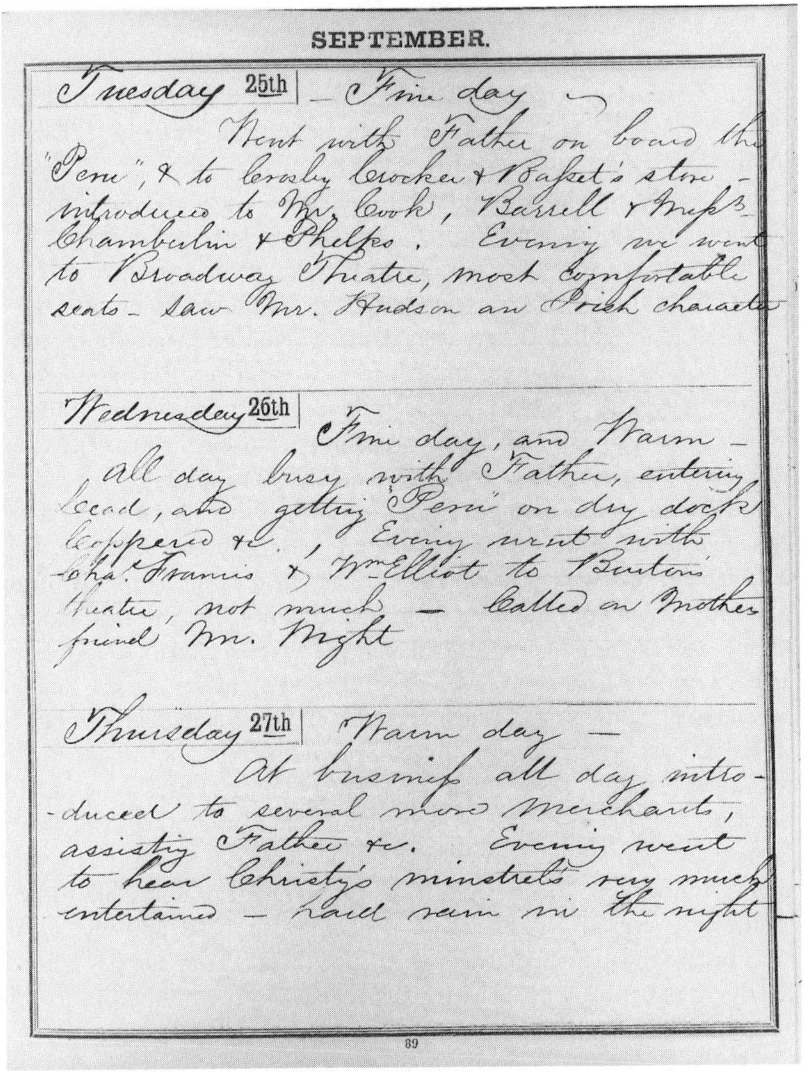

Figure 3   Diary of James Cunningham, 1849. Formats such as three-days-to-a-page enforced habits of regularity and brevity among writers. Courtesy of the American Antiquarian Society.

of their vocations in the clergy, medicine, or the law, and especially business, which, with its daybooks, ledgers, invoices, bills of lading, receipts, and correspondence, was particularly identified with penmanship. As Thomas Watts declared in 1716, "writing is the *First* step, and *Essential* in furnishing out the Man of Business." Until the late nineteenth century, clerks still saw a good hand as essential to success in business.[32] Clerks learned penmanship because it was a virtual prerequisite for a career in business. As we shall see in chapter 5, only in the late nineteenth century, with the invention of the typewriter, the avalanche of specialized printed forms, and the entrance of women into secretarial positions would penmanship cease to have this symbolic importance for men entering business. The variety of "hands" in young men's diaries testifies to the fact that writing with a pen is always a technical skill acquired with difficulty. As the sheer quantity of nineteenth-century letters, journals, and diaries also suggests, however, writing ceased to be taught as a specialized, advanced form of literacy and gradually became part of the standardized, graded curriculum of the common school.

In the nineteenth century, even modestly educated young men cultivated character in the diary and other sites of literacy. In the northern United States they were likely to learn reading and writing in the home, Sunday schools, common schools, academies, and for the privileged few, colleges. Young men not only mastered the skill of penmanship but also inherited a set of values, narratives, and conventions that allowed them to invest their practices of reading and writing with moral consequence. Our engagement with texts of all kinds is mediated by the expectations we bring to them, within educational and spiritual traditions that furnish us with what Larzer Ziff terms "pretexts" for literacy.[33] In taking up these ephemeral artifacts, my concern lies not with the prescriptive and normative quality of moral instruction that clerks such as Hoffman, White, and Belding received through mass education: the didactic program drilled into children by McGuffey Readers, for example, or the new kinds of psychological and physical discipline enforced by the common school and other institutions. Rather, I wish to explore how ordinary individuals understood and pursued moral authority for themselves by self-consciously imagining life to be a tabula rasa, by inscribing character in the empty pages of their diaries. Character became an incremental and schematic process of self-analysis, a material object of writing for which a man was personally responsible, inexorably accountable.

Middle-class clerks in antebellum America did not write diaries because they expected to become famous, or because they thought they would be remembered by the world after they were gone. They wrote diaries to exercise some control over the uncertain and changing world in which they found themselves. In doing so, they benefited from means of advanced literacy that had long identified moral authority with exclusive and hierarchical forms of cultural capital: the blank book; pen and ink; the facility with penmanship; the space and time to write; habits of reading and writing; and elite forms of moral knowledge and ethical practice concerned with correction, self-examination, and civility. Prior to the nineteenth century, a small number of highly educated men cultivated this capital of character in the service of duties incumbent to their social position. How was the meaning of character transformed in liberal democratic culture, as it became identified with habits of mass literacy? What consequences did quotidian objects such as the diary have for how young men shaped their lives as stories, for how they understood and pursued a moral life amid the pressing demands of the ordinary and the everyday?

Memory and the Commonplace Tradition

No pretext was more fundamental to literary practices of character in the nineteenth century than the humanist ideal of education described in ancient Greece as *paidea,* and in Alexander von Humboldt's Germany as *bildung:* the perfecting of human nature through active development of the rational faculties and moral virtues. In some of his last works, Michel Foucault explored an ancient humanist tradition of ethical practice he termed "the care of the self."[34] In this tradition, individuals used acts of reading, writing, and speaking as what Foucault termed "technologies of self," to alter their thoughts or conduct to achieve some particular idealized version of the self, such as wisdom, happiness, or purity. As with the Apollonian injunction to "know thyself," these technologies allowed students of liberal education to enter a self-conscious relationship to their own actions and desires, to cultivate a moral Other as a functional object of rational habits and practical intentions. To the extent its tools and institutions remained the exclusive property of the ruling class, humanist ethics was, as one critic points out, "a means of self-empowerment and of exercising responsible power over others," a caste system of moral authority in which "your superiors were your moral betters."[35]

The diary is a technology of the self that has an ancient genealogy in Western culture. "One of the main features of taking care of the self," Foucault observed, "involved taking notes on one's self to be reread, writing treatises and letters to friends to help them, and keeping notebooks to reactivate for oneself the truths one needed."[36] These ancient notebooks, the Greek *hupomnemata,* were scrapbooks for daily meditation that were compiled by the individual to constitute the self as an ethical subject. The ancient cultivation of self demanded active and diligent habits of attention, because, as Plutarch observed, the individual could be oblivious to his own moral disorders, or diseases of the soul, or mistake these vices for virtues— taking anger for courage, envy for emulation, cowardice for prudence.[37] Ethical tools such as the hupomnemata enabled students to bring habits of rational attention to their own thoughts and actions. These practices allowed them to step back from the experience that had absorbed them and to analyze it with a calm, objective detachment. For this reason, the ancient care of the self, as Foucault suggests, is most accurately captured in the image of the watchman, following Epictetus, or the administrator, following Seneca, rather than in the modern image of the psychoanalyst. Serving as a reminder, or reproof, for the "activation" of truths, these notebooks helped students to cultivate a capacity for self-government, imparting consistency to the mind and focusing attention on actions and motives. As another scholar has noted, the hupomnemata were "precisely *not* constitutive of individual identity" in its modern sense, but rather collectively authored bits of wisdom meant to guide one's conduct and self-management. They were one of a variety of "ethical techniques designed to build up virtue . . . through the slow accumulation of habit."[38]

In classical humanist pedagogy, the hupomnemata became codified in the genre of the commonplace book, which formalized the habits of controlling one's thoughts as a rationalized system for memory. Aristotle and Quintilian advised students to collect excerpts from their reading and study and to organize them under subject headings. These notebooks were often described as a portable form of memory, allowing students to efficiently store maxims and arguments from commendable authors. Students used the subject headings in these books as loci, or places where "common," accepted knowledge might be located for easy "recall" when students came to develop their arguments in speech and writing. In this way, commonplace books functioned as repositories from which one could draw evidence and examples of style, as primary resources for developing one's facility with the elements of classical rhetoric known as invention or discovery. The value of the knowledge stored in commonplace books was often defined in monetary terms. The word "treasury" applied not only to money but also to "treasuries of reading and in particular anthologies," and to memory more generally, which Cicero described as "the treasure-house of all things." Within the commonplace tradition, knowledge was like money, deposited in "the safe-keeping of memory," as Quintilian put it, its value indexed to future use and circulation. The commonplace book, like the ideal of the universal library, linked the individual student to the collective memory of *humanitas,* the precious and finite inheritance of tradition.[39] The commonplace model assumed that knowledge circulates within an economy of scarcity; its worth only increased as it survived the test of time, in the respect and deference students continued to pay to it.

Since their basic subject was the moral life, commonplace books guided individuals in the ethical process of building character. "The commonplaces are understood here to be habits of thoughts, habits of character," as Mary Carruthers has observed, and "one cannot think at all . . . except in commonplaces."[40] To copy a quotation was to borrow from the experience of others—to draw on the accumulated capital of received wisdom, in order to cultivate those habits of thought and expression that gave the ideal of "character" its particular content in a historical and social context. With the advent of printing, commonplace books became an entrenched part of the school system, as works such as Erasmus's influential *De Copia* (1550) disseminated a standard way of indexing one's memory to the collection of quotations in Latin. Unlike other kinds of Renaissance compilation literature, the "commonplace book was part of the initial intellectual experience of every schoolboy."[41] The commonplace tradition was further popularized by John Locke's *A New Method of Making Common-Place Books* (1706), which encouraged young men to develop methods for storing and retrieving knowledge already deemed to have objective, intrinsic value.[42]

Like the students in the ancient schools of philosophy, or the gentlemen trained by Lockean precepts in the eighteenth century, young men in nineteenth-century America learned to see the discipline of writing as intrinsic to the process of moral education. To write in diaries in nineteenth-century America is to identify with rational habits of thought: it is to become an administrator or judge or accountant, wielding the sovereign power of reason over the disarray of the unexamined life, the disorder of experience. Within the competing ethical pretexts of literacy, however, there are different ways that the habit of writing was rationalized as a virtue. The commonplace-book tradition encouraged writers to "verbalize present experience in the language of familiar moral paradigms and with reference to a cultural history shared by writer and reader."[43] For elite men, this reference point was education in ancient languages and literature. From the sixteenth through the mid-nineteenth centuries, that education made the "familiar moral paradigms" of classical humanism elementary to the training of young men for the professions and, more generally, for their assimilation of aristocratic identity. As Locke wrote in 1693, "Latin I look upon as absolutely necessary to a gentleman."[44] Within the humanist tradition, the habit of writing obtained its particular meaning as a male virtue—both as a practical means of ethical power and as a symbolic form of social distinction—from its association with the classical curriculum and the mastery of ancient languages.

The diary of George Jaques (1816–1872), a gentleman farmer who settled in Worcester, Massachusetts, gives us a particularly clear example of the survival of this Latinate tradition in nineteenth-century America. Jaques was born in Brooklyn, Connecticut, attended the Leicester Academy and Drury's School in Pawtuxet, Rhode Island, and graduated from Brown University in 1836. Jaques's diary offers a stark contrast to the diaries of merchant clerks who did not have the benefit of his extensive education.[45] In the college-preparatory track of the academy and in early American col-

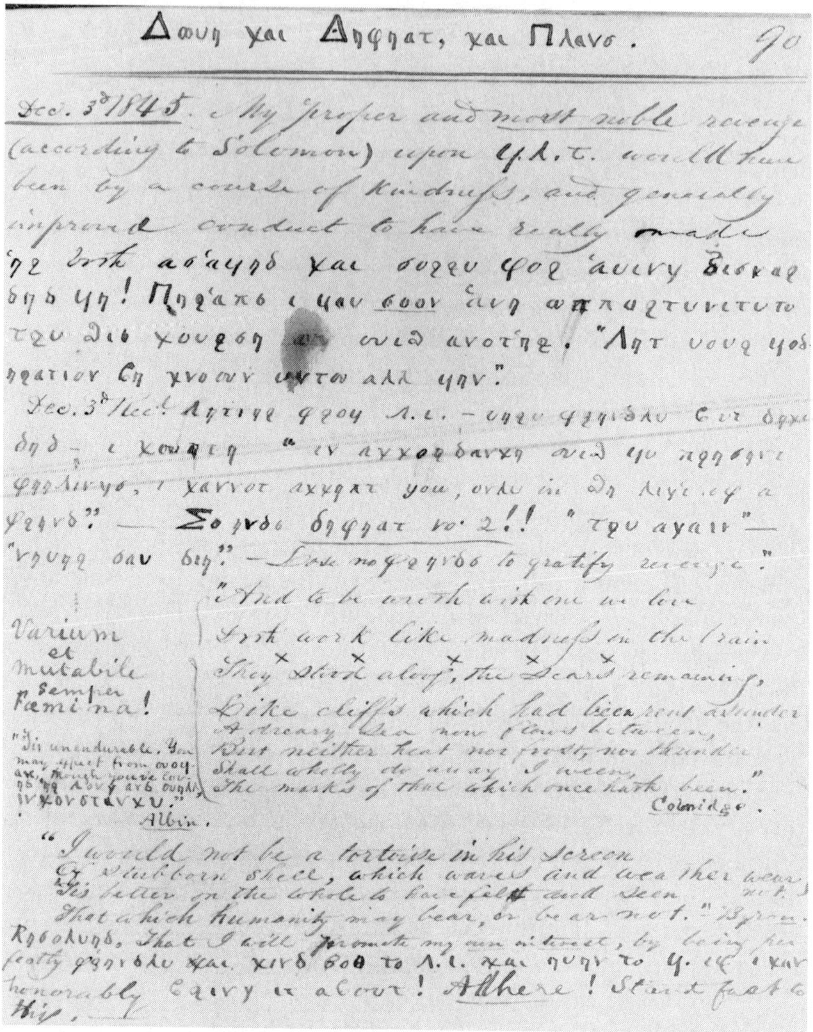

Figure 4 Commonplace book of George Jaques, 1845, entry on page 90. For centuries, gentlemen used Greek or Latin lettering as a secret code in their diaries, using their privileged education to create a zone of privacy accessible only to their social peers. On this page, Jaques consoles himself after a romantic rejection with tokens of learning, quoting from Virgil's *Aeneid* ("fickle and changeable is woman, always"), Coleridge's *Christabel*, and Byron's *Don Juan*. Jaques uses Greek letters to write English words. Vowing to make "her both ashamed and sorry for having discarded ye!," he exclaims, "So ends defeat no. 2!! 'Try again'—'never say die.'—lose no friend to gratify revenge." Courtesy of the Winterthur Library, Joseph Downs Collection of Manuscripts and Printed Ephemera.

leges, habits of thought and character were identified with Greek and Latin, and students' lives were taken up with memorization and recitation of ancient grammar, etymology, and philology.[46] In the diary and memorandum book he begins to keep in 1840 at the age of twenty-six, Jaques writes down maxims and quotations that offer ethical guidance on how to live. By writing them down in Latin and Greek, however, Jaques practices a proficiency in classical languages that was the special prerogative of his gender and class (fig. 4).[47] The learning of ancient languages was thought beyond the capacity of women, while it raised a high bar for moral and mental achievement and sorted men according to the sheer discipline and will it required.[48] By copying bits of ancient wisdom in his diary, Jaques claims an abstract kinship with an elite, cosmopolitan circle of gentlemen who not only have access to the books of classical humanism but also the ability to assess their value within a personalized system of reference. The manner in which Jaques indexes his diary with headings at the margins of the page bespeaks a learned confidence in his ability to accumulate moral insight that, whether taken from ancient texts or from his own life, he assumes to have an objective worth. By employing both the form and the content of the humanist tradition of ethical reflection, George Jaques can "own" his experience and value it as an elitist form of cultural capital.[49]

Few young men in nineteenth-century America had proficiency in ancient languages, any more than they had access to Jaques's private collection of books, or the training and leisure for study that would enable them to possess this knowledge as wisdom. Ordinary clerks were acutely aware of the moral authority and social prestige that the classical curriculum conferred on members of the traditional professions in the ministry, education, and the law. Jonathan Hill (1818–1890), for example, was working as a clerk for a Worcester lawyer when he looked around him and assessed his prospects:

> I am twenty three years of age without money or friends without a collegiate education (although it is my purpose to have one) with talent far below the mediocrity, in the office of one of the most eminent practitioners in the commonwealth, employed in the study of law. I am surrounded by three or four other students in the offices who have enjoyed the advantages of a public course of study, which places them in their own minds in a situation so far above mine that I am excluded almost entirely from associating with them. They seem to look upon me as scarcely worth of passing notice—as one belonging to the common herd, having no claim upon the favorable notice of more "illustrious personages." Nor are these views entertained merely by these "exclusives" but by all who consider themselves in a higher grade, whether others acknowledge them so or not. Thus am I situated, cast aside, rejected, despised. And for what? Anything that I have done to merit all this? . . . A consciousness of superiority in their own minds is all that has caused the disparity in our situations. And yet I will give them more cause than that.[50]

From college education and a "public course of study," young gentlemen acquired not only functional skills in advanced literacy but "a consciousness of their superiority in their own minds," a superiority premised on the exclusion of less "illustrious" clerks such as Hill from higher education. Nothing symbolized this superiority more than a facility with writing Greek and Latin. The lawyer who narrates Melville's "Bartleby, the Scrivener" refers twice to a bust of Cicero he keeps on a shelf above his desk, perhaps a trophy of academic achievement in ancient rhetoric. The bust is a totem of the eloquence and character that made the Roman lawyer and statesman an enduring exemplum of civic distinction to nineteenth-century Americans.[51] As Hill struggled in his spare time to master Latin from his "situation" in a law office, he would similarly seek to marshal the power of classical learning in his diary. Hill had "had a bit of a flame up" while reading Cicero," but was "determined to stand my ground + think I shall come off the victor if I so will, for according to Publicus '<u>Possuit qua proste videntur</u>.'"[52] This daily struggle defined the worth of writing as the accumulation of the received treasure of culture.[53] As they wrote such phrases in diaries, both Hill and Jaques identified the moral authority of character with the force of will it took to master Latin vocabulary and grammar.

In contrast to the elitist erudition that, as in Jaques's diary, was cultivated within the commonplace tradition, the diaries of clerks in nineteenth-century America seem poor in content. They transcribe in an aimless way a homely education in the English vernacular, made up of occasional lectures, chance encounters with books and periodicals, interesting conversations or incidents, accounts of the weather, and trips to the countryside. Nevertheless, the habit of memory rationalized by the commonplace tradition survives in diaries of merchant clerks as a disposition toward the potential value of experience. Every diary demands that its author make judgments about what thoughts and actions deserve to be saved for a future moment. The Boston clerk Bradley Cumings (1811–1876) begins his diary with quotations on friendship, romance, and familial love. His neglect of this task, either in the reading or in the copying, soon impels him to define his purpose more narrowly—"to record only such events as may be of real use or gratification to me for reference to."[54] To best care for the self requires that one objectify and analyze one's life within textual forms, to identify through the act of writing what is "of real use or gratification," whether by copying bits of text into a commonplace book or making mental notes in the course of living. As the record of daily news and momentary thoughts, a diary functions as a sort of memory. With any given "entry," the recording of experience becomes part of the body of wisdom whose primary "real use or gratification" is for making "reference to." Benjamin Tilton (1817–1900) distinguishes his journal from a "regular diary" when he notes that his purpose is to "record, for my own satisfaction, such circumstances and events as, at the time of their occurrence, seem worthy of note; that memory may be refreshed at subsequent periods in reviewing the days that shall have passed."[55] As a means of "refreshing" memory, Tilton's diary embodies the future perspective he will have someday about his past. According to the humanist aesthetics of memory, care for the self survives in an abstraction of the past, for which the diaries of ordinary people provide "reference" and "refreshment."

In the diaries of antebellum clerks, events and actions in one's life are scrutinized through a continuous process of note-taking and reading. William Hoffman seized every opportunity for self-culture as he passed through a series of jobs in upstate New York that eventually landed him a job in Manhattan as a merchant's clerk. At a boardinghouse in Great Burlington, he came across a book "treating the philosophy of the great philosophers and distinguished men of antiquity." Moved by the example of men who brought their "complexity of mind" to bear on "simple, ordinary occurrences," Hoffman emulated their example by seeking to cultivate a "complexity of mind" in the midst of exhausting agricultural labor.[56] For example, he writes on 8 March 1848: "In the afternoon I read until it was time to perform my chores"; on 9 March, "The most part of the day I have attended to reading and writing. [I] perused Fowler's monthly pamphlet which comes to the office for J. Martin, it generally contains rather good and digestible reading matter, but occasionally maintains some few principles which we cannot consistently follow and adhere to . . . the odd principles and measures of ultraism. Fowler has some good ideas and should be treasured up in our memories." On 10 March, he resists going fishing with an acquaintance: "Told him I could not until I finished my writing . . . Retire at ten in my lonely room."[57]

As tools of memory, diaries invested ordinary striving with philosophical dignity, enabling young men to transform their reading and their personal past alike into a fund of wisdom on which they might draw. When clerks such as Hoffman record their experience for future "reference," they invest their present experience with potential value, as a source of practical guidance to which they may need recourse. Squeezed in after hours of work, pursued as one moved from one town and clerical position to another, reading and writing were obviously considered crucial means of advancement or "improvement."[58] Both the "ancient philosophers" and Lorenzo Fowler's *American Phrenological Journal* offered Hoffman guidance about his future conduct. He noted with each that these works "should be treasured up in our memories." Because it is within the "simple, ordinary occurrences" of one's life that taking care of the self must be accomplished, the diary functions here as a memory book, for harvesting from present uncertainties the future capital of character. Like the principles set forth by the ancient philosophers or the nostrums of self-improvement retailed in Lorenzo and Orson Fowler's empire of phrenology manuals, periodicals, and consultation services, one's experience gains value from being saved. Whatever material rewards they may bring in the workplace, writing in one's diary, and reading the books and periodicals that nourished it, were means of gaining advice—for elucidating some "principles" that young men might "consistently follow and adhere to."

By writing in diaries, young men are taking stock of experience—however banal and commonplace—for its prospective worth. This is why so many diaries kept by clerks begin with a highly self-conscious statement of purpose, like that written by James Whittier (b. 1816) in 1830:

> August 3 I have this day begun to keep a Diary, or journal of the principal events which may fall under my observation. I intend to record a little every day, if I can find a little that is worth recording. I shall not confine myself wholly to things in which I am concerned but shall keep a "kind of" record of what happens in the world, and also the state of the weather. If any one sees this, they must not expect to find anything more than common for the one who keeps it is young, and not much used to writing composition; still he hopes that there may be something recorded that will bear perusal.[59]

While the Latin commonplaces that George Jaques copies from Cicero and Horace have an objective cultural value that is validated by hierarchical institutions of advanced literacy, Whittier can only hope "that there may be something recorded that will bear perusal." His apologia to an implied reader—"If any one sees this"—suggests his uncertainty about what distinctive value or interest his diary can have for others. It also suggests the degree to which the accounting of a life assumed a moral omniscience, figured as the retrospective objectivity and superior reason exercised by future reading, whether by others or by oneself. In a literal sense, these clerks were writing for posterity, ambivalent about what future value their lives might have but determined to leave a moral inheritance: the imprint of character in a "'kind of' record" and even, according to the contemporary belief in Lamarckian genetics, in the traits of descendents who would presumably read it.

In the tradition of humanist education, moral insight is always in scarce supply, something to be saved up and protected from the ravages of time, from the ease of forgetting. It requires a diligent, active attention to the long-term value of what we read and observe—an appreciation for "future use" rather than short-term gratification. It also assumes that the objects and tools of literacy—books, libraries, diaries alike—are means of storing knowledge. A blank book is a place to record events and knowledge, to bring to the fallible human memory the enduring and habitual support of writing. By selecting and recording thought in order to facilitate its retrieval, writing plays a supporting role to the creative work of memory, to a process of thinking or discovery that is distinct from the merely instrumental and passive work of inscription. Writing allows young men to accumulate from the rush of days the abstract wealth of knowledge, to appropriate its worth to the ends of self-improvement by reproducing it in ever more personal materials for "reference."[60]

Self-Examination and the Devotions of Literacy

In *The Confessions* Augustine developed perhaps the most influential pretext of literacy in Western culture, a pretext aligning spiritual exercise with ascetic modes of reading and writing. As Brian Stock has demonstrated, Augustine found from his encounter with the word of God a model of literacy practice that differed in form and motive from the classical humanist pedagogy that dominated his life before his conversion to Christianity. In and out of the classroom, his reading and writing had been guided by a secular taste for the humanist texts of antiquity. Augustine's conversion led to his renunciation of sensual pleasures and of the material deference to tradition fostered by tools such as the commonplace book. In using the Bible for meditation, Augustine discovered that reading could foster ascetic discipline rather than merely satisfying the carnal appetite for aesthetic pleasure. Reading with a religious motive to reform himself, he learned to separate the text from its material form, absorbing its meaning into his quest for spiritual transcendence and ethical commitment.[61] If in the commonplace tradition one compiles knowledge for future reference, in the Augustinian tradition one writes to evaluate where one stands from the universal perspective of spiritual duty. Motivated by the ascetic pretext of self-examination, diaries are tools for renouncing worldly desires for the timeless truths of providence, the durable convictions of faith.

Where the humanist tradition taught nineteenth-century clerks to value writing for the knowledge it allowed them to accumulate, Christianity taught them to narrate a life's progress and to spiritualize the habits of literacy. The Reformation made Augustine's introspection a ritual duty for laymen as well as priests, entrusting individuals with their own spiritual direction and making writing integral to spiritual devotion. Puritans wrote spiritual autobiographies and kept journals, seeking evidence for "their place in the divine plots of election and reprobation," as Ian Watt notes, assessing every moment of their experience "as potentially rich in moral and spiritual meaning."[62] In the same way that daily changes of weather might reveal the hand of Providence, self-examination held one's spiritual destiny in suspense. In the personal narratives of Mary Rowlandson and Jonathan Edwards, or the diaries of John Winthrop and Samuel Sewall, no salvation was possible without a relentless scrutiny of one's motives and intentions. As writing became integral to spiritual devotion, diaries fostered a heightened attention to subjective feeling. Thus for Jonathan Hill, the duty of reflection required not only that he review events in his life but that he do so in a particular state of mind or attitude, with the deliberate sincerity of what Protestants called a "prepared heart." As Hill writes on New Year's Eve, 1845: "I am not quite in a fine mood for making the reflections appropriate to the passing moments."[63] As writing became integral to spiritual devotion, from the spiritual discipline of writing young men acquired a taste for the process of self-analysis that often survived the weakening of religious conviction. As a result, nineteenth-century diaries identify character with the interior, psychological strategies of reflection that one finds in the eighteenth-century novel and the modern confessions of Jean Jacques Rousseau, Samuel Pepys, and Samuel Johnson.

In nineteenth-century America, Sunday schools became a primary site where children learned to master the rudiments of self-examination, using a linear, narrative framework of accounting. For evangelical Protestants such as Lyman Beecher, Sunday schools became ideal venues for bringing Christian character to ever larger (and captive) audiences of young children. By the first decades of the nineteenth century ministers were becoming increasingly involved in the teaching and management of Sunday schools. With standardized curriculums, denominations used the schools to teach their distinctive doctrine and theology, because out of political expedience new state-sponsored common schools adopted a more generic Protestant orientation (teaching students to read the Bible, for example, while avoiding an overly sectarian gloss). There was a new emphasis on eliciting conversion through "new means" of exhortation and example, which gave children as young as five a precocious knowledge of the conventions of spiritual biography.[64] Sunday schools made children more likely to interpret their experience in narrative terms, as a spiritual struggle for grace. The diary of an unknown seventeen-year-old student from 1833 begins with a narrative of childhood conversion that formulates in miniature some of the genre's standard features: "My first serious impressions I date at the time when I was about 8 years old, whilst speaking reading Sabbath school book suddenly I was so struck with a sense of guilt and sinful state that I expected to go to hell immediately."[65] Christian pedagogy helped to make writing a means of devotion that brought together the highly emotional "impressions" of sin and grace with a progressive accounting of moral identity. That identity emerges in clerks' diaries both as an achievement of will and as radical uncertainty punctuated by the rising and falling of spirit—something Benjamin Tilton evokes in his 1841 diary when he exclaims, "How fluctuating is our happiness."[66]

Self-examination entailed the moral evaluation of one's life from an omniscient perspective outside the self. Like Benjamin Franklin's list of virtues, regular note taking on the self allowed writers to assess where they stood in relation to the standards of religious obligation, and to recommit themselves to spiritual and moral progress. Occurring at regular intervals of time, the practice of self-examination dramatizes the accounting of experience as an incremental narrative process. "Another year gone!" the diary of Jonathan Hill exclaims. "Have we fully improved the moments of the old year? And if we have not have we distinctly enough noted them to make the correction in the new? For one I wish my answers could be more satisfactory to the monitor within."[67] "Monitor" was a standard term for conscience that, well into the nineteenth century, described pastoral supervision and instruction received from ministers, teachers, and parents as an objective, internalized standard of spiritual and moral responsibility. As the noted scientist and Cincinnati resident Daniel Drake described his mother's moral training, "Thus my monitor was always by my side, and ready with her reproof, or admonition, or rewarding smile, as occasion or opportunity arose."[68] Although he was no longer under direct parental and pastoral supervision, Hill had internalized their discipline as "the monitor within." As the formality of his entry suggests, Hill appraises his life in the voice of moral conscience—the voice institutionalized in Sunday schools and Christian homes through the habit of writing.

As Hill noted, self-examination in a diary has an instrumental purpose for moral development: "These are questions which really involve the whole matter of responsibility + the determination of these interrogations will also determine our true situation in relation to our duty towards God + our fellow men." We take notes on the self to discover our "true situation." The act of writing assumes an imperative to scrupulously account for "the whole matter of responsibility." The determination of "these interrogations" in one's diary is a way of distilling the moral will—"our duty towards God + our fellow men." The key point for Hill is that one cannot write merely from a mechanical sense of duty. The point of self-examination is not knowledge but rather the process of determination, the finding, for which it is the occasion. Taking responsibility entails more than calculating answers to mechanical questions, or checking a list of virtues of the sort Benjamin Franklin depicts in his *Autobiography*. It entails putting one's self in the state of mind that this interrogation "requires," persevering from the details to the "whole matter" of accountability. To write in a diary is to render one's account in relation to others and to God. The habit of reflecting in one's diary allows one to realize one's "true situation," an existential and moral awareness of our "relation" that we embody through conviction and action. Moral duty, to others and to one's self, is distilled by the determination to write.

Young men write in their diaries not merely out of inclination or pleasure, or with an eye to the credit it may eventually bring one's character in an office of clerks, but from a moral obligation to their faith, as a ritual exercise of sincerity. Self-examination takes place at regular intervals of the calendar, most commonly at New Year's and on one's birthday. Invariably, if a young man is inclined to self-examination at all, the longest entries in his diary will be on one of these two days. Albert Lane Norris (1839–1919), a Harvard graduate who worked as a clerk in the early 1860s before going to medical school, includes a "review of experience" at the end of each month, when he indicates his mental tally of "several duties and enjoyments together with some cares."[69] This inventory becomes slightly more extensive in his year-end reviews. His entry for 1 January 1862 reads: "In store today as usual and on summing up the experiences of the past year I am pleased with much of my life and prosperity in a worldly point of view but when I contemplate the hidden things of the Soul in any Christian life walk and progress I feel as I long have felt that I am not in the street and place that a truly Christian man should be."[70] The values and rhythms of Protestant devotion provide Norris with a stable and predictable framework for moral accounting. Writing is an instrument of his spiritual life, rather than a substitute for it. As we shall see, more secular clerks turned to their diaries with impatient demands for signs of worldly "improvement" or literary "interest." The routine and regularity of Norris's accounting bespeaks his faith in a providential order, that he can always compare his own location against "the street and place" of the "truly Christian man."

Like maxims of classical philosophy, the Christian pretext of self-examination provides a framework for ethical decision. For more pious youths such as Norris, self-examination is a spiritual duty owed to God. It brings us to an accurate understanding of our values and where we stand in relation to them—discerning, for instance, the difference between a "worldly point of view" and the "hidden things of the soul." For those clerks who were less inclined to traditional ascetic distinctions, self-examination produces a detailed inventory of one's "progress" within the world. On his birthday in 1848, William Hoffman writes:

> And the past year as I look back upon it & reviewing it shows me clearly how the greater part of my time has been spent. I have duly improved it in some respects & in others I have not. I have not labored steadily physically & not sufficiently mentally. And in taking a review

I find many errors committed which might have been shunned. . . . I have many errors committed and the evil course that I have hitherto led before me + now it is for me to answer whether I shall pursue a different course from what I have. Tomorrow morning is the beginning of a new year and as I enter the gates of tomorrow morning am I to commence anew and enter on the performance of my incumbent duty? With more than ordinary interest.[71]

In "reviewing" the past year and seeing "clearly how the greater part of my time has been spent," Hoffman performs his Christian duty, becoming accountable to his own potential (or more perfect) self, as a rational creature capable of improvement and reform. This moral accounting culminates in moments of ethical decision, as when Hoffman declares "now it is for me to answer," and asks himself, "am I to commence anew and enter on the performance of my incumbent duty?" He makes similarly dramatic avowals a few days earlier, noting on 6 March that he "drew up several resolutions which I have in my possession & are of a nature which is calculated to remove all corruption from my morals; & moreover to instill me with purer, nobler, & higher feelings than I ever before possess[ed]—They are to embrace the strictest character of obligation which I am required to follow, as I subject myself to its governing laws I am not allowed, or will not allow myself to heedlessly violate."[72] As clerks turned to their diaries to monitor their progress with birthday and New Year's resolutions, the regularity of entries becomes a measure of faith. Between their scrutiny of the past, and their uncertainty about the future, clerks commit themselves to the "strictest character of obligation" with the temporal discipline of writing. In Christian accounting, a life acquires its moral value from the discharge of duty, the *presence of resolve* that writing—no less than other ritual devotions such as prayer and song—makes possible.

When clerks found themselves estranged from formal religion on theological grounds, or simply bored with the routine familiarity of church services, reading and writing became alternative modes of spiritual devotion.[73] The diary of James B. Blake (1827–1871) demonstrates some of the complex ways in which ascetic practices of meditation became identified with the somatic experience of literacy. A clerk at a Boston gasworks who would later become mayor of Worcester, Blake invested his diary writing with spiritual authority. Still living at home, he refers repeatedly to the family library as a "sanctum" for "repose" and introspection. On Sunday, 26 January 1851, Blake writes:

This evening I spend in the library enjoying myself to my heart's content, for I love to be alone at times, and to look into my own heart, and study the impulses of my own nature; nothing is so good for a

young man I think as reflection, self examination; to look within himself at times, and to ponder over the past; to cull over all his life and to
place the mis-spent hours in front, and keep them there in view as
warnings, to guide him though the dark unrevealed future; and what
season is better adapted for this than a Sabbath evening, in the twilight, at home. God grant that I may pass many sacred hours like the
present.[74]

Each week during the Sabbath, his library becomes the scene of spiritual exercise: Blake transposes the setting, rhythm, and form of traditional devotion to the practice of literacy. He frequently attended Unitarian services,
summarizing and commenting on sermons in his diary. But it was the solitary hours spent in his library looking "into my own heart," not the time
passed in church, for which Blake reserved the term "sacred." He invokes
"my sacred library" with a formality and regularity that a more orthodox
Protestant would reserve for a Sabbath service. Indeed, Blake stayed home
on Sunday, 12 January, to write on "illuminating gas" in his library: "and I
must say that I think I have received more benefit than I should have had I
attended church." As if to justify staying home, Blake goes on to criticize
"Sunday religion" and "professional Christians" for not cultivating the
spiritual exercises and ethical reflection that his own literary devotions evidently afford him: "Give me the man whose whole life is a perpetual Sabbath, who has conscience every day in the week, and is governed by its
dictates; who lives a Christian life, who practices whatever he professes;
who is governed and directed by a high tone of moral character, who would
not exchange his soul for any pecuniary benefit; it is such a man that I
honor and respect." Like Augustine in the ascetic mode of reading, Blake
identifies ethical agency—the man "governed and directed by a high tone
of moral character"—with introspection. He associates this ethical agency
with the material process of meditation itself, divorced from interpretation
of a religious text. It is not the mere profession of faith or observance of religious duty on Sundays but the act of reflection, continuously available to
Blake through "sacred hours" of reading and writing in the library, that potentially transforms life into a "perpetual Sabbath."[75]

   A technology of self, Blake's diary allows him to aestheticize solitude as
a ritual occasion for meditation. As with the "the lonely room" to which
William Hoffman consigns himself, the writing of diaries creates an experience of isolation conducive to ascetic contemplation. Only when we are
alone do we begin to sense the immanent, spiritual value of the present moment. Having substituted the library for the church, Blake's entries on Sundays and weekday evenings spent in solitary "repose" are written in the
present tense, rather than in the past tense with which clerks typically

record the events of their days: "This evening I spend . . . ."; "This evening
I am enjoying myself in my library" (3 May); "This evening I spend in a
very satisfactory manner to myself in my library alone, reading" (9 May); "I
find myself here in my own pleasant library, made sacred by studies" (4 December). The act of writing brings Blake and other clerks into a timeless
present of self-consciousness of the sort that typifies prayer. Albert Lane
Norris, for example, uses his diary as a medium for prayer when he writes
on 31 December 1858: "And in summing up the whole year it has been one
of happiness in that health has been given with other blessings to mother
Rufus and me. Oh, that I might live in constant communion and acceptance with my heavenly father. Amen."[76]

At such moments, the diary both records meditation and is its very instrument, as if solitude only becomes spiritual when clerks have pens in
their hands, the blank page before them. As it unfolds in the present
tense, the diary becomes an accounting of self-consciousness, of an individual's sensory experience of literacy. This may explain the curious pleasure some of these clerks take in the materiality of writing, as when Blake
writes on 8 March: "This evening finds me in all my glory reposing within
the sacred precincts of this library, far removed from the din of [the] city,
away from a rattling orchestra, secluded and happy, enjoying the peaceful
thoughts which so naturally and copiously flow from a contented mind."[77]
Clerks use the habit of writing to see the flow of thought and feeling, especially when they are falling asleep. Jonathan Hill writes on 15 August
1841:

> It is now between one + two o'clock at night. Occasionally the
> sounds of sweet music fall upon my ear. What is more delightful than
> to hear good music at the still hour of midnight. All is still and quiet.
> Every note falls distinctly upon the ear without a sound from aught
> else to break the harmony. Music at such a season sends forth a kind
> of inspiration whose influence no one can deny—softens the feelings
> and fits the mind for reflection and heightens that zest already imparted by the silent hour of night. We now view the scenes of our past
> and present adversity with feelings indicative of resignation—we feel
> that they are only chastenings for our own good, tempered + fitted to
> our natures by a kind and indulgent parent who knows what is best
> for his children.[78]

Writing at the twilight of thought, with an acute sense of silence and solitude, Hill uses his diary to dramatize a consciousness of self that, like
Blake's, trades in the Romantic aesthetics of solitude. As with Charles
French's "comparative independence," writing in a diary not only records
acts of meditation, reverie, and desire, but becomes the means for their rit-

ual enactment. The habit of writing allows these clerks to cultivate an existential awareness of their location in time and place, a literary presence of mind.[79] Clerks cultivate moral authority through their *sense* of literacy. As with Blake's "sacred hours," the experience of writing makes the rhythm and mood of spiritual devotions transparent, palpable in the feeling of solitude.

Time Is Money: The Value of the Future

Diaries are instruments for keeping time that, along with the almanac and the clock, helped to divorce the coordination of social time from eschatological (or nonhistorical) time. "With the development of human-made time-meters," the sociologist Norbert Elias observed, "the relative autonomy of social timing in relation to the timing of non-human physical events increased."[80] Societies ceased to regulate their activities by the movements of the moon, the tides, and the seasons, looking instead to abstract conceptions of time for frames of reference and standards of measurement. From this perspective, both the classical humanist and the Christian devotional traditions motivated clerks to use their diary as a device for moral timing, to coordinate and evaluate the development of character against linear measures of progress. Men cultivated their moral identities by accumulating the precious knowledge of the past, for instance, or by narrating their progress to what Albert Norris called the "street and place" of Christian duty. In both senses, the timing of a diary serves to reconcile one to sources of moral authority that, like the movements of the seasons and changes in the weather, were indifferent to individual intention. To keep a diary in this way is to locate one's self within an impersonal temporal design, to submit to the persistence of tradition or to the order of providence.

Without the steady rhythms of agricultural life to order their lives, the ambitious and insecure clerks who came of age in the market revolution carried their characters with them, in the pages of their diaries. Young men moved constantly in a restless search for work that left little time for the education and faith that supplied other men and Christians with traditional measures of moral life. Like William Hoffman, they might catch whatever stray bits from "ancient philosophers" they came across in strange boardinghouses, without having the benefit of George Jaques's private library or college training. So too, they might cast a periodic "glance on their faults and make earnest resolutions to do better," without finding the solace and assurance that James Blake enjoyed every Sunday in "the sacred precincts" of his father's library. In the expansion of the senses or the display of erudition, writing in diaries attests to the debt that liberal education has always owed to the social privilege of leisure.[81] Hoffman does not have the time for study through which Blake and Jaques assume their ennobling obligations to *civitas* and God: "Monday Tuesday Wednesday & Thursday," he writes. And yet, as they account for what little freedom they have outside work, clerks develop an acutely possessive sense of its value as a personal loss: "I do not have time I do not have time." Even when a young man's character remained poor in the traditional content of moral life—maxims of classical learning, the conviction of faith—it might become, through habits of rational management, rich with time.

In addition to the motives of humanist pedagogy and Protestant piety, ordinary young men brought to the timing of their lives habits and methods of clerical practice. In this sense, nineteenth-century diaries betray the legacy of distinctly modern forms of knowledge inaugurated by the codification of double-entry bookkeeping in the Renaissance. As Mary Poovey has argued, this innovation made a rhetorical argument about the social authority of merchants: "Accuracy and virtue [were] equated with writing according to rule." Through an "effect of accuracy" based on numerical precision, correctness, and detail, merchants sought to secure to their morally dubious vocation a reputation for honesty and fairness. Whereas classical humanist rhetoric and religious piety tended to reproduce various forms of status hierarchy, bookkeeping formalized a more egalitarian system of public accountability around norms of objectivity and neutrality. A ledger displayed the creditworthiness of the merchant by making visual claims about the status of facts and the calculus of "real" values, "reiterating in its very form the symmetry and proportion with which God invested the world."[82] In adding up the facts about their lives, clerks reproduced the spatial and temporal imperatives of bookkeeping, making the daily discipline of writing a measure of moral authority, of one's practical orientation to the business of life.

In their daily recording of the weather, diaries kept by ordinary people employ the system of temporal accounting popularized by the almanac. In the early modern period, the almanac was as ubiquitous in Anglo-American households as the Bible, and printers such as Benjamin Franklin issued new editions virtually every year. In many of its portable forms, the nineteenth-century diary is a personal almanac designed for general or commercial use, rather than for farming. Amid the printed calendars, timetables, lists of Sundays, statistics on population and distances between cities, one may find interleaved handwritten pages containing terse observations on the weather or tasks accomplished. Many nineteenth-century diaries retain with the almanac the mechanical functions of timekeeping, marking the days and months, noting the daily shifts in temperature and precipitation. In his *Autobiography,* Franklin writes of making a "little Book" that functions like the almanac. Including a table of virtues as well as a "scheme of employment" where "every Part of my business should have its allotted time," it allows Franklin to take stock of the moral life and to organize time in an efficient and economical way.[83] As Franklin emphasizes, it is the clerical method of his "plan" that gives him practical power over his moral identity, bringing transparency and discipline to one's stock of virtues, no less than to more tangible goods. The remarkable lesson that Franklin learns from his book is that the application of rational means to any facet of experience makes it available for deliberation and correction.

Writing by the prosaic rules of daily life, young men applied economic metaphors to the management of character. Enos White began several of the longer narrative entries in his diary with financial statements: "It is now about 4 years since I commenced in the shoe line . . . I shall have made about 200 dollars." He then proceeded to figure in broader terms the profit and loss of his life: "I have thought long back that I had much to complain of in sickness and bad luck in business but now coming to sum up the whole and learning how I stand I have much to be thankful for and ought not to complain. I see so many around me who a short time since seemed to be prospering in business and sailing along finely who now are failing and losing all they ever had."[84] With stoic reserve, the bookkeeper looks to apparent facts about a life such as physical health and prosperity. He assumes that one can readily calculate the value of experience at regular intervals in the way that one measures the profit and loss of an enterprise. William Hoffman declared a clerical motive at the outset of his diary, when he wrote in a "Preface" to his journal of 1848: "March the first. . . . I commence again (as it is all important) to record the proceedings of each day. The design of the Author is to keep a strict account of the transactions and occurrences of each day—God—Bad—or Otherwise—believing that such a course if rigidly adhered to will be highly beneficial in the end—in short for future reference."[85] From this perspective, to keep a diary is to "keep a strict account" of "transactions and occurrences." The moral value of this accounting lay not with the content of one's entry—the "determination of our true relation to God and man" of which Hill speaks—but on the degree to which it conforms to a businesslike method. This accounting had a benefit for "future reference" more immediate and less abstract than the memory afforded by the commonplace book. It turned one's attention to objective signs of one's condition, rather than to more intangible and amorphous concerns of the spiritual life, what Norris termed the "hidden things of the soul." The bookkeeper's ethics of accuracy, neutrality, and efficiency discouraged meditation and speculation for self-consciously "practical" ends of measurement.

In the myriad ways in which they "register" and "record" for "reference," clerks plot their experience within a linear framework. Like the Christian tradition of self-examination, the accounting interprets experience from a narrative perspective that makes almost any detail or observation a potential sign of one's development or progress. It carries a faith—like providence—that one's experience will become legible and coherent as a moral identity with the passage of time. For an entry about birthday resolutions from 17 March 1848, for example, William Hoffman uses the calendar to subject himself to rational discipline: "I am strictly to discharge those duties which are strictly incumbent upon me with renewed vigor & habits that I have nurtured that are not of a desirable nature must be wholly discarded—& that only which is for my moral + intellectual enhancement be fed + thus I may lead a useful life + add muscle to my physical mental and moral enhancement."[86] Hoffman values his "physical mental moral enhancement," but he narrates its progress not according to the ebb and flow of religious conviction but according to the regular method of the calendar. From this perspective, self-improvement is standardized and regulated as a duty by the calendar and the clock. Clerks evaluate their lives and habits by adhering to a "strict" schedule, measuring the rise and decline of stable values ("physical mental and moral enhancement") at regular intervals (one's birthday, New Year's Eve). By charting the progress of the "useful" life in yearly, monthly, weekly, and daily increments, diaries transform abstract time into personal property, capital that must be invested or else lost. As Hoffman continues:

> Time is transitory. Life is transitory & we cannot too eagerly seek the opportunity of improving it as it passes & that may be all that we can do every year—every month—& every day that passes can never be redeemed: + if passed without being improved & is thereby lost, is lost for ever & never can we redeem it—if it be the time lost so much the worse for ourselves but on the contrary if improved to result in some good production we have then spent it as we should & to some good purpose.

Hoffman tangles together personal and abstract time, making his birthday the occasion for impersonal observations about the nature of time and what "we" ought to do with it. His diary indexes quantitative or objective measures—a person's age, "every year—every month—& every day that passes"—to qualitative results of how one has "improved" and "redeemed" time. Time's forward motion enforces an urgency on moral development: to not put days to some good purpose is to have lost them forever, "so much the worse for ourselves." To make one's moral improvement rational in this way is to make the prospects of success and failure alike as unavoidable and inescapable as the time we lose, the fates we incur, "every year—every month—& every day."

Holding clerks to the standard of rational methods and habits, the writing of diaries made clerks personally accountable for their management of time. To "improve" oneself requires applying to experience the rational measure of the calendar. As they anxiously watched the days pass and tracked their repeated vows, declarations, and resolutions, young men assumed responsibility for their "enhancement" or "improvement." Edward Tailer (1830–1917) writes on 1 January 1850:

> For who can see a new year open upon him, without being better for the prospect, without making sundry wise reflections, on the step he is about to take towards the good of his being? The man who does not at least propose to himself to be better this year than he was last must be very good or very bad indeed. And only to propose to be better is something, if nothing else, which is the first step towards amendment. But an act, to propose to do well, is in some sort to do well positively, for there is no such thing as a stationary point in human endeavor; he who is not worse today than he was yesterday is better. And he who is not better is worse.

New Year's vows and resolutions are forms of ethical decision: not to reflect on the steps one is taking, not to propose to do well, is to have already done worse. As Tailer notes, "there is no such thing as a stationary point in human endeavor." To write in one's diary is to become aware, with painful exactness, that you are either rising or falling, winning or losing. For almost all of these clerks, money becomes the most obvious measure of progress, and Tailer repeatedly complains about his salary: "There is not a day that passes during which I do not imagine that I might better my situation as a clerk and receive an ample compensation for services rendered."[87] As they calculate the profit and loss of each passing day, clerks come to see fate as a zero-sum game.

When nineteenth-century clerks wrote in their diaries, they were engaged in a form of self-analysis, but one that proceeded from different assumptions about identity, perception, and cognition than those bequeathed to us by Freudian psychology. The story "Imaginary Conversations" (1843) from the *Knickerbocker* magazine dramatizes an epistemological dilemma of which young men were personally, and often painfully, aware. In this dialogue between a "Youth of Twenty" and a "Man of Forty," two personas offer their very different, and ultimately unreconciled, perspectives on life. Romantic and naïve, the youth affirms the "omnipotence of will," but is rebuked by the adult who, tested and chastened by experience, has resigned himself to a more narrowly realistic view of his limitations and possibilities. "The whip, the rein, and work," he grimly warns his own boyish former self, "will soon break down that proud spirit of yours, and you will trot along obediently and patiently." The dialogue ends with each refusing the other's counsel. The twenty year old vows "never again to admit . . . to my thoughts" this "phantom, as of one troubled in sleep." The forty year old vows to disown "the strange desires and indefinite longings" of youth that continue to haunt him, so as to remain "contented with my little routine of daily toil."[88] Moral life emerges from an internal struggle, between the impulsiveness of youth and the wisdom of age, between hope and resignation. We enact this struggle over time, as an ongoing dialogue between a present self and a future self, our impulses and desires for the future at odds with the prudence and caution earned with age. Reckoned from multiple, alienating perspectives in time, character requires that we learn to bring our present self into continuous "communion" with our future self, that we make ourselves personally accountable to the future. As clerks such as James Blake and Jonathan Hill wrote in the present tense, their diaries became an iteration of their contingent, superseded selves.

As the dialogue suggests, young men had a narrow window of opportunity for achieving this communion with one's future self. The perennial refrain of conduct books by ministers and teachers, designed to help youth build character, was that one's choices in the present moment were freighted with enormous consequence for who one becomes in later life. In conduct books such as T. S. Arthur's *Advice to Young Men* (1847), as in Charles French's diary, the age of twenty-one assumes special importance in the moral enterprise of character, as that moment in a youth's life "when body and mind are of sufficient maturity to allow him to act efficiently and wisely for himself." It is a mistake to confuse adult freedom with license, to enjoy one's self now and then "assume the more important and real business of life," because "all which precedes in a man's life goes to make up his character in all its subsequent formations."[89] With his newfound power to "act efficiently and wisely for himself" came the urgency to acquire and correct habits before they became fixed aspects of adult character. William James would affirm the same lesson at the end of the century when he wrote: "Could the young but realize how soon they will become mere walking bundles of habits, they would give more heed to their conduct while in the plastic state. We are spinning our own fates, good and evil, and never to be undone."[90] No trait was more celebrated in the antebellum literature of character building than decision. This was what Rufus Clark termed "executive force in the soul," and so many other counselors of youth termed "energy" or "force" of character.[91] But, as "Imaginary Conversations" reminded its readers, the "omnipotence of will" that was unrestrained by mature judgment would lead to bitter resignation in middle age. Since whatever one did would have lasting and permanent effects, Arthur wrote, "calm and sober reflection, and not thoughtless self-indulgence, should distinguish every young man at this time."[92]

When clerks wrote in their diaries, then, they were claiming varying degrees of moral responsibility for their character, seeking to assert some control over who and what they would become. If, as the conduct books so frequently noted, men's success in life depended foremost on the habits they cultivated while still young, writing in a diary becomes a moral obligation to their character. Jonathan Hill writes, even when he has nothing to say, because he has at least performed the habit of self-examination. He writes in November 1845: "I might without any great violation of the truth say 'Ditto' of today and let it go at that. But perhaps it may be better that I should make at least a show of something while I am about that I may not stand accused of neglect by my poor journal."[93] To understand a lapse in writing as a failure or "neglect" of a habit is to interpret one's experience against a temporal imperative of improvement. Regardless of the often-despairing moods in which Jonathan Hill finds himself, or the exhaustion and lack of time that keeps Hoffman from his journal, clerks write to cultivate the rational will. Indeed, like Charles French's vow to "win," the act of accounting is a way of taking one's future into one's own hands: it puts amorphous desires into the shape of a formal plan, a schedule in which duties are, as Hoffman puts it, "strictly incumbent" and must be "strictly discharged." It is a practice of sublimation.

Shaped as it was by the ethical pretext of accounting, the habit of writing became a practical way of realizing one's moral potential: it distilled the otherwise abstract obligations of moral life into quantitative measures and material gestures of literary practice. By taking stock of his life, a clerk could compare his "situation" and "place" against normative expectations for self-development that were both material and moral. Writing was a duty one owed to one's moral Other and a tangible way of achieving communion with it. If "rigidly adhered to" according to "strict" methods of temporal accounting, as Hoffman put it, the habit of writing became an investment in character: an exercise of the rational judgment that young men assumed would bring them success and respect. Because "there was no stationary place in human endeavor," as Tailer wrote, the neglect of this duty meant that one was already falling behind, already losing at the "real business of life." The frequent frustrations that these young men express about their own writing—the frequency and length of entries, their quality or "interest"—took place against this implacable urgency to cultivate "effective and wise" habits, to nurture a rational will. By writing in their diaries, young men were acting in the immediate moment to secure the long-term capital of character, practicing moralized habits of literacy that they believed would have real-world consequences for their futures and their fortunes.

At a crucial stage in their progress to adulthood, ordinary young men used diaries to manage their lives as a moral enterprise. In the accumulation of motives and mixture of strategies with which they did so, we can see an emerging comprehension of historical time as personal. The survival of humanism taught a reverence for and deference to tradition, setting for George Jaques and Jonathan Hill a standard of perfection against which the efforts of modern individuals continually fell short, a model for social prestige based on privileged access to the treasure of the classical past. The Christian pretext of self-examination taught young men like James Blake the sacred dimensions of time and space. The act of writing placed young men in an eternal present, releasing them from anxious preoccupation with the profane world through an acute consciousness of providential or divine order—the dilation of time we feel in the present tense of spiritual devotion, in the presence of grace. By contrast, the moral imperatives that accompanied the rise of liberal individualism taught clerks to value most that time they had yet to lose. By allowing them to quantify the value of ordinary lives, the quotidian aesthetics of accounting enabled these young men to earn the fortune that awaited them. In this sense, modernity produces futures: the potential and uncertainty of the blank page becomes at once the standard of individual progress and a promise that the ordinary has a story to tell.

Equality of Aspiration

Each of these ethical traditions furnished ordinary young men with practical strategies for accounting the value of everyday life, in ways that challenge simple distinctions between the spiritual and the material, the normative and the particular, the form and content of moral authority. Evolving from one day to the next, with changes of opportunity and mood and inclination, the writing of ordinary men gave moral life aesthetic shape in the objects and rituals of literary practice. In choosing to write, and deciding how to do so, young men sought both to make particular moments of time useful as the capital of character, and to measure their progress against a temporal framework of development. A clerk might salvage from his busy day the wealth of knowledge, lessons from great books and from ordinary life to be treasured for future "reference." He might convert mass-produced objects like the blank book into a spiritual medium of transcendence, finding moments of conviction, consolation, and hope in the presence of writing. Even in the absence of grace and classical maxims, a clerk could invest in his own future by performing the habit of writing with diligence and regularity. In these and other ways, clerks used diaries to give moral value and direction to their movements in market culture, managing the self as though it were an enterprise whose ultimate success or failure depended on the accuracy and interest of their accounting.

By the nineteenth century, the humanist ideal of character had acquired a newly egalitarian resonance as a result of broad intellectual changes in politics, psychology, and religion that helped to shape a modern vocabulary of moral will. The republican revival of civic humanism emphasized the importance of moral virtues in the formation of citizens. As Daniel Howe notes, "as the scope of American democracy widened, so too did the practice of self-construction."[94] Expansion of citizenship in the early years of the United States brought with it widespread innovations in moral pedagogy, which gave new importance to early childhood and the specific role that mothers could play in the education of citizens. The philosophy of the Scottish Enlightenment helped to universalize the capacity for self-making as an attribute of "common sense," of ordinary faculties of reason and moral sense. Finally, as Max Weber would argue in his landmark study of capitalism's debt to religion, the Protestant ethic of the calling—which held believers spiritually accountable for the use they made of their talents— helped to disseminate a secular model of self-improvement, the goal of which was, as Howe puts it, a chosen "ultimate identity" and a "full realization of human powers."[95]

This model of self-improvement was intimately tied to practices of writing that were themselves democratized. For George Washington and other members of the eighteenth-century gentry, writing accrued social credit: it was a means of assuming duties incumbent upon hereditary status. As writing became more common, however, it became an instrument of self-creation within a fluid world of social and economic possibility. As Ben Franklin wrote in his *Autobiography,* "Prose writing has been a great use to me in the Course of my Life," "a principal Means of my Advancement." As a printer's apprentice, Franklin taught himself to read and write "at Night after Work, or before Work began in the Mornings; or on Sundays," patching together an education that members of the eighteenth-century elite assumed as an entitlement. By copying prose from the pages of *The Spectator,* Franklin learned a lesson that would make his Autobiography a founding text in the American mythology of success: like the quality of a person's writing, identity is a matter of style. An artisan not only gained access to the books of his social betters but to the power to actively reshape one's self for an audience, a "means of advancement" uniquely identified with the facility for writing.[96] For Washington, that skill with writing inscribed a youth's character in the status hierarchies of colonial society, according to the prescriptive rules of aristocratic duty and cosmopolitan taste. For Franklin, by contrast, "character and credit" followed from the individual's rehearsal and practice of social roles, in the same way that dexterity with prose followed the diligent emulation of commonplace texts. In Franklin's hands, writing is not an observance of social duty but an assertion of republican freedom from a dependence that is both cultural and personal. Like Benjamin Rush, Thomas Jefferson, and other advocates of popular education in the early republic, Franklin celebrated the egalitarian power of self-making as the central principle of nationalist ideology, as when he praised the proliferation of social libraries like his own Library Company of Philadelphia for improving "the general conversation of the Americans," making "common tradesmen and farmers as intelligent as most gentlemen from other countries."[97]

Filled with evangelical and egalitarian faith in the self-realizing power of the individual will, hundreds of conduct books extended to a new mass audience of middle-class readers values of gentility and self-improvement that had, throughout the eighteenth century, justified citizenship as the exclusive prerogative of aristocratic elites.[98] Earlier in the century, these books were concerned with adapting aristocratic norms of character for a more democratic audience. John Grigg's *The American Chesterfield* (1833) claims on its title page to have made "alterations and additions suited to the youth of the United States."[99] In their nationalist campaign to prove that young men in America could become gentlemen, however, conduct books addressed readers in more inclusive terms as "boys and young men," and increasingly identified character not with prerogatives and duties attached to hereditary status—to their conduct as "gentlemen"—but rather with a capacity for self-transformation in a context of economic and social mobility. Consider the radical nature of William Alcott's invitation to self-improvement in his often reprinted *The Young Man's Guide* (1838): "Let me repeat the assurance that, as a general rule, *you may be whatever you resolve to be*." Arguing for the importance of "decision of character, independence of character, and consistency of character," Frank Ferguson's *The Young Man* (1848) insisted that "the qualifications demanded are *entirely within your power*."[100] As it was promulgated by ministers, educators, and many other authors of conduct books, this facile middle-class optimism about the potential for self-invention and social mobility accompanied new anxieties about the authenticity of identity in a world of "confidence men."[101]

As young men sought to account for character in the pages of their diaries, the liberal devotions of freedom became identified with the objects and practices of mass literacy. Like Franklin, nineteenth-century clerks made the act of writing a "principal means of advancement" by accounting for potential futures and possible lives. Liberal ideology promised that any-one could acquire the self-realizing power of character and the economic and social rewards that it seemed to warrant. The proliferation of objects such as the diary helped to reconcile older humanist and religious traditions of ethical practice to new contexts of social mobility and education. It also made young men more likely to personalize moral authority, to identify character with duties owed to one's self. By writing in diaries, clerks held themselves morally accountable for how they spent their time: the senses of duty, guilt, aspiration, and failure became as reflexive as a dialogue with an internal monitor, as implacable as decisions that had to be made each day. The quotidian practices of literacy furnished an educated middle class with what Richard Fox has described as the "continuous process of internalizing the social controls that earlier societies had lodged in explicit communal commands." Among liberal Christians in particular, "the severe judgement earlier exercised, in thunderbolt fashion, by God" gave way to endless dialogues with one's moral Other, to the fear of never adding up to any-thing.[102]

As liberal ideology made the aspiration of character available to ordinary young men, so technologies of self such as the diary made them responsible in unprecedented ways for calculating the moral interest of their lives. That so many young men began diaries in their late teens and early adulthood at-tests to the tremendous importance that literacy came to have in young men's negotiations of new freedoms and responsibilities. To write was, in a simple way, to will one's life as a story of progress, to force the time of one's own story to move according to a normative schedule of moral develop-ment. The pressure to make their lives a story of progress made young men acutely aware of their stasis in the social and economic landscape. N. Beek-ley, who left Morristown, Massachusetts, to work as a clerk in Boston, wrote an entry on 31 December 1849 that was repeated countless times by clerks as they tallied their prospects: "Here is the end of another year. The end of 1849. How rapidly the time has flown since this day one year ago! What changes have taken place, in some instances for the better, in others for worse. Even as regards my humble self there has been somewhat of a change, but only as it relates to my situation, in all other respects there is no change with the single exception of being a year older. No richer nor poorer, nor no nearer being married."[103] That these diaries lack a system of reference besides the impersonal passage of time underscores how uncer-tain the personal future could seem, how anxious the search for one's own story could become.

For young men finding their way to adulthood, independence was, as Charles French put it, always "comparative," a moral autonomy relative to the a priori conditions—social and economic, physical and spiritual—in which they found themselves, stuck. Nothing was more acute for these young men than the essential fragility of futures that seemed bound to "wheels of fortune turning," as Enos White put it.[104] A Boston clerk, Bradley Cumings, divides much of his journal from the 1830s between accounts of the weather and the incidences of bankruptcy, madness, and suicide among his peers.[105] The real possibility of failure haunted clerks as they continually tallied their prospects and shifted restlessly for better positions and higher pay. After trying for months to obtain a loan from friends and relatives, Jonathan Hill sought to temper his desperation in stoic resignation: "I know well what it is to have the grip of poverty fixed upon me and the approach of the specter will have but little effect comparatively."[106] As failure and bankruptcy became newly visible and predictable features of the social landscape, clerks were more often despairing about their prospects than they were confident of winning.

As their path in the economy diverged from the linear plan of rational progress, fate became something for which individuals were personally responsible, a fortune that was one's own to win or lose. A New York clerk named Charles Rogers compared himself against school friends like Eastman "who is in business and succeeding fairly," or Reed "who is succeeding well at bookkeeping." He could only conclude: "I am not equal to my aspirations in business and almost wish I have never seen New York City." On the day Rogers lost his job at a retail store in Manhattan—things go from bad to worse for him—his unexpected incantation of traditional piety suggests an ominous and despairing fatalism more than humble submission and resilient faith: "God's will be done." Even as he was turned away from one dry goods store after another, and saw his plan to attend West Point thwarted, Rogers continued to turn to his diary with fresh resolve for his future: "I must have some new project to think of or I should be so lonesome as to hardly stay in New York."[107] Even as discouragement seemed to come from every quarter, Rogers continued to feel a moral obligation to his self-improvement that is apparent in his vows of determination—"I shall," "I must." Though he was near the end of his rope and would soon leave New York, he started to learn Spanish. And like thousands of other aspiring businessmen, he joined the New York Mercantile Library Association. As young men sought to account for their lives against middle-class norms of social and economic success, writing and other practices of literacy became devotions of the will, means of becoming "equal to my aspiration," as Rogers puts it.

Writing allows for a kind of self-analysis that reading does not, and in Franklin's hands and the clerks who followed in his wake, it became a means of producing the complex subjectivities required by market culture. "I am not equal to my aspiration": in Rogers's words, we see how implacable the pressure to succeed could become for young men, how easily the abstract promise and potential of the future became a measure of personal failure. As they charted their haphazard itinerary to an elusive freedom, Rogers and other young men found themselves trapped in a competition against time to realize their moral Other in daily habits and conduct. Pulled between moral duties and worldly desires, between the anonymity of public life and the intimacy of private life, a man not only had to manage the fractured demands of modern life in the inventory of his days, but indeed to "equalize the contradictory demands of self, family, market and national interests *in his own person*."[108] As a result, character became less an identity with a particular framework of value than a process of managing competing motives, of moving across multiple narratives of the self, navigating the contradictory roles and values generated by market culture. Making their haphazard way to uncertain futures, young men swam in a field of cultural debris, among remnants of ethical systems from which they fashioned a complex, fragmented sense of identity. As diaries allowed them to evaluate their lives from multiple perspectives in time—the deep past of tradition, the timeless present, the uncertain future—young men made equality with one's self the purpose of moral accounting. As the power of individual will became, at least for literate white men, more accessible and abstract, the responsibility to one's moral Other took root in the ever-widening cracks between intention and action, the material and the spiritual, progress and stasis.

How easily the promise that *you can be anything* becomes a taunt. Calculated in the ledger of the diary, against diffuse and shifting frameworks of value, the measure of character became interior to the self rather than exterior to it, a dividing of the self rather than its synthesis. For these young men, the moral life was an incremental process of self-realization, of becoming equal to one's aspiration through habits and objects of literary practice. Writing was an exercise of will organized around increasingly flexible, personal rules of moral difference—like the distinction between a younger and an older self. As long as one retained the aspirations of youth, the will would chart its own path to freedom; as the *Knickerbocker* story suggests, however, this path had resignation as its melancholy end. As they lost the romance of youth, grown men learned to trot obediently in the well-worn ruts of custom, purchasing experience at the cost of desire. Once they were harnessed to adult responsibilities of work and family, most young men would stop writing in diaries.

In the diverse ways in which they were shaped by ethical pretexts and historical conventions, the diaries of these young men begin to suggest how the democratic practice of moral life was shaped by institutions and practices of literacy. As the coin of character circulated more widely in nineteenth-century America, it became an increasingly standardized object of mass education and consumption. The remainder of this book examines how moral life was transformed, both in the pages of diaries and beyond them by new forms of speaking, writing, and reading in contexts of leisure and work. Young men learned habits at home and school that domesticated the objects of mass literacy, lending the otherwise impersonal experiences of mass culture new kinds of affective power and social consequence. They attended lectures by Emerson, joined voluntary associations such as the New York Mercantile Library, and struggled to reconcile their professional aspirations with the changing conditions of clerical work. Across many sites of leisure and work, sociability and domesticity, young men learned to identify the moral authority of middle-class manhood with the exercise of literary taste. Amid the displacements of market culture, Charles French, James Blake, William Hoffman, Benjamin Tilton, Jonathan Hill, and many others cultivated the capital of character in the prosaic rituals and spaces of everyday life, in the quotidian aesthetics of literary practice.

Chapter Two
Forms of Feeling: Habit, Leisure, and the Domestication of Literary Taste

On board a ship bound from New York to Richmond in June of 1842, sent by his boss to recover debts, Henry Patterson (1819–1897) noted in his diary that "to pass the time (as I have got through all my reading) I occasionally take hold and haul in the rigging with the sailors. This is hard work, but good exercise."[1] Like writing in his diary, joining the New York Mercantile Library, and attending lectures, this is just one example of the ways that Patterson found to occupy his leisure. For middle class men, free time was not merely a privilege but a moral test. If you do not have to work—for a few hours in an evening, for days at a time during a ship's voyage—what do you do? As a passenger and as a clerk in a Manhattan dry-goods store, Patterson possesses both the physical strength and the initiative to direct his energy into channels besides recovery or sleep—to read, for example, or to appreciate a sailor's "hard work" as "good exercise." In this instance, he performs the same activity as a sailor but experiences it as "occasional" recreation rather than as the routine exertion of work. The sailors do not choose to pull in the rigging, since it is but one of many duties required by their employment. For Patterson, getting some fresh air, mingling with the crew, and hauling in rigging are forms of play that he engages in only after he has finished his own proper work of reading and writing. By playing a sailor, then, Patterson affirms his own middle-class standing and his white-collar status, as an educated clerk who works with his head rather than his hands. As he accounts the value of time in his diary, the sailors become an anonymous chorus against which Patterson claims distinction as an individual. Not unlike Richard Henry Dana in *Two Years Before the Mast* (1842) and Ishmael in Melville's *Moby Dick* (1851), Patterson transforms his experience of the voyage into a literary romance, filling pages of his diary with rapturous accounts of the sea and the new feelings it awakens in him.[2]

This innocuous moment from Patterson's voyage represents a profound, reflexive commitment to what I am calling literary leisure: one redeems the value of experience through the cultivation of taste across multiple sites of education and recreation. As we have seen, clerks developed a moral identification with literacy through ethical and spiritual imperatives to account for the self in one's diary. This chapter explores the habitual nature of this identification, exploring how character came to be rationalized by the movement from youth to adulthood, through the exercise of literary leisure. Like the "good exercise" of pulling in a ship's rigging, this exercise was a form of recreation, but unlike manual activity it produced social and moral capital. In this sense, Patterson's accounting for time was governed by the larger paradox of middle-class leisure. The call to character becomes most exacting and unappeased when a clerk is free to spend his time as he pleases: its moral imperatives have been internalized as an instinctual, reflexive obligation. Young men such as Henry Patterson, no less than the women with whom they shared sites of education and recreation, responded to this call at home and at school by acquiring habits of literary practice.

Punctuated by the rhythms of sociability and intimacy, the exercise of literary leisure transformed middle-class leisure into moral work: the shaping of a literary ethos demanded diligent application, practice, and tireless improvement. The impetus for this work came from the nineteenth-century ideal of "nature" that conflated the organic process of individual development with both the cultivation of taste and the progress of civilization. In his 1855 lecture to the Boston Mercantile Library on "Practical Life," Edward Chapin described this ideal as sort of a physiology of culture:

> There is a class of men who are merely living, at least what life they do realize is little more than the diffused life of nature, the life of the plant and the shell-fish, the unconsidered life of the brute—not that higher life, not that self-organized personality whose energies are kindled by its own reflex consciousness. . . . Men are never changed, never moved by the mere dry light of intellect, till it moves upon the affections and the will.[3]

Chapin assumes that the imperative of independence—to become one's own person, "the self-organized personality"—depends on the capacity for critical reflection. At the same time, the achievement of moral maturity entails the control of lower "impulses" (the sexual instincts or brute passions of our animal nature) by higher, mental faculties of reflection. Chapin associates moral agency with "reflex consciousness," without which one remains a part of the "unconsidered" life of nature. Yet this capacity to be

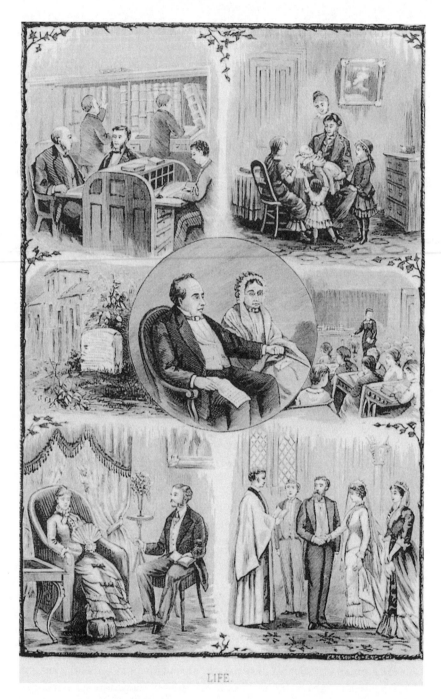

LIFE.

Figure 5 "Life," the front-piece engraving from *The Imperial Highway; or, the Road to Fortune and Happiness with Biographies of Self-Made Men, Their Business Traits, Qualities and Habits* (1883). From the writing on the tombstone to the open books of Scripture and literature, implements and emblems of literacy are present at each stage in the lifecycle of the "self-made" man. As the illustration suggests, the cultivation of domestic happiness in the private sphere became the primary end of middle-class character.

"self-organizing" relies not merely on the exercise of "dry intellect" but on the kindling of energies by the affections and the will. In their transition to adult maturity, young men sought to become "self-organizing" in economic and social life by cultivating a particularly literary taste for leisure.

Why did young men such as Patterson make literary recreation a priority during their free time and associate it with the power of being "self-organizing"? With the elaboration of state-sponsored mass education, the rise in living standards, and the proliferation of information and entertainment in the marketplace, the "literary" assumed not only new meanings but new social forms. From the broad historical perspective of what Norbert Elias has called the "civilizing process," or which Richard Bushman has more recently termed the "refinement of America," a mass audience of middle-class consumers gained access to a cultural propriety, to gentility, that had been the preserve of aristocratic elites. As training in elementary literacy became pervasive and standardized, the middle class came to mark the life cycle according to particular habits of literacy. An illustration at the front of *The Imperial Highway* (1883), an elaborate, all-purpose book of moral instruction designed for the parlor, represents a man's progress in life through various sites in the literary landscape (fig. 5).[4] From the nursery and the clerical office to the parlor and the cemetery, these sites form the very constellation of character, the orbit in which "life" finds its moral gravity. At the center of this orbit, the home became a shrine for a "fervent, Romanticized middle-class faith" in "the spiritual power of reading and writing."[5] Men and women wielded this power in the service of a transcendent moral ideal of domestic intimacy, which represented both an expression of natural sympathy and an achievement of socialization, wrought by ritual devotions of literary practice.

At every stage of the life cycle, middle-class people gave literary practices new social forms and emotional content for everyday life. A new infrastructure of mass literacy made particular kinds of writing, reading, and speaking habitual to the development of individuals, and naturalized the affections and the will as the literary performance of character. This chapter considers how literary practices altered the ways that young men identified with the social world and organized their emotional experience within it. It describes the "kindling" of consciousness, as Chapin put it, from two directions: as a development over time, in which institutions socialized young men and women into habits of literacy, and as a development over space, in which individuals exercised literary tastes across multiple contexts of leisure and sociability. Analyzing the relationship between writing and self-discipline, the first part of the chapter demonstrates how the moral pedagogy of the home and the school became the "reflex consciousness" of a "self-organizing personality." To come of age was to advance in time toward the ideal of "improvement." In moving beyond sites of family and school, young men such as Henry Patterson experienced leisure as an exercise of literary taste, critically reviewing diverse forms of reading, writing, and speaking.

As they acquired habits of literacy across time and space, young men received an extended education in the proprieties of gender and class, bridging the divisions between public and private by which scholars have typically mapped their world. With literary practices increasingly focused around domestic life, norms of gender and class were naturalized as habits of thought and feeling. The habitual exercise of literary taste trained young members of the middle class to identify moral credibility with emotional transparency in the home, with a development of the affections and will that had domestic sentiment as its seemingly natural end. By learning to associate identity itself with moral progress within a hierarchy of literary skills, young men such as Henry Patterson relocated the moral authority of character from the public sphere to the domestic sphere. As a mass audience gained access to cultural capital, moral discrimination attached less to work and action in public life and more to leisure and feeling in private: character became a peculiarly domestic object of literary performance.

The Drill of Nature

Students in late eighteenth-century America continued to use the same awkward writing tools used by medieval scribes. The cost of paper encouraged them to keep their commonplace books relatively small, by comparison with the sometimes elaborately bound diaries kept by nineteenth-century clerks. As Michael Halloran has pointed out, the "physical recalcitrance of old-style writing tools necessitated a two-stage composing process: first think out very carefully what to say, then write it down, ideally getting it exactly right the first time."[6] This recalcitrance is reflected in the conservative nature of the eighteenth-century commonplace books one finds in America. Richard Hewlett's book from 1767, for instance, contains social, legal, and religious forms of discourse that comprise the major uses that he will have for writing over the course of his life. Following the model inscribed by his penmanship instructor, the twelve-year-old Richard copied out the prayers said before and after meals, a certificate of indenture, a receipt, and seven versions of promissory notes (fig. 6).[7] In a literal sense, his writing is a discipline of propriety, in which the primary social obligations he will assume become legible in the practice of penmanship. The "knowledge" Richard's book collects for future reference is inscriptive rather than inventive, devoid of creative expression or reflection. Within a scriptural econ-

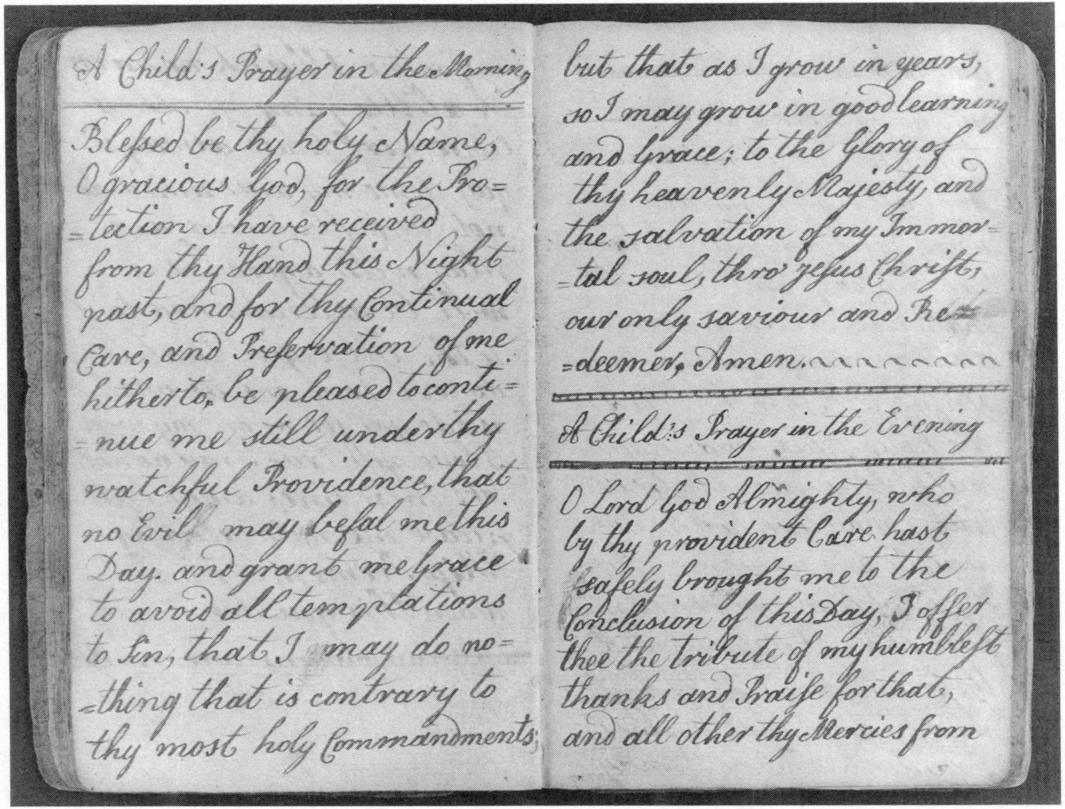

A Child's Prayer in the Morning

Blessed be thy holy Name,
O gracious God, for the Pro=
=tection I have received
from thy Hand this Night
past, and for thy Continual
Care, and Preservation of me
hitherto, be pleased to conti=
=nue me still under thy
watchful Providence, that
no Evil may befal me this
Day. and grant me Grace
to avoid all temptations
to Sin, that I may do no=
=thing that is contrary to
thy most holy Commandments;

but that as I grow in years,
so I may grow in good learning
and Grace; to the Glory of
thy heavenly Majesty, and
the salvation of my Immor=
=tal soul, thro' Jesus Christ,
our only saviour and Re=
=deemer, Amen.

A Child's Prayer in the Evening

O Lord God Almighty, who
by thy provident Care hast
safely brought me to the
Conclusion of this Day, I offer
thee the tribute of my humblest
thanks and Praise for that,
and all other thy Mercies from

Figure 6 Commonplace Book of Richard Hewlett (1767). In his commonplace book, Richard Hewlett practiced the rudimentary social "forms" he would need to get by in life: prayers, certificates of indenture, and promissory notes. Courtesy, the Winterthur Library, Joseph Downs Collection of Manuscripts and Printed Ephemera.

omy of scarcity, his writing is functional rather than literary, the technical facility he needs to reproduce a limited number of texts within his limited sphere of social duties. Along with the scarcity of leisure, the functional nature of scrivening precluded working youths from more advanced forms of literacy. In the early American college or in eighteenth-century salons and coteries, those forms remained the cultural capital of educated elites.[8]

Along with the invention of the reservoir pen, which made the sharpening of "nibs" unnecessary, the availability and diversity of paper goods helped to make writing a skill of basic literacy, taught to a rapidly expanding population of school children. As it was codified for school curriculums by a growing body of textbooks by professional educators, composition ceased to refer to an advanced art of belles lettres, and increasingly was taught simultaneously with other skills of literacy, as an adjunct to recitation and reading.[9] The journal became a standard tool for elementary literacy instruction, and incorporated students' own "experience" into the process of learning to write. During the 1830s at the experimental Temple School in Boston, for example, Bronson Alcott set aside time each day for writing in journals; he would collect them and frequently read them aloud, criticizing them in class. As reported by his co-worker and author Elizabeth Palmer Peabody, Alcott told one student that he wished the boy "would put more of himself into the journal." In contrast to one of the girls, "whose journal gave something of her mind," the "boy of that journal is a mere automaton; he came, he went out, and did things, but he never felt or thought."[10] Students in Alcott's classes learned to write "directly" from their own lives, to express themselves—indeed invent themselves—within the material process of writing, rather than by mastering abstract rules of rhetoric and imitating classical models. Within the Romantic pedagogy that Alcott helped to pioneer, writing should become integral to the process of education: writing is a medium for self-knowledge, an "occasion for the kind of introspection and self-analysis that would lead the youngster to the truth of his own nature," as Lawrence Cremin puts it.[11]

Behind these changes in the teaching of writing were profound cultural changes driven primarily by the evangelical revival, middle-class sentimentalism, and a newly affective, benevolent culture of childhood, in which parents and teachers turned against the harsh discipline of rules. We see in Alcott's words the new psychological priority of "experience" earlier developed by John Locke, Jean Jacques Rousseau, and the Swiss educator Johan Pestalozzi, who believed that the goal of education was to provide useful knowledge, through methods adapted to the child's maturity and experience.[12] As a result, pedagogy texts increasingly emphasized object lessons, which were seen to be a more natural style of learning than the drill of automatons, and which led to the use of firsthand experience in the classroom. Under Romantic innovations in pedagogy, journals became tools for teaching self-knowledge at the same time as they were used more systematically to teach composition. Unlike the student who collected commonplaces, the students schooled in these new methods learned that the composition of one's thoughts required looking to one's own experience. Moral insight was to be discovered, or invented, from the humble object lessons of one's own life. In *The Young Man's Guide* (1838), the reform-minded pedagogue and sometime schoolmaster William Alcott recommended that his readers carry notebooks with them, and use them not only to record events but the innumerable "thoughts, which the circumstances and incidents" of life afford. "Pages, instead of a few lines, might sometimes be written, when our leisure permitted, and thoughts flowed freely."[13] Habitual exercise helps to make visible the organic "flow" of thought, to make the mind's nature transparent in writing. The act of writing, then, distills a kind of attention to the potential value of any experience. Its worth or interest is reflected in the aesthetic taste by which one transforms personal life into an object of literary practice.

With increasing frequency, children in nineteenth-century America learned to use their journals in the classroom. On the first page of her diary from 1837, Anna Gale (1818–1851), a nineteen-year-old student at the Greene Street School in Providence, Rhode Island, declared: "Wish I was not obliged to write in my journal. My studies are not numerous, and if they were I should not be able to write anything interesting or even fit to read." Gale was "obliged" to write by her teachers, Margaret Fuller and her father Hiram, who assigned the writing of paraphrases to test students' attention in class and their memory of what they had read and heard. Gale made a tortured attempt to paraphrase Mr. Fuller's reading on the topic of happiness on 27 December, only to note on 28 December that, after reading their journals, he had said that "some greatly misapprehended what he read. I felt as if I might be guilty of this fault but I hoped my memory would not prove so very treacherous." On 10 January, Mr. Fuller surprised his class by reading aloud "some of our own production, our school journals—they were very good, but I felt for those to whom they belonged, for I imagine they would not like to hear them read before the school, even if they were perfect."[14] In her own journal, Gale faulted her own memory, expressed shame about her hasty compositions, and made earnest resolves about "how happy I should be of an opportunity to show, that I have the power, and ambition, sufficient to do better." As a result, she gradually learned to see the act of writing from the critical perspective of her teachers. In an entry made a few days before the end of the spring term, for example, it becomes clear the degree to which, after only a few months, Anna Gale's repeated use of the journal in the classroom had socialized her into a facility for writing.

It is not the praise, the favor, or admiration of the world that I would seek—that would be too cold, and hollow. I am content to have one, good, true, and faithful friend. But I will make it my aim silently and unobstructively to win, for myself, the approbation of infinite purity; this I fear cannot be done, so long as I remain inactive. I intended to have avoided this train of thought, but I could not write without allowing my mind to wander at its pleasure. And now that I have thus made these feelings—these resolutions, public, let them serve to remind me that as they were serious, they must also be proved to be firm, and sincere.[15]

At the outset of this exercise, Gale valued journals because they belonged to students as "our own production." She now values the journal as a means of self-expression. Gale can now write without self-consciousness or embarrassment because she has shifted her ownership from an object that she values for its privacy, to a practice that she values for making "these feelings—these resolutions, public." She no longer writes because she is "obliged" by her teachers, but from a free and spontaneous impulse: "I could not write without allowing my mind to wander at its pleasure." The imputed spontaneity of this process corrects her original intention to "avoid this train of thought" and brings her, as though by the progress of nature, to a moral truth about herself—a truth understood not in modern psychological terms of confession but in pedagogical terms of improvement.

Gale's diary anticipates the new pedagogy that would unfold in nineteenth-century classrooms, transforming the act of writing from a largely passive tool for the inscription of knowledge into a unique means of gaining access to the nature of thought itself. The newfound freedom with which Gale writes in her diary, under the real or implied surveillance of her teacher, reproduces the moral training purveyed in the classroom. To make seemingly private feelings public is to redeem the pleasure of a wandering mind as socially useful and morally instructive as the resolutions against which Gale will hold herself accountable. Who is this "one true friend" for whom Gale sacrifices the "approbation of the world" but her moral self—that "monitor" of conscience as it was often described in textbooks of moral philosophy or conduct manuals—for whom she will strive for the "approbation of an infinite purity"? To write "freely" is to adopt the literary conventions learned in the classroom as expressions of one's own voice, and to internalize the institutional obligations we owe to teachers as duties owed to one's future self, to one's moral Other. As it mirrors the language of her teachers, Gale's journal makes moral realization the literary object of self-expression. It substitutes the implied presence of this moral Other or monitor for the presence of other people, for the worldly society from which Gale would—with humility and modesty prescribed as female virtues—resign.

The teaching of writing as a basic tool of literacy helped to institutionalize a Romantic orientation toward self-discovery. The organic growth of the individual was inscribed as a habit of literacy, a progressive and self-reflexive improvement in facility, developed across a spectrum of institutions and social locations. Like the diaries of young men, Gale's journal realizes the moral Other of character through a self-conscious discipline of literary practice. Both this process of self-realization and the pleasure of wandering thought that warrants it as "true" depend on written avowals of sincerity. Her ephemeral feelings become "serious" as "resolutions": the action of her writing rather than its content serves the moral process of self-monitoring and reminding, of being "proved firm, and sincere." As one's facility with a pen mirrors thought and feeling, words obtain their moral power by becoming instruments for correction and improvement. As the practice of writing became a standard feature of early schooling, young men and women learned to see language as a transparent medium for subjective experience and social obligation. In this way, writing is not only a technical literacy skill but an instrument that students use to turn the moral duties of the classroom and the home into pleasures of a wandering mind. Rational discipline becomes the affective play of nature, and private thoughts become objects for public performance.

Letters and the Debts of Family

After 1830, a distinctively middle-class ideal of domesticity converged with educational reformers' efforts to do away with corporal punishment, producing a theory of socialization that Richard Brodhead has termed "disciplinary intimacy." As Brodhead, Nancy Armstrong, and David Miller have argued, silent reading and the novel in particular became in the nineteenth century a preferred means for the discipline of bourgeois subjectivity.[16] More significant for the emergence of "disciplinary intimacy" than a new middle-class taste for the particular genre of the novel, however, was a new emotional and social investment in the *practice* of literacy. Within the curriculums of common schools and academies, young middle-class men and women came to identify the "nature" of social and emotional experience with the habitual, repetitive discipline of literacy. This discipline was enforced by the external authority of the teacher or the parent, but for the successful student it was internalized as obligations owed to one's self, developed in habits of writing and reading outside the classroom. As journals and compositions became a standard feature of basic literacy training, learning to write became a social exercise, an extended process that stretched across multiple stages of a young person's socialization into middle-class life.

In the correspondence of Brady Morse (b. 1834), a clerk living in San Francisco in the 1850s, we see how a young man's continual practice of writing extended school discipline to family relationships. Equating the moral autonomy of character with economic and social independence, young men in nineteenth-century America increasingly found themselves at a geographic distance from their childhood homes. For Morse's family in Charlestown, Massachusetts, the arrival of a letter was a collective event, and it would be read aloud to gathered family members and neighbors in the parlor or kitchen. Because postage costs were prohibitive, Morse typically sent several letters in the same envelope, and often included multiple letters on the same large pages of paper.[17] Although the exchange of letters reminded Morse and his family of the distance between them, it also opened up possibilities for new kinds of literary proximity. Morse's letters cultivate proprieties of intimacy, addressing the topic and tone of his writing to the gender and age of his recipients. In his correspondence with his father and his oldest brother, for example, Morse writes about the practical difficulties of finding work and improving the use of his leisure time. While these letters seem anxious and serious in their concern with what he calls the "particulars of my affairs," his letters to his mother revolve around picturesque evocations of domestic life. "May the happy time of our again meeting find you all in the enjoyment of a good health to which I look forward to, as one of the happiest events of my life."[18] Like so much of the writings of young men, Morse's letters to his mother develop an abstract, sentimental vision of home that is at once predictable and impersonal, nostalgic and familiar. In a context of geographic mobility, the letter assumed new centrality in the middle-class home as a means for cultivating relationships with family, friends, and neighbors which, as Joan Hedrick has noted, were both "attenuated and intensified through distance."[19]

The letter intensified familial relationships primarily by serving as a medium for moral admonition and guidance. The advice that Morse received in letters from his parents followed a gendered division of labor. His mother addressed his religious and spiritual needs while his father ministered to his struggle for success. A letter to his mother begins: "I intended to have replied to your letter last evening, but knowing your ideas about using the Sabbath for such purposes I delayed until this morning" (19 April 1855). He goes on to assure her that her role in his life remains the same, no matter where he is: "A word of encouragement coming from you is ever welcomed by me, and may you be spared these many years to give me your advice and warnings whether I am with you, or whether thousands of miles lay between you and the wanderer, who is ever uppermost in your thought and prayers." Even at great distance, Morse can be the dutiful son by heeding his parents' advice, and he uses his letters to demonstrate his deference and respect for their moral authority. To his father, he writes: "As regards my success in life, you mention in your letter of August 11, I must say that I only wish to meet with success enough to make a little money. If I cannot get it in a right manner, I do not want to get it, I would not want to do anything that my brothers would be sorry for in after life" (14 October 1853). Indeed, what else should a young man say to earn his father's approval? Similarly, in a letter to his brother, he says that he has "met some old Boston faces" such as the Ingalls boys: "I have not associated [with them as] they are very dissipated and will hardly do to rank with respectable men" (29 April 1854). Reassuring his parents that he remains loyal to the precepts they have imbued in him, Morse uses his letters to give his news the spin of character, what David Riesman termed that "internal gyroscope" by which the modern middle class equipped its children for the world of liberal capitalism. In every letter he sends home, Morse seeks to earn his family's affection by sustaining their moral confidence in him.

A letter home, then, was more than a transfer of information between individuals. It was a performance of social forms, enacted through the literary conventions of the "separate spheres." While all his family members receive the same "news" from San Francisco, the process of writing and reading by which this news is relayed enforces patterns of domestic deference. That process instills awareness of what concerns you and what does not, of the kinds of knowledge and forms of feeling from which your age and sex preclude your direct participation. Correspondence, in other words, is an exercise of address that teaches Brady and his family respect for the boundaries of propriety. Brothers and sisters learn how to present themselves differently between mother and father, parents assume custody of their respective spheres of influence over their children, and all are reminded of the limits and prerogatives of their individual roles within the family. Trained in the idiom of domestic affection, Brady's letters present competing, if not contradictory, versions of his identity that seem to mirror the desires and expectations of the loved ones at home. He bids his mother to accept their separation as though it were a fate of providence: "should our destiny be different we must try and abide by it." To his brother, however, Morse frankly admits the importance of money and work in his decision to leave: "It is useless for you to urge me to return home. What could I do if I should do so? Whatever may be my success here, it is wise for me to remain, than to 'come home' as you all say, where I never could be contented" (19 November 1855).[20] His exchanges with his father turn to the philosophical theme of composure, affirming the ancient virtues of manly character—perseverance, integrity, action, and bearing up under pressure: "I have not 'wavered my peak' but 'put the stick hard down, and kept her to it.'" With each letter home, Morse practices a facility with the forms of social address and locates his identity within a web of roles and obligations.

Morse's letters embody domestic propriety in the literary practice of writing letters, as respect for the discipline of habit. As Morse sends dozens of letters home, familial proprieties of gender and age are reflected in the technical facility for writing. A series of letters from 1 March 1855, for example, are concerned almost entirely with the discipline of penmanship. To his brother Edward: "I am very proud to see that you can write so fine a letter as your last proved you show a great improvement in your penmanship and your grammatical construction is very good indeed." To his brother Ammi: "I wish you would write me even if it is only two lines. You must practice yourself in writing all you can, mother tells me you have been a good boy." Corresponding with his mother, he lends his hand to the homework of writing, evaluating the letters of his siblings, monitoring habits, enforcing discipline, and suggesting topics for composition. On 31 August 1854, for example, Morse tells her that "I was much disappointed in not receiving a letter from sister, who I expected would give me a minute description of all she saw and did at the [July 4th] 'Celebration' so please tell her it is not too late." In a letter of 18 December 1855, Morse writes that "I was greatly pleased with Ammi's letter and ask you to see that he writes me frequently, as by so doing it will improve him much, he only needs a little practice for him to write well, the language he chose is very good." On the same paper, he writes his youngest brother Charlie: "This is the first letter Brady has received from you written with a pen, and you do not know how proud he is to think that Charlie can write such a letter so that you can tell me next spring about the garden. Be a good boy and mind what your pa and ma tell you, and they will say what a good boy Charlie is." And to his brother Ammi: "I am much pleased with your letter, with the penmanship, and composition, all the words were spell [*sic*] correctly, and if you will only be patient, you will soon be able to write a very handsome letter. I will not repeat the advice which I gave you in, I think, my last letter to you, about using your spare time, you probably know that as well as I do. I expect by the next steamer to get an account of your Thanksgiving, the way in which you spent it." But as Morse's correspondence suggests, domestic propriety demands the repetition of advice, that siblings express their care for one another in an economy of admonition, disappointment, and improvement. In the drill of nature, pedagogical imperatives circulate as tokens of familial affection and respect.

As they extend from the classroom into the home, exercises of literacy provide a moral discipline of domestic intimacy. They train boys and girls to respect hierarchies of age and gender as obligations of literary propriety. They teach young men such as Morse to appreciate otherwise abstract and impersonal norms of moral improvement as the basis for emotional exchange in the family—to associate the propriety of writing with competition for love. This becomes apparent in the subtle rivalry in which he seems engaged with his next youngest brother, Edward: "I was impressed and happy to see what a fine hand you write. Yours surpasses mine, and if the others don't look out, you will be the best penman 'in the crowd'" (28 April 1854). Writing brings the struggle for success home in the contest of hands, as a personalized obligation that will be measured and judged on paper. At a moment when Brady still did not have a job, while Edward had landed a plum job keeping books for a prestigious firm in Boston and Ammi was winning medals in school, Brady wrote to his father that: "I am happy that Ammi and Edward are doing so well. They are improving so much. I shall be of 'no account' beside them" (15 April 1854). As he competes with his brothers for their father's approval, Morse reveals the emotional costs that came with the accounting of character. Family affection is rationalized according to the impersonal language of the marketplace.

Once Morse leaves home, then, the emotional bonds he shares with his family become newly present and visible through the habit of writing. Through the exchange of letters, he learns to identify the proprieties of writing with the obligations of domestic life—to see literary practices as emotional duties. In a letter he wrote shortly after he arrived in San Francisco, Morse suggests the ways that writing disciplines family affection:

> I wrote on the fifteenth of this month, and told you that I had received but one letter from father, since then the Mail has arrived, and still no letters from you, I cannot think what can be the reason, for I know you must think how anxious I am to hear something from my friends, you should see the crowd around the Post office, when the mails are ready for delivery, and notice the lines formed, some nearly a quarter of a mile long, each poor fellow waiting for his chance to come to see if there is any news, from the "loved ones at home." And then to be oblige [*sic*] to go away without anything, as I have done, is very annoying. (29 May 1853)

Morse suggests that his mother and father have failed in their parental duty, but where does that duty lie? "Surely you know how anxious I am," he says, and yet by their failure to write his parents have expressed their seeming indifference. As a mode of social exchange, letters entail the duty of reciprocity—a duty for which he scrupulously accounts by beginning every letter with an acknowledgment of a previous letter, which references every letter to the ongoing process of social exchange. The prompt reply to letters makes the otherwise intangible compassion, sympathy, and love of one's family suddenly palpable, present or absent as a literary exercise. The prevalence of the facility for writing makes friends and family members emotionally accountable to one another according to objective criteria of exchange—the duty to write when one has the means to do so. It makes the medium of the letter a competitive arena for the exercise of family duty among other young men at the post office (fig. 7). As Morse suggests, not all of the poor fellows waiting for news are "obliged to go away without anything, as I have done." Morse rebukes his parents for their neglect not only by directly stating how "very annoying" it is but also by sending them an acute portrait of his isolation. In a culture that conferred respect through the observance of social forms, Morse's commas punctuate his distress like telegraphic code from across the continent.

Letters intensified emotional ties among distant family members by making the affective obligations of the middle-class family transparent in the practice of literary discipline. To receive a letter is to incur an emotional debt. Morse writes to his brother Edward: "I am much oblige [sic] to you, for the letter, and wish to be under this obligation every mail" (28 April 1854). Morse fills his letters with apologies and explanations for not writing sooner, with careful notation and dating of letters received, and exhortation to all of his family members to perform their duty by writing to him. The performance of this emotional duty is rationalized according to proprieties of gender and familial roles, as correspondents discipline one another not only for the content of their letters but also for their facility with a pen. By scrupulously maintaining his handwriting in letters to his youngest siblings and to his mother, Morse makes social rank and emotional bonds within the family visible as script, in the propriety of literary form. Morse seems to confine his concern for handwriting to domestic exercises of respect, however. When he writes his brother on 29 April 1854 about finally finding work, Morse apologizes repeatedly for the quality of his writing—"excuse great haste"—and leaves ink spots all over the paper, as though by carelessness to inscribe the restless striving to which he presumably owes the slight success that comes his way (fig. 8). Or to his father, on 15 February 1854: "I write in such a haste that I can hardly read my own writing. I hope you can." As he communicates with his peers in the world of white-collar work, Brady feels free here to dispense with his concern for his "hand" as though it were a mere formality, secondary to the pressing demands of work. With the ink spots and untidy scrawl of this letter, Morse permits himself a lapse in form because he has learned to associate propriety of writing with the moral discipline of domesticity, and with mothers in particular. As we shall see, clerks would increasingly identify morality with nos-

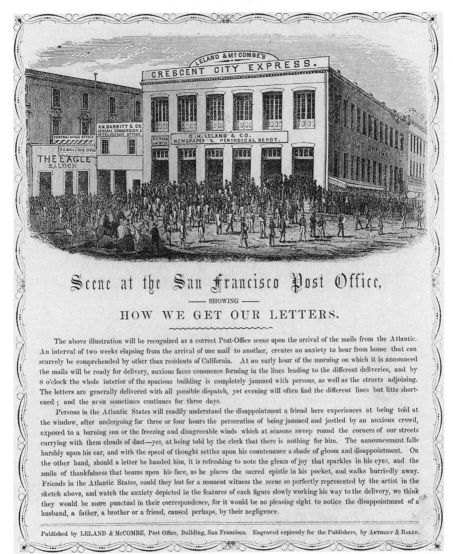

Figure 7   Scene at the San Francisco Post Office (1854). As they emigrated to the West Coast following the Gold Rush, the habit of letter-writing assumed a central role in the emotional lives of young men. Courtesy of the California Lettersheet Collection, Huntington Library.

talgia for childhood, among maternal exercises of socialization for which the public world of adult men seemed to have little use.[21]

As Morse's letters suggest, the facility for writing became a ubiquitous medium for moral discipline, infusing pedagogical norms into the emotional life of the middle-class family. By formalizing propriety as deference

Figure 8   Letter from Bradford Morse, 1854. "Excuse great haste": Hurrying to finish in time for the mail, clerks allowed lapses in the propriety of their "hands," leaving scrawls and ink spots on their letters as marks of their engagement in the pressing affairs of business. Courtesy of the American Antiquarian Society.

to familial rank, the domestic discipline of writing helped to privatize respect for social forms. These exercises were increasingly organized around the affective and moral bonds of domesticity. As pedagogical values became the lingua franca of private life, letters and other modes of social facility identified affective norms of domestic life with moralized obligations of literary habit. These obligations included the duty to write often, to excel at penmanship, to correct grammar and spelling, to emulate commonplaces of gender, to remark on the lives of others as an object worthy of studied attention, and always, inexorably, to "improve." As domestic affection was increasingly mediated by practices not only of writing but also of speaking and reading, Anna Gale, Bradford Morse, and other young men and women became personally accountable and emotionally responsible for self-development. The journal or the letter is less an expression of intimacy than its exercise: they enact intimacy in habits of literacy.

As Morse's haste in writing to his brother only begins to suggest, boundaries of class and gender in nineteenth-century America came to be reorganized within the evolving landscape of literacy. Albert Norris, for example, was educated at Harvard and worked as a clerk for a few years in Boston in the late 1850s before becoming a physician. The scrawl in his diary suggests an indifference to the propriety of forms fostered among children at home and school (fig. 9). Locating the value of their work in the mind, young men aspiring to professional success such as Norris could afford to lose their habits of the hand. As I argue in chapter 5, penmanship would lose its economic value for white-collar work. Although it would retain vestigial importance in twentieth-century pedagogy until the advent of word processing, penmanship ceased in the late nineteenth-century to be a significant mark of moral distinction among professional men. Duty to the form of writing and other modes of literary practice would, perhaps, seem a vestige of subordination to teachers and parents that upwardly mobile youth necessarily outgrew—a kind of manual labor suited to scriveners and female secretaries rather than self-made men. Certainly, fathers did not distinguish themselves by the frequency or length of their correspondence to distant children. If "brevity is the soul of wit," Morse joked to his father about one of his father's memos, "you are the most witty man in Boston."[22] So too another clerk who had migrated to California, E. B. Howe, commented on his father's general disengagement from his life, in a letter from 23 June 1872: "Your letter of the 13th did not reach me until the 21st (my 29th birthday, by the way) and it took me greatly by surprise, both by its contents and by the infrequency of your favoring me with your autograph."[23] With the divergence of a male sphere of white-collar work from the domestic sphere of leisure, the concern for form and propriety would be increasingly privatized, if not feminized, in the literary cultivation of domestic feeling.

The Profit of Pleasure

In order for this discipline to be automatic and natural, it had to begin early. Boys and girls were socialized into literacy in nineteenth-century America. Depending on where and when they lived, individuals received simultane-

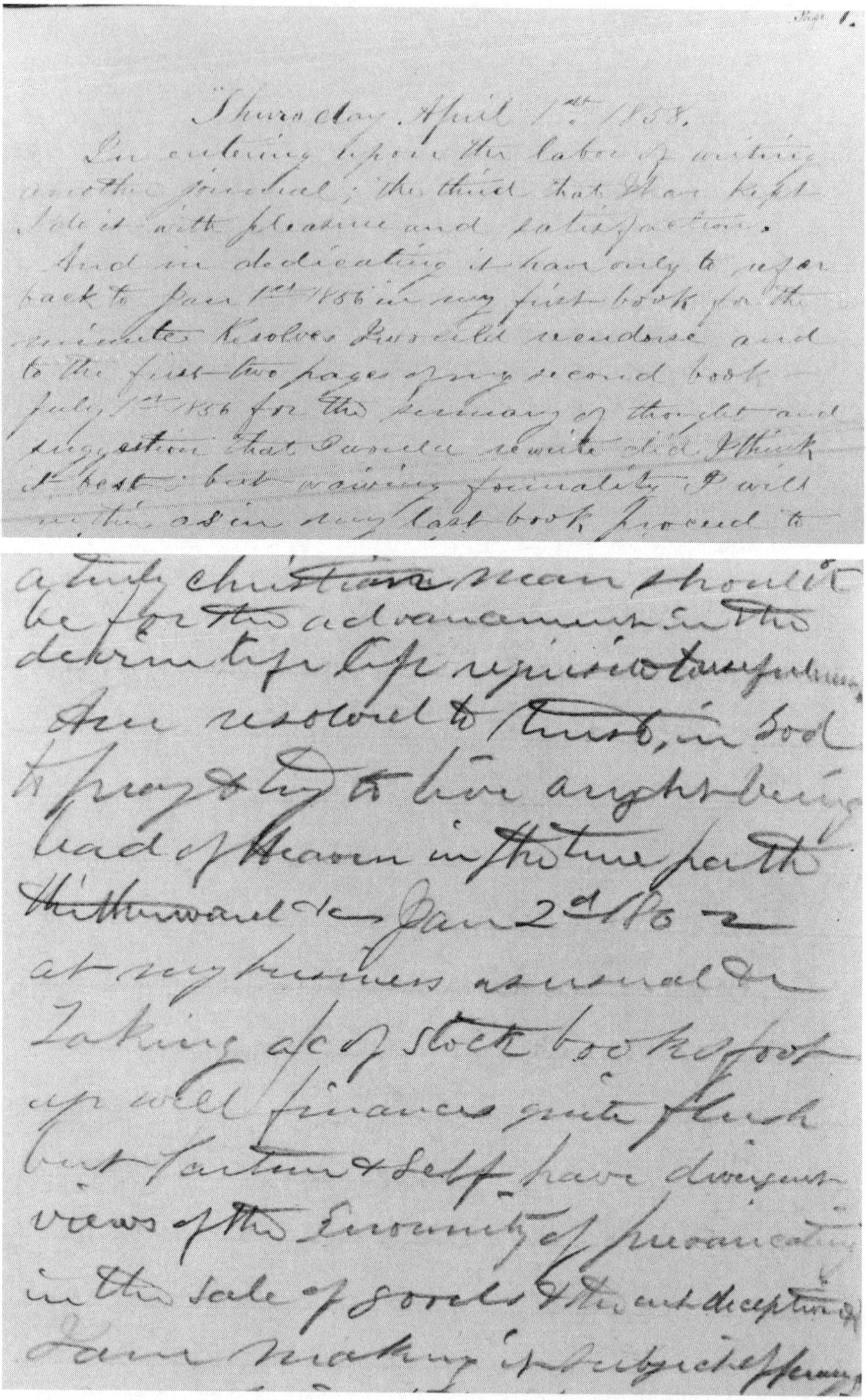

Figure 9 Diary of Albert Norris. Penmanship was a technical skill that young men could afford to lose as they left business for other careers. Above, an entry from Norcross's diary in 1858, when he had recently graduated from Harvard University and was working as a clerk in Boston, and below, an entry from 1862. This decay of habit suited his eventual entry into the medical profession, which has become notorious for its illegible "scrip." Courtesy, the Winterthur Library, Joseph Downs Collection of Manuscripts and Printed Ephemera.

ous training in reading, writing, and speaking. To learn how to read, for instance, was to identify with the performative qualities of a text: the voice of your mother as an infant, for instance, or your own voice and the voices of fellow students pronouncing words and sentences aloud from McGuffey Readers in the classroom.[24] With the advent of a mass culture of printed goods, the middle-class home became a literary institution. Books served as props for rituals of life transition and as tools of sociability during both work and leisure, as decoration in textual themes and scenes portrayed in illustrated prints and other consumer goods. Books and other luxury items that saturated domestic spaces were enlisted, as Ronald and Mary Zboray have shown, for "traditional social ends of maintaining social networks of family and community."[25] The children who reached adulthood in this world read books aloud to one another, shared diaries and letters, and engaged in conversation.[26] So too they took notes on sermons and lectures they heard, recited poetry from gift annuals, and in other ways "poached," as Michel de Certeau puts it, from the commons of mass literary culture.[27] In the habits and values of literacy it nurtured and rewarded, middle-class domesticity promoted the sharing of literary tastes between young men and women, and codified character in values of gentility—in the "standard" or "correct" usage of words promoted by etiquette books, anthologies for practical elocution, and dictionaries.[28] Horace Mann's curriculum for the common schools of Massachusetts conflated drills in literacy with respect for middle-class Protestant norms of civility and character development, as though "politeness was always inseparable from handwriting and spelling and that learning to write one's name was inseparable from morality and spiritual salvation."[29] Genteel propriety was promoted in the moralistic and sentimental literary curriculum purveyed both in the classroom and outside it in institutions such as the lecture hall and the New York Mercantile Library.

In analyzing the participatory nature of nineteenth-century theater, Lawrence Levine has reminded us that "culture" refers as much to styles of attention as to objects, partaking of class-oriented prerogatives and expectations; the audience for culture is always engaged in a complex performance of its own sensibility.[30] It is not only the dissemination of knowledge in particular venues but its *performance* within particular social contexts—the Enlightenment salon, the private academy, the collegiate literary society or debate club, the common school, the middle-class parlor, private and public libraries—that gives modes of discourse their symbolic and functional authority. That authority manifests itself not only in the abstract possession of knowledge—what one knows from having read books—but in the development of new affective and social norms for literary practice and cultural taste. The silent text, read in solitude, would become the modern academy's paradigmatic object for the definition and interpretation of literary value. Henry Patterson and his nineteenth-century peers, by contrast, defined "the literary" within a spectrum of activities that included not only silent reading but myriad forms of writing and speaking. Across diverse contexts of intellectual recreation, young men defined literary value in terms of practices rather than objects, for its moral and affective utility in fostering intimacy and social trust.

Young men understood the capital of character as an investment of time. For young men to build their characters required that they find ways to "improve" themselves outside of home and the school, in the midst of ten- or twelve-hour workdays. Bradford Morse writes to his parents on 15 February 1854, "to tell you how I spend my spare time," because they were "anxious to know how I live." He details his sleeping arrangements (on a cot, in the store where he works) and some of the routine of his diet (breakfast of steak at 7, no coffee), and assures his parents that he goes nowhere and keeps no company that might exert a bad influence ("I am 'old solitude'"). Most importantly: "I spend my time mostly in reading and study."[31] Like the diaries of other clerks, Morse's letter is a history of his moral life addressed to his future self, the mature judgment of moral omniscience. Following the path of Ben Franklin's self-making, he demonstrates his capacity to monitor his conduct in the absence of parents and teachers, and reproduces the central tenets of their training. Because fate was cast from the habitual pattern of choices and actions, time was a capital resource—to be invested in one's future character, spared and spent in exercises of literary leisure. When Morse congratulated his brother Edward on his success in finding a clerkship, he repeated the imperative of extracurricular improvement: "You must study your school books the same as if you were at school, you must learn all you can" (2 June 1853).

As they moved across a spectrum of educational and social institutions, young men learned to invest their time by cultivating habits of literary taste, and to see leisure as their major opportunity for moral work. Like other clerks, Henry Patterson carried his diary with him out of the school and the childhood home where he had first learned to use it, recording and commenting on different forms of leisure in New York City throughout the late 1830s and 1840s. How did this clerk spend his time in literary practices, and what qualities made these practices useful for building character? From many sites in the urban landscape, Patterson developed a critical vocabulary that defined the literary value of his leisure habits by their moral utility, as exercises of the affections and the will. He acquired a "reflexive consciousness" by locating literary interest not in objects but in the process and style by which one attends to them. Literary leisure obtained its moral "profit" as it became an active exercise of individual taste, rather than the passive reflex of instinct.

The most rudimentary term in Patterson's critical vocabulary, "pleasure" distinguishes many of his activities as forms of leisure. Before he has learned the relative degrees of pleasure—the many reasons one might describe an event as "pleasing"—Patterson distinguishes the value of the events he records by noting their difference from "my usual monotonous business pursuits." Aside from occasional notes about personnel changes, Patterson's work in a Manhattan dry goods store took up the largest portion of his life yet remains for the most part invisible in his diary. He mentions putting castor oil, mustard, and pepper in bottles, and one day notes that he had gotten through taking stock of store goods, "to my great joy."[32] This monotony of work represents a sameness of daily life that, it seems, cannot be redeemed through reflection in his diary. The attention that Patterson lavishes on his record of recreation suggests, in contrast, that any activity acquires meaning by the simple fact that it happens outside of work. Consequently, he records a whole range of diversions in order to validate their "pleasure." "I spent an hour very pleasantly in conversation" with two unnamed women and a man. When Patterson saw two acquaintances at a wedding, he "amused myself with conversation (which by the way was carried on in sometimes so loud a voice as to attract general attention)" until the bride and groom arrived. He noted that he was "very pleased" with a Mr. Grinnell—he went to hear him speak twenty times. He had "rare fun" boxing with his brother, practicing "almost every evening in the past week after we closed the store."[33] By accounting for these diverse activities in his diary, Patterson claims ownership of his free time as moral capital. The hours he spends at work as a dry goods clerk do not belong to him, but his wages enable him to buy the leisure on which the cultivation of character depends.

Patterson casually viewed his literary pursuits not as another kind of work but as a "pleasurable" diversion, which he chose as willingly as other forms of amusement. Indeed, his work continually threatens to absorb more of his day. "Monday our hour of closing . . . changed to 9, a very unpleasant arrangement, as it deprives me of a valuable leisure hour every evening. Tuesday I did not go to store after tea, but attended debate." Under these circumstances, Patterson learned to experience all of his leisure pursuits as interchangeable diversions. One Friday evening, he made social calls with his brother but found no friends home. Patterson then went to the Mercantile Library "to look at Audubon's birds, and came home at ten." After another Friday evening's "great deal of merriment," he passed up the chance to meet again with "the company" the next night and "stayed home writing an essay on currency, and on Saturday did same."[34] In writing about currency on weekend nights (which he probably presented to the debate club to which he belonged), Patterson takes a moral pleasure in renouncing mere fun, perhaps with an eye to his own future role on the civic stage. Because of the pressure that his work life exerted on his leisure, Patterson learned to differentiate among his various activities and distinguish their relative value. For example, when his debate club has a dinner at a restaurant, complete with champagne, speeches, and songs, Patterson writes that "the evening to me was a delightful one, and I hope profitably spent." In noting his pleasure, Patterson also suggests a qualification.

Not all evenings "delightful to me" are "profitably spent": time, in the now familiar accounting of character, is a speculative investment, the return on which remains a hope to be realized in the future. The profit of time spent now is measured by moral criteria rather than by gratification. The slight shadow cast by the profit motive on his dinner party falls more profoundly across the entire diary, as Patterson assiduously inventories the precise spending of free time, as though accounting itself could yield profit from leisure. "Last evening," he writes, "I spent over an hour in conversation with the Miss Livingstons at their house"; "I was under the necessity of wasting an hour and a half under the sound of a man . . . who was one of the most ill qualified speakers." At Peale's Museum, he "stayed an hour, was pleased laughing at the greenhorns, but with nothing else, and spent the remainder of the evening reading at home."[35] Patterson's careful attention to the passage of time represents his leisure activity as a quantifiable resource that must be invested in his self-improvement. When he tells of failing to "hear any preaching which I considered sufficient remuneration for the expenditure of time," it is a form of self-rebuke as much as a critique of the sermon. This occasion has failed to bring "sufficient remuneration," and so his time has been spent poorly.

Patterson suggests a variety of ways in which the use of leisure could bring returns to character. For example, the mere repetition of an activity was likely to reduce his interest in it. The term "as usual" denotes the potential to induce boredom, as in his "usual monotonous business pursuits" or "we amused ourselves as usual on such occasions." Patterson's decision to stay home writing about currency instead of going out with his friends suggests a preference for spending his time in a less predictable (and therefore more rewarding) manner than seeing "our usual circle" and passing another "evening as pleasantly as usual." If an activity ceased to engage Patterson as it became routine, the unexpected and surprising similarly heightened Patterson's appreciation. During a visit to northern New York, for example, he notes that he "passed the evening in conversation very pleasantly" with a Frenchman so that "to my astonishment it was almost midnight," finding himself almost locked out of his hotel as a result.[36] This anecdote suggests that a conversation succeeds to the degree that it becomes a sort of concert among the parties, absorbing in equal measure their exertion and attention, and temporarily suspending their awareness of ordinary time. He describes a recital by the singer Mr. Russell as "exceeding anything else I ever heard." Similarly, at a lecture on architecture, Patterson found himself "quite interested, instructed and unexpectedly gratified with the evening's entertainment."[37] In this instance, the interest and instruction are the more gratifying for their unexpected novelty. To lose track of time becomes the ultimate measure of value, profit beyond accounting.

Patterson appears to have attended most of the churches in New York City, using sermons and lectures alike to cultivate a literary taste for topics, speakers, styles, and contexts that would make his time profitable. He found Reverend Burchard's church, with "such goings on, clapping, stomping, etc. as I never witnessed" to be "more like a theater than a place for the worship of God." If Patterson disdained such crowd-pleasing sensationalism, however, it was less from religious scruples than because it did not suit his taste as entertainment. At a Catholic service, "I didn't pay much attention, except to the music which was splendid." Back on Unitarian soil he was chagrined to hear a "good sermon *read,* by a Mr. Lunt," but he was nevertheless consoled in being "very much pleased with the building"—"by far the handsomest, and most splendid, comfortable one I ever was in." In 1841, he writes of going to the new Church of the Ascension, where he was "pleased with the appearance of things (the sermon I did not hear, as my thoughts were entirely engrossed by my debate)," which awaited him the following Tuesday.

After Patterson joined the New York Mercantile Library, he began attending lectures more frequently and became involved with the Jefferson debate club. He increasingly evaluated both sermons and lectures according to their literary "interest." Thus, one sermon, despite its "well chosen and flowery" language, "abounding in metaphysics," "had so little impressiveness and depth and earnestness of feeling that he [the minister] left no distinct pleasurable or profitable emotions acknowledged in my mind." "Depth" and "earnest feeling" corresponded to the degree a speaker intellectually drew in and emotionally engaged Patterson, inviting him to acknowledge the "emotions in my mind." A sermon by Orville Dewey (a Unitarian minister who lectured frequently at lyceums and mercantile libraries) succeeded because "it aroused every mental faculty to strenuous exertion and excitement, and while imparting new and elevating thoughts, it also added vigor and strength to the mind and moral sentiments."[38] Patterson links literary recreation with mental "arousal"; its pleasure elicits the active reflection necessary to mental and moral improvement. Patterson writes of Henry W. Bellows's lectures in a similar vein: "His opinions are so entirely correct, his ideas so original, his expressions so clear and forceful, and his illustrations so happily chosen, that I was quite delighted and the subject is even yet continually on my mind, furnishing me with a great deal of pleasure."[39] Bellows's ability to continually surprise him with his originality helped the clerk to assimilate these ideas and keep them "continually on my mind." The lecture's effective "delight"—forceful expression and happily chosen illustration—makes it a continuing source of reflection. The most "interesting" investment of time reaps the profit of further reflection rather than momentary sensation or diversion. Thus, Patterson wrote of an "animated conversation" about whiskers with his brother and another man that he remembered weeks afterwards. At the same time, he noted that he did not "derive much profit from" a sermon he had heard days earlier: "At this moment I cannot even recollect the subject of it."

As his ongoing assessments of Henry Bellows's lectures demonstrate, the literary "profit" of leisure depended on whether it furthered his desire to "improve." Bellows was a prominent Unitarian minister and frequent speaker on the lecture circuit. With Frederick Law Olmsted, George Templeton Strong, and other patricians, he became prominent in the 1850s and 1860s in promoting various reforms of urban culture.[40] In a series of entries beginning in December 1841 and spanning the next two years, Patterson carefully compared Bellows's literary efforts in the lecture hall and at church, while gauging his own progress as a critic of oratory. After hearing Bellows for the first time at the Mercantile Library, he wrote: "On Tuesday, heard Henry Bellows deliver the best ["in all respects," crossed out] discourse as a whole I ever listened to: subject, 'the capacity for education, a distinguishing peculiarity of man' . . . His ideas were all so original, so perfectly in accordance with my own, and so clearly and beautifully expressed, that I was quite delighted." Patterson's excitement about the lecture appears here to derive from a clearly expressed originality that seems to "perfectly accord" with his thinking, as though he has suddenly found his "own" ideas articulated by someone else and given back to him for further consideration. A month later Patterson is "quite delighted" with a sermon by Bellows, "quite as much as on the occasion of his lecture before the Library Association," while in another lecture, concerning the influence of trade on character, Bellows "even surpassed himself."[41] Seeing Bellows over the span of months, however, Patterson becomes more discriminating. In July, he writes that he was "not pleased" with Bellows, due to "a repetition of ideas I have heard him express before"; four months later, he writes that a Bellows sermon was "not a practical one to me, as his discourses usually are, but I admire the ingenuity and correctness of his argument, well-chosen illustrations, and the strain of pure practical morality which pervades all his productions." Patterson's prior familiarity not only raises the threshold for originality but stiffens the criteria against which his reading judges Bellows's discourse as entertaining: the "delight" he once experienced has been tempered to a more academic "admiration." We might surmise here that novelty was crucial to how lecturers made a name for themselves, but difficult to sustain as their routines became familiar.

Within a spectrum of literary practices that also included writing, lectures, and conversation, how did Patterson understand the "profit" of reading? With the rapid institutional and technological developments of the antebellum print market, the "diffusion of knowledge," as it was called on both sides of the Atlantic, was simultaneously local, regional, and national. One might see Emerson on one of his lecture tours, or read a summary of his lecture in the local newspaper, or buy a volume of his essays that had been shipped by train from the major publishing centers in New York, Boston, and Philadelphia. One might, furthermore, see a review of the volume in a journal such as *Hunt's Merchant's Monthly*. The eclectic assortment of topics and interests that typified the popular lecture was reflected in Henry Patterson's recreational reading, which included such works as J. B. Say's *Political Economy*, Charles Dickens's *Old Curiosity Shop*, James Fenimore Cooper's *The Spy*, Malthus's *Essay on Population*, J. L. Bulkingham's *America*, and books on the laws of nations and chemistry. Patterson's expansive and inclusive cultural concerns are reflected in the book review section of *Hunt's Merchant's Monthly*, in which assessments of Emerson, Whitman, and Hawthorne appeared throughout mid century alongside reviews of sentimental novels, gift books, manuals on farming, textbooks in the physical sciences, and sundry other works.

When Patterson read these works at the New York Mercantile Library, in his room during weeknights or on Sundays, or on vacation at his parents' home in New Jersey, he did so within a social framework of received opinion. In his choice of reading he might be directed in particular topics by reviews in periodicals such as the *Knickerbocker* and newspapers such as *The New World*, against which he developed his own views by differentiation or agreement. Having read through a now obscure book and "digested it sufficiently to form an opinion," he declared *The New World's* criticism "perfectly just and sufficiently lenient throughout." Patterson also noted that because Dickens's *American Notes* "has been the theme for conversation and for newspaper criticism for several days past, and by the press and individuals has been condemned as trifling," he was "disposed to be dissatisfied with it." Instead, he recorded in his diary his own lengthy review of the work, concluding that "it is only because his words are *truth* that we wince under them so much."[42] Patterson's interest in particular texts was stimulated by topics and speakers he came across in the lecture hall. Thus, when Orville Dewey spoke on William Ellery Channing, "whom I have lately been engaged in studying," Patterson's reading was abetted by the lecturer's explication. When he sought out two volumes of Orville Dewey's discourses, or gave close attention to a story of Henry Bellows published in *Knickerbocker* magazine, he had already been impressed with the public speaking of both men.

Within this context of competing genres and modes of discourse, the literary value of any text, whether printed or spoken, was predicated on its moral credibility. Modern critics tend to see readers as responding to genres of literature, judging a text according to the consistency and quality with which it meets formal values of appreciation. Certainly nineteenth-century critics were equally attentive to the particular formal and narrative qualities of the literature they read. As Nina Baym has shown, for example, the "novel" referred to a plot narrated in prose and was most frequently accompanied by the concepts of "denouement" and "interest"; verse, on the other hand, would provoke concern with style, diction, imagery, and sentiment. In the nineteenth century, however, it was more important to assess a text as a whole, and to respond to its broadest unit of meaning. The first duty of the literary critic was "to determine the moral tendency" of a given work.[43]

Even for middle-class readers, the habit of reading was rationalized as an exercise in moral taste. Some of Patterson's most extensive praise for a fictional work went to a short story by Henry Bellows, "Edward Alford and his Playfellows." Patterson writes: "The plot is simple, and to me without interest. But the great value of the article . . . which caused it to enter so deeply, and with so happy an effect into my mind, is the principles which it inculcates and illustrates, on a variety of subjects, principally education and collaterally religion and the philosophy of life in general." Questions of literary form are pragmatic, concerned with the way particular aspects of fiction, such as plot and character, serve moral purposes of inculcation and illustration. Patterson's review of his reading shifts questions of worth from the textual object to the process by which the story "enters deeply." Like the directors of the New York Mercantile Library in their defense of fiction, Patterson believes that moral truths are more effectively imparted in the congenial garb of leisure reading rather than through the rigors of "study."

Evaluating texts for their "moral tendency," Patterson subordinates an aesthetic taste for the distinctive features of fictional form to a moral taste for the "principles" they convey. Patterson valued the specific qualities of fiction to the degree they helped one cultivate moral discrimination. When his literary club debated the "injurious effect" of reading fiction, Patterson offered a qualified defense: "I expressed my opinion as a general rule that they were of more benefit than injury, by cherishing and producing a love of literature." While "a great many instances did occur when it was carried to excess and proved highly injurious," Patterson argued that these were "only exceptions to the general rule." The "benefit" of novels, as the managers of the New York Mercantile Library would also argue, is that they encourage a taste for reading and better literature. When not balanced by other kinds of reading, however, the pleasure of fiction becomes an end in itself, carried to "excess." Patterson defines literary value with a utilitarian calculus of benefits and injuries that figures moderation and balance—the *rational* exercise of taste—as the proper end of any love of literature. At another point in his diary he describes the press's interest in "the most minute details" of sensational news in terms of bodily health, as appealing to "morbid cravings," feeding "unhealthy excitement," and "gloating over accumulated horrors." Like other antebellum critics who condemned the new mass-circulation penny papers, Patterson analyzes their lowbrow appeal in the terms of propriety, that middle-class moderation always threatened by "excess." Implicit in Patterson's judgment of the penny press is a deep distrust of verisimilitude. During a visit to New York's Academy of Fine Arts—"to see exhibition of Niagara Falls with <u>Real Water</u>, stay'd five minutes, and were [*sic*] thoroughly disgusted in that time"—it is precisely the clumsy ambition to achieve verisimilitude that Patterson finds so offensive: "So silly, so ridiculous, and childish an exhibition I never before witnessed." In this instance, the ambition to portray reality is "silly" and "childish," trading on a superficial, naïve taste for the illusion of reality rather than a mature and sophisticated appreciation of moral truth. When healthy rather than morbid, reading exercises the moral constitution, balancing pleasure with instruction, formal means with moral ends.

In his reading as well, then, Patterson measures the pleasure of leisure according to its literary "profit" for building character—for its elevating thoughts, which bring vigor and strength to the mind and moral sentiments. Reading Dickens's *Old Curiosity Shop*, he declared that the plot "has no interest to me—the characters are many of them amusing, some well depicted, others extravagant and unnatural. . . . but the chief value and beauty to me lies in that tone of deep feeling, generous love of humanity, equality and liberty, and highest standard of morality which pervades the book."[44] Here Patterson offers his definition of the literary value of literature. Rather than sustaining the reader's identification with a novel's particular reality, Dickens's plot and characters serve as vehicles for a "chief value and beauty"—the feeling, principle, and morality that, like a "tone," "pervade" the story's representational elements. Conversely, when he turns to the nonfictional *American Notes,* Patterson especially responds to Dickens's fictive style, "that quiet humor, and most comic and novel style which characterize all his writings . . . and render them attractive to me, pervade this throughout, enlivening the description, rendering the narrative instead of dry historical and statistical details a continuous succession of amusing incidents, interspersed with some valuable information and sound and useful reasoning."[45] Dickens's literary achievement lies in having used narrative and stylistic devices to animate or "enliven" otherwise "dry" history and statistics, as a vehicle by which "valuable information" and "useful reasoning" are rendered "attractive to me." Patterson declares that "His distortions of truth are unimportant, arising from his desire to make a good story." The truth that Dickens distorts in his nonfiction is as superficial and ephemeral as the devices of novelistic realism: "his words <u>are truth</u>," but obviously not a literal truth, as Patterson's emphasis here confirms. Unlike the sensational realism of the penny press, Dickens's work uses the formal resources of fiction to represent a higher, moral truth.

Reading acquires its literary value, then, when it becomes an exercise of moral taste. It fosters the 'inculcation" of moral truths or "principles" assumed to be universal but which require the critical discernment of individual readers. Access to the moral profit of reading requires exertion of the will. The worthiness of Bellows's prose pertains to how well it conveys timeless and universal truths about human nature. At the same time, this worth must be *earned* by active effort, through "careful reading, profound meditation, and practical application." So too with Dickens, literary worth becomes a function of one's perception of moral truths, and entails critical effort by the individual. For those "who can enter into his feelings and sympathize with him and appreciate his vivid and high-toned sentiments with regard to those subjects he treats seriously, [*American Notes*] will add to his already high reputation as a man of good principles and correct ideas, and an author of unusual ability and diversified powers." Patterson's account of reading suggests that literary leisure is, finally, a test of autonomy that links moral distinction to the exertions of those "who can enter feelings," sympathize, and appreciate. In the midst of competing forms of mass media and the popular tastes to which they appealed, independent judgment asserts the reader's moral sense. This kind of reading reproduces genteel propriety, valuing moderate pleasure and refined "feeling" rather than the "excess" of passion and unreflective instinct.

Identified with the moral profit of the affections and the will—what Edward Chapin termed "reflexive consciousness"—reading was also valued and practiced as a social exercise. Patterson's reading often proceeded in tandem with conversation as one type of social recreation enjoyed in the company of friends. An evening at Doctor Halsey's house "passed to my entire satisfaction," with "checkers, reading, prints, conversation, and c [etc.]." In Suckasunny, New Jersey, he spent an afternoon with family and friends "conversing, reading, enjoying ourselves." He noted that he was "much pleased with the evening enjoyment" after he spent two hours with a Miss Wright, "reading poetry aloud, conversing, and occasionally moistening my organs of speech with some lemonade." After listening to a Miss Livingston read poetry by the best-selling N. P. Willis, Patterson declared that "I never experienced the beauty of good poetry to so great a degree before, owing perhaps to my peculiar situation"[46]—his romantic interest in the reader. As these instances only begin to suggest, the reading of printed texts proceeded not only in solitude and privacy but across many sites of middle-class recreation, sociability, and courtship.

Within many contexts of middle-class leisure, the moral authority of printed words was, as we shall see with Emerson's lectures, identified with qualities of rhetorical performance that effaced distinctions between orality and print, form and content, textual object and reading subject. Books might be described as "pleasant companions during the long winter evenings." The analysis of written language was often referenced to the features of spoken language. "Punctuation performs for language, when written or printed, the combined offices which pause, emphasis and inflection do for it when spoken."[47] Particularly in the case of poetry such as Longfellow's *Hiawatha,* it might "unfold its melody without the aid of music," and sing itself. The distinctive feature of a written text, suggested by its flexible approximations of oral forms, lies in its portability. Through the constant company of a book, a reader conveniently maintains his engagement with social discourse—even when he's away from friends or outside of the lecture hall. For example, a Boston clerk wrote of putting *Hiawatha* "in a side pocket":

> This little volume has since been a traveling companion with us for many hundred miles. It has been read and re-read,—read in silence, read aloud, read to the lady we love, and ladies we do not love. Those horrid old Indian names, that gave us so much trouble when we first met them in our cursory examination, lost all their jaw-cracking terrors, when we came to them in regular course. The measure so indicates the pronunciation, that there can be no mistake about it. Wah-wah-staysee, Minnehaha—what can be more euphonious than these Indian names? It is really a pleasure to pronounce them.[48]

For this reader, the versatility of *Hiawatha's* text derived from the built-in vocal cues of its rhyme scheme because, like so much popular nineteenth-century poetry, it was meant to be read aloud. This small volume not only primes this reader for potential sociability—teaching him to pronounce difficult words, and to do so with enthusiastic pleasure instead of timidly ironic horror—but also figures in actual encounters. Comprehension here is understood in terms of social performance, not as silent decipherment. A writer's great accomplishment was, through devices such as "animation" and "illustration" in the case of prose, or "measure" and "charm" in the case of verse, to bring the sense of life to words otherwise mute and inert. Also note that this clerk attributed his early difficulty with this text to "cursory examination"—a kind of appraisal endemic to silent, solitary reading that depends primarily on the quick movement of vision over abstract alphabetic code.

Mastery of Longfellow's text, by contrast, becomes possible within a voice oriented model of reading: acquiring "familiarity" in the "regular course" of literary leisure is conducive not only to a more sophisticated appreciation of this text but to the reader's own spontaneity within social exchange. Curiously, the company of *Hiawatha* seems to inspire a compulsive process of reading on the part of the clerk. A book in one's pocket is an ever-present companion; the promise that one need never be alone. Despite the book's seeming insistence on being read, it arouses no irrational passion, no engrossed withdrawal, but accompanies the clerk out into the world, making itself heard by potentially large groups of otherwise unrelated people. The word "read" here punctuates the listing of different contexts (which are alternately romantic and illicit), the methodical sequence of the book's reading seeming to lend continuous "measure" to the otherwise disorderly variety of experience. Moreover, the book tutors the young man in elocution, transforming his disdain for "jaw-breaking" words into an appreciation of the poem's "euphonious" beauty.

As Carol Gilligan has argued, moral development follows patterns of gender socialization, promoting autonomy and competition among boys and mutuality and cooperation among girls—modern patterns of differentiation that remain haunted by the nineteenth-century ideology of the separate spheres.[49] For Henry Patterson, moral development reflected his socialization into gendered norms of propriety, "progress," and taste. In their anxious drive to become self-organizing and to account for the "profit" of leisure, young men exercised literary taste as a form of self-assertion. Critical judgment enacted a male style of will typified by action and initiative, rather than the passivity and deference that psychologists and moralists attributed to the female mind. Girls were frequently admonished to avoid too much mental exertion for the sake of their health; as Brady Morse wrote his mother, "I am proud to hear that little sister has done so well at school. She must not study too hard" (12 October 1853). The pleasure and profit of leisure for a young man depended, by contrast, on whether and how it engaged what Edward Chapin termed one's "protean" and "plastic" capacity for "reflex consciousness." Because the cultivation of character required the assertion of individual will, reading remained merely a passive rather than an active "use" of knowledge, unless one articulated a personal engagement with social discourse. Terms such as "pleasure," "profit," "animation," and "conversation" describe the relative success of a form of literary leisure in motivating the *individual's* engagement in the social production and circulation of knowledge.

The Art of Conversation

The literary habits acquired by Henry Patterson, Bradford Morse, and Anna Gale were not new to the nineteenth century, nor were they unique to the United States. The development of commerce and the adaptation to the new psychology of a consumer society before 1800 nourished in Europe a "culture of sensibility," as Barker-Benfield has noted, characterized by "the aggrandizement of feeling and its investment with moral value" in the religious, economic, domestic, and literary arenas.[50] As one consequence, throughout the eighteenth century the merchant was the object of an innovative cultural idealism, in which men altered their gender roles in the interests of commerce by cultivating heterosocial politeness and sensibility. It was for this reason that British moralists and novelists, particularly in the latter half of the eighteenth century, would impugn the nouveau riche "man of fashion" as the harbinger of social decay. With this new stereotype, the merchant functioned as a scapegoat for the ill effects of rapid social and economic change; his popular image offered moral lessons about new ways of making and spending money.[51] Although the reception of these values in the American colonies was strongly shaped by unique social and political circumstances, mercantile elites in the new world similarly sought to secure and legitimize social advancement through material refinement and the pursuit of "genteel" tastes, aristocratic pretensions, and European fashions.[52]

In eighteenth-century etiquette and conduct books, a young man becomes a gentleman by learning to comport himself with propriety and civility, according to values exemplified by polite conversation. In addition to general issues of social deportment such as "elegance of expression" and "graceful utterance," the Earl of Chesterfield's often-reprinted *Principles of Politeness* includes thirty-five "Rules for conversation"; George Washington's hand-copied "Rules of Civility & Decent Behavior" is subtitled "In Company and Conversation." As nineteenth-century conduct books extended precepts of aristocratic gentility to ordinary readers, they made literary habits and social norms of conversation central to the propriety of character. In William Alcott's *The Young Man's Guide,* for example, the "Rules of Conversation" take precedence over "On Books, and Study" in the chapter on "Improvement of the Mind," and culminate with the imperative that "what you say be strictly *true*." And as his chapter on "Social and Moral Improvement" suggests, it is particularly in heterosocial company, beginning with sisters and mothers and culminating in marriage, where conversation helps to achieve the moral end of a man's education: "Without such society his manners can never acquire the true polish of a gentleman,—general character, dignity, and refinement;—nor his mind and heart the truest and noblest sentiments of a man." If he "would profit from the society of young ladies," it is the "duty of a young man to introduce topics of conversation which are decidedly favorable to mental and moral improvement."[53] When the New York Mercantile Library erected its new building at Astor Place in the 1850s, it included a "Conversation Room" to facilitate such interactions.

As gentility was democratized for a mass audience in nineteenth-century America, young men sought to cultivate a literary taste for the social forms of middle-class life. In calculating the value of leisure for moral and mental development, young men gave particular importance to conversation. Among the quotations that the Boston clerk Bradley Cumings copied into the front of his diary was that "Conversation is the daughter of reasoning, the mother of hearts, the bond of friendship, the nourishment of content, and the occupation of men of wit."[54] As Henry Patterson's ubiquitous references to conversation suggest, the success of any social encounter depended on the quality of talk it made possible. Throughout his diary he displays an acute sensitivity to the boundaries of his social world, carefully recording his encounters with people whom he does not already know. He complains, for example, that a wedding he attended was "too fashionable, too formal, the company was too much of it strange to me." After passing an evening "with conversation, sacred music, pictures, engravings," in the company of "mostly young women," Patterson further notes that he was "introduced to strangers," with whom he had "moments of conversation." He describes a visit to a Mr. and Mrs. Curtis: "Lady very precise in her manners, and the gentlemen being a stranger to me, conversation was not very animated, but rather flagged for want of spirit." Although conduct books testify to some general anxiety with which Americans faced nineteenth-century urban environments filled with strangers,[55] Patterson's account is striking less for a fear that individuals may seek to deceive him than from his disappointment that nothing is produced from these encounters. Of a Friday night party, he observed: "The company were nearly all strangers to me, consequently I felt no interest in the proceedings, and was not at all pleased with the way in which my time was misspent."[56] He gets no purchase with strangers.

Parties, lectures, and the Jefferson debate club were comfortable, predictable contexts for engaging in the meaningful intellectual exchange of conversation. In social contexts such as the lecture hall or the salon, individuals' familiarity with tacit and informal rules facilitated the joint production of knowledge. A party at the Wennans, Patterson noted, was "not a pleasant one to me, the company, being so many of them strangers to me, flagged; the whole affair was very spiritless, or else I was so, and my imagination communicated the same tone to external things." As Patterson intuits, the "flagging tone" of the company results from the circular logic of discourse, where an individual's imagination and external reality mutually sustain a "spiritless" communication. Facing people he does not know and whom he will never see again in a small space violated this basic requirement. Like many people confronting the random anonymity of the public world, Patterson could be hesitant and inhibited as a result. Nothing ventured, nothing gained: yet the faces of strangers could make the risk of any emotional and intellectual venture unacceptably high. One understands Patterson's relief when he runs into a Mr. Williams from Drakeville and "talked with him a few minutes. It is very pleasant to meet a person from near home, even if I have not been well acquainted with him."[57]

Conversation acquired its particular literary value for antebellum clerks to the degree it fostered sociability. As Patterson explains: "And who has not been at once surprised and delighted by the coruscations of wit, and lively repartee, the earnest expression, and original thought, the welling up of fancy, learning, and humor, from the secret and unknown springs of a mind usually accounted reserved and taciturn, when subjected to the present stimulus of excitement, and surrounded by the atmosphere of congeniality and appreciation."[58] The spontaneous liberty of conversation allows strangers to suddenly become known to each other, but it must be exercised with discrimination. Conversation requires the "present stimulus" that provokes a "welling up" from the "unknown springs of the mind," rather than polite formalities. To become a literary art, conversation must combine facility with freedom, stimulating inspiration that brings "surprise" and "deeper interest." To experience it one must have a prior knowledge and expectation, an "established order" from which one may purposefully depart. In this instance Patterson expects to become taciturn at a party that is too formal, too full of strangers. The environment must provide an atmosphere of "excitement" and "congeniality," to which one must be receptive. Yet to experience delight or elicit it from others requires us to employ cultivated skills such as wit, repartee, humor, earnestness, originality, and learning. It requires what Emerson admired as "shrewdness" and "power of face," the ability to quickly assess and navigate a social situation.

True "liberty" in language is the license that artists earn only through a thorough knowledge of their media, by "acquiring mastery over that most musical of all instruments, the human tongue," as a Boston clerk described it in an article for the *Mercantile Library Reporter*.[59] As a "fine *art*," conversation must be distinguished from "talk necessary" (for transacting business of all kinds) as well as from "talk involuntary, to which we are subjected by those who seem afflicted with a sort of colloquial hemorrhage." It is "the rational means of occupying and improving the time, when individuals, few or many, for a season are thrown together in company," and may be of three kinds, the "chatty, the argumentative, and alloquial." Of these three alternatives, "Familiar, easy chat, is at once the most agreeable," but the most difficult of the three:

> It is impossible, save among those on about equal terms, from long acquaintance, congeniality of feelings, or similarity of pursuit. When such come together, in any number from two to twenty, the current of their conversation will be the weather, individual and general health, the domestic occurrences or business of the day; the sermons, conversations or amusements of the week; the fashions; the prominent state of national topics; recent discoveries in sciences; new books published; art; literature; morals or philanthropy, according to the intelligence or acquirements of the company, the time when, and the place where.[60]

Chat allows people to feel at ease socially. What makes it difficult is the freedom conferred by the seemingly automatic familiarity of those on "equal terms": depending on the participants and the occasion, chat may be about anything, and so books, art, and literature are as likely to become topics for conversation as the weather. Familiar conversation stages one's engagement in discourse as an organic consequence of acquaintance, congeniality, and similarity. The "literary" here is less a specialized body of studiously acquired knowledge than an improvised and sophisticated taste for sociability. The other types of conversational art are inferior because they make it more likely that an individual will disrupt such easy familiarity. As a sort of intellectual fencing, argumentative conversation can make discussion "doubly profitable: it sharpens and quickens the intellect, confirms or corrects our opinions, removes doubts, and enables each to participate in and share the experience of all"; and yet, it may easily fuel combative tempers and become a "dispute."[61]

Conversation offered a compelling model for all literary activity because it exemplified this culture's profound commitment to language as a medium of social cohesion.[62] As the third category of "artful talk" implies, any form of knowledge had the potential to enhance an individual's sense of authority while disrupting the voluntary interaction so essential to "familiar" social exchange. In *alloquial* talk, one person's speaking dominates discourse. He "compels your attention, or at least your silence, by mere nimbleness of tongue, force of lungs, and unblushing effrontery." The knowledge and experience acquired about conversation as an "art" mitigate the potential for coercion because they train one more broadly in the art of social exchange—to offer cooperation and seek assistance, to assume joint responsibility in the production of knowledge. "There are many men of well-filled and willing minds, who require a little judicious 'drawing out,' to contribute by their store of thought, observation and anecdote to our instruction and amusement."[63] The subservience of individual "effrontery" to mutual amusement, and the contribution of one's own thought to a greater good, reinforces an essentially economic model of literary skill. Mastery of conversation may bolster one's literary authority but it remains a potentially negative skill unless put into social circulation, adding to the common "store" of thought.

Conversation generates a surprise of feeling that compels reflection in Patterson's diary. He records the unexpected pleasure of chance encounters or conversations, separating them from others that go unnoticed, and distinguishing them from those experiences that disappoint him. For example, in one entry from 1843, he describes a picnic with friends in exemplary terms: given "good appetites, high spirits, mutual good feelings, habits of unrestrained intercourse with each other, overflowing wit and mirthfulness," Patterson asks, "who would be otherwise than pleased?" Besides elaborating on what contributes to a successful social encounter, Patterson expresses his own participation in normative terms, as if excusing any merely personal pleasure he might take from the event: "Who would be otherwise than pleased?" Instead of dispersing, however, the group spent the evening together, their "time pursued in the dullest, most unsocial manner imaginable."[64] Patterson makes an aesthetic judgment about his experience, evaluating its success or failure in "improving time." The correlation he makes between boredom and an "unsocial manner" here suggests the degree to which the success of a social encounter depends on what in the French salons of the eighteenth century was termed *esprit*, or what Voltaire called *raison ingénieuse*.[65] This esprit animates a meaningless occasion into a pleasing one characterized by wit, mirth, and unrestrained intercourse. It turns otherwise wasted time to the profit of individual and social stimulation. Patterson's picnic suggests the fragility of our emotional engagement in the social enterprise. As his commentary avers, sociability and knowledge must serve one another if leisure is to be spent well.

In evaluating the literary worth of conversation, Patterson invariably uses the term "animation" to describe the engaging and versatile use of language in public. It describes the ability to marshal argument and take a side, frequently about public issues on which many citizens would have been widely read. At his grandfather's house, Patterson notes, "I had an animated discussion on the subject of the tariff and free trade. I supported the latter, and all the rest the former." In discussing his debate club as well, Patterson took special pride in his ability to take both sides in an "animated dispute" over any one of the perennial conflicts of American politics. He supported capital punishment and the proposition that men exert greater moral influence than women. He rejected the idea that wealth exerts greater influence than knowledge or that commercial endeavors are less favorable to the development of the mind than agriculture. The oratory of lyceums and library associations tended to avoid broaching truly divisive ("sectarian") issues in the interests of collegial unity, and Patterson similarly valued his debates not because they developed particular convictions but because they refined an extemporaneous facility with oratory. He "was quite highly complimented by the judges, and my production was said to be the most able one yet presented, which was quite flattering, and I was appointed a regular debater"; he "made a short extemporaneous speech . . . the decision was in our favor." In his diary, he included lengthy quotations from his "unprepared" arguments in "lengthy animated" debates, pointing out the literary polish of his impromptu wording: "I took the view that," "My argument was something like this."[66] The commentary on political, economic, social, and moral issues that typified public discourse about character in Patterson's debates as well as in the lecture hall and in the annual reports of the mercantile libraries provided a common reservoir for social discourse. As a literary attribute, "animation" harnessed individual aggression to an interest in the *form* of public debate—a commitment to democratic conversation—while minimizing the potential for conflict and dissent that might ensue. This discourse sublimated men's personal feelings to the conventions of civic speech, in abstract debates about rights and obligations in politics and business. It was precisely the abstract complacency of this model of political debate that advocates of temperance, abolition, and other antebellum reform movements sought to disrupt by using sentimental rhetoric. By giving special importance to individual testimony and direct appeals to feeling, Harriet Beecher Stowe, Frederick Douglass, and many other writers and orators made the political personal, challenging the exclusive entitlement of native-born white males such as Patterson to participate in the civic conversation.[67]

Requiring skill and spontaneity, "animation" measures one's proficiency as reader, writer, and speaker within a paradigm of linguistic expression oriented to sociability rather than to solitude. The "animation" of conversation helped Patterson overcome his habitual discomfort with strangers. For example, on a railroad trip to northern New York, he made himself "acquainted with several of my fellow passengers, with whom I had much in-

teresting and animated conversation, on the subjects principally of abolition and the tariff." Patterson uses the knowledge and skills he has acquired
outside of work to transform social encounters into literary occasions distinguished by "animated, intelligent and familiar conversation." During a
social call in New York City he finds a "Mr. Riley, an Englishman with
whom I had quite an animated discussion on international copyright"[68]—
a discussion that uncovers a path of intimacy with someone who he would
otherwise have labeled a "stranger."

Animated conversation was an exemplary model for how nineteenth-
century Americans believed literary discourse ought to be both stimulated
by and conducive to social intimacy. As the Boston clerk further explained
in his article for the *Mercantile Literary Reporter:*

> In a mixed company, where many good powers take part in the con-
> versation, in company with a few, even when two or three join in
> unrestrained, familiar, and exciting colloquies, there is the highest in-
> tellectual enjoyment. The manner, the expression, the tone, the ges-
> ture, the lively anecdote, the brilliant wit, the sharp repartee, the
> well-conducted argument, the workings of different minds, the ani-
> mation depicted on the countenances of the speakers, the natural elo-
> quence flowing from the heart, excite a deeper interest, and make
> more lasting impressions of pleasure on the mind than the perusing of
> a book in solitude, however elegant or agreeable be the style, and
> however exciting or instructive be the theme.[69]

The "perusing of a book in solitude" in effect demands from the reader the
same "study and care" that resulted in the writing of it, so far as he must follow the "rules of rhetoric, the observance of which is necessary in writing."
Conversation seems more natural than reading because it is unpredictable.
"Greater liberties . . . naturally follow" from conversation: "we plunge in
medias res, uttering the thoughts which first arise in the mind, and expressing them in the language which first occurs . . . Then, letting ideas follow in
their natural order, we may dwell on any one of them as long as we please,
and bring up everything that relates to it, without interrupting any established order."[70] Animated conversation succeeds as a joint production of
"intellectual enjoyment" to the degree it frees participants from the discipline of rhetorical and social forms alike. "Unrestrained" colloquies among
"different minds" are conducive to a "natural eloquence," and more accommodating to the possibilities of spontaneity and surprise than written
discourse. The "deeper interest" of conversation follows not from what
one hears but from the intimacy that becomes possible only through natural expression. The "animation" on the participants' faces indicates with

"familiar" directness the "flowing from the heart." As we shall see with Emerson, it is not abstract ideas but the evidence of thought and feeling in a person's rhetorical presence that elicits and validates interest.

As a general literary attribute, "animation" denoted freedom from rules that constrain written expression, preventing the authentic or "natural" expression of feeling. From this point of view, a reader's encounter with written prose suffers from a social liability analogous to an encounter with strangers. The established order of written language—"a certain precision or conciseness of language, a certain conformation and dependence of sentences and parts of sentences, which, for the most part, having the appearance of study, would, in conversation, be thought stiff, pompous and affected"—necessarily modifies the spontaneity and "familiarity" of language that typifies good conversation. By the logic of literary leisure, prose writing lost its "appearance of study" as it incorporated the freedom and familiarity of sociability into the text. "There are some kinds of writing, the great merit of which consists in an easy flow of thought and language, such as should characterize good conversation." The pleasure of social exchange, with its "more lasting impression" on the mind, offers a metaphoric incentive to unrestrained engagement with prose. As they aspired to the ideal of "animation," both writing and speech became transparent media for that "natural eloquence" that gives society its pleasing and instructive forms.

In this way, conversation and other habits of literary leisure standardized the proprieties of discourse while making freedom from formality the measure of intimacy. As we have seen, Henry Patterson evaluated his social encounters according to the relative "animation" and "familiarity" they produced. So too, the literary value of listening to a lecture or reading a story was measured against the rhetorical qualities of social presence evoked by the *manner* of the text—the way it allows one to "enter into" the author's feelings, as Patterson noted of Dickens. As with Patterson's reading, middle-class conversation obtained its moderate and rational "pleasure" by balancing the aesthetic with the practical, the artifice of form with the spontaneity of "nature," the individual will with the social affections. Directed over time by the pedagogical imperatives of improvement, and organized across spaces of recreation such as the parlor, the lecture hall, and the library, the emotional habits and moral proprieties of middle-class intimacy became exercises of literary leisure.

If Henry Patterson generally valued an aptitude for conversation, he especially valued it in women. Two women impress Patterson with their "good conversational powers, habits of observation and much propriety of conduct." We can surmise that he applied different criteria to the form as well as the content of his exchanges with women. When he critiqued his

talks with other men, Patterson would remark on their unexpected familiarity or on their significance in touching on issues of public and national
interest. During his encounters with the Frenchman in Albany or with
strangers in a railcar, Patterson could find himself at once pleasantly surprised by and absorbed in conversations about economics and politics.
With women, by contrast, he stresses the formal "propriety" of conversation, the value of style. He finds the "acquaintance and good feelings" of
two ladies "worthy of cultivation and calculated to be of much benefit to
a young man situated as I am, by calling into action and developing the
finer feelings of his nature, refining his manners and taste, purifying his
morals."[71] Ideas are not of concern, any more than the experience of fellowship, however transitory. Instead, the acquaintance and feelings of these
women have an instrumental value for his own improvement, "calculated
to be of much benefit" by training him in the correct forms of heterosocial
conduct. In 1842, Patterson describes the "novelty" of being "engaged in
conversation for three hours" with an apparently voluble and outspoken
Englishwoman, who was "free and easy in manners, occasionally even
transgressing our standard of propriety in her conversation."[72] He admires
this conversation for qualities that might characterize a memorable encounter with another man, such as a spontaneity and interest that "engaged" him for three hours. At the same time, Patterson admonishes the
Englishwoman for precisely those qualities that made their conversation
exceptional—her violation of "standards" and "manners" of gender, of the
formal "propriety" that ought to govern a young man's exchanges with respectable women. The process of conversation matters to Patterson as an
opportunity for practicing social judgment, quite apart from the specific
subject discussed, the women's individual personalities, and indeed his personal response to them. Patterson appeals to generalized norms of gentility
and gender to define what social relationship is worthy of cultivation and
why; he values the process of conversing with women as a resource for "calculating" his improved self, as he puts it. As it calls into action, develops, re-
fines, and purifies character, conversation acquaints Patterson with the finer
feelings, nature, morals, and manners—what he already aspires to as "a
young man situated as I am."

   Like other forms of literary leisure, the literary pleasure of conversation
is defined in terms of moral discipline. To be "improving" of the will and
the affections, conversation must cultivate a taste for the proprieties of gender and class. Like Patterson, a Philadelphia bookkeeper named N. Beekley
judged women with whom he passed his time by their facility with conversation. In his diary in 1849, for example, he wrote that he "passed the
evening with miss K. R-y. She is one of the few, very few, young ladies with
whom an evening can be spent most agreeably without either music or

dancing."[73] While working as a law clerk in Hartford, Connecticut, George Watson Cole (1850–1939) complained to his diary that "I find so much conversation that is, as it seems to me, superfluous that it is very tiresome to drag though it." He then wrote on 1 December 1874: "No music tonight but a quiet chat with Louise for an hour or two and then the usual separation for the night—I believe that there is a destiny in our acquaintance and love for she is the one of all I have ever met who has secured my deep and heart-felt admiration and love." The "quiet chat" they have, without the distractions of other recreation, becomes the warrant of his "deep and heartfelt admiration and love." Two years later, on 6 August 1876, after reading the first volume of *Daniel Deronda* together, Cole and Louise "went out into the woods and stayed till six o'clock. Had a serious interview that terminated happily."[74] For Cole, intimacy is indexed to the "chat," "serious interview," and other sorts of conversation he has with his fiancée. In a similar way, James F. Fiske (1841–1909), a native of Holliston, Massachusetts, associated the quality of conversation with degrees of emotional engagement, declaring on 11 April 1857 that he and his fiancée Stella "had a splendid talk and we had a chance to express our feelings fairly plainly. If any one should happen to see this I should not wonder if they would think that I was love crushed or something else but its no such thing I only write my honest sentiments."[75] As Fiske's diary begins to suggest, courtship was among other things a *literary* institution, representing the romantic transcendence of the emotional reserve and genteel proprieties that normally regulate heterosocial intercourse. Like Cole's "serious interview," Fiske's "splendid talk" becomes a transparent medium for emotional exchange, for the consummation of natural sympathy between lovers. Self-conscious that his writing of "honest sentiments" in his diary has, like the plain expression of feeling in their conversation, become too candid and personal, Fiske abruptly changed the subject: "the reservoir caved in this afternoon."

Like other forms of literary practice, conversation takes place within liminal spaces of development, socializing young men into an intimacy organized around moral proprieties of middle-class taste. Habits of literary leisure such as conversation were morally improving because they enabled young men to cultivate that "natural sympathy" on which the happy union of husband and wife would ultimately depend. These habits helped young men to repress what Edward Chapin termed the "brute appetite" for sexual gratification by fostering a specifically moral interest in intimacy. Note, in this regard, how the New York clerk Edward Tailer writes in his diary about the engagement of one of his friends:

What delightful reflections are offered to the study of a moral and philosophical mind by the innocent amours of two young persons who know no other emotions for their actions than the pure inspirations of the nature and the heart. The strictest chastity presides at the first interviews, a word, a glance, a whisper, the pressure of trembling hand, are now the enjoyment of happiness. . . . As their visits are more frequent, and the physical love is increased, which it is by the excitement caused by their meetings, their interviews are more numerous, their conversations become longer, more delicate, more intimate, a reciprocal and exclusive confidence is established between them . . . they embrace, their hearts palpitate, a secret fire consumes them, and they finally vow to taste legitimate pleasure after swearing eternal fidelity to each other before the altar. The above case is suitable no doubt to the one in which "Ein and Joe" [nicknames] now find themselves, and may the future promise as legitimate and lasting pleasure as the few months of their engagement has thus far been fraught with.[76]

Conversation occupies a central place in this history of love. It is both a medium of social feeling and a measure of the moral value of the intimacy that results: "Their conversations become longer, more delicate, more intimate, a reciprocal and exclusive confidence is established between them." Tailer dignifies the progress of intimacy as a sequence of "interviews," proceeding from "a word, a glance, a whisper" to the "final vow" of fidelity at the marriage altar. "Physical excitement" here is conducive to union of mind and heart—"a reciprocal and exclusive confidence"—rather than a merely sexual union; the lovers' facility for conversation protects the "innocence" of their love and consummates it in the "legitimate" outcome of marriage.

What makes intimacy an object of beauty for Tailer is the consanguinity and subtlety of moral taste that issues from it. As a moral ideal rather than a physical act, intimacy requires that two individuals subordinate brute instinct to an improved facility for "longer, more delicate, more intimate" conversation; this collaboration in mutual improvement allows them to transcend their self-interest and physical desires in the natural evolution of moral sentiment. So too, Tailer's account of his friends' engagement is, itself, an exercise in moral discretion. He displaces his own voyeuristic, sexual interest in the "trembling," "palpitating," and "consuming" nature of sexual passion to the higher, more innocent pleasure of literary taste—those "delightful reflections" offered to the study of a "moral and philosophical mind." As is so often the case in the nineteenth century, the histories and desires of specific individuals are made predictable by the normative conventions of domestic sentimentality. Like Tailer's writing about it, the middle-class art of conversation brings self-control to the brute within, taming lower impulses with a higher consciousness of propriety.

What made the pleasure of heterosocial intimacy "legitimate" was, essentially, the exercise of literary taste. For middle-class Victorians, moral life tended to melodramatic struggles between light and dark; the battle for character was an internal one of the will, each Dr. Jekyll wrestling his Mr. Hyde. Given the baroque formality of the moral codes that governed respectable relations between the sexes, erotic experience that fell outside the path of propriety would be normalized by literary habits. As Richard Fox has suggested, the infamous Beecher-Tilton adultery scandal of the mid-1870s hinged on the ways in which spirituality, friendship, and sexuality become entangled in "silky webs of endearment." The intimacy that liberal Protestants achieved in the Romantic movement's language and seductive rituals of domestic literacy was a slippery slope, proceeding from the "interviews" and "mutual confessions" that bound Theodore Tilton to his wife Elizabeth in early years, to the physical and emotional pleasure surrounding their exchange of letters, to the civil charge of "criminal conversation" that he brought against Beecher for adultery with his wife.[77] "Conversations" and "interviews" were not merely euphemisms, draping naked desires in an elaborate garb of literary discretion that now looks like hypocrisy or repression, but the names for a new frontier of erotic play. When a New York clerk, Richard Robinson, carried on an affair with the prostitute Helen Jewett in the 1830s, they exchanged a series of letters laden with the conventions of bourgeois marriage, trading in "legitimate" exercises of literary taste. By combining sexual license with such moral pleasures, as Patricia Cline Cohen observes, even illicit behavior "gave inexperienced young men an accelerated study of the rituals of bourgeois courtship—learning to read and write love letters, to seek favor by means of gifts, to bend two heads over one poetry book, to defer gallantly to women, to flirt, and more."[78] Through conversation, writing, and reading, young men and women remade intimacy into the play of literary taste.

Sentimental Pathos and the Conventions of Intimacy

Respectable young men acquired a moral taste for leisure. They wrote in their diaries or read in the solitude of the boardinghouse; joined libraries, debate clubs, and literary societies; attended lectures and sermons; wrote letters to distant relatives and friends; and engaged in animated or familiar conversation with strangers, friends, and lovers. As they did so, they also acquired a taste for conventionality—what we might call a feeling for social forms, an attachment to normative patterns of gender and class. There was, of course, nothing particularly new about the journal, the letter, the lecture, or conversation as forms of discourse. What was new in the nineteenth century was their ubiquity and intensity of use by a mass audience, an audience educated within an increasingly common set of literary conventions. Through multiple stages of maturation, both men and women learned to identify the nature of thought and feeling with reflexive habits of literacy, rehearsing their lives according to a script of middle-class propriety. That script became widely available through mass print culture, standardized in the literary values and practices of domestic sentimentality.

As they left their parents to search for lives in distant cities, young men learned to master an emotional reserve as evidence of self-reliance. Note how Beekley records in his diary the incremental stages of leaving home: "Arose about 5 o'clock. Mother got up about 5 ½ clock and covered my trunk for me. Had breakfast a little after 6. Cogswell came after my trunk and valise about 20 minutes past 6. About ½ past I left home. I found it pretty hard to keep from crying on leaving the home of my childhood." As though watching himself from the distant future, Beekley crafts a sentimental drama "of leaving the home of my childhood" that subsumes the impulse to cry into manly stoicism. Pain or regret about leaving home, when "it was hard not to keep from crying," is consigned to the past tense by the detached, present-day determination of his moral Other: "I have resolved to be as manly as possible about it."[79] Through literary practices, young men learned not only to break the emotional bonds that tied them to the past, but also to manage emotion as a kind of literary capital, to be invested gradually in the negotiations of newfound intimacy. Early in the century, after exchanging diaries with Ebenezer Grovesner, New Jersey resident Rachel van Dyke complained: "to read my journal I may almost say that with a few exceptions you read my heart," while the diary of her future husband was "merely a register of time."[80] As it became more certain that they would share their futures with a particular woman, however, men revealed themselves more fully within the Romantic theater of domestic privacy. Indeed, their success in creating their own homes depended on their dexterity with emotional expression.

As they learned to value literacy as a facility, repetitively practiced throughout their movement to adulthood, young middle-class men were trained in habits of feeling. They entered a social geography that associated masculinity with reserve and reticence in public, while encouraging self-revelation and sentiment in private. "Victorians designated the street and marketplace as regions of expressive control," as Karen Lystra observes, "the parlor as a middle-landscape of self-restraint; and the inner sanctum of the home as the locus of freedom and the open heart."[81] As young men confronted the contradictory demands of this social geography, they associated this open heart with the domestic forms of literary practice. Recalling his first separation from his family, Edward Ayer (1841–1927) wrote about how, as an eighteen-year-old soldier in 1860, he received his first letter from home:

"On receiving my mail at Council Bluffs, I dared not trust myself to open it before anybody, so I took it and went off in the big sunflowers, towards the Missouri river, away from everybody, sat down alone, and read the letters over, of course, crying most of the time."[82] By the time Ayer received this letter, he knew that he had to restrain his feelings when in the company of men. Lest a display of sentiment make him seem childish or unmanly, he improvises a private space in which to open the letter. Feeling here has social parameters: there are boundaries to the "trust" of others and of oneself, which become palpable in where one chooses to read a letter. "Crying most of the time" once he is alone, Ayer exercises a literary taste for feeling, organizing emotional expression around tokens and habits of domesticity.

The middle-class literary landscape that took shape during the nineteenth century made domestic intimacy the goal of a man's social and moral development. In spaces of literary leisure, young men practiced the trust, confidence, and candor on which their eventual marriages would depend. As Ellen Rothman has pointed out, middle-class courtship was dominated by a vision of romantic love that "stressed mutuality, commonality, and sympathy between man and woman—precisely those qualities most likely to bridge the widening gap between home and world." Husbands and wives increasingly inhabited separate worlds of work and home, so it became imperative that young men and women develop shared tastes and interests during their courtship. "By feeling at liberty—indeed, under obligation—to share their inner selves young men and women could lessen the distance that divided them."[83] Domestic intimacy required a cross-gender identification that would bridge diverging spheres of public and private. In this context, intimacy was not merely the result of instinctive desire or spontaneous feeling but a collaborative performance of sincerity and sympathy, forged from the Romantic conventions of literary taste. As they exchanged books and diaries as tokens of affection, men and women developed new emotional standards for intimacy, creating a shared sense of self from collective practices of reading and writing.[84]

As they developed their literary tastes across a spectrum of media and social spaces, middle-class men and women were engaged in a peculiar, oddly public kind of moral work—the production of domestic intimacy. Literary leisure had a moral trajectory, moving young men from the anonymity of public life to the emotional trust idealized by the middle-class home. In his diary, Benjamin Tilton continually romanticized the bonds of family. At one point he notes of his future bride's family that "the love and affection that swells in and governs that domestic circle is domestic happiness portrayed." At another point, he admires the "love and affection so pleasing to witness between brother and sisters—mutually reciprocated between them and their parents."[85] Tilton has little personal experience with Mary's family, but his familiarity with the generic image of "domestic happiness" allows him to judge their particular "portrayal" or enactment of it. He can recognize and be "pleased" by aspects of domestic affection—that it ought to "swell in and govern" the group's relations, for example, and that it should be reciprocal. When young men idealized marriage, it was not as an abstract obligation but as a duty to the universal moral laws of nature. As Edward Tailer wrote in his diary on 7 July 1852: "The perfection and sincerity of friendship can only be found in the marriage state, where an identity of interest shuts out all petty jealousies, and a unity of thought, sentiment, feeling, and conduct exists." Domesticity appeared to these young men as a unique opportunity to achieve the highest development of their nature: an arena for perfect friendship, where individual identity dissolves in the marital "identity of interests," a "unity" of thought, feeling, and conduct. Young men moved toward this moral destination of the home, then, by developing a literary taste for the transparency of private language and feeling—for that natural sentiment of domestic ideology on which the credibility of middle-class character would increasingly depend.

Literary taste was, finally, an expression of moral sentiment that was held to be universal to human nature. Note how a clerk reviews a lecture by Henry Ward Beecher at the Boston Mercantile Library: "There are natural sympathies and generous sentiments in every breast which instinctively respond when rightly appealed to. No one understands this art better, or practices it so skillfully as Mr. Beecher. The feelings of childhood, the memories of home, the love of a mother, the beauties of nature and the calm delights of the country, are subjects which no artist can paint in more vivid colors than himself."[86] This praise of Beecher's eloquence suggests how fully literary leisure was built around the predictable familiarity of sentimental discourse, commonplace topics of moral consensus that were linked to "natural sympathies and generous sentiments." And yet, these natural sympathies and moral sentiments remain merely latent until they are "skillfully" or "rightly appealed to"—at which point they become the "instinctive" response to what now seem to be the most tired clichés of sentimental literature. Through the judicious appeal to commonplace moral precepts, the lecturer thus gained an emotional access to his audience that was intimate and individual but also typical and universal—the "instinctive" and "natural" response "in every breast."

In responding to Beecher's eloquence, middle-class audiences attached moral value to the conventionality of sentiment: feeling was most authentic when it was commonplace, an expression of natural sympathy that was at once contrived and spontaneous. Like Beecher's lectures, young men traded in sentimental commonplaces to render their personal response to otherwise impersonal norms of social discourse. Once transposed to even the briefest entry in a diary, otherwise spontaneous effusions on the beauty of passing landscapes and seascapes become flights of literary fancy. "The evening was cold," Tilton writes, "and the full moon in all its majesty was wending its course through the brilliant stars like diamonds were twinkling from the clear blue arch of heaven."[87] So too, young men painted their childhood in the predictable light of pastoral nostalgia. At the age of twenty-four, Tilton writes of returning to "the home of my childhood," to "mingle with those who <u>were</u> near and dear, to wander over the ground I had often trod before; or sit on the green sod by the 'little brook' where with hook and line my first fish I caught. Well do I remember the joy and surprise my unexpected success occasioned me." Recollection of specific events, or frustration about the alienation he might have felt from this simpler, carefree world are subordinated here to aesthetic appreciation of a timeless, idealized past. Continuing in this vein, he returns in memory to "thread the winding path to the 'Freeling Mill,' and by the side of the 'dam' watch the smooth sheet of water as it glided over rumbling and foaming into the stream below."[88] His concern is not in recalling those who "<u>were</u> near and dear" but in rendering picturesque moments and affecting sensations that are, in his recollection, best appreciated in the implied presence of an omniscient social audience.

Through practices of literary leisure, young men learned to value seemingly private and personal experience as objects of literary taste. The diaries of young men not only demonstrate their familiarity with the terms of domestic sentiment but their identification of these sentiments with the habits of literary practice. After Tilton became engaged to Mary Baker, for example, he began referring to himself and his fiancée as "the Bride and Groom." He further embellishes their attachment with an assortment of sentimental endearments: "two hearts that have beat in unison," "her whom I fondly loved," "her whom I have chosen as my first love." Tilton coyly describes their betrothal as "moments of happiness which the silent gushings of the imagination can best express"—speaking in his diary about something best expressed by silence. This stylized language obviously did not represent the extent of Tilton's relationship with Mary, since despite the "gushings" of imagination he soon admitted his unfamiliarity with her: "The bride improves on acquaintance, she appears to be amiable in her deportment and agreeable in conversation."[89] At the very least, Tilton's apparent relief at the bride's improvement suggests how his romantic endearments had a cultural purpose distinct from his particular acquaintance with her. Mary's personal qualities of deportment and conversation were peripheral to the literary pleasure he took in their romance. Literary conventions of family and romance furnished these clerks with formulas of het-

eronormative affect, which our own mass culture of sentimentality continues to retail to young men and women.[90]

Sentimental commonplaces were not passively absorbed through reading and other modes of middle-class leisure and consumption, but developed actively through dexterous exercises of literary taste. Directed by the
relentless imperative of improvement, the habitual exercise of literary
leisure taught young men and women to identify the "nature" of feeling
with its repetitive practice. As a result, the emotional lives they represent in
their diaries and letters are characterized as much by elaborate forms of propriety and evasion as by earnest sincerity and idealism. Tilton writes frequently of his "fond and devoted mother," noting the "feelings of anxiety
for her absent children which none but a mother knows," while only once
alluding to her debilitating rheumatism. This sort of specific information,
and the realism it might convey, is of little account for Tilton's literary purposes. So too, in mentioning the death of his sister, Tilton writes not of her,
nor of his relationship with her; instead, he offers a series of generic sentiments meant to sustain a critical detachment: "But who can describe the
feelings of a husband thus unexpectedly deprived of one who was 'near and
dear.' One who was to share in his joys . . . Of our happy circle she was the
first, on whom grim death had cast his withering mantle."[91] The particular
reality of his own mother's condition, his sister's death, his disillusionment
with Mary and many other topics are assumed, evidently, to be types of personal knowledge that are irrelevant to the increasingly literary process of
cultivating character in the domestic sphere.

Why does Tilton speak in his diary about "gushings of imagination" that
are "best expressed" through silence? As the letters and diaries of these
young men demonstrate, domestic feeling did not become sincere or natural until it became an object of literary discipline. Intimacy does not
emerge in these diaries, as it does in our modern idiom of privacy, through
the whispered tones of the special confidence or the privileged confession
to our friends and therapists. These young men arrive at knowledge of their
personal identities and values by literally talking themselves into the moral
obligations of middle-class domesticity. When Tilton's sister dies, he describes the loss from the perspective of his bereaved brother-in-law: "Who
can describe the feelings of a husband . . ." He converts personal loss into
an impersonal lesson on the nature of the familial roles he will eventually assume. Bearing witness to a child's death similarly moves him to identify
with his future life as a father, but in that case the spectacle of his own potential grief unnerves him so much that it calls the entire enterprise of family into question. Familiar verbal postures such as "near and dear" distance
one from the pain of loss. By translating this incident into a sentimental

form, Tilton can speculate about a husband's role and the relationship binding him to "one who was to share in his joys," and prevent himself from dwelling on the specific fate of his brother-in-law. The conventionality of social discourse enabled young men to convert personal experience into useful knowledge. As it became the insistent, commonplace topic of literary practice, sentimental taste enabled young men to prepare for the social roles they would assume as adults. Habits of literary leisure taught young men to invest the moral obligations of character with emotional conviction, initiating them into a feminized rhetoric in which one could rehearse the moral duties of domesticity.

Organized across time and space in habits of socialization and exercises of leisure, literary practices became the medium of middle-class emotion. From their intensive training across multiple sites of education and sociability, young men learned to see reading, writing, and speech as a transparent means for self-expression and social exchange. Thus we find Henry Patterson in 1842, sitting with his fiancée Eleanor, listening to a sermon by Henry Bellows: "My heart involuntarily swelled with joy and gratitude, to be once more seated under the sound of his voice, breathing forth words of hope, consolation, and guidance, with her by my side who is dear to me as life, and whom I was sweetly conscious was with me, in spirit, in love, and in a just appreciation of and sympathy with the truths to which we were listening."[92] In an instant, years of social training that kept men and women at a distance give way to an "involuntary" swelling of feeling that brings them together. The boundaries of the individual self that Patterson had so assiduously built through his literary exercises of the will dissolve "in spirit, in love," in becoming "sweetly conscious" of "her by my side who is dear as life." If middle-class people increasingly saw character in the public world as opaque—hidden within a duplicitous world of confidence men—they came in such sentimental devotions to see it as excessively transparent; we cannot know what Eleanor felt or heard, beyond Henry's conviction of their unity of feeling and thought. In their literary patterns of courtship, however, men and women "simultaneously denied/transcended their sexual difference," and defined the individual self "primarily in relationship to others."[93]

Patterson's communion with his beloved is both literary and spiritual, elicited and sanctified by Bellows's words as they "are seated under the sound of his voice." After avidly following Bellows in the lecture hall, Patterson had begun to attend his sermons, attracted to a speaking style that he elsewhere praised as "so eloquent, and so feeling."[94] As we have seen, Patterson had acquired a "just appreciation" for moral truths outside of church, but at this moment his experience of those truths blurs distinctions we might make between sacred and secular, religious and domestic. Like the words that men and women crafted for their letters and diaries, or read in sentimental prose and fiction, or exchanged in animated conversation, the words that Patterson hears derive their spiritual power and emotional force from a faith in literary practices that was, as Richard Fox observes, both middle class and Romantic: "middle class because it emphasized individual autonomy; Romantic because it located autonomy in growth towards ever more fulsome expressiveness—an expressiveness modeled by their favorite novelists or poets. Middle class because it stressed internalized self-control . . . Romantic because it imagined that individual independence, control, and expression were compatible with, and indeed undergirded by, wider webs of organic solidarity, beginning with the soul union of two lovers."[95] With school, family, friendship, and romance mediated by institutions and habits of mass literacy, young men learned to associate moral authority not with the assumption of public duties but with natural sympathy in private—subjective experience authorized by institutions and practices of literary leisure.

A developing American middle class came to identify the cultural capital of literary leisure with the inexorable development of one's moral nature. As they trained young men and women to move within the middle-class geography of intimacy, literary habits were naturalized as habits of mind and heart: the play of wandering thought in a journal; the emotions released by the sound of a voice. As they acquired a facility for literacy, and attached moral value to its habitual exercise in social contexts of leisure, young men such as Henry Patterson, Benjamin Tilton, and Bradford Morse achieved the conviction of character. Through their "exertions" and "exercises" of literary taste, the moral commonplaces and affective obligations of sentimental domesticity became compelling forms of self-realization, the personal achievement of a normative individuality. The middle-class home was the destination of a youth's moral and mental "improvement"—the threshold of adult independence and mature responsibility, when boys became husbands and fathers.

Within the new institutions and practices of mass leisure, ordinary people came to organize their personal and social lives as literary experience, learning to claim the moral authority of character within new economies of gender and class. To an unprecedented degree, technologies and institutions of mass literacy made particular kinds of writing, reading, and speaking both habitual and conventional—seemingly as natural as gendered patterns of affective experience and social obligation, as implacable as the middle-class will to improve. The complex facility for advanced literacy that young men and women acquired taught them to identify the moral obligations of adult life with the inexorable progress of the maturing mind, the sincere expression of the heart. The reflex consciousness that young men cultivated through practices of literary leisure gave aesthetic pleasure its moral utility, the passive consumption of culture its productive emotional end, the impersonal commonplace its personal interest. By making conventions of gender and class individualized habits of thought and feeling, habits of literacy made the values and institutions of domestic privacy morally compelling and emotionally irresistible. Young men and women came not merely to know the roles expected of them as adults but how to play these roles with conviction.

In the middle-class home, the boundaries of propriety were physical, enforced by the norms of gender and class. They were also imaginative, commonplace sentiments and stylized conventions of expression that, for a mass audience of readers and writers, transformed the private sphere into a stage for literary performance. As they mastered habits of literacy, young men increasingly relocated the authority of character from the public world, with which it had been engaged throughout the eighteenth century, to the domestic sphere. The self-consciousness with which ordinary young men played their domestic parts, however, may suggest less the fall of public man, as Richard Sennett and other scholars have argued in their histories of bourgeois life, than its relocation indoors.[96] The pleasure and guilt that attended domestic propriety had an emotional and psychological resonance very different from honor and reputation, which were valued within the aristocratic duties of character. Character was privatized and personalized, becoming a psychological process of self-realization rather than a normative process of social accreditation.

Nothing is more striking about young men's presence in the middle-class landscape of literacy, however, than its temporary, provisional nature. As they struggled with the haste and anxiety of a business world that respected male autonomy more than propriety, young men would eventually excuse themselves from habits and rituals that, at home and school, had socialized them for the feelings and duties of middle-class "life." Adult men became too engaged with the "haste" of their work lives to write letters to their children, or to continue the habit of writing in diaries much past their mid to late twenties. In another illustration from *The Imperial Highway*, a husband and father sits alone in the parlor, surrounded by the members of his family as they engage in the practices of literacy and sociability that came to distinguish "A Happy Home" (fig. 10). As his wife tends to one child, siblings do their schoolwork, and the eldest daughter sings at the piano with a gentleman caller, the man of the house reads his newspaper, preoccupied with worldly affairs. Indeed, as Edward Tailer became a successful New York merchant and bank director, his diary was taken over by public life: in 1860 he began pasting clippings from newspapers and other printed sources in its pages, leaving his personal entries shorter and fewer in num-

A HAPPY HOME.

Figure 10   "A Happy Home," from *The Imperial Highway* (1883). Adult men become distant, if not absent, figures in the literary landscape of the middle-class parlor. As members of his family pursue leisure, education, and sociability around him, the father sits in splendid isolation, absorbed in the cares of the public sphere.

ber.[97] In the meantime, as Thorstein Veblen observed in *The Theory of the Leisure Class* (1899), the "conspicuous consumption" and etiquette that defined middle-class aspirations became the special charge of adult women. Wives and mothers composed polite letters, practiced ornamental scripts for invitations and calling cards, and in other ways enforced genteel norms of gender and class to which respectable men delegated their increasingly symbolic claims to moral distinction.[98] By the late nineteenth century, middle-class women dominated the membership of the New York Mercantile Library, just as they became the primary constituency for lectures sponsored by the Chautauqua movement and the reading groups organized by women's clubs in communities across the United States.[99] As practices of reading, writing, and conversation were naturalized in practices of literary leisure, young men would find the domestication of character in the private sphere at odds with, if not irrelevant to, the demands of work in the public sphere.

Chapter Three
Popular Philosophy and Democratic Voice: Emerson in the Lecture Hall

Like thousands of other young men before the Civil War, Benjamin Tilton had come to New York City with hopes of achieving success in the new world of urban capitalism. He worked as a clerk in a series of dry goods stores before he eventually opened up his own hardware establishment. Like so many other ordinary people whose personal writings survive, largely unread, in libraries and archives across the United States, he wrote a diary in which he sought to interpret the world in which he found himself. In 1841, at the age of twenty-three, he began his diary with a narrative of his moral life—the life that began when he left his family at age seventeen and went searching for work. He came to New York City from New Jersey in 1835, he writes, in order to gain an opportunity for "further advance-ment." In leaving home and taking up the uncertainties that awaited him as a merchant's clerk in Manhattan, he was "eager to pass from the quiet of a country village to the tumult of a city life." Inevitably, the big city assaulted the naive youth's senses with the "noise and confusion of rattling carts," with a bustle and activity that make even the busiest of childhood homes seem an idyll of peace and tranquility. Months after his arrival in New York, Tilton would experience more "tumult" when the economic crisis of 1837 suddenly put an end to the boom times, as well as to the speculations about personal "advancement" on which young men staked their futures.[1]

As Tilton later recognizes, the vicissitudes of a civic life organized around the marketplace are intensely personal. He follows his description of the economic "revulsions" of 1837 with an extended meditation on his own emotional and moral condition. Concluding that economic prosperity had depended on speculative bubbles and willful delusions, he found that the prosperity of the soul—its happiness—depends on emotional and psy-chic states that are themselves tenuous and insubstantial:

How fluctuating is our happiness. At times the soul feels so light, so buoyant—so forgetful of all troubles real or imaginary (and the latter is by no means the least source from whence they arise) and again so gloomy—so oppressed. How the soul then struggles to obtain light through the dark cloud of uncertainty that envelopes it. To free itself from the bondage of oppression. At times I have felt ready to exclaim "why was I born and for what cause came I into the world?" Such a feeling of consciousness of my "shortcomings" of my inability to render happy or give enjoyment to a single being. The gayety that floats around meets with no response within me. All seems doubt and uncertainty. For whom do I live? Save the hope indulged in for the power to add, in the feelings of the heart, its tribute of happiness to a fond mother—none! Yet hope swells in the human heart, whispers encouragement and inspires it with renewed energy; sweetening the present in the gilded prospects it anticipates in the future. How true are these lines,

'O hope! Sweet flatterer! thy delusive touch
sheds on afflicted minds the balm of comfort
Relieves the load of poverty—sustains
The captive, bending with the weight of bonds
And smooths the pillow of disease and pain.'[2]

Like Max Weber with his famous image of the iron cage in *The Protestant Ethic,* Tilton finds man's freedom held hostage by the speculative habits of modern capitalism. At this moment, Tilton's diary transposes reflections about the illusory nature of economic value into an allegory about the "captive" soul—about the fate of his own moral autonomy in an unpredictable economic and social world. "How fluctuating is our happiness": Like the sudden shifts of fortune, it gives way to the despair and alienation that Tilton evokes by quoting a passage of sentimental verse.[3] The soul aspires to a conviction that, like the material values of economic life, proves to be ephemeral. The "bonds" and "load of poverty" lie finally not in the material world but within the "afflicted minds" of human reason itself. In these moments of metaphysical doubt, Tilton ceases to respond to the "gayety that floats around me," to feel the obligations he bears in being loved by others and in inhabiting a social world. Tilton is so acutely aware of his "shortcomings" as to question the very purpose of his life: Why was I born? For whom do I live?

Tilton's diary records a loss of philosophical composure that strips his actions of purpose and empties his beliefs of conviction. We might attribute Tilton's "fluctuations of happiness" to a bout of loneliness, and to a taste for emotional drama, both of which now seem very typical of late adolescence in modern America. We might interpret his words from a contemporary point of view, as a crisis of "identity." The boy is merely lonely, in other words, and the formulaic and conventional terms in which he expresses this mood confirms for modern readers the seeming banality of the moment. And yet, the drama of moral identity—of how, as Emerson puts it, the "soul becomes"—will necessarily look prosaic when seen in the contexts where ordinary people struggle to fix their values, against the limited resources by which individuals find their identities and cultivate character. The middle-class pursuit of character proceeded from the exigencies of market culture. No less than the thousands of young people who face uncertain and lonely prospects in today's job market, Tilton was chasing hope.

Lamenting the "fluctuations of happiness," Tilton expresses a desire to escape the captivity of his own thoughts and perceptions—to be freed from the "poverty" of subjectivity. From this perspective, Tilton's reflections should be understood in the context of simple questions about moral epistemology and individual autonomy that have been an enduring concern of Western philosophy. Recent historians of philosophy, such as Pierre Hadot, Michel Foucault, and Martha Nussbaum, have sought in related ways to redescribe Western thought from the perspective of an ancient tradition of ethical practice. Hadot's analysis of the Hellenistic and Roman schools of philosophy, for example, asks that we set aside the modern idea of philosophy as a purely theoretical activity concerned with discourse, and reconsider it from a holistic and functional perspective. To study philosophy among the ancient Epicureans or the Stoics was to practice what Hadot terms "spiritual exercises" concerned with attention to the present, meditation, friendship, and training to face death, directed toward the pursuit of wisdom. "In their view, philosophy did not consist in teaching an abstract theory—much less in the exegesis of texts—but rather in the art of living." As practice rather than theory, the art of living had a therapeutic dimension, concerned with the transformation of personality and the acquisition of new habits of perception and behavior. The classical practice of philosophy demanded the alteration of one's lifestyle in the everyday world because, like all spiritual forms of knowledge, it aspired to the experience of conversion: a transcendent, self-conscious liberation of the self "from the state of alienation into which it has been plunged by worries, passions, and desires" in the everyday world. "The 'self' liberated in this way," Hadot adds, "is no longer merely our egoistic, passionate individuality: it is our moral person, open to universality and objectivity, and participating in universal nature or thought."[4]

As with the "spiritual exercises" of the Epicureans and the Stoics, the ideological content of philosophy should not be separated from historical forms of pedagogy. The acquisition of knowledge has to be responsive to the practical imperatives of learning by living. As Hadot has emphasized, ancient philosophy concerned itself with the cultivation of an attitude, with an orientation or disposition, rather than with those concepts and ideas that we might be inclined to segregate as the "content" of philosophy. All of the ancient schools agreed that man, "before his philosophical conversion, is in a state of unhappy disquiet," and for all, "happiness consists in independence, freedom, autonomy. In other words, happiness is the return to the essential: that which is truly 'ourselves' and which depends on us."[5] Happiness, then, is not a "feeling" or a "mood" from our own psychological perspective, in which the self transparently reveals its desires and conflicts through the spontaneous expression of emotion (or, alternatively, represses this subjective data through conscious control or neurotic displacement). It is a philosophical object that must be fashioned and cultivated. Each of the ancient schools used particular strategies to "live and think according to the norm of wisdom." To engage in spiritual exercises was to discover one's "moral person," to claim an integrity and autonomy as an ethical agent that was explicitly identified with the cultivation of reason and self-discipline. Happiness and wisdom are not only ideals or feelings but convictions that one carries into the world.

What does it mean to practice philosophy in a modern democratic culture? How were the terms of this conversion of the self altered within the social and economic context of market culture? Or, as Stanley Cavell has recently asked: "What happens to philosophy if its claim to provide foundations is removed from it—say the founding of morality in reason or in passion, of society in a contract, of science in transcendental logic, of ideas in impressions, of language in universals or in a formalism of rules?" Cavell has argued that Ralph Waldo Emerson and Henry David Thoreau, by addressing themselves to the relative "poverty" of American culture rather than to Europe's wealth of learning, inaugurated a new direction for philosophical inquiry concerned with "the common, the low, the familiar." This new direction entailed a shift in the practice of philosophy: democratic philosophy takes literary forms that, by revising European Romanticism for the particular conditions of the New World, resist the ways in which modern scholars constitute philosophy as a genre of knowledge, a tradition of discourse. As we shall see, Cavell's own interpretation of how an Emerson essay "conceives its work to be realized"—of how we understand his work as "attracting the human (in practice, his individual readers) to the project of becoming human"—can benefit from a fuller description of the institutional and social context in which philosophy found democratic forms.[6]

In nineteenth-century America, the practice of philosophy found a mass audience in the lecture hall. Tilton was one of thousands of persons who would hear Emerson speak, and go on to record his encounter with the Sage in his diary. Many people continued to find consolation and guidance in the traditional sermons they heard at church, as they had for centuries. But increasingly, the search for wisdom and happiness encompassed a secular appetite for "rational amusement" and "useful knowledge," and was fueled by an obsession with spoken eloquence. With the Lyceum movement, which began in the late 1820s, and with the spread of other agencies for adult education such as mercantile libraries and young men's associations, public lectures came to be offered in cities and towns across the United States. In the lecture hall, ministers such as Henry Ward Beecher and ex-ministers like Emerson carved out a new vocation as public intellectuals, achieving regional and even national name-brand recognition as their speeches were marketed through newspapers and packaged in books. When Emerson left his first position as minister of Boston's First Congregational Church after only six months, he drew on his professional training in the homiletic tradition to build a new institution of civic education. He made what Peter Gibian terms a "counter-Augustinian conversion from theology to rhetoric, from a calling as minister to a new vocation as lecturer."[7] While helping to win respect for oratory as a literary genre with its own distinctive American tradition, Emerson and other popular speakers used the lecture to develop a kind of secular ministry. "I look upon the lecture room as the church of today," as Emerson himself put it.[8]

Like writing in a diary, or borrowing a book from a library, attending a popular lecture was a means of spiritual exercise or a technology of the self—a practical means by which ordinary people sought to define and exercise moral agency. Emerson's middle-class contemporaries did not assume, as recent critics have, that his central message about the moral warrant of nature was incompatible with their interest in common sense rules for success.[9] Rather, they understood the development of character as an ethical project, demanding the cultivation of one's moral person within the everyday world. Because Tilton could not with lasting confidence take his economic or social place for granted, the quotidian pursuit of happiness, independence, and success became his occasion for philosophy. Students of the elitist, ancient schools of philosophy were protected from the prosaic but urgent problems faced by those of another caste or gender. Detachment and asceticism, of the sort idealized by classical thought and sustained in the early American college by the study of Greek and Latin, were luxuries that nineteenth-century clerks could not afford. Young men such as Tilton sought to build character not as an abstraction but in the midst of "the real world"—which the Platonic tradition has always sought to renounce—in the struggle to find work and love.

The knowledge about character purveyed by Emerson and others in the lecture hall was a vernacular philosophy, a moral pedagogy concerned with imparting wisdom about right modes of conduct in the volatile world of market culture. Its purpose was to guide Americans in the democratic art of living under capitalism. As it was developed in the written, printed, and oral modes of literary leisure in the commercial marketplace, this discourse potentially extended philosophical capacities to a broad democratic audience. To develop this proposition, this chapter discusses briefly the theme of composure—or the right disposition of one's faculties—in Emerson's later work. On the popular lecture circuit, and in texts such as *The Conduct of Life,* Emerson used imagery drawn from business life to develop a philosophy that addressed the epistemological dilemmas and ethical opportunities of market culture. To Tilton and other young men, he offered practical guidance on the conduct of life. To appreciate Emerson's status as a philosopher among his contemporaries requires that we appreciate the particular terms in which they described his effect and that we understand the centrality of the lecture hall in the building of middle-class character. By appreciating the multiple formats of Emerson's reputation and the variety of ways that audiences read and practiced what he presented to them, we gain a less static picture of Emerson as a transcendentalist, and a fuller sense of the literary landscape in which he worked.

The lecture hall was a privileged arena for the acquisition of moral conviction in nineteenth-century America. Seeing Emerson in the lecture hall entailed a complex range of intellectual and emotional engagement on the part of the audience. Emerson's appeal to young men such as Tilton depended on a commitment to rhetorical eloquence that, in its epistemological assumptions and modes of engagement, diverged from modern text-centered values and practices oriented to the solitary, silent reading of books. The knowledge about character that Emerson dispensed in the lecture hall only became moral to the degree it exemplified a philosophical attitude, an *ethos* that ordinary people might bring to the business of living. Our own ways of reading Emerson, in other words, cannot speak for the manner in which audiences responded to him in the lecture hall or, more broadly, how they valued the moral use of knowledge for building character. By considering alternative ways of reading and hearing Emerson, in his time and in our own, we can appreciate in new ways how different literary institutions and practices invest certain kinds of knowledge with moral authority. In the lecture hall, Emerson sought to locate sources of advice and conviction outside the learned professions where they had traditionally resided. In asking what happiness and wisdom might look like amid the tumult of modern life, he helped to redefine the practice of philosophy for democratic culture.

Becoming Whole: The Struggle for Composure

Like Ulysses sailing within range of the Sirens, individuals coming off farms to bustling commercial centers such as New York or Philadelphia in the decades before the Civil War found themselves facing a challenge of self-command. They needed to engage not merely in "self-control" but to compose themselves in the midst of an unpredictable and dangerous world—and to commit themselves to a vision of the future despite their limited experience, despite their own untested natures and capacities. Before the financial collapse of 1837, it had seemed to Benjamin Tilton that the epic of economic progress prophesied by the boosters of the mercantile profession was indeed coming true. "Man's ambition" was building railroads, "ploughing every river with floating palaces of steam . . . shading the ocean itself with numerous sails spread out to the breeze." Tilton's words echo the countless celebrations of liberal progress which, as a member of the New York Mercantile Library, he might have heard in the late 1830s and early 1840s in lectures on "The Morals of Mercantile Life" or read in periodicals such as *Hunt's Merchant's Monthly.* So too, Tilton's observations about the 1837 crisis repeat their moral admonitions about the dangers of speculation: "The chain was complete; and had each class pursued their legitimate calling, no link need have been broken." Because people want to get rich in a day, they forsook "legitimate business" and branched out into "wild speculations for 'townlots' and 'mulberry trees.'" In the end, Tilton writes, "Reality was abandoned [for] dreams of immediate wealth . . . Onward they rushed, until too late they discovered they'd been pursuing a shadow."[10] A "legitimate calling," according to Tilton's theory, sustains the optimal engagement of one's faculties with "reality." The chain of prosperity is broken by the disordering of individual perception, the "abandonment" of reality that ends in the too-late shock that what one took as certain and true as golden wealth was illusory. Given the incidence of bankruptcy, madness, and suicide in the urban business world, self-reliance, trust in one's own perceptions and judgments, was no academic matter.

By equating the moral "legitimacy" of a calling with a composure of the senses, Tilton assumed with many of his contemporaries that temperament and capacity suited workers to particular vocations. What distinguished the businessman from the lawyer, the doctor, the minister, and indeed any of the learned professions was a practical style of thinking powered not by the reading of books but by a heroic command of the individual's senses in the midst of experience. The volatile economic climate and fluid social possibilities of America made its citizens familiar with "intellectual toil . . . intense mental exertion, a profoundly thoughtful life," as the Unitarian minister Henry Bellows put it.[11] As they navigated the risks of business life, and were tested in the crucible of "action," young men traded on the capital of character—the physical and psychological resources by which individuals made experience a moral enterprise. As they were purveyed by conduct books, business manuals, fiction, periodicals, biographical sketches, and lectures sponsored by mercantile libraries and lyceums, heroic images of the merchant repudiated long-standing doubts about the legitimacy of commerce and gave clerks without college educations new role models suited to the expansion of liberal capitalism. Offering Tilton and his peers guidance in the work they were undertaking, writers and educators sought to claim for business the moral authority traditionally associated with the learned professions while disavowing its elitism.[12]

In developing this theme of composure in his lectures and writings, Emerson asked what it means to practice philosophy in a democracy. Like the boosters of the business profession, Emerson was by the middle of the nineteenth century invoking images of enterprise in order to locate moral heroism in the everyday life of market culture. Recent scholarship has tended to read Emerson's use of metaphors drawn from business life as expressing his ideological accommodation to liberal capitalism. Ever since Steven Whicher's *Freedom and Fate* (1953), critics have seen an ideological transformation in the body of Emerson's work. From romantic optimism and the revolutionary social implications of an earlier, radical brand of individualism in such earlier transcendentalist essays as "Nature" and "Self-Reliance," Emerson moved toward the social conservatism and cultural complacency attributed to his later essays and lectures. Sacvan Bercovitch, for example, notes that Emerson's later works "collapse the ambiguities" entailed by his earlier utopian individualism, completing his "journey into ideology" with "his more or less outright identification of individuality with industrial-capitalist 'Wealth' (1851) and 'Power' (1860)."[13] Mary Cayton argues that this ideological accommodation was effected in particular by the enormous celebrity that Emerson achieved on the professional lecture circuit by the 1850s, giving lectures on topics such as "Wealth," "Character," and "Eloquence." As Emerson sought to meet the demands of his audience for "practical knowledge" that would build character, "culture" came to be understood and practiced as "the consumption of well-known texts and performances," and the foremost American philosopher became antebellum America's primary, and most influential, spokesman for bourgeois individualism.[14] Even Richard Teichgraeber's sympathetic defense of Emerson as a "connected critic" of liberal capitalism paradoxically assumes a similar perspective, noting that by the 1850s the "nobler values

he attributed to culture and soul thereby turned out to provide an unin-
tended but nonetheless reassuring apology for acquisitiveness, inequality,
and exploitation."[15]

Rather than seeing the evolution in Emerson's writing solely as evidence
of an ideational shift, we might also see it as a self-conscious adaptation of
civic education to the requirements of democratic literary practice—an expression of a changing *idiom* of philosophy. As Stanley Cavell has argued
since *The Senses of Walden,* Emerson and Thoreau inaugurated a particularly American tradition concerned not with the formulation of abstract
discourse but with exemplifying in their thinking and writing the "task of
philosophy." They use an ordinary language for a philosophy concerned
not with arguments, not with the Continental tradition committed to accumulating a canon of objectively certain knowledge, but with a *style* of
philosophy, an "intimacy with experience" and an "economy of living."[16]
If we grant that a truly democratic philosophy must engage the epistemological problems that inhere in what Cavell calls the "habitat" of ordinary
experience, then it becomes possible to recognize in Emerson, as Cornel
West does, a "leveling of the subordination of common sense to Reason,"
which gives "primacy to power-laden people's opinion (*doxa*) over value-
free philosophers' knowledge (*episteme*)."[17] As both Richard Teichgraeber
and George Kateb have recently suggested, Emerson should be read as a reformer who wanted to correct his society's narrow view of success. In his
example and his advice, he argued for the necessity of making idealism relevant to everyday life. For Emerson, this meant bringing moral aspiration
"into the language of a society where wealth, power, profit, and property
now comprised the reigning 'theory of success.'"[18]

If historians and critics have tended to interpret the middle-class discourse of character in terms of status-seeking individualism, for Emerson it
constituted a sophisticated but pragmatic system for management of the
self, a set of strategies for responding to the problems of knowledge and decision making that arise in market culture. Like Benjamin Tilton and Henry
Bellows, Emerson sought to analyze and respond to the conditions of market culture. He understood the practice of character in business as providing an egalitarian alternative to an elitist, aristocratic tradition of European
education. It was not by reading but through attention to their own experience that individuals would learn the skills and capacities they needed to
become democratic citizens. Particularly in later works delivered on the lecture circuit and published as *The Conduct of Life* (1860), Emerson repeatedly invoked the imagery of enterprise in order to define distinctive ethical
processes and objectives for moral life in America. He sought to explicate
just which dispositions, given the freedoms accorded to individuals in the
market, make the pursuit of selfhood in a democratic culture "legitimate."

Unlike promoters of mercantile character, Emerson was concerned less with associating these states of attention with a particular profession than with identifying them as quintessentially American, as representative of a democratic character. He sought less to moralize business than to rationalize moral consciousness for a mass audience.

In his later lectures and essays, Emerson continually returned to the imagery and psychology of work, transposing the philosophical and abstract imperative to care for the self into the most immediately pressing, material key of experience. "As soon as a stranger is introduced into any company," Emerson declares at the opening of his essay "Wealth" (1860), "one of the first questions which all wish to have answered is, How does that man get his living? And with reason. He is no whole man until he knows how to earn a blameless livelihood."[19] What is "blameless" and what are the conditions of "livelihood" for becoming a "whole" person? To defy the sirens of economic life was to evince composure of one's faculties. This composure had to be distinct from a person's work, to mark an individual's bearing or ethos in private as well as in public. Emerson does not turn to manual labor—romantic visions of farm life, dusty peasants, or grimy factory workers—for his model of labor. "How does that man get his living?" Emerson asks. The inability to tell from his appearance indicates that it is not physical labor in which he is engaged, but work of the mind, and therefore easily concealed within the apparent ease of the body, the apparent freedom from work in which middle-class success is so often clothed. This more general ease in the market economy testifies finally not to any monopoly that businessmen have on wisdom but rather to a more universal equanimity in the face of contingency. For Emerson, the self pursues its vocation by learning to attend to material facts and act from the imperatives of nature, under the command of one's eye, one's mind, one's hand. As is so often the case with Emerson, a deceptively simple exhortation here becomes a series of challenges that spiral outward in their complexity: "He fails to make his place good in the world, unless he not only pays his debt, but also adds something to the common wealth. Nor can he do justice to his genius, without making some larger demand on the world than a bare subsistence. He is by constitution expensive, and needs to be rich" (989). The passive restraints that usually typify economic morality—"earn a blameless livelihood," pay as you go—become positive obligations, elusive in their implications, of going beyond "bare subsistence," of *needing* to be rich. What has making one's "place good" to do with making demands on the world? What does it mean to add to the "common wealth" or "do justice" to one's own "genius," and how can these be compatible aims?

What the merchant embodies for Emerson is a particular sensory disposition toward the material world, or what we might call a somatic intelligence. "An infinite number of shrewd men, in infinite years, have arrived at certain best and shortest ways of doing, and this accumulated skill in arts, cultures, harvestings, curings, constitutes the worth of our world today" (996). The businessman exemplifies this "shrewdness"; the successful merchant is one who recognizes that "Property is an intellectual production," and that "Commerce is a game of skill, which every man cannot play, which few men can play well." For Emerson, however, the businessman is merely representative of this more universal potential we all have to be "shrewd" in our dealings with experience. He invokes white-collar managerial work as a trope for the potential efficiency with which an individual mind can engage with experience, and so "arrive at the best and shortest ways of doing." It is not any merchant, but "the right merchant" who has the "just average of faculties we call *common sense*" (996–97). In reading such phrases it is easy to overlook the precise implication that words such as *right* and *just* have for Emerson's argument. As we saw with Benjamin Tilton's meditations about the "fluctuations of happiness," perception is attended by risk and fallibility. Thinking that you are right, having a hunch that things will go your way—these are worth no more than the merest daydream should they diverge from what comes to pass. To be *right* is a categorical imperative of *common sense*—it results not from any amount of individual intention but rather from the moral ontology that nature has built into human cognition, in that precise "average of faculties" that can be called *just*. Emerson subtly admonishes those speculators who would be immodest in their pride of vision, who have forgotten the essential delicacy of our senses, the frailty of human perception that has not proved itself by becoming *common* insight.

The legitimacy of economic activity depends on ordering the senses, on what Emerson terms its particular "application" of mind to nature: "the art of getting rich consists not in industry, much less in saving, but in a better order, in timeliness, in being at the right spot" (989). Like the care of the self, Emerson's idea of vocation is not a matter of contemplation but management: its peculiar "art" depends on acts of perception, analysis, and execution, by which one discovers a better "order" and "timeliness" or transforms what might otherwise be happenstance *being* into an opportunity for the active exercise of judgment and will, into being at the right spot. Vocation for Emerson exemplifies the exertion of individual will once it has been caught, as all of us are, between the "bare subsistence" of material reality and spiritualizing idealism, or the need to be "rich." A just use of one's faculties, being right: business is for Emerson a metaphor for how we confront realities that are not within our control. Not unlike the diaries of merchant clerks, Emerson represents experience as a zero-sum game. We pit our shrewdness less against one another as against the brutal, objective facts and consequences of our actions. "The game requires coolness, right reasoning, promptness, and patience in the players." By characterizing commerce as a "game of skill" Emerson emphasizes that one's success or failure here, as in life in general, is primarily a consequence of the efficacy of one's faculties, and not a matter of chance. "There is always reason, in the man, for his good or bad fortune, and so, in making money" (997). At the same time this metaphor generalizes the nature of shrewdness beyond a particular profession. Any "union of thought with nature" (996) acquires both the risks and the dignity of this game once it has been invested with such a moral disposition of the senses. To be shrewd is to play life itself as a game, never losing sight of the vulnerability of our perception, always seeking to master the problems of knowledge and conviction posed by life's changing circumstances.

Emerson invokes business not to make a religion of money but to illustrate how vocation is a secular form of devotion. Its moral basis is founded not on faith but on that enigmatic combination of reason and instinct, of speculation and practicality, that any person evinces in being shrewd. In a culture without a modern vocabulary for diagnosing the complex processes of psychology, Emerson finds a practical and accessible illustration of somatic intelligence in business. "The problem is, to combine many and remote operations, with the accuracy and adherence to the facts, which is easy in near and small transactions; so to arrive at gigantic results, without any compromise of safety" (997). The skillful player moves in two directions, toward the "adherence," observation, and analysis of immediate facts and sensory experience, and also toward the execution of "many and remote operations," to a simultaneity of attention that often depends on intuitive judgment and savvy practicality rather than a strictly rational accounting. Common sense becomes an "operation and adherence" of the faculties that is potentially universal in its availability, an adaptive intelligence that is intrinsic to any one person's experience of living his or her life. "Nature has her own best mode of doing each thing, and she has somewhere told it plainly, if we will keep our eyes and ears open" (1008). One acquires shrewdness through a patient, watchful proximity to the evidence of experience. Shrewdness requires becoming an apprentice to the operations of nature and temporarily sacrificing one's conceit of autonomy, rather than maintaining the "ignorant willfulness" with which one pretends that one has total freedom to act, as though the world will simply respond to the rules one dictates. "Success consists in close appliance to the laws of the world, and, since those laws are intellectual and moral, an intellectual and moral obedience" (997).

By suggesting that the "laws of the world" are innately economic, Emerson is also suggesting that common sense, the right use of one's faculties, is not the monopoly of a professional class or a learned elite. As the phrase "intellectual and moral obedience" suggests, Emerson is not simply using economic processes of specialization and the division of labor as crude metaphors for individual development and self-mastery. "The rule is not to dictate, nor to insist on carrying out each of your schemes by ignorant willfulness, but to learn practically the secret spoken from all nature, that things themselves refuse to be mismanaged, and will show to the watchful their own law" (1007). In this sense a vocation is discovered in a given form of work, rather than decided on—when we "learn practically the secret spoken" by "things themselves," seeing what "all nature" shows and refuses.

> Nature arms each man with some faculty which enables him to do easily some feat impossible to any other, and thus makes him necessary to society. This native determination guides his labor and his spending. He wants an equipment of means and tools proper to his talent. . . . Let a man who belongs to the class of nobles, those, namely, who have found out that they can do something, relieve himself of all vague squandering on objects not his. (1003, 1004)

While this "native determination" or "talent" entangles us within the intellectual and moral laws of the world, shrewdness requires a self-conscious detachment from those laws. To realize a vocation is to achieve a state of self-knowledge that exacts a moral obligation: this knowledge is not so much an economic resource, to be valued for its scarcity in the market of expertise, but rather "obedience," a commitment to "nature's own best mode of doing things." To be shrewd, an individual finally must have the discipline to "relieve himself of all vague squandering on objects not his" as though the focus and concentration necessary to do this are not in fact work but a form of "relief." Emerson's imagery seems to associate both efficacy and "relief" with a partial disengagement from certain kinds of experience—from those objects and efforts that use up one's faculties instead of being useful to them, squandering one's attention in a diffuse vagueness of purpose. In phrasing these imperatives in passive terms, Emerson emphasizes the qualities of stoic composure that distinguish the self within its vocation. Character thus emerges from vocation and the elimination of wasteful occupation, composure through "means and tools proper to his talent." To maximize the efficiency of one's faculties in the application of mind to nature creates wealth, Emerson says, but in a larger sense this process allows one to discover the laws of nature and to utilize them fully, at the service of each person's moral nobility or "genius." "Nobles" are not natural aristocrats, but those who have found out that they can do something, whose pursuit of self-interest makes them "necessary to society."[20] To compose one's senses is to make one's claim to the common wealth of nature "legitimate."

It is the particular combination of close observation and patient stead-fastness in common sense that transmutes a mere job into a vocation, a way of making money into a moral way of being. The ability to separate one's self from the pressing cares of work, to be at ease in one's vocation, be-speaks a *moral,* as opposed to merely rational, discipline of mind. To have achieved "character" is to have articulated an identity apart from the exi-gencies of experience, to have become a "whole man" despite the necessity to work and, as Marx so forcefully argued, despite the alienation that can come with it. Emerson defined "character" in these terms in an 1865 essay of that name: "Character denotes habitual self-possession, habitual regard to interior and constitutional motive, a balance not to be overset or easily disturbed by outward events and opinion. . . . it points to what no event can, that is, a will built on the reason of things."[21] For a self to achieve its vocation is to become "whole" within the immediate and pressing exigen-cies of experience—not through a respite from work but through the "self-possession," "balance," and habitual attention to "motive" that testifies to a moral engagement of the senses with all facets of experience. For Emer-son, then, it is not material wealth that one achieves from the pursuit of vocation but the wisdom that accumulates from spiritual exercises of char-acter. Vocation is the composure of the senses required for the care of the self, an internal equanimity in the midst of experience, a "will built on the reason of things."

In his later work in general, as in his essay on "Wealth," Emerson in-creasingly responded to the ethical challenges of liberal culture by formu-lating the moral imperatives of character in a manner squarely directed to the young men among whom he became so popular. Individuals must strive to realize their "wholeness" in the very midst of society, where eco-nomic relationships exact the most brutal compromises between depen-dence and autonomy, where the seductions of status and mobility incessantly distract us from our moral person. We might see this vernacular philosophy of character as merely an apologia for laissez-faire capitalism, with its exhortation to individual responsibility, its commitment to liberal freedoms that have been or continue to be denied to working-class people, its didactic faith that the values of white Anglo-Saxon Protestants are supe-rior to those of other peoples and cultures. Indeed, the revival of the con-cept of character in late twentieth-century debates about moral life and civic duty has made it difficult not to read this earlier discourse as the pre-history of a brand of political and social conservatism. However, contem-porary uses of the concept should not obscure the fact that nineteenth century discussion of character was concerned primarily with the extension of the capacities by which individuals might exercise their liberty as demo-cratic citizens. As Emerson's later lectures and essays powerfully recognize, for prospective members of the middle class the problem of how to live—as a worker, as a member of a family and a community—became the essentially rhetorical task of how to *act*, how to realize one's character in the dynamic and uncertain world of market culture.

Modes of Civic Education

The lecture on "Domestic Life" given by Emerson in 1843 "was one of the best delivered" before the [New York Mercantile] Library this year," Benjamin Tilton wrote.

> There is much originality both in thought and reasoning with Emerson. He handled his subject with much ability. He described the state of childhood—its innocent pursuits by which it obtains knowledge which is its power; with its schools and proper base it forms its pyramids; those who come in its sway are an easy prey for its irresistible powers of persuasion, by which it increases its power of locomotion, imitating its older brethren in "riding reform on the back of all flesh."[22]

At the time he heard Emerson, Tilton had become preoccupied with his courtship of Mary Baker, and was perhaps contemplating the domestic duties he would assume with marriage. As he moved into adult life, he perhaps looked back with nostalgia at his own childhood while also considering the prospects of fatherhood. It is not surprising that in his diary Tilton took special interest in this lecture rather than in the dozens of others he attended in his early twenties. It may be a little more surprising to find Emerson so publicly probing the joys of childhood a year after the death of his son Waldo, and a year before he published the brooding and fatalistic account of his grief in "Experience" (1844). But in Tilton's summary of the lecture, Emerson anticipated that essay's concern with the limits of subjectivity: "In the domestic circle he remarked truly that wealth alone does not produce happiness; but a cheerful industriousness and contented disposition. And that our poverty lies, chiefly, in <u>feeling pain</u>." As we have seen, Tilton had made his own reflections on the "poverty" of conviction, the way that our knowledge of the world and our place in it can be undone by changes in mood. With Emerson, Tilton found in the popular lecture hall someone whose "originality in thought and reasoning," with "much ability" in handling his subject, spoke "truly" to his deepest need for moral guidance.

In its gloss on what he heard, Tilton's diary reminds us that truth has a social history.[23] We create knowledge and control access to it within historically specific cultures of literacy. Particular institutions, values, and practices supply us with the means of recognizing an idea or fact as "true," and constitute knowledge as a form of power in social, economic, political, and religious life. By attending a lecture by Emerson, Tilton gained access not merely to knowledge but to a way of valuing knowledge. He invested Emerson's words with the authority of truth: those ideas we paraphrase, the commonplaces we quote, the words we underline. For the young men who flocked to hear Emerson speak at mercantile libraries, young men's associations, and lyceums in cities throughout the northern and midwestern states, particular words acquired moral status as truth within the social context of the public lecture hall, according to the values of rhetorical performance. What might Emerson's career in the lecture hall tell us more generally about the forms that moral knowledge takes in a mass culture?

Trading in the topics of enterprise, character, and domestic life, Emerson's appearances on the professional lecture circuit were part of an emerging genre of popular recreation and adult education. The "public lecture" by which Emerson, Henry Ward Beecher, and others became national celebrities sought to explain contemporary life in antebellum America. Unlike the traditional itinerant system of lecturing, the "public lecture" that emerged in the antebellum years was situated, as Donald Scott has observed, "within a cluster of social meanings and ethical prescriptions."[24] Within this new genre of public address, a set of literary and moral norms were shared by certain performers as well as by the expanding audiences that turned to them for edification, instruction, and inspiration. By the 1850s the lecture circuit had become a commercial business that allowed celebrities such as Emerson and Henry Ward Beecher to make a comfortable living, but it had also become the venue for a new sort of professional vocation. We might, under these circumstances, see Emerson's choice of vocation as not only an expedient move for liberally educated men of letters facing diminished career options, but also a pioneering effort to create a niche within the commercial marketplace for general, secular learning. The emergence of this new place in the literary landscape represented not the debasement of intellectual authority but rather its popularization for a mass audience.

The "professional lecturer" exemplified a model of intellectual authority fundamentally at odds with the new kind of professionalism that would, from the 1870s onward, come to define formal intellectual life. Lecturers such as Emerson thought of themselves as cultural spokesmen encompassing the world of knowledge in a "forum organized and accepted as a fully legitimate agency for creating the 'intelligent progress' that was thought to guide American democracy." Professors in the new research universities, on the other hand, "divided the cognitive universe into discrete and fairly well-bounded disciplines," orienting themselves to isolated quarries of scholarship, pursuing "truth and science free from the interference of those outside the professional community." As Scott suggests, this new model of intellectual authority "institutionalized a sense of an unbridgeable cognitive gap between professionals and nonprofessionals" by transforming the production of genuine, valid knowledge into a positivist endeavor best left to specialized experts.[25] Today, we acquire skills as solitary readers and autonomous thinkers through years of compulsory and voluntary schooling. A professional culture of literacy shapes the particular attentions we exercise as citizens: the active judgments we make about certain ideas, the social norms that informally shape our inclinations and values, the dispositions that invest our commitments to these values and ideas with their practical consequence. It does this by training citizens in epistemological norms and methods of inquiry oriented to the solitary, silent, and intensive reading of printed texts. These methods and values are acquired over years of training within institutions of higher learning, in general seclusion from the television and radio talk shows, book clubs, motivational seminars, and the like that have come to furnish most Americans with food for thought.

We can only read Emerson's work today, of course, and we typically do so in silence and solitude, according to hierarchical norms of expertise and professional authority in the academy. A major reason that we have had difficulty appreciating Emerson's later work is that historians and critics alike interpret it according to modern literary values and methods concerned with the lexical sophistication, symbolic complexity, and imaginative originality of printed texts. Note, for instance, that Cavell uses this model of reading as a primary trope for the activity of philosophical discourse in which Thoreau and Emerson are engaged: their writing "realizes itself daily under their hands, sentence by stunning sentence. . . . Such writing takes the same mode of relating to itself as reading and thinking do, the mode of the self's relation to itself, call it self-reliance."[26] It might be more accurate to say that *we* realize their writing through our reading, applying highly sophisticated hermeneutic and conceptual skills 'sentence by sentence.' As exemplified by Emerson, these skills typically involve explication of particular phrases and passages, inventories of references and allusions across the corpus of a writer's work, and the invocation of a biographical telos that gives an author's career shape and direction. Finding Emerson's ideological position has depended *implicitly* on literary judgments about the declining literary quality of his later, more popular, work generated for the lecture circuit. Maurice Gonnaud made a typical judgment of Emerson's last phase when he suggested that in *English Traits* (1850) and *The Conduct of Life* (1860), "Emerson has at last made peace with the world and its rules. They have the serenity of an Indian summer," lacking "the impetuosity, the sparkle, the boldness that won the younger and more rebellious Emerson friends and foes of equal fervor."[27] Emerson's strongest work as a writer is typically understood as coinciding with his transcendentalist, idealist phase, which is usually described as ending with the existential crisis and disillusionment of "Experience." These judgments of the literary quality of Emerson's later work are largely implicit because there has been relatively little sustained scholarly engagement with "Wealth" and most of his later essays.[28]

Emerson's modern literary reputation on the page and in the lecture hall reflects his identification with the ideology of liberal individualism with which he has been linked repeatedly in the twentieth century. Recent academic appraisals of Emerson's later essays extend a tradition of modern cultural criticism that began in the early twentieth century and was directed against the literary inheritance of the genteel tradition and the values and tastes of a middle-class audience—both of which seemed to be epitomized by Emerson's work. Van Wyck Brooks, for example, found Emerson to be a singularly unusable piece of the American past. Instead of using idealism as a restraint on self-interest, Emerson ushered in a "thorough-going, self-reliant individualism," his work having all the "qualities of the typical baccalaureate sermon . . . addressed to the private virtues of young men." H. L. Mencken would similarly blame Emerson's appropriation by the 'booboisie' on defects of his literary style. Emerson's philosophy, Mencken wrote in 1930,

> seems to be made precisely for the lunch-table idealists . . . men who would be all too easily satisfied by its almost incomparable sweep of soothing generalities [and] vast marshaling of sugary and not too specific words . . . I can imagine nothing better suited to the spiritual needs of used-car dealers, trust company vice-presidents, bath fixture magnates, and the like, gathered together in the sight of God to take cheer from one another and shove the Republic along its rocky road.[29]

To dramatize the banality of Emerson's work, Mencken and Brooks invoked images of the hortatory tradition—the baccalaureate address, after-lunch speeches, Rotary and Chamber of Commerce orations, and other debased, modern venues of civic discourse. As Emerson's soothing generalities circulate in these oral venues of middlebrow uplift, his ideological use by the cultural establishment has come to be seen as a consequence of their literary medium and style—of the promiscuous ease with which they lent themselves to citation by used-car salesmen and bankers (fig. 11).

Modern scholars have had difficulty appreciating just how audiences in the nineteenth century valued what they heard in the lecture hall. "Contemporaries rarely described the personal benefits of the pursuit of

EVERY MAN HIS OWN PRINTER.

With one of our presses, and the material accompanying it, every man can do his own printing, thus saving much time and expense. Circulars containing full information about these Presses, prices, recommendations, &c., mailed free on application. Specimen-books of types, cuts, borders, &c., &c., 10 cents. ADAMS PRESS CO., 53 Murray Street, New York.

A GREAT OFFER!!

HORACE WATERS, 481 Broadway, N. Y., will dispose of ONE HUNDRED PIANOS, MELODEONS, and ORGANS, of six first-class makers, including Chickering & Sons, at *Extremely Low Prices, for Cash*, during this month, or will take from $5 to $25 monthly until paid. Instruments to hire.

HINKLEY KNITTING MACHINE

FOR FAMILY USE—*simple, cheap, reliable.* Knits Every thing. AGENTS WANTED. Circular and sample stocking FREE. Address HINKLEY KNITTING MACHINE CO., Bath, Me., or 176 Broadway, N. Y.

Fishing in American Waters.

Opening of the Season for Angling and Fish-Farming. To the angler or the fish-culturist Scott's book on "Fishing in American Waters" will prove a real *vade-mecum* in every thing about angling and breeding fishes.

Sent throughout the United States, postpaid, for $3 50. HARPER & BROTHERS,
Franklin Square, N. Y.

VINEGAR.—HOW MADE FROM CIDER, WINE, Molasses, or Sorghum, in 10 hours, without using drugs. For circulars, address F. I. SAGE, Vinegar Maker, Cromwell, Conn.

FRENCH and ENGLISH INSTITUTE.—The first-class Boarding-School for Young Ladies, 278 Clermont Avenue, Brooklyn, N. Y., will open Sept. 19.
M. GIRAUD, Principal.

TROY FEMALE SEMINARY.—This Institution offers the accumulated advantages of over fifty years of successful operation. For circulars apply to JOHN H. WILLARD, Troy, N. Y.

EMERSON says, "Trade has grown supple to the borders of fraud." Try us. Sales large. Exclusive agencies. Sells at sight. 5000 in use.
DUDLEY & ROCKWELL, Buffalo, N. Y.

$240 per month to Agents. 15 entirely new articles, staple as flour. Samples and instructions free. C. M. LININGTON, 88 S. Halsted St., Chicago.

MICROSCOPES. Illustrated Price-List sent free on application. T. H. McALLISTER, Optician, 49 Nassau St., N. Y.

$60 A WEEK paid Agents in a new business. Address SACO NOVELTY CO., Saco, Me.

ONLY $10 A MONTH REQUIRED to own as fine a Farm as there is on the American Continent. Address SOUTHERN LAND CO., 432 Broome St., N. Y.

W. D. WILSON & CO., 327 Pearl St., N. Y., furnish Printing Ink for *Harper's Weekly* and *Bazar*.

WATCHES. $10

...E WATCHES—Best Imitation of Gold ...—excellent timekeepers—Price $10. ...S—Very handsome—Good timekeepers ...ed and sent C.O.D. with privilege of ex... A descriptive Catalogue & Price List of ...ERS & Co., 197 Broadway, New York

and Gennesareth, &c. A Canoe Cruise in Palestine and Egypt, and the Waters of Damascus. By J. MACGREGOR, M.A. With Maps and Illustrations. Crown 8vo, Cloth, $2 50.

FREE RUSSIA. By W. HEPWORTH DIXON, Author of "Her Majesty's Tower," &c. With Two Illustrations. Crown 8vo, Cloth, $2 00.

THE HISTORY OF HORTENSE, Daughter of Josephine, Queen of Holland, Mother of Napoleon III. By JOHN S. C. ABBOTT, Author of "The French Revolution," "History of Napoleon Bonaparte," &c. With Engravings. 16mo, Cloth, $1 20. *Uniform with Abbotts' Illustrated Histories.*

THE BAZAR BOOK OF DECORUM. The Care of the Person, Manners, Etiquette, and Ceremonials. 16mo, Toned Paper, Cloth, Beveled Edges, $1 00.

THE LIFE OF COUNT BISMARCK, Private and Political. With Descriptive Notices of his Ancestry. By Dr. GEORGE HESEKIEL. Translated and Edited, with an Introduction, Explanatory Notes, and Appendices, by KENNETH R. H. MACKENZIE, F.S.A., F.A.S.L. With upward of 100 Illustrations. 8vo, Cloth, $3 00.

FRESH NOVELS,

PUBLISHED BY

HARPER & BROTHERS, NEW YORK.

RECOLLECTIONS OF ETON. By an Etonian. With Illustrations by Sydney P. Hall. 8vo, Paper, 50 cents.

VERONICA. By the Author of "Aunt Margaret's Trouble," "Mabel's Progress," &c. 8vo, Paper, 50 cents.

CHARLES READE'S NOVELS, COMPLETE. Harper's Library Edition. Complete in 3 Vols., 8vo, Green Morocco Cloth, $6 50 per set.

Hard Cash.—Griffith Gaunt.—It is Never Too Late to Mend.—Love Me Little, Love Me Long.—Put Yourself in His Place.—Foul Play.—White Lies.—Peg Woffington, Christie Johnstone, and Other Stories.—The Cloister and the Hearth.

W. M. THACKERAY'S NOVELS, COMPLETE. Harper's Library Edition, with Illustrations by the Author. Complete in 3 Vols., 8vo., Green Morocco Cloth, $6 50 per set.

Vanity Fair.—Pendennis.—The Virginians.—The Newcomes.—The Adventures of Philip.—Henry Esmond.—Lovel the Widower.

THE NEW TIMOTHY. By WM. M. BAKER, Author of "Inside," "Oak Mot," "The Virginians in Texas," "Life and Labors of Daniel Baker," &c. 12mo, Cloth, $1 50.

TRUE TO HERSELF. By F. W. ROBINSON, Author of "Stern Necessity," "Poor Humanity," "Mattie: a Stray," "Christie's Faith," "Carry's Confession," "No Man's Friend," &c. 8vo, Paper, 50 cents.

JOHN: A Love Story. By Mrs. OLIPHANT, Author of "Agnes," "Chronicles of Carlingford," "The Minister's Wife," "Life of Edward Irving," "Brownlows," &c. 8vo, Paper, 50 cents.

MAN AND WIFE. By WILKIE COLLINS, Author of "Armadale," "Moonstone," "No Name," "The Woman in White," &c. With Illustrations. 8vo, Paper, $1 00; Cloth, $1 50.

MISS THACKERAY'S WRITINGS, COMPLETE. The Writings of Anne Isabella Thackeray. Illustrated. 8vo, Paper, $1 25; Cloth, $1 75.

KILMENY. By WILLIAM BLACK, Author of "In Silk Attire," "Love or Marriage?" &c. 8vo, Paper, 50 cents.

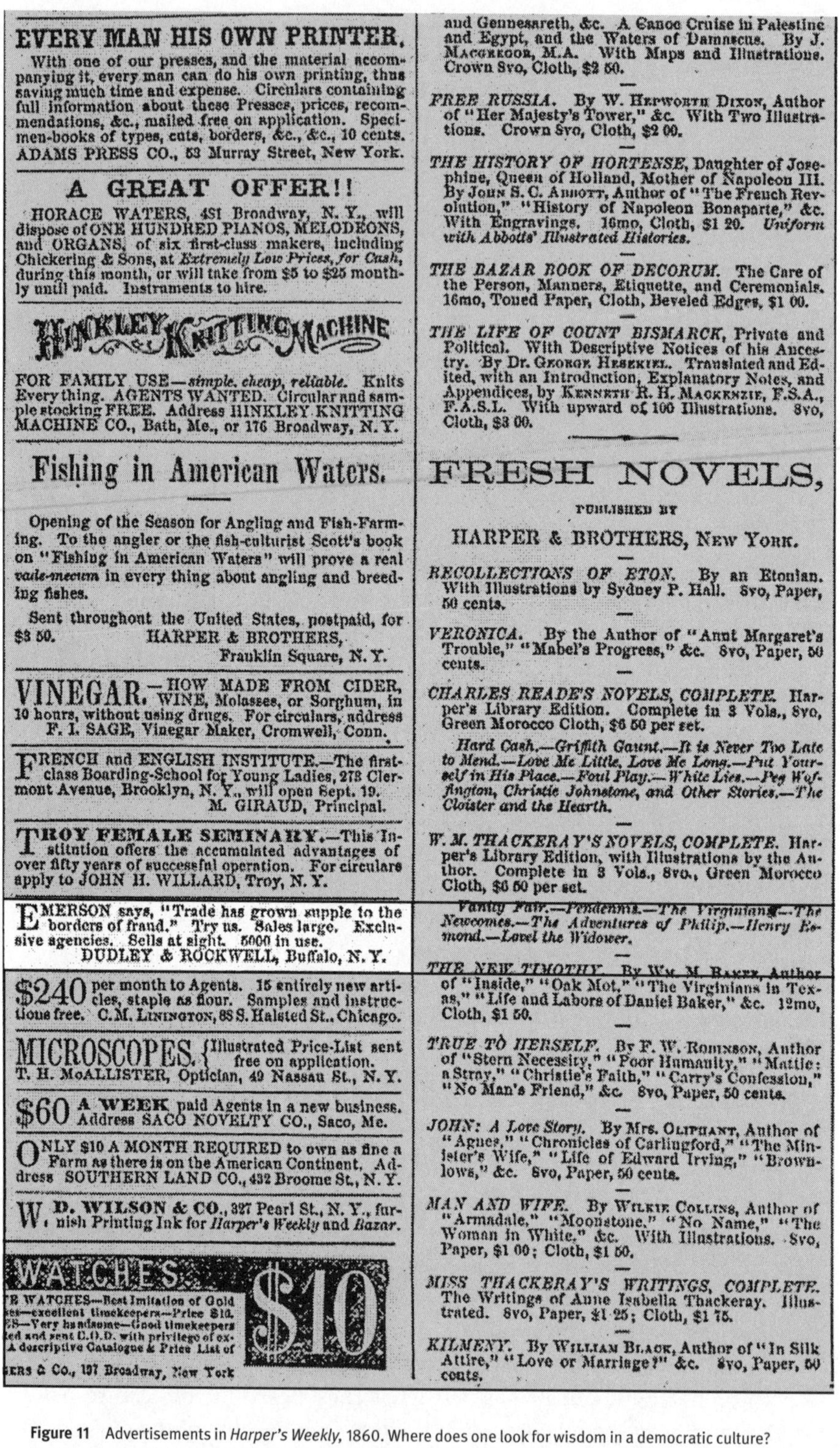

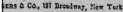

Figure 11 Advertisements in *Harper's Weekly*, 1860. Where does one look for wisdom in a democratic culture? Emerson's words surface as a sales pitch, surrounded by advertisements for watches, etiquette manuals, clothing patterns, "fresh novels," and other consumer goods requisite to the outfitting of middle-class character.

knowledge," as Joseph Kett has observed, "beyond general statements that it would build character."[30] In analyzing some reviews of Emerson's many appearances in the Midwest (including lectures on "Wealth" delivered before the Mercantile Library Associations of Cincinnati and St. Louis), Mary Cayton has argued that the building of character from the lecture platform had a largely symbolic function. What Emerson intended as a "means of moral reform whose warrant was a unique spiritual understanding of nature" was heard as "common sense rules for attaining individual and social success." The commercialization of the lecture system that helped to make Emerson a "personality," Cayton argues, also resulted in a flattening of his ideas.[31] Emerson's philosophy became a commodity that was readily absorbed into young men's pursuit of genteel taste and middle-class status. In a similar vein, Kett suggests that the immense interest in "useful knowledge" in the lyceum and other venues of adult education "was a way for individuals to advance within the professions," "a means by which occupational groups guarded their flanks by aligning themselves with genteel culture." A Latin quotation here, a historical anecdote there: the display of liberal learnedness leant a patina of culture to the upwardly mobile.[32]

Critical attempts to rescue Emerson from his own popularity inevitably locate a more authentic philosophical or artistic truth on the printed page, blaming the mass media of a middle-class consumer culture for the distortion or watering down of his message.[33] Cayton, for instance, puts Emerson's printed text for "Wealth" against newspaper summaries of his lectures in Cincinnati, in order to illustrate how the process of self-culture became a product. Within the "new international bourgeois way of life" created by institutions of mass consumption, "culture was a state to be achieved, a status to be acquired, no longer a process of self-awareness and introspection." That process is implicitly identified with solitary reading rather than the "misapprehension" that occurred in the lecture hall.[34] Teichgraeber's account of Emerson's influence in the 1840s is argued entirely from his reception and dissemination in religious and literary periodicals in England and America. He dismisses the idea that Emerson's efforts on the lecture circuit contributed to the growth of his *intellectual* reputation, which is measured by his standing in elite organs of print culture. As is so often the case, Emerson's "philosophy" is divorced from the popular audiences whom he so assiduously courted and with whom, as I argue, he was actively engaged as a thinker. "The potential for half-readings [of Emerson] was latent in his approach"—another way of saying that we are more adept at reading Emerson than were his popular audiences at hearing him in a lecture hall. Emerson's deep words were thus "misread" or "half-read" by his popular audiences "as justifications for an existing social and economic order."[35] As they translate Emerson's "voyage into ideology" into a story of

literary decline, modern critics invariably cast the spoken word as an inferior mode of intellection. In their analysis, the medium of the lecture hall
was more conducive than print to the passivity and dumbing down that
scholars often attribute to forms of mass consumption.

In mid-nineteenth-century America, neither Emerson nor his middle-
class audience assumed that expertise in the silent reading of texts was requisite to a moral use of knowledge for self-making. In fact, the intensive
work of solitary reading that they associated with "study" was if anything
considered to be an impediment to the acquisition of a moral disposition to
knowledge—a conviction of character—that gave the practices and values
of literary leisure their tremendous social and personal consequence. Reading Emerson within a modern context, mostly in high school or college
courses, bears little resemblance to the "reading" of his work that took
place in the nineteenth-century lecture hall. No doubt, many young men
went to hear lecturers because they wanted to gawk at celebrities. No
doubt, many people fell asleep, sat confused or bored, or passively heard
what Emerson had to say, as they frequently do in high school and college
classrooms today.

It is also true, however, that ordinary men and women brought a sophisticated critical attention to oral texts in the nineteenth century. That attention drew on a familiarity with pulpit eloquence as well as a more general
cultural obsession with myriad forms of rhetorical performance during a
period that one author has referred to as the Golden Age of Oratory. Inside
the nineteenth-century academy and college classroom, rhetoric "was the
classical art . . . of public discourse," standing "very near if not precisely at
the center of pedagogical concerns." Commencement exercises included
"exhibitions" of oratorical eloquence, as they still do today. The values of
the neoclassical oratorical tradition were disseminated across the spectrum
of formal and informal educational settings by "speakers" and "readers"
such as Caleb Bingham's *The Columbian Orator,* which had been reprinted
dozens of times by the time Frederick Douglass got his hands on an edition
while still a slave. Outside the classroom as well, American culture was profoundly committed to the art of oratory. Young men formed literary and
debate clubs in which they competed with one another for rhetorical distinction; Americans attended public orations in huge numbers, while the
press followed speeches in the U.S. Senate and on the stump with the sort
of detail it now reserves for professional sports. Political speech was "spec-
tacular mass entertainment," and orations were "often reprinted and
widely distributed, to be reviewed, studied, recited from memory, and ap-
plauded as the cultural equipment most basic to every citizen in the new
democracy."[36] Following F. O. Mathiessen's argument about the importance of oratory in the American Renaissance, a few scholars have recently

suggested that antebellum writing was decisively shaped by a national fascination with the democratic power of speech. What really distinguishes American literature of this period from British literature was a cult of eloquence committed "to the public function of the writer and of literature," as Peter Gibian puts it—eloquence that aspired to the "rapturous union of speaker and mass audience." In mid-nineteenth-century America, the public function of literature was served by the mass medium of speech.[37]

The notes that clerks took in their diaries about lectures and sermons efface modern distinctions between "moral" guidance and "practical" advice, between mere consumption of ideas and critical introspection. After several years of attending lectures at the New York Mercantile Library, for instance, Henry Patterson actively "reviewed" the texts he heard in church and in the lecture hall. In his diary he included not only summaries of arguments made and examples given, but also a complex inventory of stylistic gestures, physical presence, and vocal quality. Of one speaker Patterson noted that "flowery" language could not compensate for a lack of substance, for a "very uninteresting, uninstructive and pointless piece of declamation." And yet a speaker's concern with the authority of the written word could lead to a disaster like Colonel Stone, who "just reads his discourse in a monotonous, unattractive style, scarce taking his eyes from his manuscript except to lose his place when he does."[38] As his comments on sermons and lectures suggest, Patterson's criteria for the literary success of a lecture depended on the speaker's rhetorical presence. Patterson was resentful that the famous scientist Benjamin Silliman's "oratorical powers are nothing, his style of speaking is of the paternal kind, such as a teacher would use toward his pupils and is too rapid and indistinct to be quite agreeable."[39] As Patterson and other clerks affirmed repeatedly throughout their analysis of written and spoken texts, rhetorical skill was crucial to securing the active engagement, appreciation, and scrutiny of individual listeners. Prior to the advent of modern forms of mass spectacle, ordinary people were 'literate' in the medium of public address as mass audiences are today with television and movies.

In his critiques of lectures, Henry Patterson often applied his critical skills as much to the speaker's body as to his text. His strong dislike for Mr. Moffit's "hackneyed" lecture on the origins and power of the English language was clearly informed by a less literal 'reading' of his character: "Not at all pleased with lecture, his subject, or the manner in which he treated it. I understand him to be a man of at least a very doubtful character, and his physiognomy plainly indicates it." In 1842 he went to see James Fenimore Cooper plead his libel case in court in part to appraise in person the character of the author he had already evaluated in print: "Fifty five, inclined to corpulency; a distinct, forcible and very easy speaker and a good logician, but I thought with no good claims to eloquence." While listening to a lecture by the minister Orville Dewey, Patterson similarly inventories the author's physical appearance. "Mental power, cultivation and refinement of intellect, depth and originality of thought" are "denoted" as much by the "unusually well-formed" head of "this fine specimen of manly duty" as by Dewey's discourse. Patterson was particularly impressed by the formidable ethos projected by Daniel Webster. "All [his] intellectual organs developed to [a] remarkable degree," Webster's "scowling and forbidding" aspect, "never relaxing into a smile," denotes "deep and habitual thought, close observation and a calmness and self-possession which necessarily arises from a conscious capacity to judge all things correctly, without being imposed on by false appearances." Patterson's detailed description here was a claim to his own "capacity" to discern the truth from appearances, so as to declare that "I consider his the strongest, best balanced mind in this country."[40] By invoking the particular categories of phrenology, Patterson reinforced his confidence in his powers of interpretation.

Rooted in the "new rhetoric" of the late eighteenth century, an aesthetics of "natural" eloquence flourished with this popular rage for oratory, leading audiences to reject the self-conscious formality and erudition associated with the academic study of books in favor of Romantic tendencies toward authentic feeling and expression. A speaker's main priority was to move people. As Edward Channing put it in his *Lectures to Harvard Seniors,* a successful oration required "a popular tone . . . an adaptation to various minds." The speaker needed to achieve emotional credibility with audiences, "to avoid what might be called a literary style, as distinguished from a natural one," as Henry Ward Beecher advised Yale divinity students.[41] Language had to be effective as communication. In a lecture by the Unitarian minister Henry Bellows (of whom he became a devoted follower), Patterson took exception to even a "slight touch" of transcendentalism, "which is incomprehensible to my understanding." Transcendentalism in the 1840s evidently had acquired public notoriety as an esoteric school of thinking. Its self-conscious and hermetic status as abstract theory aroused Patterson's resistance, because for him intellectual reflection had to be *portable:* the difficulty of merely comprehending a text diminished the possibility that he would find it relevant later or that memory might preserve it. Orville Dewey's sermon succeeded on these grounds because it was not "abstruse and difficult" but "practical," giving Patterson ideas to take away, reflect on, and apply to his experiences beyond the lecture hall.[42] What made lectures about the commonplaces of character "practical" were qualities of rhetorical eloquence by which they engaged and inspired the moral imagination.

Emerson pioneered a role for the public intellectual in market culture, but he did so primarily on the lecture circuit rather than on the printed page, which twentieth-century scholars habitually privilege as a medium of intellectual authority. As the testimony of his contemporaries makes clear, Emerson's literary genius was understood in terms of his effectiveness in the lecture hall, the "truth" of his words indexed to the practice and values of rhetorical eloquence.[43] This fact should matter to us, I argue, because it forces us to question tacit assumptions that guide modern readings of texts from the past, and it helps us to see Emerson's literary work within the historical context of philosophical practice. As Margaret Fuller recognized in her review of *Essays: Second Series* (1844), Emerson's lectures resembled classical forms of civic ritual that in many ways were alien to modern epistemology. Critics objected to the lack of conventional scholarly exposition in an Emerson essay, she noted, because "They did not see that Pindar's odes might be very well arranged for their own purpose, and yet not bear translating into the methods of Mr. [John] Locke."[44] By introducing a reference to a classical tradition of oral performance to our appreciation of silent, printed texts, Fuller suggests that the literary "genius" of Emerson's work lies in its particular pedagogical appeal. Like the odes of the ancient poet Pindar, Emerson's essays are forms of spiritual exercise: they stage wisdom in ways that defy the literary standards and epistemological norms by which we have come to value modern knowledge. A major interpretative problem for modern scholars (and one faced by my own reading of Emerson's essays and lectures) is that we only have access to Emerson's printed words. Today, we necessarily read within the institutions and practices of liberal education, according to specialized uses of "the methods of Mr. Locke."

With its attention to the physical and vocal qualities that literally embody moral authority in the credible ethos of a particular orator, a still-vital tradition of neoclassical rhetoric helped nineteenth-century readers to see Emerson's printed essays as transcriptions of oratorical eloquence. The defects of organization and logic that "often confuse the reader," as Theodore Parker noted in one review, were, as many critics discerned, a function of the original oratorical ambitions of Emerson's writing. "It would in truth have been a marvel if Emerson had excelled in the virtues of the written page, for most of his published work was originally composed and used for the platform," the English critic John Morley declared in 1881.[45] The Sage could be accessed and enjoyed within an expanding marketplace for leisure because Emerson made forms of intellectual stimulation and provocation accessible as recreation—made the lecture hall "the purest organ of intellectual entertainment," as Bronson Alcott put it in 1882. "The highest compliment we can pay to the scholar is that of having edified and instructed us, we know not how, unless by the pleasure his words have given us."[46] The ways in which Emerson made edification and instruction a "pleasure" were defined against the process of reading silent, printed texts, according to social and sensory qualities of rhetorical performance. Where the silent reading of Emerson might become hermetic and difficult, requiring our individual skills for textual exegesis, hearing him became a pleasure of a distinctly communal nature for which one required no special preparation—the collective experience of *we* and *us* afforded by a mass medium of *intellectual entertainment* (fig. 12).

In similar ways, James Russell Lowell's 1861 review of Emerson's *The Conduct of Life* for the *Atlantic Monthly* defines Emerson's literary genius by his effectiveness as a performer in the lecture hall. Emerson work displays an uncanny eye for telling phrases—"a diction at once so rich and so homely as his I know not where to match in these days of writing by the page"—because he is not in fact "writing by the page." We best appreciate an essay by Emerson, Lowell's review suggests, by reading its textual form as an evocation of the social context in which it first came to life. When he went as a young man to hear Emerson speak in the late 1830s, Lowell recalled, the spectacle of the lecture created a sense of moral community: "those faces, young and old, agleam with pale intellectual light, eager with pleased attention. . . . I hear again that rustle of sensation, as they turned to exchange glances over some pithier thought."[47] Seeing other faces alight with intellectual excitement, hearing the rustle, exchanging glances: these details qualify some of those extratextual factors that for Lowell are intrinsic to his experience of Emerson's literary "sensation." Like Alcott, Lowell saw that what distinguished Emerson was his accessibility, his rare capacity to affect a diverse mass audience: "I know none that can hold a promiscuous crowd in pleased attention so long as he. As in all original men, there is something for every palate."[48] Lowell confessed little regard for what he calls the "peculiar style of thought or phrase"—"here and there, a certain thinness and vagueness of quality"—because his own discrimination as a reader was not primarily about understanding the lexical content of Emerson's often confusing verbal formulations. "Some of us may hear more than the mere words, are moved by something deeper than the thoughts." Indeed, popular literary discernment in the nineteenth-century lecture hall concerned itself with incantory power, with being moved and hearing what lay beyond "mere words."[49]

When read in the light reflected from the aura of Emerson's physical presence, in the shadow cast by his reputation, Lowell's critical terms suggest the nineteenth century's distance from twentieth-century assumptions about literary value. Linking Emerson's lecture schedule to the cycle of the seasons, Lowell compares an announcement of a new course of lectures to "those forebodings of spring that prepare us every year for a familiar nov-

A TYPICAL COOPER-UNION AUDIENCE DURING THE LECTURE SEASON.

Figure 12 "A typical Cooper-Union audience during the lecture season," undated halftone from unknown source, ca. 1870s. Throughout the mid-nineteenth century, the public lecture was a popular form of education and entertainment. Museum of the City of New York, Print Archives, gift of Louis Arata.

elty, none the less novel, when it arrives because it is familiar. We know perfectly well what we are to expect from Mr. Emerson, and yet what he says always penetrates and stirs us, as is apt to be the case with genius, in a very
unlooked for fashion." What Emerson says may be "known perfectly well"
in advance; indeed, without some prior familiarity with Emerson's work,
his disjointed style might seem merely disorganized. But clearly Lowell values the immediacy of "impression," the force of oratorical presence that
transforms the familiar into a novelty that "penetrates and stirs" us in "unlooked for" ways. The physical form of Emerson's speech is its content.
"We do not go to hear what Emerson says so much as to hear Emerson,"
Lowell declares. With "that thrilling voice of his, so charged with subtle
meaning and subtle music. . . . there is a kind of undertow in that rich bari-
tone of his that sweeps our minds from their foothold into deeper waters
with a drift we cannot and would not resist"; the artfully "deliberate utterance" that makes us "partners in the labor of thought, and makes us feel as
if the glance of humor were a sudden suggestion, as if the perfect phrase
were there on the desk as unexpected to him as to us!"[50] In an era when
mechanical and electrical means for reproducing speech at a spatial and
temporal distance from its utterance did not yet exist, this voice of Emerson's becomes the symbol and instrument of his moral power, an expression of the continuity and surprise that nature brings us. You can see what
Emerson says there on the page, but do you hear him?

Like music, to which it was often compared, an Emerson lecture was
knowledge of the moment.[51] Aphoristic phrasing, anecdotal exposition,
colloquial wit, elliptical organization, and the like conspired to engage an
audience through the visceral immediacy of "pleasure" and "sensation,"
rather than through the abstract "methods of Mr. Locke." Identifying
voice rather than text as the primary medium of creation in these spaces defines writing as a species of rhetoric. The aesthetic of natural eloquence
imagines the literary to be, like conversation in the salon, a shared "labor of
thought" within the community of the lecture hall rather than the solitary
production of one individual's ideas or style. This "labor of thought" is
shared between author and readers because true eloquence exacts obligations from all members of a rhetorical community. It requires that what is
already familiar become moving and persuasive in "unlooked for ways," as
though it were a novelty. Such familiarity promises consistency of quality
but must be articulated anew every moment—a rhetorical ethos that must
be both recognizable and newly compelling. Authors make their appeals
"promiscuous" in the crowded spaces of the lecture hall and the commercial market of readers.

To speak of Emerson's literary style in the latter half of the nineteenth
century meant appreciating his eloquence, the rhetorical means by which he

and his audiences invested the vernacular practice of philosophy with the visceral intimacy of social engagement. Thus in his review of *The Conduct of Life* James Russell Lowell continually indexed the "impression" of Emerson's words to the mysterious charisma of his physical presence. "If ever there was a standing testimonial to the cumulative power and value of Character (and we need it sadly in these days), we have it in this gracious and dignified presence. . . . For us the whole life of the man is distilled in the clear drop of every sentence, and behind each word we divine the force of a noble character, the weight of a large capital of thinking and being."[52] Literary authority manifests itself as though the words were a physical expression of the "whole life of the man" in the same way that sweat and tears are "distilled" from the body. Language gains its particular force from the "weight of a large capital of thinking and being." A printed text in this instance refers not to a solitary moment of creation but to the ongoing production of character, the "presence" of an author that is at once physical and social.

Lowell's assessment of Emerson makes an explicit equation between eloquence and moral authority. In their commitment to the power of voice, Lowell and others valued the immediacy of moral suasion, whereby identification with a consensual community took precedence over the sovereign autonomy of individual subjectivity. The consummate proof of Emerson's success, of the persuasive impression of his ethos, is the fact that his words enable Lowell to *lose* his individual identity as a reader. In Emerson's 1858 oration on the poet Robert Burns,

> every word seemed to have just dropped down to him from the clouds. He looked far away over the heads of his hearers, with a vague kind of expectation, as into some private heaven of invention, and the winged period came at last obedient to his spell. "My dainty Ariel!" he said murmuring to himself as he cast down his eyes as if in deprecation to the frenzy of approval, and caught another sentence from the Sibylline leaves that lay before him ambushed behind a dish of fruit and seen only by nearest neighbors. Every sentence brought down the house, as I never saw one brought down before . . . I watched, for it was an interesting study, how the quick sympathy ran flashing from face to face down the long tables, like an electric spark thrilling as it went, and then exploded in a thunder of plaudits. I watched till tables and faces vanished, for I, too, found myself caught up in the common enthusiasm.[53]

Lowell testifies to Emerson's genius not by watching it from a remove but in losing the sense of himself that critical detachment makes possible, in becoming "caught up in the common enthusiasm." He renders this transformation, significantly, as a kind of blindness, in which "tables and faces vanished," in which "an interesting study" gives way to an "excited fancy" that has left him with only his hearing. In listening rather than watching, Lowell has like those "nearest neighbors" gained an imaginary nearness to those Sibylline leaves from which Emerson himself catches his sentences. And yet at the same time, the watching, the visible presence of sympathy in others, is a necessary prelude to the proximity to thought—getting close to Man Thinking—which listening finally secures.

Force of literary expression is gauged here by the animation of a collective space of discourse by a voice, real or imaginary, whose moral conviction is both provoked by and responsive to the natural familiarity and congeniality of civil society. In praising the essays of Michel de Montaigne, Emerson similarly invoked images of social exchange to describe the eloquence of a written text: "It is the language of conversation transferred to a book. Cut these words, and they would bleed; they are vascular and alive."[54] Montaigne's thinking does not ornament itself with the self-conscious literary conceits of "Cambridge men who correct themselves, and begin again at every half-sentence, and . . . pun, refine too much, and swerve from the matter to the expression." This writing gets to the "matter" of thought not because it seeks autonomy of "expression" but because it seeks engagement with others. "One has the same pleasure in it that we have in listening to the necessary speech of men about their work, when any unusual circumstance gives momentary importance to the dialogue. For blacksmiths and teamsters do not trip in their speech; it is a shower of bullets." In measuring his literary success, Emerson, like Lowell, looks beyond "mere words" to the moment these words become "necessary speech"—as direct, important, and urgent as the words men use as they go about their work. A shower of bullets, an electric spark thrilling as it went: Emerson's language distinguishes itself as an irresistible spur to "being and doing," as thought so fully entered into human dialogue that it becomes as "necessary" as the driving of horses or the operation of telegraphs.

The imagery of voice represents literary effect as making an entire community palpable: words compel conviction through the evidence of the senses, by assimilating the subjective activity of reading into the social experience of feeling and thinking. The commonplace notion in the nineteenth century that books could become "companions" to a solitary reader follows the same logic by which a text can be heard as "talk": words matter, they can matter, when, as in thinking, listening, and speaking, they partake of the vitality of social life. What Emerson praises in Montaigne's writing, and Lowell praises in Emerson's, are variations of what the French salon termed *esprit* and valued above all else in the art of conversation: the vitality with which language retains its human and moral dimension, its primacy as an act of communication rather than representation.[55] "Montaigne talks with shrewdness," Emerson writes. His prose is real to the extent that it "brings us *life*" and "distills the whole man," retaining the human presence that gave it utterance, conveying the social motives that animate it. To hear written words as "vascular and alive" is to discover anew the potential for language to insinuate itself into consciousness as though it were flesh and blood. Books, as Emerson writes in the essay of that name in *Society and Solitude* (1870), "take rank in our life with parents and lovers and passionate experiences, so medicinal, so revolutionary, so authoritative—books which are the work and the proof of faculties so comprehensive, so nearly equal to the world which they paint, that, though one shuts them with meaner ones, he feels his exclusion from them to accuse his way of living."[56] The intimacy achieved with such exemplary books tutors readers in the cultivation of character.

In Lowell's recollection, Emerson ushered his auditors into a moral community by using the lecture hall as a medium of spiritual communion. Prior to audio and visual technologies of reproduction that now allow us to revisit, analyze, and objectify qualities of aesthetic engagement, knowledge of the moment bore the peculiar transcendental authority of spiritual inspiration, indeed of conversion: a sudden, unique event excites and overwhelms the senses, leaving conviction in its wake. For those who had seen Emerson speak, his writings remained haunted by historical encounters with the "seer" or "prophet." Like many others, Lowell recalled the transforming impact Emerson had on his intellectual life without much remembering the particulars of his philosophy. Emerson "put us in communication with a larger style of thought," "made us conscious . . . of whatever bit of soul might be in any of us"—and he did all this through an eloquence that transcended printed forms of discourse intended for silent, solitary reading. Emerson "freed us, in short, from the stocks of prose in which we had sat so long that we had grown well-nigh contented in our cramps."[57] Emerson freed us from the "stocks of prose": The newfound conviction that Lowell acquires in listening to Emerson—his becoming conscious "of whatever bit of soul might be in any of us" and communing with "a larger style of thought"—translates the experience of grace into a cognitive movement between modes of literary discourse. In writing about Emerson's impact in the lecture hall, Lowell is describing a secular conversion experience.

In an age when the modern system of mass production, distribution, and consumption of books was coming to maturity in the United States, Emerson's hortatory efficacy—his ability to engage a democratic audience, and to seduce middle-class souls into the love of wisdom—was located in the specific medium of the lecture hall rather than the printed page. In its power to provoke an intellectual awakening that resembled the experience of conversion, Emerson's work is best appreciated, as Margaret Fuller first suggested in 1844, within an ancient hortatory tradition of spiritual exercises:

> In the union of an even rustic plainness with lyric inspirations, religious dignity with philosophic calmness, keen sagacity in details with boldness of view we saw what brought to mind the early poets and legislators of Greece—men who taught their fellows to plough and avoid moral evil, sing hymns to the gods and watch the metamorphoses of nature. Here in civic Boston was such a man. . . . In New England he thus formed for himself a class of readers who rejoice to study in his books what they already know by heart.[58]

Alluding to Hesiod's *Works and Days,* the mode of reading Fuller cites— memorizing by heart, as a way to "rejoice"—is, like singing hymns to the gods, a ritualized means of spiritual devotion, an aid to reflection that reacquaints "civic Boston" with the dispositions of philosophical composure: wonder, courage, confidence, peace, exultation.[59] As they continued to be influenced by the Protestant faith in the mysteries of grace, nineteenth-century Americans still believed in the power of decisive moments to transform our way of being in the world.[60] Increasingly, worldly young men such as Tilton sought this experience outside of the traditional venues of orthodox piety and religious evangelism, using the lecture hall and other mass media of character as a means of spiritual exercise.

The Eloquence of Moral Life

It is no coincidence that Emerson's work loses its literary interest for modern scholars just at the moment when he came to have a unique credibility as a public intellectual among his contemporaries in the lecture hall. Drawing on general assumptions about the ideological nature of middle-class consumption of knowledge that would build character, critical consensus about the "dumbing down" of Emerson's later work has made it easy to overlook Emerson's most urgent question for modern readers, and for professional academics in particular: How do individuals cultivate character in a democratic culture, within the conventional values and mass institutions of the marketplace? The intensive work of solitary reading that typifies the modern academy is at odds with the cultivation of a moral disposition toward one's own experience—a conviction of character—which was at the heart of the democratic project of citizenship to which Emerson, Thoreau, Whitman, and so many others were committed in nineteenth-century America. Most people today only read in this way when under the duress of the classroom, where they master ways of reading texts that are incommensurable with the cognitive demands and discursive habits that exist outside of the professional culture of literacy. For example, we reward students for a mastery of printed texts, which is itself unresponsive to the egalitarian argument in Emerson's practice of philosophy. The pervasiveness that silent, solitary reading now has in our academic life makes it appear to be a superior mode of practicing philosophy, but it is simply the dominant form in our historical moment. As we shall see in chapter five, the currency of solitary reading and "writing by the page," as Lowell put it, were secured by the development of a modern literary sphere organized around print media, the specialization of academic study, and professional authorship.

The terms of Emerson's success in his own time tell us much about the politics of literacy through which ideas and dispositions acquire their appeal within the spaces of mass culture. The liberation of spirit and thought from the constraint of "mere words"—from "stocks of prose," from the "methods of Mr. Locke"—was the fundamental intellectual framework within which Emerson's contemporaries understood the civic function of literature. For this reason, some of Emerson's readers understood his work as an escape from a modern intellectual culture already captive to the rationality of reading, imprisoned in the iron cage of printed texts. As contemporary reviews of Emerson make especially clear, the popular values of nineteenth-century literary culture remained committed to the *idea* if not always the fact of an author personally addressing a crowd that extended only so far as the average person's hearing and vision. This meant, on the one hand, that the printed essays inevitably seemed "less directly powerful, as [they were] more distant from the source"[61]—that Emerson's voice could seem diminished by its transposition to the seemingly cold medium of the printed page, his words received through a more abstract cognitive process of solitary reading. On the other hand, these nineteenth-century values define eloquence as an intrinsic feature of moral life: moral authority is always finally embodied in persons, not in privileged access to liberal education or in hierarchical regimes of literary taste.

Both inside and outside the nineteenth-century lecture hall, writing and speaking served the ends of moral cognition not only by imparting information but by modeling the reader's disposition to knowledge, exemplifying in theme and form a philosophical attitude, a composure of character. As Pierre Hadot reminds us, Greek and Roman philosophy did not abstract ideas from the humble, human medium of the speaking voice. Dialogue, exhortation, maxim, meditation, prayer: all of these were means of giving words not just rational credibility but spiritual force. The oral dimension of ancient philosophy was not meant primarily to convey information or represent ideas but to produce psychic effects, "to form more than inform."[62] So too literature's expressive power in this context depended not only on its verbal argument but also on what Hadot calls its *psychogogy*—the multiple and various means by which a teacher seduces the soul to the love of wisdom. These included traditional *rhetoric*—formal means of persuasion through continuous discourse—as well as *dialectic,* models of discourse that depend on the student's initiative in the task of education. As people listened to Emerson and responded to what they heard in their journals, they each took up the task of philosophy for themselves, and entered a dialogue with their moral Other.

Emerson located moral authority not in some silent, solitary moment of creation for the printed page or in the acquisition of abstract knowledge, but in the voices of spoken eloquence, the democratic art of presence. Throughout his later essays and lectures exploring character, culture, and social ethics, Emerson insisted that moral authority is rhetorical. In one of his popular lectures given repeatedly in the 1850s, Emerson declared that eloquence is "an example of the magic of personal ascendancy": "What we really wish for is a mind equal to any exigency."[63] He illustrates the "magic" of eloquence by invoking images of personal confrontation under extraordinary circumstances.

> You are safe in your rural district, or in the city, in broad daylight, amidst the police, under the eyes of a hundred thousand people. But how is it on the Atlantic, in a storm—do you understand how to infuse your reason into men disabled by terror, and to bring yourself off safe then?—how among thieves, or among an infuriated populace, or among cannibals? Face to face with a highwayman who has every temptation and opportunity for violence and plunder, can you bring yourself off safe by your wit, exercised through speech?[64]

This sketch is a parlor-game charade, a playing with moral authority that asks us to impersonate a heroism that the circumstances of modern life no longer afford. Emerson wishes to remind his comfortable middle-class audience—protected by police, safe in their anonymity—of the visceral meaning of "exigency": have you felt the imperative of heroism, and could you respond to it if you did? These sensational and extreme scenarios belie Emerson's larger claim, which is that we admire not so much the unique, charismatic individual in rhetorical performance, but the qualities of a "mind equal to any exigency." These qualities are potentially universal, but called from us in moments of duress. However absorbing these moments appear in their dramatic intensity, each becomes just another scene in the ongoing performance of character. We admire individuals who have transformed themselves into examples of universal capacities, who have embodied qualities of moral composure. To cultivate such a presence in our own lives would be to contrive the quotidian circumstances we confront at work and leisure into crises of silent film melodrama: to endure catastrophe with the insouciant stoicism of Buster Keaton, to escape every peril with the athletic poise of Pauline. Thus does Emerson seek to reawaken a sense of *moral exigency* to which many citizens, complacent in their safe suburbs, are numb. Eloquence enables one to "bring yourself off safe" from a world hostile to individual autonomy of every kind. As Benjamin Tilton discovered in his own crisis of composure, that world keeps us hostage in more mundane and insidious ways than the threats of cannibals and pirates. Tending to boredom, desperation, despair, and perpetual "fluctuations of happiness," the anonymous and rationalized barbarism of market culture disables the rational faculties, undermining those forms of human presence and conviction we most value: dignity, courage, wisdom, and compassion.

Emerson argues that we should see our public and private lives as rhetorical occasions, arenas for the moral performance of character. Dramatic encounters with highwaymen and cannibals offer a hyperbolic version of what Emerson calls the "power of face," the rhetorical power of presence exercised in the smallest units of society. "What a difference between men in power of face! A man succeeds because he has more power of eye than another, and so coaxes or confounds him." Emerson waxes on about the "eloquence" of eyes and faces because he associates rhetoric with a more general efficacy of social being. With the serenity of a poker face, "a man this is who cannot be disconcerted, and so never play his last card, but has a reserve of power when he has hit his mark. . . . Men and women are his game. Where they are, he cannot be without resource."[65] Emerson offers a metaphor for contests for power that occur in democratic culture: not a contract, not a public sphere of reasoned discourse, but a high-stakes poker game in which citizens play one another like so many "resources" to be exploited. We play this game for profit, certainly, but no less for the instinctive pleasure that we take in hitting our mark, our satisfaction in the elegance of the play itself. This metaphor evokes Herman Melville's cynical portrayal of democracy as a riverboat full of tricksters and dupes in *The Confidence Man* (1857). Emerson has another purpose, however, which is to adulterate his earlier transcendental optimism in self-reliance with a cautionary and pragmatic realism. Recall Emerson's early claim in "Self-Reliance," that "this one fact the world hates—that the soul becomes." Here, he wants us to recognize the odds against us, the odds against the soul's becoming, in democratic culture. As his later work argues in complex ways, character entails the effective exercise of moral eloquence, a shrewdness or composure that must be learned, mastered, and inhabited. This practice of character is the proper object of civic education in a democratic culture, the *techné* of philosophical play that lends the game its egalitarian and utopian stakes: "The greater power of face would accomplish anything," confounding "merchant, banker, judge, men of influence and power,—poet and president," unseating sovereigns and abrogating constitutions.

Emerson invokes the natural "power of face" to dramatize the politics of character in democratic culture. By addressing the rhetorical game of social life, Emerson is making us see again that the extreme and ordinary interactions we have with one another are occasions for philosophical practice. "The eyes of men converse as much as their tongues," Emerson notes in "Behavior," "with the advantage that the ocular dialect needs no dictionary, but is understood all the world over."[66] Part of the reason that Emerson makes character the medium for democratic philosophy is that it 'speaks' this universal language of the body, a grammar of expressions, dispositions, and convictions that—because it is "natural"—defies its monopoly by educated elites or demagogues. Emerson repeatedly emphasizes that eloquence pertains not to the art of public address as mastered by professional statesmen, theologians, and men of letters, but to the moral credibility of individual character within everyday life. "Every man is an orator, soever long he may have been mute," and "so probably, every man is eloquent once in his life." The great promise of democratic culture is the freedom it allows ordinary people to acquire the moral authority once reserved for the traditional professions. Anyone might inspire and lead their fellow citizens by the eloquence of their example and actions, the performance of character.

In print and in person, Emerson asked his middle-class audiences to see the moral life as an art of presence, a latent eloquence that is every individual's right and duty to claim. The democratic freedom of voice is merely theoretical, however, unless all citizens have equal access to the institutions of literacy and technologies of self that make the realization of character, or what Emerson calls the becoming of the soul, possible within a modern environment. The inequalities of education and opportunity that deny the liberal promise of freedom to so many Americans manifest themselves in the contests of character we encounter daily. The practical politics of character, then, is about how we go about constituting a just society in a democratic culture where the "power of face" renders every human relation a contest of wit, a conversation or confrontation among intimates who are not at equal liberty to speak, and who are unequal as well in their tastes, education, talents, and moral virtues. For Emerson, the democratic right to influence our collective destiny comes with the moral obligation of individuals to divine and express character, their particular eloquence, as they play the incessant games of social life. From this perspective, it makes sense to describe Emerson's work as George Kateb recently has. With their apparent contradictions and defects of reasoning, his essays are "impersonations," each enacting a particular "mood" with its own valuable, but partial, perspective on the problems of democratic self-care. We come to exercise a true self-reliance through the incarnation of, or sympathetic identification with, the many voices of a democratic culture. Skeptical of the sufficiency of any one of these voices, the individual realizes moral agency by achieving self-trusting independence from the particular roles and social inequalities of the world we inhabit.[67]

Knowledge gains moral authority, then, from the rhetorical force with which it manifests itself within ordinary experience. In democratic culture, knowledge does not become wisdom until it becomes conventional, accessible to diverse audiences, repeated and relayed through impersonation, engaging as a social and practical discourse. This may be what Lowell meant in his praise of the repetitious familiarity of Emerson's work, when he noted that "genius" was one of the few things "that multiply rather than weaken the force of their impression by iteration."[68] We can find an illustration of what Emerson means by returning to the diary with which this chapter began, and to the individual who made of it both a record of his "fluctuations of happiness" and an instrument of his struggle for composure. Benjamin Tilton's questions—What should I do? For whom do I live?—lie at the heart of young men's struggles to find a place for themselves in mid-nineteenth-century America. With varying degrees of skill and self-consciousness, clerks sought to answer such questions when they wrote in their diaries, learned the art of conversation, joined mercantile libraries, attended lectures by Emerson, and engaged in other modes of spiritual exercise. The economic freedom that democracy theoretically ensured to all adult white males was empty unless individuals cultivated their moral autonomy: the ability to learn from their experience of market culture, to emancipate themselves through moral imagination and literary practices of the will.

By attending a lecture by Emerson and writing about it in his diary, Tilton gains access to a moral identity and to normative values that his experience of modernity had put into question. Defying simple distinctions between reading, writing, and speaking, his readiness "to exclaim" in despair is transformed into a literary performance. The image of the captive to which he turns is a quotation of sentimental verse that he might have copied from a periodical at the Mercantile Library, or from one of the many gift albums and "annuals" that became popular in the domestic circles of middle-class leisure. The soul captive to the body, the chain of prosperity, a fond mother, material values that become "shadows": Tilton's diary dwells in the sentimental conventions and commonplaces of spiritual resignation and melancholy. The literary value of these commonplaces does not inhere in the object or text from which they are taken, but in the rhetorical gestures that make them useful and practical for the art of composure. The importance that sincerity has in Tilton's performance has much to do with why modern scholars (typically modernist in their aesthetic tastes) have had difficulty appreciating this discourse about character. The repetition of didactic verse allowed individuals to embody a philosophical conviction of character, when one's own perceptions and values seemed merely subjective, fragile, and fluctuating.

The sentimental conventions that dominated literary leisure in nineteenth-century America offered middle-class men and women instrumental means for the rhetorical practice of character. Commonplace texts offered examples of reflection, sincerity, and conviction from which young people learned to claim their own moral voice. As Tilton writes "How true are these lines" and copies sentimental verse, he moves from his own experience to a claim about the human condition in general: he quotes from his own despair. The conventional pieties and sentiments that circulated through the mass media of print and the lecture hall allowed Tilton to escape the existential "poverty" of subjectivity, furnishing him with tools for his own performance of character. The ephemeral insight that Tilton paraphrased from Emerson's lecture acquired its value as wisdom not through interpretation and introspection as a textual object but through its social circulation as literary ethos. Like the quotation of verse, the underlining of sentiments he hears from Emerson—"that our poverty lies, chiefly, in <u>feeling pain</u>"—relays moral authority from textual objects to rhetorical practices—those hortatory arts of emphasis, repetition, credence, assertion, and exhortation that build the convictions of character. The "use" Tilton makes of promiscuous insights from mass culture fosters a personalized aesthetics of presence that throughout the nineteenth century was valorized as eloquence.

What makes some sentiments and maxims "true," from this point of view, is the manner in which they trade in the affective knowledge that is already in wide social circulation, bringing the common currency of social discourse to life as the particular presence of ethos and pathos, in the performance of character on the multiple stages of literary leisure. One paradox then of these sentimental commonplaces is that it was precisely those topics that were so highly visible, so seemingly impersonal in their ready social currency, by which people discovered their moral convictions about the nature of happiness and the purpose of their lives. As they wrote about courtship, the domestic circle, solitude, and the landscape, young men transformed their letters and diaries into stages for rhetorical performance. Tilton underscores his familiarity with the literary conventions of sentimentality through his repeated use of quotation in his diary—"charmed scenes of childhood," "Home," the "near and dear," the familiar or social "circle." It seems important to him to emphasize the derivative, secondary relation his own writing bears to normative forms of social discourse. He quotes not to suggest an ironic distance from this discourse, as a modern reader might expect, as to "prove" his sincere identification with it through the evidence of his literary exertions. We see this as well in his capitalization of terms such as "Mother," "Brother," Sister," "Bride," and "Groom."

At every site in the middle-class landscape of literacy, writing, reading, and speaking were less autonomous skills to be differentiated and specialized than they were reflexive, cognate forms of rhetorical performance. As they were experienced in relation to essentially Romantic, conventional values of middle-class privacy, even solitary reading and writing became oddly self-conscious forms of utterance. On one night in November 1841, after withdrawing from the "social circle assembled around" the "bright fire," Tilton declares: "But to enjoy retirement—to be alone at times is a greater pleasure, then to our own room I betake myself, draw the table before the little grate in which a cheerful fire is burning and with book in hand (my ever welcome companion) enjoy the evening in silence; or with pen ink and paper employ myself as at present." Here and elsewhere, literary practices unfold as silent dialogues between a clerk and his book or diary. To speak of books as friends or companions, as these young men so often did, suggests the degree to which they identified "true" expression with the loyalty, trust, honesty, and other virtues of social intimacy. At another point, Tilton interrupted his reflections about Mary Baker to declare: "But hold! I am thinking out loud, though in the quiet recluse of my own room."[69] Even in the quiet and solitary "recluse" of writing a diary, moral reflection takes place as a self-conscious "thinking out loud," in which the credibility of one's thoughts and feelings are tested by performance in the ever-present company of one's moral Other.

What difference does it make for thinking to be done "out loud" through the practices of literary leisure? The rhetorical practice of literary taste naturalized norms of character as habits of feeling, expressed at leisure and increasingly in private, rather than habits of action undertaken in public life. Tilton's facility with quotation enables him to make new or unsettling experiences predictable and useful to his future. In August 1842, Tilton obliquely describes a walk on the beach with his brother and the woman who would become his fiancée, coyly designated as "M." The water at the shoreline, he writes,

> sought to kiss the retreating foot steps of the lingering admirer who strolled along the smooth white beach. . . . Never can I forget the pleasure of that delightful walk. It swelled with fond anticipation of the future. May these golden visions be realized. These illuminating visions of the future that occasionally flit before the mind to cheer me

on in life's rugged path—to soften the hours of despondency which at times depress me. But I will cast them off, that I may enjoy life, which now begins to assume a more pleasing garb and exert myself to realize if possible those lovely anticipations.[70]

By becoming associated with "illuminating visions" an otherwise momentary "pleasure" and "delight" generates tangible choices about one's future. Like the other picturesque episodes and often-repeated sentiments expressed in Tilton's diary, the walk on the beach becomes memorable by being transposed to his diary as a lyrical moment that changes his attitudes toward a woman. Tilton's use of this moment on the beach exemplifies the fundamentally moral function of literary taste. In the diary's record of this episode, we see how writing can transform an otherwise ordinary experience—a walk on the beach—into a compelling scenario of personal fulfillment, a set of "fond anticipations" that Tilton would set out "to realize" through his courtship and eventual marriage to Mary. Such events and feelings only become memorable and "useful" in a rhetorical sense of "thinking out loud," in allowing a young man to commit to his choices and to take meaning from them. Sentimental affect inspires him to pursue "illuminating visions," to commit to domestic happiness as a moral ideal that can "be realized" in the context of his own life. Tilton used the resolution and hope afforded by the habit of writing and other literary exercises to sustain his "exertions" in the social realm: courtship and marriage to a woman who, according to modern precepts of intimacy and feeling, remained a relative stranger to him. In a world and at a stage of life when all values could seem uncertain or "fluctuating," then, literary practices gave Tilton and other young men moral certainty and emotional resolve, but they did so within the increasingly private eloquence of middle-class life.

However banal the self-fashioning they produced may seem to present-day readers, the diary and the lecture hall were modes of spiritual exercise, tools for casting off despair over what was beyond one's control, in order to realize moral conviction, a hope for the future. Through the rhetorical practice of character, ordinary people such as Benjamin Tilton found opportunities to recover the moral drama at stake in their quotidian experience of modernity. In striving to answer the question "How should I live?" Benjamin Tilton is not merely a consumer of ideas about character but a practitioner: he uses his diary to give voice to his own moral striving. The habits and capacities that constituted "character" were developed through literary performances that transformed the ordinary search for work and love into opportunities for moral heroism. When young men wrote in diaries or attended lectures, they found, like James Russell Lowell, that knowledge was most compelling and *transforming* when it was characterized by features of a rhetorical eloquence that seemed to free their minds from the "stocks of prose"—to speak to their spiritual ambitions.

The discourse about character promulgated in lecture halls and the mass culture of print reflected popular engagement in and demand for practical moral advice. Unlike the elitist and sectarian schools of classical philosophy, this discourse was disseminated through an immense variety of media: conduct books, etiquette guides, moral tracts, lectures, the songs and images of sentimental culture, penmanship instruction, the "sciences" of phrenology and physiognomy, stories and novels, sentimental poetry. We would normally not think of any of this as philosophy, as it has come to be defined by the methods and norms of professional academic discourse and pursued in the intensive, analytical reading of a relatively small canon of printed texts. Through these ordinary occasions and objects of intellectual leisure, middle-class people acquired for themselves convictions that, they hoped, would guide them through life's trials. The didacticism that distinguishes this discourse and so alienates the modern scholar from its central moral precepts is, from this point of view, a feature intrinsic to the ancient hortatory tradition of giving advice. The practice of philosophy is necessarily evangelical, the very opposite of a professional body of knowledge, which has estranged modern academic philosophy from its roots in spiritual pedagogy and its practice as the art of living.

In asking why Emerson's popularity in the lecture hall should matter to us now, I wish to suggest how literary institutions of mass media made the practice of philosophy newly relevant for democratic culture. The fact that so many middle-class people such as Benjamin Tilton found Emerson's performances, both in print and the lecture hall, "useful" may suggest more a consummation of his philosophic project than its frustration. An 1852 issue of the *American Phrenological Journal* praised recent lectures delivered by phrenologists Lorenzo and Orson Fowler, noting that they had given audiences "wise, practical, and friendly instructions about ourselves, and the true way of keeping and improving ourselves, physically, mentally and socially." The journal went on to interpret the success of Emerson's public lectures in similar terms, as making "*practical* wisdom" available to a general public through their distinctive rhetorical appeal.

> R. W. Emerson's lectures on the Conduct of Life attest, likewise, in subject and treatment, to the demand of the age for *practical* wisdom, though it be transcendental at the same time. His audiences have been larger and larger, and such as it is an inspiring pleasure to sit among; so much intelligence, original character, refinement, culture, and humanity, is rarely concentrated by the magnetism of one original man. Everybody speaks of the eminent practicality of these

lectures, especially the third and fourth, of which the themes were "Wealth" and "Economy." There is exquisite wit, as well as wisdom, in his sententious lessons, and *ad hominem* illustrations. Everybody leaves in good humor, though nobody escapes unhit; and you go away more serious, and more hopeful from these truly poetic oracles, not of sentimentality, but of *hard fact.*[71]

As the reviews of contemporaries suggest, Emerson was popular largely because he could he tease moral implication from its homely hiding places. His "natural" style imbued his words and ideas with the conventional, "familiar" ring of truth necessary to persuade people to reform their own conduct, to convert citizens to the democratic project of caring for the self. A lecture by Emerson let few "escape unhit" by the "poetic oracles" of "hard fact," let few be unmoved by the "inspiring pleasure" of "practical wisdom." By developing the natural eloquence of his own literary form, Emerson responded to the philosophical yearnings of ordinary people who, in pursuing myriad forms of literary recreation, sought moral purpose for their lives.

As mass media of character, the diary, the lecture hall, and the printed book served the ends of philosophical practice by circulating a rhetorical ethos that transcended the limits of textual form. For this reason, Theodore Parker, Emerson's contemporary, suggested that the fundamental message of Emerson's essays was exemplified by the unwavering *tone* that animated them. "In all Emerson's works there appears a sublime confidence in man," a "calmness and serenity" that Parker attributes to the composure of their author's character: "He is evenly balanced and at repose. A more tranquil spirit cannot be found in literature. Nothing seems to fret or jar him, and all the tossing of the literary world never jostle him into anger or impatience."[72] For those who never heard Emerson speak, it is this sublime, philosophical equanimity of Emerson's ethos that explained the compelling force of his texts—when even read by a German critic with no idea of their author's reputation. "How could I be so captured and enthralled; so fascinated and bewitched," Herman Grimm asked in 1861 about a volume of the collected "Essays" he had deciphered with the aid of Webster's Dictionary:

> Emerson fills me with courage and confidence. He has read and observed, but he betrays no sign of toil. . . . He is a perfect swimmer on the ocean of modern existence. He dreads no tempest, for he is sure that calm will follow it; he does not hate, contradict, or dispute, for he understands men and loves them. I look on with wonder to see how the hurly burly of modern life subsides, and the elements gently betake themselves to their allotted places.[73]

The use that popular audiences made of Emerson's work was essentially spiritual, for the possibility of composure it embodied for listeners and readers alike.

For Tilton and for so many others making their way in the world of market culture, there was (and continues to be) an existential challenge at stake in the practice of character: to realize moral autonomy, which is so delicately poised between the heart's swelling and the "poverty" of the senses. The middle-class practice of character concerned itself primarily with the cultivation of philosophical attitudes, with moral dispositions such as independence and happiness and hope. Like Tilton's reflection on the "use" of hope by which the heart "whispers encouragement" and "sweetens the present," these attitudes often require nonrational means of kindling one's energies, beliefs, and faiths, bulwarks against rational doubt or disabling melancholy. This spiritual use of intellectual recreation, addressed to "fluctuations of happiness" and what George Kateb calls the "mood" of philosophy, would by the twentieth century find itself estranged from the textual focus and critical procedures of formal literary criticism. It is worth noting that although Van Wyck Brooks railed against the "superannuated boyishness of the Emersonian tradition" in his literary criticism, he would later produce a *Life of Emerson*. In its didactic, "stylized paraphrases" of Emerson's work, Brooks's biography resembled the simplistic pirating, and even the spiritualist channeling, of the Sage's more devoted adherents, like E. E. Emmons, whose *Light of Emerson* offered "two thousand quotable thoughts" and "many virile epigrams" (fig. 13). Written in the midst of a nervous breakdown, Brooks's *Life* suggests that he had gained a new appreciation for the use of Emerson's hope.

Emerson and other artists and public intellectuals in nineteenth-century America imagined market culture as an egalitarian arena for philosophical practice, where individuals might become expert in self-composure—become both more serious and hopeful, as the *American Phrenological Review* put it, and so cultivate their autonomy in spite of the oppressions of modernity. The American discourse about character sought to revise an elitist model of moral authority associated with the European tradition of liberal education. As Emerson increasingly argued in his later, popular essays and lectures concerned with character, every democratic subject must have the opportunity and responsibility to claim moral authority as their own. While he disagreed with Emerson's taste in poetry, Walt Whitman praised his own touch of "Emerson-on-the-brain" as a "stage of exercise" necessary for any youth aspiring to autonomy: "No teacher ever taught, that has so provided for his pupil's setting up independently—no truer evolutionist."[74] Not unlike the students of the ancient philosophers, these young citizens, as Fuller put it, "receive his influence as a help and incentive

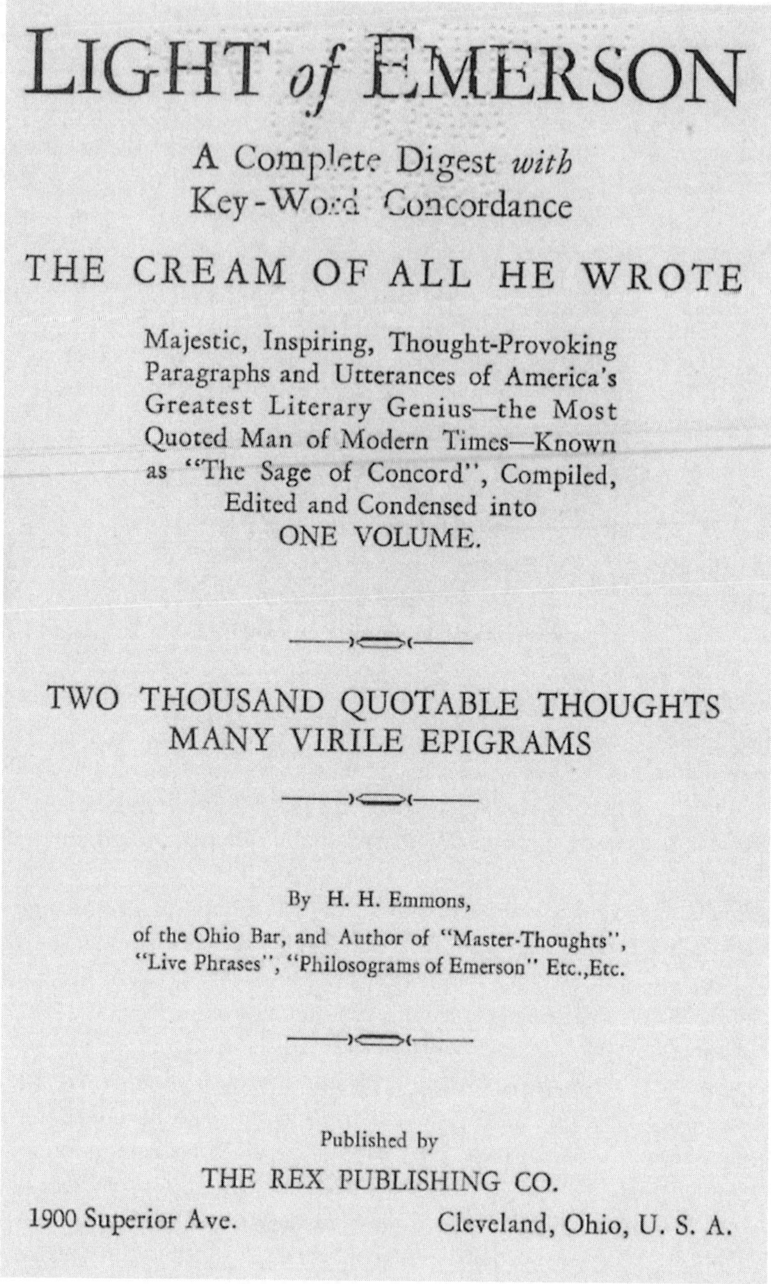

LIGHT of EMERSON

A Complete Digest with
Key-Word Concordance

THE CREAM OF ALL HE WROTE

Majestic, Inspiring, Thought-Provoking
Paragraphs and Utterances of America's
Greatest Literary Genius—the Most
Quoted Man of Modern Times—Known
as "The Sage of Concord", Compiled,
Edited and Condensed into
ONE VOLUME.

———)⊂⇒(———

TWO THOUSAND QUOTABLE THOUGHTS
MANY VIRILE EPIGRAMS

———)⊂⇒(———

By H. H. Emmons,

of the Ohio Bar, and Author of "Master-Thoughts",
"Live Phrases", "Philosograms of Emerson" Etc.,Etc.

———)⊂⇒(———

Published by
THE REX PUBLISHING CO.
1900 Superior Ave.   Cleveland, Ohio, U. S. A.

Figure 13 Title page, *Light of Emerson*. Published in 1930 by H. H. Emmons, *Light of Emerson* is a compendium of "Majestic, Inspiring, Thought-Provoking Paragraphs and Utterances" by "the most Quoted Man of Modern Times." While Emerson's essays became a staple of literary studies in the modern academy, his words also circulated as digestible sayings in a modern tradition of popular wisdom and advice. Ranging from *Bartlett's Quotations* in the nineteenth century to the maxims of self-help gurus and corporate consultants in the twentieth century, this tradition of pop philosophy is rooted in the moral authority of the spoken word, in contrast to the solitary reading and writing emphasized at every stage of modern formal education.

to a nobler discipline than the age in its general aspect appears to require."[75] The awakening of individuals to both their poverty of condition and their moral aspirations is the starting point for civic engagement and the practice of freedom in a democratic community.

If, as Herman Grimm suggested, "the ocean of modern life" demands the sort of calm exemplified by Emerson in his essays, it is also true that we are not all such able swimmers. Tilton and other young men looking for white-collar work in bustling cities could rely on few of the institutions and resources (health insurance, credit cards, college education, and so forth) by which today's middle class seeks to stay afloat. Because it was experienced through mass-cultural institutions of literary practice such as the lecture hall, the vernacular philosophy of character divorced moral authority from the elitist privilege of liberal learning to which it had been tied. Neither the social credibility of knowledge nor the conviction of commonplace truths were achieved through the solitary, silent reading of texts. Rather, conversion to one's moral person—to the demands of wisdom and happiness—was realized by seeing Emerson speak in a crowded hall, by speaking aloud to one's diary, and through the many other means by which nineteenth-century Americans learned to quote from experience. By making each individual's experience of the market an object of philosophical taste, modes of rhetorical practice such as the diary, the letter, conversation, and the popular lecture helped to make the practice of character in America—the art of presence—more democratic.

Chapter Four
Making Society out of Books:
The New York Mercantile Library
and the Enterprise of Reading

In 1853 the *New York Times* ran an editorial about the proposed relocation uptown of a popular circulating library. "Should the Mercantile Library Company decide to occupy the Opera House" at Astor Place, joining the Astor Library, the New York Society Library, and the Historical Society, the largest book collections in New York City would be within a stone's throw of one another. "No arrangement could be more satisfactory to the literary man by profession," the editorial declared. "His sedentary habits will not be over tasked" by hunting down a source, and so "it becomes easy to be learned and lazy at the same time." Midtown Manhattan would become the fashionable locale for "spectacled young men of pale complexion," and a "market will exist there for the acquisition and exchange of ideas." But the proposed move would have less salutary benefits for "those who do not study but only read; in whose lives literature is an incident and not an aim, an amusement or a solace, and not a business":

> Certainly, the centralization of our stores will be a source of inconve-
> nience to promiscuous and un-methodic readers, to whom books are
> merely time-killers. Young men may be tempted to forego the trou-
> ble of procuring them, if they are not at hand, and supply their place
> with a dangerous study of the book of city life, whose illuminated
> leaves are the theatre, drinking-saloon, and gaming parlor. . . . If
> books are to be an attraction from such mischiefs, the attraction
> should unquestionably be found in the thickest of the evil, courting
> the eye of the tempted. The managers of the Mercantile Library As-
> sociation are maturely advising upon the subject. All these points will,
> doubtless, have their full weight. If the balance be struck in favor of

removal, the civilization of the Fifteenth Ward may be regarded as complete. It will presently hold all the wise men of Gotham.[1]

This editorial offers us a bird's-eye view of the urban world to which thousands of young men came in the middle of the nineteenth century. That world is a landscape of literacy, where libraries and books in general loom large in the lives of individuals and the communities they inhabit. Cultural reformers have argued since the emergence of mass educational systems that books are mediums of moral pedagogy: to absorb children in the pages of textbooks or literature is to protect them from the book of urban life. In making this argument, the editorial recognizes something that has often been overlooked in histories and theories of reading: the experience of reading, and education for civic and moral ends more generally, takes place within a dense landscape of "attractions." A young man in the city had many options for how he spent his free time, and it was precisely this freedom from the supervision of parents and employers that made leisure the fundamental moral dilemma for not only his self-improvement but for the general progress of civilization in Gotham. In this context, a library was no mere collection of books but a temple in the civil religion of American individualism. In the pages of books young men would find redemption from drinking, gambling, and prostitution—social pathologies that middle-class Protestants increasingly attributed to the defective character of ethnic, working-class neighbors. In the soaring neoclassical spaces of libraries and other sites of public culture, the opportunity to build character became a democratic right rather than an aristocratic privilege—but only if books served the "amusement or solace" of "promiscuous and unmethodic readers." The specialized study of books as a "business" by "professional" men of letters met needs very different from the casual reading of ordinary people who, as the editorial's sarcasm about pale bookworms suggests, have *real* business to attend to. Like writing in diaries, the reading institutionalized by the Mercantile Library was a technology of self that allowed a young man to give his leisure practical value and moral purpose—to inscribe his character in the book of city life.

As the *New York Times* editorial suggests, the history of this institution offers us an episode in the public life of literature, a microcosm of the politics of culture in nineteenth-century America. This politics of culture is concerned with issues of access and value: Who should have access to books in a democratic culture? What value does reading have in the moral formation of citizens? By raising these questions, the editorial offers us a useful snapshot of the history of reading within a particular social world, a picture not so much of how people read books than of the contested meanings they brought to the practice of reading. The vision of the editorial is, like that of any snapshot, a static and partial version of history, simplifying a complex social world in two-dimensional clichés that lend themselves equally to melodrama and satire. The clerks who used the library are cast as plebian "sons of toil," as if they were republican yeoman farmers pushing plows rather than clerks pushing pens, ambitious strivers pursuing their self-interest in ethically challenged fields of American commerce. But like the violent tableau that illustrated the sensational fiction and drama of the period, this partial picture of the social landscape has a heuristic value, distilling from otherwise small questions about the management and location of a library the schematic and urgent plot of moral history. The lampoon of the scholar reminds us that most Americans at this time habitually associated some styles of reading with the inequalities of aristocracy. Scholarly "ease" and "laziness" symbolized privileged access to cultural goods and a professional monopoly on the moral authority traditionally conferred by liberal learning—the authority of the "professional man of letters," which was denied to most working people who were struggling with the pressures and distractions of the book of life. In a democratic culture, the editorial asserts, moral authority must "be found in the thickest of the evil, courting the eye of the tempted." Reading must become an "attraction" in the marketplace for leisure.

Behind this seemingly arcane debate about where to locate a library in the nineteenth century is a question that remains a pressing one for early twentieth-first century America: How can we construct a civic culture amid the social havoc that historians and sociologists have identified with the process of capitalist development? Scholars increasingly have drawn attention to the intricate connections between media, civic identity, and economic development. Benedict Anderson has argued that no factor was more important than print capitalism in making it possible for "rapidly growing numbers of people to know themselves, and relate themselves to others" in the new bureaucratic and commercial vernacular of nationalism that emerged in the eighteenth and nineteenth centuries. As the first "modern-style mass-produced industrial commodity," the book "created that remarkable confidence of community in anonymity which is the hallmark of modern nations," continually reassuring the literate middle class of the tangibly immediate reality of its imaginary association with other citizens.[2] From this perspective, the mass medium of print, working in tandem in America with a middle-class ideology of the domestic sphere, nurtured a private, individualistic sensibility. This sensibility allowed people—amid the temporal, spatial, and social dislocations of rapid economic development—to identify themselves with what scholars have recently described as "a fictive, shifting, imaginary community," where the "impersonal links" of "sign and symbol" replaced traditional forms of social cohesion.[3] Whether concerned with the "implied" or "ideal" reader posited in the reader-response literary criticism of Jane Tompkins and Steven Mailloux, or seeking like Cathy Davidson, Michael Denning, and Janice Radway to connect books to social constituencies, much scholarship on the history and theory of literacy has similarly analyzed reading as the abstract cognitive act of solitary individuals creating imaginative communities with one another.[4] This chapter alternatively takes an institutional perspective on literary community, situating the act of reading within a specific social and intellectual environment that changed dramatically over the course of the nineteenth century. What forms did reading take and what value did it have for the moral lives of young businessmen?

Founded in 1821 by prominent merchants for the benefit of their clerks, the New York Mercantile Library Association was the largest, oldest, and most successful of the dozens of mercantile libraries established in cities and towns across the nation before the Civil War. Like libraries for mechanics and apprentices, mercantile libraries were devoted to "useful knowledge" and "rational amusement," but they served expanding communities of merchant clerks and other young men from the middling ranks, rather than tradesmen or artisans.[5] Like many other nonprofit benevolent and educational institutions founded throughout the nineteenth century, these libraries opened up to Anglo-Protestant elites new channels of leadership and social control free from the interference of elected officials and the church. Through the circulation of annual reports and informal social ties, these mercantile libraries formed a loose network that contributed to the development of a national culture, oriented to the sensibility of a managerial middle class.[6] Not unlike the physical spaces of schools, playgrounds, museums, parks, and other public sites of secular culture, the New York Mercantile Library helped to institutionalize the capacity for self-government, or character, within a context of mass leisure and education, and gave particular forms of reading new social meanings and moral functions for manhood.

Despite its origins in paternalistic philanthropy, the New York Mercantile Library became by the 1850s an enterprise of reading competing within a crowded field of leisure activities. It devoted the largest percentage of its collection to novels, and would increasingly open its doors to women and others outside the business community. By following aggressive and innovative strategies of marketing and circulation, it achieved a success that was unprecedented among private circulating libraries. By 1871, its reading room was crowded with as many as one thousand visitors each day. Because this institution was owned and operated by its members, it offers a rare opportunity to see how young businessmen understood the role of literary practices in their own moral and professional development. Between 1821 and 1880 almost sixty individuals served as president of the association; the reports they made each year on the progress and the status of the library, while officially representing the board of directors, as well as the views of the hundreds of members who had elected them, allow us to listen to otherwise ordinary individuals speak about the role that reading played in their experience of market culture. The institutional records, collection catalogs, members' diaries, as well as lectures and orations sponsored by this and other mercantile libraries describe the moral utility that reading came to have for middle-class clerks and illuminates the social dimensions of the literary landscape in which they moved.

The Mercantile Library did relocate to Astor Place in 1855, although it remains unclear whether the Fifth Ward held all the wise men in Gotham as a result. For decades before and after its relocation, this institution played many roles in the lives of young men who could take neither learning nor leisure for granted. Following in the tradition of the social libraries that began with Ben Franklin's Library Company of Philadelphia, the Mercantile Library pooled resources for the education and refinement of working youth. Unlike many social libraries, the Mercantile Library owned its building, which furnished a comfortable and hospitable reading room "to accommodate all who are desirous of reading there in preference to their lodgings." In addition to improvements in lighting and ventilation, the managers continually altered and expanded the space to render it "popular and attractive," adding new carpets, tables and chairs, various engravings and artworks, and eventually female attendants to "materially promote the comfort of visitors, and secure the perfect and necessary order of its furniture."[7] The physical comfort of the library's rooms mirrored its members' aspirations to middle-class gentility more effectively than the rooms most of them rented in boardinghouses. In this sense, the Mercantile Library was a sort of social club where young men could mingle with their peers on a casual basis, albeit under the silence-enforcing supervision of attendants.[8] As with the innumerable voluntary associations that sprang up in the antebellum years, the Mercantile Library appealed to what Tocqueville saw as a peculiarly American appetite for joining organizations. The elections, meetings, and informal literary and debate clubs sponsored by the library provided an outlet for the competitive and aggressive sociability of boyhood, while helping to ease clerks' transition to the more abstract, verbal world of commerce and the formal proprieties of middle-class domesticity.[9] With its regular series of lectures and classes, the library also served as a school of adult education, extending the benefits of liberal learning to working men—something public universities would do following the Morrill Land Grant Act in 1863. Young men primarily used the room during their tea or dinner break, and after work until ten o'clock in the evening when "the desks and tables are well-filled, and the silence is broken only by the continual rustle of leaves."[10] And although it continued to restrict membership by gender, age, and vocation—to the diffuse category of "clerks"—the library functioned as a fraternity, linking generations of young men in a sense of institutional tradition and professional identity.

By asking who the proper audience for literature is and how it could be served by the institutions of civic life, the New York Mercantile Library helped to form the social and professional norms of middle-class character. In the first part of this chapter, I explore the manner in which the mercantile library commodified the practice of reading for a mass audience. As they faced the dilemmas of managing a voluntary membership organization, the young men who served on the board of directors and various committees learned that success in the library business meant supplying intellectual recreation within a competitive urban market of leisure. The second part shows how the library claimed for businessmen a moral authority traditionally associated with the learned professions, while marketing a style of literacy appropriate to those "who do not study but only read," as the *New York Times* put it. Although mercantile libraries pursued goals of self-culture and improvement shared by other contemporaneous reform movements, their primary goal was not to provide a philanthropic refuge from the dislocations of urban life but to socialize young men into a newly self-conscious business profession. The third part of the chapter suggests how the commercialization of leisure by the mercantile library contributed, like the pervasive extracurricular literary clubs and debate societies of antebellum culture, to the emergence of a "middlebrow" style of literacy that formed a bridge between the older belletristic culture and newer currents of popular literary taste. Attempting to cultivate character while continuing to satisfy the tastes of readers within the mass culture of print, the managers of the Mercantile Library articulated a new framework for understanding the moral epistemology of reading. In practice, if not always in theory, the policies of the Mercantile Library revealed the novel's utility as an instrument of social knowledge and ethical practice, prior to and distinct from the sacralization of literary art in the later nineteenth century.

The New York Mercantile Library offers a case study of how modern individualism came to be produced by institutions and practices of liberal culture. The emergence of liberal democratic states coincided with a shift in the locus of governance from traditional forms of political coercion to the bodies and identities of citizens: in the modern state, individuals claim their freedom by governing themselves. Like so many other modern institutions of civic life, the Mercantile Library redefined the relationship between freedom and moral authority for a mass audience, transforming the pursuits of taste and knowledge in the print market into exercises in self-govern-ment.[11] Within institutions such as the Mercantile Library, reading for character was subjective, a developmental experience of imagination and discipline, and social, a form of community and collective identity forged out of the dislocations of market culture. Commercial signs, printed money, newspapers, and many other urban media for the printed word made reading a promiscuous, inclusive activity shared by an anonymous and heterogeneous urban public.[12] Within this context, however, the abil-ity to master more advanced forms of literacy—literary taste—in sites such as the parlor, the lecture hall, and the library, became a new means of social differentiation. In seeking to make reading both popular and useful for the urban middle class, the New York Mercantile Library helped to turn moral life into an object of leisure and entertainment in the marketplace.

Circulating Libraries and the Business of Books

Praising mercantile libraries for their "great and indispensable service to the interests of literature," a federal report in 1876 described how these insti-tutions had helped to open up access to books. But if these "social libraries" for young men had been a "further step in cheapening and popularizing knowledge," they had clearly outlived their purpose, and now faced a crisis of competition with the emergence of free public institutions.[13] With a dis-tinct sense of irony, the report blamed this crisis on unprofessional manage-ment. If these mercantile libraries were to survive, they obviously required more "business-like ways of dealing with the emergency—a doctrine pecu-liarly appropriate to institutions managed by businessmen. . . . Such man-agement makes a pork business successful." The author of the report, F. B. Perkins, had served as assistant librarian for the New York Mercantile Li-brary. Now ensconced at the Boston Public Library, the flagship of the pub-lic library movement, Perkins judged his former employers by invoking his own authority as a professional librarian:

> They are conducted by rapidly changing boards whose members are often mere youths. Their affairs are taken in hand once a year and dealt with by a meeting of the members, whose votes [are] cast dur-ing an exciting canvas for officers of the library . . . Such methods do passably well in associated enterprises, conducted by experienced businessmen. . . . Yet there is sometimes a good deal of . . . intriguing at the annual elections to oust one party or person, or to introduce another. Sometimes the executive force is changed in a similar man-ner. Sometimes, on the other hand, there is too much apathy, and the

machine moves in a rusty way in the hands of managers disinclined to give it the requisite care and energy.

Reflecting the era's spirit of civil service reform, Perkins implies that the interests and resources of the community are best managed by a professional cadre of civil servants, impervious to "exciting canvases" or rapid changes in administration.[14] Such paternal disinterestedness coincided with the professionalization of library work. Businessmen, in short, did not know the business of libraries, whatever they might know about the business of pork. It took the skilled, committed, and neutral hand of a specialized librarian to keep the machinery running with the requisite efficiency and energy.[15]

Rather than viewing mercantile libraries within the context of antebellum philanthropic and educational reforms and as an intermediate step in the democratization of knowledge, I wish to explore how, as "associated enterprises" run by young businessmen, they invite us to recover alternative meanings related to institutional contexts of reading. Like other social libraries, mercantile libraries generally borrowed corporation charters because they were the commonly accepted legal form for associations.[16] New York City's Mercantile Library Association was a common law corporation formed in 1823; it made rules concerning its membership and controlled how it disposed of its income from dues, which after overhead costs were met were used to purchase the books.[17] Upon joining the association and remaining in good standing, a clerk in effect became a temporary shareholder of literary property and services that he jointly owned with other members. Through his vote in annual elections for the association's president and board, he participated in the independent government of a nonprofit, private corporation. The New York Mercantile Library was only one of many institutions founded through nonprofit corporate charters.

While this legal status was shared by many other kinds of organizations, including bridges and turnpike companies, it was particularly meaningful for young businessmen. The New York Mercantile Library was a training ground for business organization, where young men self-consciously managed the library as a nonprofit, commercial enterprise. This is apparent from the annual reports, which gradually assumed the ritualized formality of modern corporation literature: endless restatements and qualifications of the library's mission; recapitulation of its history and veneration of its founders; taking credit or delegating blame for its performance over the year; anxious attention to signs of decline, and exaggeration of signs of growth; the demonstration of expertise and the solicitation of approval from the shareholder-members. The association functions as the protagonist of this genre, as the report from 1823 suggests: it "is not merely an abstraction—a skeleton—inanimate and powerless, designed only to attract the public eye, or subserve a selfish ambition, but endowed with substance and vitality, it is capable of useful action, and productive of positive good. . . . The desire for useful knowledge, which is actively diffusing itself among all classes, should receive every possible encouragement by a cheap, prompt, and adequate supply of the instruction demanded." Even by 1835, the "action" and "production" of this library was conceptualized within the neutral language of economic organization: cheap, prompt, adequate supply. As "a splendid example of the results attainable by associated effort," the library's reports lent themselves to ever more precise and technical presentation, in turn reinforcing the directors' impersonal detachment from their story. "In making statistical and other statements," they claimed to be "guided by the simplicity of facts," avoiding "assertions which might in any way overrate the numerical or real degree of our strength, operations, or progress."[18] In this way the association indeed became an "artificial person" whose vital signs were 'scientifically' measured in the various tables and budgets that predominated in the reports by the 1850s.

Within the generic language of enterprise, the managers used the library to develop a managerial sensibility. From the point of view of the young men who ran it, the mission of the institution became its own growth: "It is not possible for us to remain stationary. We must advance or we must retrograde," it was often stated. "The motto of our institution should ever be expressed by the single word 'Action!' . . . the animating power . . . of the class to which we belong." The tendency of these young businessmen to view the library primarily as an economic vehicle and to pursue an aggressive policy of expansion was reflected in their experimentation with the institution's form and purpose. Over forty years the managers of the library continually adapted to changing circumstances, diversifying its offerings with "attractions" "sufficiently interesting to induce permanent membership." They sponsored lectures, stocked a comfortable reading room with hundreds of domestic and foreign periodicals, offered classes on subjects ranging from accounting to gymnastics, and displayed natural and mineral curiosities, engravings, statuary, paintings, and a collection of celebrity autographs.[19] The managers sought to diagnose the various 'policy' factors that might contribute to the success of particular endeavors. To "popularize" lectures, for example, it was necessary to "present subjects of a varied and interesting character," marketing them to the general public and to targeted special groups such as female academies.[20]

Taken together, the annual reports represent a managerial case study, an ongoing effort to articulate an institutional analysis of the enterprise of literacy in a competitive marketplace of leisure activities. The report from 1851 noted that since 1839 the library had been in an "unhappy state of affairs, aggravated by the effects of indiscreet measures" of some previous boards. It went on to attribute the current revival of prosperity to what it called the "present system of management":

> A prudent care over the expenditures; an active system of prosle-tyzism [*sic*] by means of advertisements and other modes of attracting public attention; an anxious endeavor to satisfy the wants of members, as well in the purchase of the books they may require . . . as in securing to them, full opportunity of obtaining them at the desk when called for: in fine, an earnest effort to make new members, and by increasing the literary resources and advantages of the Institution, retain them when they have joined . . . Experience having shown the efficacy of the system adopted . . . we indulged in no rash experiments, nor rejected knowingly any means or appliances likely to be conducive to its welfare, because they were new.[21]

This observation explicitly articulates the otherwise implicit, improvisational management philosophy that characterized the direction of the New York Mercantile Library. To have "efficacy," managers must adopt a "system." They must be able to execute that system while adhering to the original plan, deducing lessons from the institution's past experience, considering new options without engaging in "indiscreet measures." However commonplace such lessons may seem now, they illustrate how fully these clerks valued their work for this library as a means of developing management skills. It was a place where young men learned how to work with others, to perform cost-benefit analysis, and most of all to appreciate the 'law' of supply and demand. After the association moved to its new building at Astor Place, the managers even got to sit in their own corporate boardroom (fig. 14).

The directors of the association demonstrated that "business-like" ways could make a library as successful as a pork business, long before F. B. Perkins admonished these "mere youths" for their supposed inexperience. The library began in 1820 with two hundred members and as many books; by 1854, it had 4,500 members and a collection of more than 40,000 volumes, with an estimated circulation of 130,000. During the height of its success in 1875, the association had over 8,300 active members, while the library had become the fourth largest in the United States, containing more than 160,000 volumes. With its annual lending of over 200,000 volumes, it had become for a short time the largest circulating library in the country. The library could not have handled such traffic had it not resembled "a depot where business is transacted with mercantile dispatch and regularity," as *Scriber's Monthly* described it in 1871 (fig. 15).[22]

Book-purchasing strategy was the most important component of the

Figure 14   The Board of Directors Room, where hundreds of young men learned to speak and act as businessmen while perfecting the "policy" and "system" of the New York Mercantile Library. *Scribner's Monthly*, 1871.

directors' evolving "system" of management. Nowhere was the tension between the original benevolent mission of the association and pragmatic business practice more apparent than in the effort to define a policy for buying books. The first annual report of the New York Mercantile Library Association stated that its objective was "the dissemination of knowledge and the cultivation of intellect." Consistent with this, the official criteria for book selection classified fiction as of secondary importance to "standard and classical works, such as would impart . . . a tone and character of usefulness."[23] Serving as a repository of enduring cultural wealth, the library would value works of biography, history, travel, and science in opposition to prevailing popular taste, as a "voice of wisdom that makes itself heard" amid the chaotic and unorganized reading culture outside the library walls.[24] "Many young readers, who were otherwise wont to devour pages of romance alone" had in standard works and useful knowledge "received

Figure 15 The impressive circulation desk resembled a "depot where business is conducted with mercantile dispatch and regularity." *Scribner's Monthly,* 1871.

the first impulse to faculties which would have lain dormant and neglected." A fundamental assumption here, inherited from the moralistic condemnations of fiction throughout the eighteenth and nineteenth centuries, was that different kinds of reading matter corresponded to particular mental faculties. Where higher faculties required active stimulation by an external 'improving' agent, a taste for romance expressed the reader's susceptibility to corruption, the potential for rational faculties to be undermined by an excessive desire. The "crude productions" of fiction were "suited merely to the gratification of an unnatural appetite for the marvelous."[25] Where romance feeds an already existing and potentially debasing weakness, history and science provoke and draw out—speaking to the young reader, as it were, in the paternalistic, improving 'voice' of wisdom.

This hierarchy of literary genres was reinforced by an association of higher "faculties" with the capacity for rational improvement. Standard works "constitute 'food for the mind' of those who are truly solicitous for improvement"—implying that they become nourishment only to those who were, in their solicitude, both suitably tractable and capable of independent initiative. In contrast, the "appetite" for fiction is nonrational and almost physical in nature, and as such is not amenable to cultivation or control: fiction readers "gratify their tastes" and soon become "satiated with mere works of fancy."[26] If, as we saw in chapter 1, the moral investments in character entailed an essentially abstract accounting of one's future self, the benefits of "study" and "standard works" were always defined according to the enduring value of culture. In 1852 the St. Louis Mercantile Library Association advised its members to read with their eyes on the gold standard of knowledge:

> Study to gain the untold wealth of wisdom, for that is a species of wealth that never depreciates—that all the changes and vicissitudes of life cannot take from you. Once yours, it is yours forever. Time cannot efface it, so long as reason retains her throne. Eternity alone can only suffice to unfold the extent of its priceless worth . . . its possession will cheer your hours of adversity and be to you a source of consolation when the elasticity of youth shall have departed.[27]

The timeless and priceless values associated with study were understood to sustain one beyond the siren calls of passion and the "hours of adversity," adding to the capital of character when all forms of material capital (money and possessions, youth and health) had receded with the inexorable tides of fortune.

Regardless of these early paternalistic concerns about the dangers of reading romances, the New York Mercantile Library came to function as a distributor for the burgeoning mid-nineteenth-century fiction market. The mission to provide "useful knowledge" was contradicted even in the first years when one report noted that "it was deemed advisable, even necessary, to introduce works of fancy and imagination."[28] Young businessmen would have been especially inclined to recognize this demand for "current works" as a 'necessity' for the institution's growth and survival. Rather than merely buying rare and valuable standard works, the library had to actively compete for readers in the contemporary book market, "whose numbers require that their wishes should not be disregarded, and who would otherwise seek elsewhere." Only by supplying the demand for fiction from both current and potential members could the library afford to subsidize the acquisition of 'higher' literature. Indeed, the low price of fiction would soon be used to rationalize purchases, since "books of fiction are the least expensive of the works we purchase" and yet had the greatest benefit in boosting membership and revenue.[29] The members wished to read fiction, which by 1870 constituted 70 percent of the books purchased by the library and probably an even larger percentage of works borrowed by readers.[30]

To realize the library's economic potential, then, the "system" of management required effacing the philanthropic mission of the association. "While we have given due attention to the collection of valuable and lasting books," the 1870 report explained, "the more prominent object has been to keep pace with the current publications of the day, following only a natural law of making our supply correspond to the demand."[31] In following the "natural law" of the market, the managers of the mercantile library elaborated a new paradigm for the library. "Our primary object has been the *circulation* of books," the 1853 report stated:

> Already we are in the way of purchasing almost every new work in general literature published in England or America, immediately after its appearance . . . [which] obliges us to procure many works of fiction which are fortunately so low in price that they cause no very great expenditure of money. . . . Great results have followed the plan adopted by the purchasing committee—that of procuring several copies of popular works, and supplying the demand for those books which were most called for. It is the only true principle of a circulating library. New books must be read while fresh.

By embracing the classification of circulating library, the managers explicitly redefined the library's purpose. Instead of claiming to improve reading or supply useful knowledge for a distinctive population of clerks, they identified the institution with a generalized clientele and served an array of functions. On these terms, the library can be understood as an early model of a modern service organization, whose "only true principle" was to get the books readers wanted while they were still "fresh." "Our province is now . . . to furnish every work, that the general public who use us, wish to read . . . whenever any book occupies a peculiarly prominent place in estimation, it should *in that very proportion,* occupy a prominent place in our purchases."[32] In this context, the distinction between intensive study and extensive reading is the difference between an institution that promotes knowledge as intrinsically valuable and one that sells services "used" by the "general public." The activity of reading here can be commercialized precisely because there are large numbers of people who do it. The public's 'wishes' can be calculated because they seem to follow a pattern which—unlike that of a specialist and the odd request for a reference work—can be analyzed in terms of supply and demand, thus facilitating the submission of library services to managerial efficiency. As though with the relief of discontinuing a product line that never sold well anyway, the managers now suggested a tone of contempt for those "standard works" that were never read but rather studied.

The New York Mercantile Library by the 1850s had become an intermediary between its members and the mass market for nineteenth-century fiction. In the rhetoric of these young businessmen, reading lost its use value and became a commodity whose profitability inhered in its quick turnover, in maximizing the number of people borrowing books in the minimum possible time. As *Scribner's* observed about the reading habits of the Mercantile Library's patrons, "Novels are read quickly and changed often, and pass through a dozen hands while more serious works are passing through one." To take the time to "study" a book was to take it out of circulation when there was a mass audience potentially waiting for that same book.[33] The library's success as an enterprise depended on minimizing the shelf life of its books, keeping them in circulation and 'producing' ever higher rates of fee-paying circulators. The library catered to the general readers who inhabited an anonymous mass "public": popular wishes registered within the walls of the mercantile library as multiple demands for particular books. The managers' policy of buying multiple copies of the same works was designed to calibrate precisely the library's supply of fiction to the contours of changing demand: "Whenever any book occupies a peculiarly prominent place in estimation, it should *in that very proportion,* occupy a prominent place in our purchases."[34] The purchasing committee measured that demand through a suggestion box established in 1847, the librarian's count of requests at the circulation desk, and informal canvassing of the membership. Their effort to accurately appraise the public "estimation" is reflected in the specific and varied purchases they made: 15 copies of Melville's *Moby Dick* in 1852; 75 of Hugo's *Les Miserables* in 1863; in 1869, 250 each of Alcott's *Little Women* and *An Old-Fashioned Girl,* 200 of Augusta Evans's *Vashti,* 75 of Elizabeth Phelps's *The Gates Ajar,* and 115 copies of Twain's *Innocents Abroad*—and for most of these there were "still more applicants . . . than we can supply."[35] This responsiveness to its members required considerable sophistication in predicting not only what books would prove popular but also when a book would cease to be in demand. The library had by the 1850s started a duplicate book sales department to raise money when works were no longer requested. As the 1870 report noted, "The one essential thing is to determine when books become useless to us, and how many can be profitably disposed of. . . . An old book to one is often a new book to another." The constant turnover in membership created unpredictable fluctuations in demand; thus, in 1870 the library had to buy an additional fifteen copies of a popular work like *Uncle Tom's Cabin* after having already sold extra copies.[36]

The innovations in "policy" and the efficiencies of the "system" that fostered the library's growth were a function of the particular manner in which its managers conceptualized and ran their institution as an enterprise. For example, rather than continuing to serve the specific interests of a particular occupational group, the New York Mercantile Library consistently expanded the size and nature of the community it served *because* they thought and spoke about it in economic terms. By the Civil War anyone who could pay the membership dues of two dollars a year, including large numbers of single women, was allowed to subscribe to its services.[37] When the association changed its constitution in 1870, introducing a new category of membership whereby "Subscribing Members" could enjoy the right to use the library and charge books out but not vote in the elections or run for office, it was merely a formal implementation of the library's ongoing effort to reach an ever-wider audience. It was also clearly a move calculated to both exploit and disenfranchise the market of women readers since they were already, as *Scribner's* observed, "among its most frequent patrons."[38] By reserving for merchant's clerks the right to vote and run for office, the new membership policy was based on the belief that the library's management required the special expertise of businessmen.

The unique success of this institution among circulating and proprietary libraries was the result of its being run as a business. This claim is borne out by the contrasting manner in which the Boston Mercantile Library responded to similar changes in the business environment. Like the New York Mercantile Library, for example, the Boston library faced competition from a new public library. When the Astor Library opened in the 1850s, the managers of the New York Mercantile Library responded by carving out a more specialized niche for itself as a "circulating library." The Astor Library was deemed to be a more fitting place for students, scholars, and others engaged in intensive "study" of particular subjects. Instead of "attempting to cater to men of that class," the Mercantile Library was "spared the necessity of such purchases" and could confine itself "to the supply of books that are to be read rather than studied, or rarely referred to."[39] Like the Astor, the Free Public Library in Boston made its book selection to suit the tastes of "mature scholars and adults." While "there is a healthy class of popular literature which is much sought after by young men, and extensively duplicated in this library," the "Trustees of the Public Library have judiciously decided it is not their duty to furnish to the public, as all its funds are required for a more standard class of literature." The fact that the Boston Mercantile Library suffered a dramatic decline in membership after the opening of the Free Public Library suggested to its managers the need to copy the example of the New York Mercantile Library by emphasizing its competitive advantage—to see itself, as an annual report put it in 1854, as "presenting such facilities as no other institution could offer to those who are in search of the current and popular literature of the day." By following this strategy, the Boston association hoped to achieve a position like that of the New York Mercantile Library, "occupied by no other library or literary institution."[40]

Although both libraries were started in 1820, the Boston Mercantile Library had far fewer members and far fewer books because its managers, unlike their New York peers, failed to learn from experience in the library business and commit to a system of management that followed from their diagnosis of the institution's strengths and weaknesses. Only a few pages after recognizing the need to provide "the current and popular literature of the day," the annual report of 1854 noted:

> A person occasionally complains that he cannot find *Ruth Hall* or Barnum's *Autobiography* in; yet his reflections on the good taste of the purchasing committee would be essentially modified, if he should consider that these books have been called for from thirty to fifty times a day; and that, in a few months, the ten copies of each now belonging to the library will be accumulating dust upon the shelves. It is entirely incompatible with the interest of a permanent public library to meet the full demand for that style of literature immediately on its publication.[41]

While partially accommodating public demand, then, the Boston library only did so on a limited scale, choosing to judge this demand as ultimately inconsistent with the "interest of a permanent public library." This ambivalence about popular demand—seen in the paltry numbers of two of the more popular works of the 1850s—followed from a paternalistic idea of the library and its civic functions that was at odds with the New York library's market-driven approach. For an institution that depended on its members' satisfaction, the hesitation in meeting readers' demands represented a failure of management. Its directors admitted their own incompetence the following year when they suggested their need for professional help along the lines suggested by F. B. Perkins in his federal report in 1876.[42] With a smug indifference to economic imperatives, the Boston Mercantile Library viewed itself not as a circulating library but a "permanent public library," for which top-down, value-driven management was presumably the only legitimate mode of operation.

Annual reports issued by the various mercantile libraries reflect alternative ways of defining the "public" for reading and different strategies for meeting its needs. The adaptation of the New York Mercantile Library's "system of management" to opportunities for growth—through expansion of membership, the diversification and specialization of services, and the policy of buying multiple copies of popular fiction—enabled it to flourish for fifty years when most social libraries failed to survive for more than a few years after their founding, or to accumulate more than a few thousand books.[43] To not deliver books when customers wanted them was to disrupt the efficiency of the library's system and betray its acquired mission as a "circulating library." If in the 1820s the reader had initially borne the official onus for reading "frivolous" literature, by the 1850s the institution bore the onus for not providing such works promptly on demand.[44] In its promotion of the timely circulation and popularity of books, the library helped in a modest way to calibrate cultural consumption for the age of mechanical reproduction, helping middle-class tastes to embrace the modern velocity of change.

Reading and Breeding for the Profession

In a country that continues to be unique in the restless movements of its citizens, wide-eyed young men who came to cities in the antebellum era became used to waking up in strange places. As one report from the Mercantile Library observed in 1853, "Most of the young men who are engaged in mercantile pursuits in this city are strangers from the country; their home is not here, their friends are not here . . . the cheerless hotel, or the scarcely more sociable private boarding house, becomes their home." In their reports, the managers often blamed declines of library membership on the periodic depressions that put clerks out of work or sent them elsewhere in search of better opportunities.[45] Particularly after 1850, hundreds of the library's members disappeared each year, "entirely disregarding their constitutional obligation" to settle the membership dues they owed. The managers made occasional efforts to recover delinquent fees from these "lost members." Despite all their "tramping . . . the going up and down imposing flights of stairs, the persistent inquiries made on their behalf, from ground floor to attic, to ascertain their whereabouts," they rarely recovered anything more than the remnants of transient lives.[46] In attics and ground floors, in boardinghouses or hotels, young men found housing where they could, and often vanished with the shifting tides of economic fortune.

Between the home they had left and the one they would presumably make, young men were outside of the familial spaces that increasingly defined middle-class identity in the nineteenth century. The New York clerk Benjamin Tilton wrote in his diary of the anxiety he felt about the constant changes of residence that accompanied the first of May, the "variety" of moving "breaking in upon the monotonous routine of everyday life." "Instead of quietly going to the store and returning to our 'home' where we may lie down in quiet repose," Tilton lamented, "we are almost inclined to doubt the existence of a 'home' so confused and 'jumbled up' in everything."

> And then to stay the first night—to sleep in a bed thoroughly shaped in one corner of the room amid the wreck of accumulated furniture of chairs, tables, bureaus, looking glasses & c. [etc.] which lie scattered around the room, presenting frightful images to the imagination (perhaps not in the best state of repose) as daylight begins to reveal, through the window, their doubtful shape to the sleepy eyes of the new occupant. After becoming satisfied of our identity—that we are not someone else; but ourselves only under different circumstances and most uncomfortably situated . . . we take a hasty breakfast and leave, fully determined to 'dine out' and if need be sleep out until things are "put in order."[47]

However much clerks may have welcomed the excitement of city life, they no doubt experienced the forced "variety" of their lives as a depressing and alienating time. Amid the disarray of rented rooms, clerks such as Tilton found themselves in a liminal state between childhood and adulthood, where perception was rendered uncertain and even identity lost its customary solidity. Tasting autonomy for the first time, clerks faced the dangerous "temptations and allurements of a populous city," as Tilton put it, which held out "rare enjoyments to the unsuspecting youth" but also the chance to "enter on a more enlarged sphere of action."[48]

If only temporarily, the New York Mercantile Library allowed young men such as Tilton to escape from the transience and isolation of their lives. After arriving in the city, Tilton found that his "unemployed" evenings "required some other source of enjoyment" than seeing relatives:

> That which afforded the best and at the same time the most rational, was the privilege obtained by becoming a member of the young men's Mercantile Library Association. . . . It now contains 24,000 volumes and 3,000 members having commenced, like many of its proprietors, with very limited means. . . . Its growing advancement holds out inducements to its numerous members whose unemployed hours from business, may be profitably spent in accumulating the means of mental improvement and substantial knowledge, from the works of eminent authors.[49]

As Tilton publicizes the library's success in his diary, the institution becomes a heuristic for moral accounting. Like its managers, Tilton understands the library's success in the same quantitative terms of volume and increase by which clerks measured the enterprise of character. Like the exercise of writing, belonging to a library puts "unemployed hours" to rational and profitable use. Amid the "monotonous routine of everyday life" as well as the lack of a meaningful "home," membership in the library enables Tilton to become a "proprietor." By sharing in the association's "growing advancement," he not only adds to his own "very limited means" but accumulates social and moral capital. As they move the rational accounting of profit and growth from a public institution to the private enterprise of character, Tilton's words evoke the ethos of a managerial middle class.

The sincerity of Tilton's interest and its prominence in his diary suggest the degree to which he saw joining the association as a turning point of his early years in New York. What exactly did a clerk get, at a cost of two dollars a year, by joining the Mercantile Library? Tilton enthusiastically describes the "privileges" of membership as "thus placing within our reach vast treasures for enriching the powers of the mind."[50] Another member, Henry Patterson, similarly recorded in his diary the powerful and exclusive sense of ownership that came with access to the library's facilities and the use of its resources: "Friday evening I went to Clinton Hall, and joined the Mercantile Library Association. I have now the use of any books in the Library, containing 17,000 volumes; also the use of the reading room at pleasure." For youths of modest means but impatient ambitions, membership meant a sense of freedom and privilege that was perhaps equal in importance to any use they made of the many volumes or the comfortable reading room. Patterson twice noted the benefits of this "excellent" and "comfortably warmed" establishment, either because he had forgotten the first entry or because of his excitement over having appropriated such impressive property for his use "at pleasure."[51] That Patterson internalized his affiliation with "this our Mercantile Library Association"—or understood it as his own, and not simply a service available for his use—is further suggested by the fact that after a few months of membership he was actively interested in the outcome of the annual elections, and that after a few years he even put himself forward as a candidate for the board of directors.[52] If for most clerks evidence of progress was hard to come by in the workplace, membership in the association brought material signs of social advancement.

By joining the library, these young men secured for themselves a stable and prestigious social location that was not only physical but symbolic. The Mercantile Library Association countered the isolation and dislocation clerks faced in their transition to the city by giving them a public status. It was through their sincere commitment to the meaning of membership that clerks became "satisfied of our identity," as Tilton put it, "that we are not another but ourselves, only under different circumstances."[53] As the 1847 report noted, "There are many belonging to this institution, far away from friends and endearments of domestic life, and what can better make up for this great privation than to be allowed to meet those of their own class, on one common ground, in one social brotherhood."[54] The institution sought to counter this social "privation," which increasingly became the cost of economic mobility in market culture. Quite apart from the knowledge it contained, every book in the mercantile library became a token of abundance, security, and affection—of a public sentiment for community that the impersonality and self-interest of modern commerce seemed to undermine. "The quiet evening hours passed among the books," as the Philadelphia Mercantile Library suggested, have been for its members "in the ever changeful scenes of life, in some degree a substitute for society in solitude, for health in sickness, and for wealth in poverty."[55] The library was also a substitute for the brothel, the saloon, the gaming table, the theater, and other sites where men could spend "unemployed hours" with ambivalence if not hostility toward the genteel domesticity of Anglo-Protestant morality.[56] When members of the Mercantile Library chose to "employ" their empty hours in the moral work of character, to occupy their hands with the pleasures of literary practice, they trod a path of manly discipline and respectability for which there were no short cuts. Although most members continued to read in the solitude in their rooms—Tilton in the evening before he went to bed, Patterson mainly on Sunday mornings—the books they had borrowed from the library served as tokens of an institutional identity.

The young men who flooded into New York, Boston, Philadelphia, and other cities seeking white-collar careers in business did not enter a ready-made world, where a corporate workplace, municipal and state educational systems, or a set of mass-advertised lifestyles organized the paths to adult success. In this context, the Mercantile Library furnished clerks with not only a comfortable escape from the "wreck" of their rooms but initiation into a "social brotherhood" that segregated them according to age, gender, and vocation, among "members of their own class." With membership in the association, thousands of strangers to the urban world acquired a symbolic propriety, a collective identity related to their work in business. The imaginary "common ground" of mercantile character represented a moral ideal of social and gender identity that was promoted not only by the rhetoric of the association and the lectures it sponsored but also by such periodicals as *Hunt's Merchant's Monthly*, in practical guides to business, and in sentimental fiction by T. S. Arthur and others depicting the travails of clerks.[57] This moral ideal asked young men to govern their behavior according to principles that had traditionally defined genteel character: sobriety, frugality, self-control, and other virtues typical of what Anthony Ro-

tundo has called the Christian gentleman. But it also embraced the autonomy, self-assertion, and devotion to work that were increasingly valued in
the competitive marketplace. Restricting formal membership to "clerks" at
least until the 1850s, mercantile libraries elaborated new virtues of manly
achievement in the particular context of clerical work. As economic specialization and commercial expansion contributed to the separation of urban
workspaces and residential areas, mercantile libraries helped institutionalize
white-collar respectability—the difference "between 'men who worked
with their heads' and 'men who worked with their hands'" that, by the late
nineteenth century, defined what it meant for a man to be middle class.[58]

In seeking to socialize young men to the norms of character, mercantile
libraries were engaged in a larger cultural campaign to renovate the moral
and social credibility of commerce. In an address to the New York Mercantile Library in 1862, a lawyer named Richard Lathers noted that all occupations that "meet the real wants of man" should be respected. "The relative
elevation of each occupation in the scale of social life," he observed, "depends mainly on the aggregate intelligence, probity and success of the individuals pursuing them respectively."

> The mere day laborer, the household servant, and those performing
> the menial duties of life, although fulfilling useful avocations, yet re-
> quiring moderate ability, and rarely possessing any marked degree of
> intelligence or genius, fix a low standard for such occupations; while
> professions requiring great mental attainments, valor, integrity or en-
> terprise, obtain a more elevated standard. The social position be-
> comes the more distinguished the more the respective occupations
> require a combination of these qualities. . . . Now, mercantile pur-
> suits not only require a rare combination of all the elevated qualities
> of civilized man, but they enlarge his views and desires. Religion, civ-
> ilization, knowledge and freedom, are the natural results of this suc-
> cessful enterprise in this field of human industry.[59]

What separates the "professions" from the "menial duties" of mere "occupations" and "avocations" is the "degree of intelligence or genius" they require. Lathers differentiates all forms of work according to a hierarchy of
nonmanual "ability" (the "elevated qualities of civilized man"); he also ra-
tionalizes the economic advantages and social prestige of the professions as
the just reward for the cultural benefits that their collective industry brings
to even the lowly servants and mechanics—the "religion, civilization,
knowledge, and freedom" that are the "natural" result of successful enterprise in commerce. The ideal of mercantile character elucidated that "rare
combination" of "great mental attainments, valor, integrity or enterprise"
that entitled businessmen to the esteem of their fellow citizens as "profes-

sionals." It explained why the "active, intelligent businessmen of the country," as Edwin Freedley put it, merited higher respect than "any other class of men in the world"—why "the merchant is the man of this age."[60]

In the sketches of successful businessmen and in the countless orations on the origins of civilization in trade, it was repeatedly claimed that only within the thriving economic life of the United States had the life of the mind at long last become egalitarian. The "fundamental peculiarity of our mental life," the Unitarian minister Henry Bellows observed, is "its popular and practical character. A studious class does not originate, control, or represent it."[61] Bellows placed the entrepreneur in the company of the Founders, as the American man of letters:

> Had they been engaged in the highest studies of the universities at home, or coping in the Old World with the abstrusest problems of science and philosophy, they could not have had drafts so deep made on all their faculties of soul and sense, could not have worked under so keen a stimulus to the intellect, or experienced so rapid and grand a development of character, as in thus wrestling with the newness of the continent, the originality of their circumstances, and the unfettered forces of human nature . . . But to produce this immense development of human enterprise, there must be an old race, with all the inbred tastes, wants, appetites, of an advanced civilization, thrown into a new home, destitute of everything but boundless opportunities. Bring the wilderness and the exile of the highest civilization face to face, and you have fulfilled the conditions of the most tremendous human energy.[62]

The civilized mind of the "old race" only gains access to this "stimulus to the intellect" and "development of character" by engaging with the tangible difficulties and opportunities of economic development. One might say that the merely schooled mind of Europe, once in America, acquires an advanced degree in management, experience with "that executive power which is the highest attribute of humanity and the distinctive mark of the American character." Accordingly, mental life becomes "practical" when harnessed to "the most tremendous human energy" released through enterprise. It becomes popular because of the expansive economic wealth symbolized by the frontier, which with its unprecedented opportunities for advancement makes each free man the executive of his own economic enterprise, an outlet for "tremendous human energy," the captain of his fate.

In celebrating the entrepreneurial spirit of Americans, Bellows's claims illustrate the nationalist ideology that emerged with the development of liberal capitalism in the United States. Despite the vociferous conflict between Democrats and Whigs over such issues as tariffs, banking, and the rise of a commercial "aristocracy," the political rhetoric of the antebellum years belied an emerging consensus about economic arrangements. A key term within this consensus was *enterprise,* which Rush Welter has described as a "national predisposition to increase individual wealth by any acceptable means" that rejected traditional moral scruples about business conduct as "old fogeyism."[63] In contrast to multiple, general applications of the term in the seventeenth and eighteenth centuries, "by the 1840s *enterprise* had pretty much disengaged itself from its much earlier associations with moral discipline, courage, and self-sacrifice," as Leonard Neufeldt notes, and become an almost exclusive referent for the "individual industry, invention, skill, and discipline, and virtue" that were the province of business success.[64] As Daniel Walker Howe has argued, eastern Whigs and especially Unitarians such as William Ellery Channing, Henry Bellows, and James Freeman Clarke lent moral justification to these qualities of enterprise, not only in terms of individual "character" through the doctrine of "self-culture" but also in terms of the national character through the political creed of Manifest Destiny. Nineteenth-century newspapers attributed the success of Stephen Girard, John Jacob Astor, Cornelius Vanderbilt, and other plutocrats to their unique skills and talents: because character determined destiny, the legitimacy of the economic system was never implicated in the explanation of a person's success or failure within it.[65] So too, the "role of merchant was justified not solely on the ground that he is materially useful, nor even on the honor and probity with which he pursues his vocation, but also because he is an agent of a more general culture that lies outside business itself."[66] Despite a passing comment that the "American attitude represented a republican and egalitarian protest against monarchy and aristocracy," Richard Hofstadter characterized that culture and the business values that generated it as fundamentally anti-intellectual: "Fear of mind and the disdain for culture" have been ubiquitous themes in business' argument against intellect.[67]

If liberal ideology excused the pursuit of wealth by making it the measure of individual character and the engine of national civilization, it also raised new questions about the roles that learning should play in a democratic culture. Bellows, for example, did not attack intellectual authority per se but rather its traditional association with literary culture and formal learning. In America, Bellows noted, men are "able to steal from professional toil only the rarest occasions for intercourse with each other, or with the Muses," yet "no class of students in the world is more accustomed to intellectual toil;—for the professional, that is, the usual life of educated men in this country is one of intense mental exertion, a profoundly thoughtful life, though not characteristically scholastic or literary." Thinking in America is not for the sake of thinking. "Men think in America because they must, not because they like to;—think, to accomplish an object, to attain a desirable end," living "in a land where Life is more interesting than Literature, and Men more promising than Books; where Thought finds its natural outlet in action, not in speculation, where Doing and Being take rightful precedence over describing and recording."[68] Absorbed in the business of living in a dynamic social and economic world, American men value thinking that disappears into the necessity of "doing and being." We have here another version of the *New York Times's* editorial about the Mercantile Library: spectacled pale young men and sons of toil struggling over access to the goods of culture.

Through the ideal of mercantile character, Bellows and others sought not only to justify the pursuit of wealth but to redefine business itself as a kind of "professional toil": to borrow for merchants the moral authority traditionally accorded the learned professions such as the ministry, law, or education, while challenging its elitism.[69] Bellows locates the writing and reading of books by the "studious class" within the rigid social hierarchy of Europe, where the absence of economic mobility strips men of the native stimulus to "action." Thinking for thinking's sake is an emblem of the undemocratic and static nature of European civilization. Like Harriet Martineau, Francis Trollope, Charles Dickens, Alexis de Tocqueville, and others in the constant stream of foreign social critics who would remark on the Americans' obsession with money-getting, the traditional man of letters was content to "describe and record." From the comfortable seclusion of the private library, he passed moral judgment on the practical imperatives of business. Bellows and other prophets of liberalism argued that mental life in the New World was not impaired by its want of literary culture but improved and transformed. "Inbred tastes, wants, and appetites," a mechanical facility or capacity that every Anglo-Saxon has as his inheritance from the "advanced civilization," provided the raw material for an entirely new kind of "literature," indeed a new kind of thinking that was most effectively realized and articulated in commerce.[70] The ideal of mercantile character at once discredited a traditional concept of "literature" ascribed to the Old World while dignifying American devotion to business as a more vital, indeed revolutionary development for intellectual pragmatism and the progress of civilization: the merchant is the American man of letters, his life of enterprise the art of democracy. Bellows argues that the moral value of intellectual life is only realized when it becomes efficacious, manifested in the "interesting" objects and ends to which a life in business afforded unique access.

At issue in this distinction that Bellows and so many others made between literary speculation and practical experience was the moral utility of academic learning. Bellows's story, "Edward Alford and His Playfellows," published in *Knickerbocker* magazine in 1842, makes the connection between modes of literacy and moral agency quite explicit. Bellows's story, like the fiction of T. S. Arthur and others in this period, traces the economic and domestic travails faced by young men. Comparing the advantages and opportunities of a rich boy to those of a poor boy, the story shows "the effect of opposite plans of education; the one the study of contrivance, the other the work of necessity." It concludes many chapters later that it is the moral capital acquired through the "necessity" of experience, rather than the privileges of birth, which produces character in the republic. The inertia and weakness of the title character results from his excessive and intensive study of books: "Edward likewise had been taught religion. . . . But his mind was so crowded with terms, and he had been taught so many words and phrases, that he had no time to think of anything else, and was glad to escape from teachers who looked so sad and solemn, and whose voices had that sepulchral sound he had heard his nurse say was heard about grave-yards o' nights."[71] Blending a republican attack on aristocratic luxury with a critique of traditional pedagogy, Bellows criticizes the death-like seclusion of the classroom as a way to defend the equality of moral potential: character cannot be purchased through elite study, but can only be learned in the business of living, where even a poor boy can become self-made. Only when intellect is freed from rote academic discipline can moral authority become available to all. Formal learning is an "aristocratic study of contrivance" that hinders a youth from acquiring the initiative, industry, benevolence, rationality, and imagination on which true success depends in the putative "real world" portrayed, ironically, by a work of fiction.

Both inside its walls, in the services it offered, and outside its walls, in the larger norms of mercantile character to which it appealed, the New York Mercantile Library Association sought to define the practical value that literature could have in the moral formation of businessmen. At each annual address to the membership, the current president of the association would offer his own version of business ethics, which would be printed and disseminated as part of the annual report. In this venue, one young man after another described reading as a form of insurance against the uncertain future, an investment in character. As the 1831 report noted, character is "more valuable than capital": "Unavoidable misfortunes may swallow up his capital; circumstances beyond his control may defeat his most judicious plans, and render his most prudent speculations ruinous, yet his character will survive the storm, safely moored beyond the reach of the tempest which has scattered his property." By cultivating character, one bought protection against the contingencies of experience. Unlike monetary forms of capital, character retained its value regardless of the unpredictable tempests in the economic realm. The association suggested that employers use membership in the library as a "test of character": if a clerk was a member, "there is confidence indulged that he is not only free from vicious habits, but that he also possesses one of the most effectual securities against the temptations of vicious companions and vicious indulgences."[72] By cultivating character in the library, young men acquired "effectual security" against potential catastrophe, whether generated from within the self, through indulgence in vicious habits, or generated from without, through the loss of property. It was this ideal that was implicit in the library's statement of mission in 1821. Against the tendency to waste the mind's "native powers in the luxurious indulgence of the present moment, let it be our nobler aim to secure those refined and intellectual attainments which alone remain when the ephemeral enjoyments of the day shall have perished with the buoyancy of youth."[73]

As literary performances, and as part of a multigenerational conversation about the meaning of business life, the managers' addresses wove Bellows's populist romance of experience into a more complex allegory about a young man's social and psychological development in the modern city. Apprenticed at an early age, the clerk had been deprived of "those studies which are suited to unfold the mind and prepare it for the intelligent exercise of its powers." He now faced the task of turning from "the allurements of pleasure, and solitary and alone, direct[ing] his mind to a systematic course of study," which required "a resolute purpose to undertake and pursue."[74] The isolation that clerks faced in the city posed a particular challenge to mental culture. "Solitary and alone," the newly arrived young man could not be expected to turn from pleasure and "direct his mind" to study. "Left to his own guidance" meant being left without guidance, "stimulated by nothing he might witness around him, either in the attainments of his superiors, or the example of his fellows." The youthful clerk was vulnerable to the influence of corrupting companions because there was no one and nothing around him to challenge his behavior, no model of conduct by which to compare and critique his own. Fundamental to these fears about the weakness of the clerk's moral will was the assumption that *individual* self-knowledge was not reliable. Left to their own devices, clerks were likely to act against their own better interests because individuals in general had too much confidence in their own judgment. "Brazen assurance may conceal ignorance from the eyes of its possessor, but not from his neighbors." Without an institution such as the mercantile library to correct that ignorance within a milieu of shared principles and expectations, the business community would have seen "places of amusement and dissipation thronged, morals destroyed and reputation with them." Having mistaken license for moral autonomy, the clerk was "cast upon the wide world with a blighted reputation," facing "naught but a dreary waste before him."[75] Mercantile libraries were therefore "places where young men, entering upon a commercial life, are to finish their education," as one clerk described it.[76] The books these institutions provided were a means for exercising the "resolute purpose" of the will, of "withdrawing the inexperienced from the unhallowed temptations that surround them."[77] Through reading, a clerk could act in the present moment to secure the capital of character, and prevent his mind from being diverted by the enticements of "ephemeral enjoyments." Like the habit of keeping a diary, the practice of reading idealized by the mercantile library was a technology for managing the self over time, a means of rationalizing character though moral accounting.

When the library's managers represented reading as an investment in character, they appealed to the mental discipline and self-control associated with formal education. By stimulating the passion of avarice, commerce tended to disable the exercise of the higher faculties. "Cultivation of superior knowledge is overshadowed by a rank and luxuriant passion for the accumulation of riches—a passion which, when carried beyond the natural bounds, becomes a vice that stifles and supplants the growth of better feelings of our nature."[78] Success in commercial life depended on the "intelligent exercise of the mind's powers" to counter its vulnerability to greed and other vices. "Unbridled licentiousness" always threatened to "cast its mildew blight upon his habits of mind, and prostrate the moral energies of his soul." As a Boston clerk declared, it was the "nature of trade" and "absorption" in business "to generate a spirit of profound selfishness. It denies the wisdom of all past time; warps the affections; and destroys, or tends to destroy, every generous impulse of our being. The result of its mastership in our community is, that multitudes of young men, inheriting their fathers' peculiarities, grow up without hearts." The only antidote, the clerk noted, was to develop the clerks' "reflective faculty," to "get our young men into the habit of thinking of something besides the accumulation of lucre," something that had the same absorbing "degree of intense interest" as making money.[79] The annual report from 1838 commented that few merchants are "regularly bred to their occupation," a fact "signally unfavorable to any other development of the intellectual powers, than was elicited by the demands of business."[80]

Both the clerk's maturation and success in business depended on his reading habits. But what sort of reading suited the regular breeding of businessmen? Unlike liberal arts colleges, the 'withdrawal' into the world of the mercantile library would have been for a few hours a day at most, squeezed in during or after a long day at work. The library had to promote the moral and intellectual interests of members during those hours without becoming another "employment . . . that shall so engross their minds as to prevent proper regard for their main vocation." What distinguished the businessman's relation to knowledge from that of the "engrossed" academic, idealistic reformer or frivolous dilettante was his pragmatic relationship to experience. For this reason, members of the Boston Mercantile Library Association felt justified in ridiculing college students' devotion to useless abstractions and ancient languages.[81] Another annual report similarly criticized the "want of practical knowledge" among public servants drawn from what it called the "unproductive classes." The mistakes in the history of government showed that "the most competent persons for such stations would be practical merchants, whose minds have been invigorated and enlightened by an attentive personal observation, combined with the results of study and reflection." What made the merchant's knowledge distinctive was the *process* through which study and reflection merged with his "attentive personal observation." Information could only become meaningful to the degree that it was "intimately connected with the very details of his business, with the routine of his daily thought." At the same time, merchants' practical experience became too narrow if it remained uncultivated by study and reflection, "so little have they traveled out of the daily routine of the counting house."[82] Reading made the difference between being driven by a passion for wealth and being able to "travel" out of the single-minded pursuits of the counting house.

The ideal of mercantile character articulated a pragmatic philosophical commitment, poised between the potential deformations of idealism on one side and the temptations of sordid passions and unreflective behavior on the other. In his work as in his life, the clerk had continually to weigh thought and action against each other, to tame automatic habits and impulses by cultivating rational will. "The merchant should possess an intimate practical acquaintance with human nature—a knowledge of the human heart—its affections and passions; he should be, indeed, a moral philosopher, although not wrapt up in the abstract speculations which both begin in the closet and end there." As the Mercantile Library Company of Philadelphia declared, "He should become acquainted with the springs of human conduct, the motives that influence the decisions of men, and the interests by which their passions are aroused, and their prejudices controlled. Well directed reading and thought will assist him [in forming] close and accurate observations of life and character."[83] For a merchant to become a moral philosopher required that degree of self-consciousness that transforms personal observation and psychological experience into knowledge about the nature of human action and interaction. Rational self-management and "intimate acquaintance" of the human heart could prevent a clerk from being driven by passion and self-interest, while it also prevented a reader from becoming "wrapt up" and trapped "in the closet" through an excessive (academic) detachment from the business of life.[84] In setting forth moral standards for mercantile character, the managers of the New York Mercantile Library developed a system of "regular breeding" that defined the form and function of reading for business life—a system that depended on the nonspecialized "cultivation of intellectual powers" outside those specifically demanded by business.

The Mercantile Library socialized young men for public life not only by promoting the clerk's identification with the abstract norms of character but by affording opportunities for the practice of community. Because sociability was understood as a practical necessity for a youth's moral development, reading in the shadow of a voluntary association made possible a collective ownership of identity different from that obtained by gentlemen in their private studies. Membership entailed not only ownership of books but a stake in the public property of character, the "common ground" of a "social brotherhood." The emotional experience of association was one of the benefits of membership espoused most consistently throughout the annual reports. As the 1853 report declared, "We have endeavored to diffuse a social feeling among our members, to do away with all coldness and restraint, and to make each individual member feel that he has a personal interest in sustaining this our Mercantile Library Association."[85] In attempting "to do away with all coldness and restraint," the directors of the library articulated a language of corporate feeling: "To prosper, popular societies like ours should be actuated by an undivided impulse of mutual good feeling, and guarded with a single eye to the common advantages, without distinction of opinion or parties, either political or religious." In suppressing the grounds for social and intellectual conflict, affection could secure individual adherence to the collective body and its goals. Since "mutual kindness" is essential to the success of "every body united for a common object," the 1839 board sought to "respectfully and affectionately remind" the membership of "the importance of cherishing unity of sentiment, energy of action, and unity of deportment, among themselves."[86] Analogies to academies of higher learning promoted public sentiment for the corporate tradition of the library. As "the alma mater of the clerks of the mighty metropolis of the western world . . . the Association is yet in your hands, and by your devotion to her best and dearest interests, must rise, or by your neglect, perish." By virtue of the library's long life and the rapid turnover of members, the library could invoke a symbolic sense of imagined community that far exceeded the actual number of members who belonged in a given year. With greater and lesser degrees of affection, some twenty-two thousand young men had graduated from the "alma mater" by 1856.[87]

For the thousands of young men without the opportunity or inclination to attend college, the mercantile library provided a substitute. In all institutions of liberal education, the seclusion of young people from the diversity, tensions, and conflicts of the "real world" provides a protective pedagogical space. Mercantile libraries, while considerably less exclusive than private colleges of the nineteenth or twentieth centuries, functioned like halfway houses, weaning young men from the domestic sphere and ushering them into the responsibilities of public life. As William Scott put it in a lecture to the San Francisco Mercantile Library Association in 1856, these libraries would continue an education "which was begun at home. . . . Here the young man far from home may find solace in a weary hour, and acquire knowledge, that it will dissipate prejudice, overthrow superstitious fears, chasten vice, guide virtue, and give grace and government to genius."[88] In these spaces between private and public life, young men had the opportunity to continue the process of moral education begun in the middle-class home. As Scott's comments suggest, the moral education that clerks received in the mercantile library embodied Locke's ideal of liberal education for a large audience of young men who, for the most part, had had limited access to books. Overthrowing fear, chastening vice, guiding virtue—these are conducive to the "grace" and self-government requisite to involvement in civic life. The social capital informally acquired at the mercantile library figured the merchant's intrinsic capacity for rational improvement; it dignified a talent and ambition for business as native "genius" rather than as impairments of moral character. If upon "graduation" members found their "hearts weaned with emotion" for their "alma mater, as it were," it was because the "heart" was understood to be the primary organ of moral education that separated savage boys from civilized men.[89] This liberal education of young men began in the home but it increasingly extended across a range of institutions that, like the mercantile library, cultivated a sentimental taste for public life.

As with many other kinds of voluntary associations, the production of character in the library was practiced as a civic enterprise, through the language and tools it afforded respectable young men for the cultivation of sentiment and sociability in an otherwise anonymous city. The ritual appeals to "harmony" and "common cause" in the annual reports, the standard exhortations to cohesive action, express the degree to which the gender identity of members was shaped by affective norms of sociability, fraternity, and collective mobilization and contention. For example, in modeling the association as a political community, complete with a constitution and amendments, elections, committees, annual meetings, and parliamentary procedures, the association provided many of its members with their first direct experience of democratic culture. At the 1842 annual meeting, Philip Hone, the ex-mayor of New York and long-standing president of the Clinton Hall Association, chastised the New York Mercantile

Association for "the spirit of faction, and strong party feeling evinced" during elections. As Henry Patterson noted in his diary, the meeting was "characterized by a want of order, turbulence, excited feeling, and a general want of dignity and consideration on the part of members."[90] As the Boston Mercantile Library Association observed, the years of "strong party rivalry" were also the years of its most rapid growth; a particularly virulent contest in 1851 brought in $300 in dues in a single day, although no one suggested that party strife be encouraged for the library's financial benefit.[91] Despite repeated appeals for kindness and unity of action, however, the elections of the New York Mercantile Library were famous for their partisanship (fig. 16). As *Scribner's Magazine* described them in 1871:

> The annual elections, however, are scenes of the most intense excitement; and, in the eyes of a young clerk, running for office in the Mercantile Library Association is only a little less important than running for Congress. There are usually two tickets in the field, the "regular" and the "Reform," the difference between which it would puzzle anybody to define. . . . Long before the opening [of the polls], the staircase is crowded with members. Canvassers press the claims of their respective parties, and thrust ballots into the hands of undecided voters. A long queue is formed with some difficulty, reaching down the stairs, and through the hall, and out into the street, and the strong force of police have about as much as they can do to keep the exuberant animal spirits of the free and unterrified electors within reasonable bounds. . . . But towards evening the contest begins in earnest. Now the uproar becomes hideous; the police force is increased; the anxiety of the election agents, as one party or the other seems to gain, rises in its intensity, and the way of the voter to the polls is beset with terrors.[92]

The remarkable fervor depicted here cannot be explained in terms of concern about substantive issues, although occasional matters of importance—whether to move the library uptown, whether to admit lawyer's clerks, whether to open the library on Sundays—would lead to heated debates at annual meetings.[93] The "exuberant animal spirits" occasioned by elections, along with the "noise, and uproar, and practical jokes" with which members awaited the final tally, suggest that the exercise of formal duties became an excuse to engage in "social feeling" for its own sake. The political subculture of the library mirrored the larger society in other ways as well, such as the rampant practice of vote fraud. Imitating the "naturalization mills" that rapidly produced voters in city elections, one popular tactic was to pack the membership rolls with one's friends before an election, in many years often increasing the list by a thousand names, all of whom would become

Figure 16 "The Annual Election—Scene at the Polls," *Scribner's Monthly,* 1871. The annual elections of officers at the Mercantile Library were, like those held for regular political office, a raucous occasion for male sociability.

delinquent in paying the rest of their quarterly dues. Repeat voting was also practiced "to an extent at which the Sixth Ward would stand aghast," and one year a room was set up in which repeaters "changed their coats and hats after every vote."[94]

As the raucous elections suggest, clerks found in the New York Mercantile Library a powerful sense of institutional belonging, a space in which to assert their entitlement to civic authority and to revise the moral status of commerce, even as they engaged in leisure activities that called both into question. Membership was conducive to a symbolic identification with advanced literacy that was affective and social. If reading might serve as rope, so to speak, by which to bind the self against youthful passions and irrational instincts, the common ground of a "brotherhood" would provide the mast and the ship for the enterprise of character. By fostering common values and "unity" of deportment, the Mercantile Library helped young men to become detached from the immediate demands of business so that they could be reflective about its ethical issues. Particularly for lonely youths in the anonymous city, the desire to belong, to share with one's peers in the proprieties of "this our Mercantile Library Association," was an incentive to critique and correct one's conduct according to collective norms of character.

In its public campaign to define the value of reading to clerks, the New York Mercantile Library helped, with other outlets of liberal ideology in the mid-nineteenth century, to invest business with moral authority. In an era when a college education continued to separate members of the ministry, the law, and education from other vocations, the library extended the capital of character to thousands of young men. By linking business ethics to particular kinds of leisure and reading, however, it helped to alter the meaning and form of public culture in nineteenth-century America. Between the elitism of pale scholars holding themselves apart from the urban crowd and the egalitarianism of the sons of toil seeking pleasure in the anonymous marketplace, the Mercantile Library forged a middle ground. The practical and symbolic capital of character sold by the library helped redefine the relationship between learnedness and moral authority, giving a particular kind of reading a new social function in the urban landscape. The mercantile library institutionalized a style of literary taste that combined the highbrow values of study with the lowbrow attractions of mass leisure, contributing to the development of "middlebrow" patterns of leisure and sociability in modern America.

The Liberty of Intellect and the Taste for Fiction

By 1848, while advocating on behalf of the infant Smithsonian Institution Library, librarian Charles Jewett had translated the distinction between "standard" works of the repository and "ephemeral works" piled up like so much "lumber" by the popular print market into a distinction between kinds of attention one could give to a text. "Reading" involved "casual perusal" "as a pastime" and was to be supplied by "circulating libraries, athenaeums, book auctions, and cheap publications." "Study," on the other hand, entailed "vigorous mental application, which is necessary in order to fully comprehend, weigh, analyze and appropriate the thoughts, facts, and arguments of an author." Where "reading" might involve perusing a larger number of books, "study" might require fewer works, more intensively examined and selectively used, but need more time for the greater exertion of mental faculties involved in weighing, comprehending, analyzing, and appropriating.[95] Jewett's distinction underscores that the taste for literature in the antebellum era was organized across a range of institutions: the private academy, the collegiate literary society or debate club, the common school, the middle-class parlor, and college, private, and public libraries.

Although all of the institutions in the literary landscape promoted the power of knowledge and the use of books for self-improvement, they did so according to competing standards of literary value. The "standard work" had demonstrated its lasting cultural and literary worth—typically through inclusion in the classical college curriculum to which most library leaders and educational reformers such as Jewett had been exposed—according to elitist norms that had been tested by decades, if not centuries, of tradition. Although not promiscuous in their appeal, such works rewarded repeated encounters and sustained the long-term interest of readers in a way that "ephemeral" works could not.[96] By contrast, works of immediate and wide interest to "the popular taste," as it was repeatedly termed, were easily accessible and for this reason only superficial in their engagement of readers and quickly forgotten. New "public" institutions such as the Smithsonian, the Boston Public Library, and the Astor Library in New York promoted the active mental exertion and application of study, a kind of reading undertaken by scholars and vested with the serious moral connotations of work. At least for their high-minded and paternalistic custodians, the purpose of public libraries was to define and defend the value of study rather than to mirror popular tastes. As Robert Gross has shown, the creation of a tax-supported institution in Concord, Massachusetts, effected a consolidation of Victorian culture characterized by "a new division of labor," in which "the 'best books' sat in the official collections, while the popular, transient works of the day were ever-present in the market stalls."[97] Tax-supported public libraries helped to institutionalize this hierarchical distinction between reading and study. Accompanied by the establishment of bureaucratic educational systems, the proliferation of colleges, and the specialization of academic inquiry in the new universities of the late nineteenth century, they contributed to the emergence of expert styles of literacy.

As we have seen, the New York Mercantile Library sold its members the "capital of character," a way of owning a social identity in a world undergoing economic and demographic upheavals. While articulating the value of reading for young businessmen, the managers faced a practical problem: they required the voluntary cooperation of their dues-paying members. Why should young men commit to values which, in effect, they were too young to appreciate? As the annual reports noted in various ways, members needed "motives to intellectual exertion."[98] Solitary and alone, what incentive did the young men new to the city have to pick up a book, to turn from pleasure and undertake the exertions of study? When the managers of the New York Mercantile Library spoke about their institution in their annual addresses to the membership, they were speaking to hundreds of clerks who had come to exercise their rights as shareholders of this joint enterprise. These were occasions not only to inform the members of the achievements of the institution as an economic enterprise, to measure and explain the laws of growth and decline in the business of libraries; they were also occasions for advertising the benefits of reading. In selling access to books, the Mercantile Library was marketing a set of values and dispositions particular to the institutional experience of reading, a style of literacy in a distinctive social setting. As they built up its lecture series, rationalized its supply of fiction, and more generally promoted the "social brotherhood" of a reading community, the library's managers were promoting the moral benefits of sociable forms of literary recreation. The Mercantile Library institutionalized a popular taste for reading as a pastime.

For decades the association emphasized the social features of its intellectual life to counter the solitude of study. As the 1835 report remarked:

> The mind, especially while young, requires variety . . . Beyond a certain point, reading becomes wearisome, and we gladly pursue our inquiries by other more congenial paths. . . . There can be no better schools for exciting emulation and developing intellect than societies for mutual discussion. We are thus enabled to compare and correct views derived from books, or instruction, and by the habitual practice of communicating our thoughts with propriety, either verbally or in writing, we acquire a confidence in our powers.[99]

These "societies for mutual discussion," with their imperative of 'communicating with propriety,' provided the best mechanism for "exciting emulation" and "developing intellect." The library also sought by the 1840s to formalize the tendency of its members to join discussion circles. One year, for example, it was resolved to hold monthly meetings "for conversational, literary and other exercises," and a conversation room was installed when the association moved into the Italian Opera House on Astor Place in 1855.[100] The lecture was the nineteenth century's most popular, and perhaps most effective, medium for packaging knowledge as a social attraction. Like the annual elections, lectures were dependably public occasions, when "immense crowds" of over one thousand might "throng the hall" of the library.[101] They also provided a forum where wider patterns of middle-class social life intersected with the theory and practice of mercantile character. For example, Henry Patterson almost always attended the lectures in the presence of women, some of whom he was courting.[102]

In their strategies and reports, the managers of the library increasingly recognized the distinctive value of leisure for cultivating character. The lecture courses, for example, offered a more "congenial" path to knowledge to the degree that they made social interaction a conduit of instruction, "beguiling the leisure of those disposed rather to entertain themselves by receiving information from others than to incur the labor of research."[103] As the 1838 report noted, the "utility of this mode of instruction" lay precisely in the qualities of performance through which it "enforced" truths "in the most effective, as well as most agreeable manner. . . . We have all listened with emotions of delight and admiration to the impassioned eloquence that has poured forth on subjects of the highest interest. Literature acquires fresh charms, and the lessons of philosophy sink deeper into the minds, when set forth and illustrated by the animated tones of the lecturer . . . and the inquisitive student is stimulated and encouraged to engage with fresh ardor in the pursuit of knowledge."[104] Intellectual engagement is represented here as a kind of social encounter in which literature acquires "fresh charms" from the "animated tones" of oral delivery—quite the opposite of the sepulchral voices of sad and solemn teachers that Edward Alford sought to escape in Henry Bellows's story. By stimulating the audience's "delight" and "admiration," a sociable form of knowledge reinforces the emotional "ardor" that is necessary to self-cultivation but that could be easily lost in the 'labor of study' incurred by solitary reading.

By the late 1840s, the annual reports formally accepted the necessity of "combining mental culture with rational amusement." If the association was to "elevate and dignify the life and character of our clerks," it also had to provide relief from their "mental privations" at work, from the "engrossing demands of business, the formality and unconcern of commercial relations, and the absence of salutary restraints."[105] While the association wished to provide members with "opportunities for completing their studies," it also realistically recognized both the scarcity of free time available to clerks and their 'mental privation' at work. Members had a "natural indisposition, after engrossing application in the counting room . . . to yield that leisure to the pursuit of studies which, to be profitable, require equal assiduity and exertion." For book purchasing as well, the 1838 annual report frankly granted the utility of "judiciously mingling entertainment with instruction" to render the pursuit of literature and science "more attractive than the haunts of pleasure"[106]—"subjects of general interest, as may relieve the tedium of severer study, or furnish . . . literary entertainment."[107] The "use of books" had to achieve an "economizing of time," informing the mind but also providing an "innocent and agreeable pastime."[108] In developing the leisure time of members, the association's acquisition policy increasingly favored "general information" and "literary entertainment" over the "severer" study of standard works.

The accommodation of pedagogy to entertainment was obviously driven by the managers' desire to foster membership growth, but it also reflected a new understanding of the moral value of leisure. Clerks cultivated the capital of character by learning to rationalize the quantity as well as the quality of their time. As we have seen, character required investment of time during that brief interlude of freedom between childhood and adult responsibility when the young man's nature had not yet hardened. While "dreams of wealth and rank" might "excite [members'] imaginations," the realization of such anticipations "depends on the proper" and "systematic employment of leisure hours." The urgency of using this time correctly was reflected in the often-repeated imperative that one's reading in the library be disciplined: "It is not sufficient that a taste for reading exists; it is necessary that it should be properly directed, and to be beneficial, a course should be deliberately adopted and steadily pursued, and while it is not necessary to discard all works of imagination, they should not be permitted to occupy the first place of attention of the young man." Juxtaposing the excitement of dreams and imagination with forms of conscious diligence, this report implies that "works of imagination" were read in a more casual way. Leisure time was used most productively when a clerk organized his mental activity into a "system," rather than surrendering to the spontaneous and undirected freedom of the imagination. Indeed, it sometimes became difficult to distinguish work from leisure in a regimen where "assiduous attention to business" had to be accompanied by an "equally assiduous application of the hours of leisure to the cultivation of the mind." But if leisure reading was not to be understood as a mere release from responsibility, it was at the same time not to compete with regular wage-earning employment. The 1840 report rejected the proposal that the association form a business college on the grounds that "any employment . . . be it ever so worthy in other respects, that shall so engross their minds as to prevent proper regard for their main vocation, must and will be considered as highly prejudicial both to them and their employers." If the library would not sponsor the formal training later provided by business schools, "the question then arises, how shall we best promote the moral and intellectual welfare of our [profession's] interests, without injuring their commercial interests?"[109]

As a technology of self-management, reading was most effective in building mercantile character when it was sociable rather than solitary, a pastime rather than the absorbing work of study. From this perspective, the evolution of the library's collection of books from a repository of standard works to a clearinghouse for ephemeral reading represented more than a displacement of pedagogic values for the sake of commercial expedience. This evolution represented an adaptation of the moral forms and values of literacy to a mass culture of recreation. As the New York Mercantile Library cornered the niche of the "circulating library," its policy of acquiring popular books represented the accommodation of an elitist theory of literary value to alternative values that exemplified the "popular taste" for reading. First, the taste for reading is a fashion and therefore inevitably suffused with motives of social inclusion, emulation, and affection—with the human appetite for sociability. Second, the taste for reading is most "popular" when experienced as a form of leisure rather than as another kind of work. The Mercantile Library's decision to devote itself to the circulation of fiction represented a gradual recognition of how the novel and the literary values it embodied could serve the practice of character in market culture.

If the library managers rarely specified how the novel would serve the intellectual and moral interests of their members, their commercial policies and their rhetorical commitment to self-culture allowed them to develop a popular psychology of reading. In their policies, they discerned how a pastime of reading exemplified by the novel could foster civic enterprise in a democratic culture. The emergence of new public institutions devoted to serving the needs of scholars and researchers facilitated the New York Mercantile Library's specialization in general-interest literature for popular reading. By 1863, for example, the library defended its positioning in the print market as a "circulating library" by invoking the ephemeral nature of fiction and other popular works. Novels are not only "the least expensive of the works we purchase," but also "the class that people care least to purchase for future use. They naturally look to a circulating library like our own to obtain them."[110] In a complete inversion of the repository paradigm, the special role of the library was now to buy the cheapest and least rare books since its patrons would find them too disposable to own for themselves; it was presumably the standard and classic works that became valuable additions to the home library or parlor because they had the "future use" that popular fiction did not have. As they were dispatched in large numbers to meet the simultaneous demands of multiple readers, novels acquired a future use in a functional, egalitarian sense. Their "future use" lay with other readers among whom they were commonly circulated and valued in the marketplace, rather than with the timeless authority of texts one "studies or rarely refers to." Despite the high-minded avowals of Charles Jewett, the public libraries that spread across the United States in the early twentieth century would eventually follow a similar path.

In its growing supply of popular fiction, the New York Mercantile Library implicitly recognized the unique expediency of novels as a form of knowledge that, like the lectures it sponsored, was effective as instruction *because* it was entertaining. That Henry Bellows and so many other ministers, reformers, and educators increasingly sought to inculcate "principles" by publishing fiction (and, in "Edward Alford," a story critical of academic pedagogy) reflected their recognition of the efficacy of fiction as a means of moral training. So too, the library managers believed that novels helped create a new kind of casual reading because they were "agreeable." One report suggested attempting to draw young men's attention away "from books of mere amusement, to those where amusement and instruction are combined, such as well-written travels, biography, and c. [etc.], where there is sufficient variety of incident to present nearly all the charms of fiction." Even with the dismissal of the content of fiction as mere amusement, there is here an incipient recognition of the utility of the form of fiction in sustaining a youthful reader's attention. By this logic, the "charms" of fiction can provide a vehicle for kinds of content that are not mere rubbish, or mere amusement: general information about the customs and manners of other peoples, or the moral truths and principles of conduct retailed in the so-called improved fiction of the 1850s.[111] For that knowledge to be useful it had to offer an incentive to the reader's nonrational faculties, and not merely hold out an abstract ideal of future satisfactions. It was by affording "an agreeable source of relaxation from the arduous duties" of the clerks that "additional force would be given to the moral influence of the association."[112] It was this logic that underlay the prevalent idea that novels created a taste for reading, providing a sort of mental appetizer (or gateway drug) by which the reader could be "conducted through the fields of romance and poetry to the more useful and instructive knowledge." As the 1853 report observed, "It is a curious fact noticed by librarians . . . that new members begin with novels and works in light literature, and from these go to essays, humorous works, then travels, history, and works of substantial merit."[113] Thus, the seductive appeal through which fiction manipulated one's irrational appetite could be used to foster a commitment to character. By acquiring an addiction to books, a young man might pick up a habit of reading frivolous novels that he could not kick, but he also obtained a habit of literacy—a technology of self-management through which he might harness his "ruling impulses" to a "resolute purpose." Over the course of decades, then, the New York Mercantile Library effected a gradual revaluation of the literary merits of fiction relative to other genres of "useful knowledge" and "standard works."

Fiction contributed a recreational "use" to this knowledge by serving as a vehicle for developing norms of middle-class sociability and gentility. Every fashion object is time-sensitive: what makes a book worth reading by this criteria are its wide social circulation and its immediate availability to consumers. Readers chose to leave the association because they were denied "what they had a right to expect, to wit, *fresh reading matter*"—access to the fiction currently in circulation. The reports increasingly recognized that members were lost because "just those books which are most talked of, and that every one is supposed to have read or wishes to read, are not always to be procured here by each member who may make application." This observation alludes to a public discourse about books "that are most talked of," as well as to the imperatives of social expectation, suggesting the blurred distinction between what one wishes to read and what one "is supposed to have read."[114] The buying of multiple copies and the recurrent use of the phrase "fresh reading matter" highlight how the particular value of fiction for the library's readers derived from its timely social circulation, from becoming something that other people were talking about and expecting you to talk about as well. The managers were especially sensitive to the "inconsiderate complaints" of their readers, sometimes "uttered in a petulant or peevish tone."[115] When insufficient supplies prevented members from participating in its popularity, a book ceased to be "fresh." For many of the hundreds of members who left the association each year, popular books were evidently not worth waiting for.

The policy of book acquisition did more than accommodate members' preference for fiction. It legitimized their 'rights' as consumers and made their literary tastes the singular focus of a system of management. As novels in particular fueled the expansion of its collections and membership, the library had become a popular place to gather for fashionable recreation. In *Scribner's* profile from 1871, an illustration suggests how the taste for popular reading was conducive to middle-class leisure and sociability (fig. 17). Simply captioned "Saturday Night," it depicts the New York Mercantile Library's circulation area full of men and women, all of whom are identified by their dress and comportment with genteel respectability. Groups of two to four people are discussing books, which are held open in readers' hands or laid open on a surface. Significantly, the illustration accentuates the popularity of the library as an arena in which men and women could socialize, gathering at the end of the week to discuss books that hold a mutual interest for them, under the glow of glass lamps and surrounded by the soaring columns of the neoclassical atrium as well as the fine wood of shelves and tables. This image portrays a fundamental disposition that came to define the taste for reading within the print marketplace in opposition to the solitude and labor associated with study. By not only defending popular fiction but installing it as a primary attraction for respectable men and women, the mercantile library and other social libraries helped, along with college literary societies and many other extracurricular institutions of literary recreation, to bring "local culture into contact with contemporary currents of taste," as Gerald Graff puts it, and "to break down genteel moral opposition to secular literature."[116]

The library's provisional acceptance of the novel emerged from the pragmatic necessity of competing with other forms of pleasure and gratification available to young men, but it was legitimized by a fundamental commitment to the practical philosophy of character: the clerk's moral autonomy in the marketplace ultimately depended on his free exercise of taste as a reader, on the capacity for social judgment that emerged from the process of self-culture. Despite the attribution of agency to texts by moral-

Figure 17 "Saturday Night," *Scribner's Monthly*, 1871. By the 1870s the Mercantile Library had become a bustling site of middle-class leisure and sociability that catered to large numbers of women.

ists opposed to the novel—that they "inculcate" or "enforce"—the success of any 'system' of character formation could be only the result of the young man's "intelligent exercise of his own mental powers," and not of the guidance of another or obedience to external direction. An early report noted that the directors had "endeavored to give satisfaction to all concerned"; although they acknowledged the "influence on the youthful of books of a reprehensible character," they bought fiction because they were also aware of "the deleterious policy of restraining the liberty of intellect."[117] In raising the specter of censorship, the report succinctly articulated the liberal policy of book acquisition that came to dominate the mercantile libraries in practice, and that in subsequent decades would come to dominate the nation's public libraries and liberal arts curriculums more generally. This new concern with freedom as a crucial aspect of the mental development of readers mirrored pedagogical innovations in other institutions such as the common school. By the 1840s, for example, educators increasingly rejected the use of physical discipline, embracing instead an ideology of literacy that defined the skill of "reading" to be a virtue that children should acquire, quite apart from any utility it might have for "study."[118]

To deny members the "liberty of intellect" would contradict the central purpose of the mercantile library and the larger commitment to character formation that it represented—which was to foster self-government. In an article on novel reading, a member of the Boston Mercantile Library argued that no education would be complete, and that no man could perform at his full capacity, without first having an "ardent love for that kind of reading which disciplines at the same time that it delights and instructs," a "passion for it, so strong that it shall be self-denial to lay down a book which demands close attention rather than take it up." In preventing a lad from indulging his taste for fiction, a coercive plan of "forced reading" destroys the passion for reading by making it into a tedious exercise that does not engage the student's mind. "Pinned down to a sober essay or a volume of history . . . he will wade through it as he would through a page of Latin grammar—toiling only because he feels obliged to toil—mechanically repeating the words, but with his mind far from the subject." This toil fails to create "a genuine passion" for books precisely because it does not absorb the young man's natural fancy and imagination.

> Boys are naturally imaginative. They look upon the world as a sort of paradise, in which trials and perplexities are unknown, and it is not to be wondered at that they are constantly laying brilliant though extravagant plans for the future. Building air castles soon becomes to them a source of greatest pleasure. . . . We believe that the pictures of life which are found in the best novels are correct, and even harmless, compared with those which are depicted in a boy's imagination. A good novel seldom paints a scene which could not, by some possibility, occur, or portray a character which does not somewhere exist. In this way it checks rather than assists the soarings of the imagination, but at the same time satisfies it. Will anyone deny that this is far better than to leave a boy's fancy to its own waywardness?[119]

"Merely mechanical" reading leaves "fancy to its own waywardness" precisely because it allows a boy to skim "over the words and sentences, without bestowing a single thought upon the facts which they embody." That waywardness of imagination can be "checked" only if "the young mind . . . fully enters in to whatever it undertakes." By satisfying the boy's natural propensity for reverie, novels can discipline the mind: they "check" its wandering because they have a greater realism than the potentially harmful "soaring" of a boy's fancy. The writer of this article also concluded that as the mind matures, the "sameness of construction" of novels makes them tedious and mechanical, exhausting "the imaginative muscle of his intellect" while leaving the rest of it "clamorous for exercise."

In the epistemology of reading that this writer explicitly articulates, each reader had to become a manager of his own mental enterprise, balancing

ruling impulses and present gratification against rational discretion and de-
ferred ends. Having grown both addicted to the taste of realism in novels
but also tired of its predictable and unrealistic delivery in this venue, the
"mind longs to feed upon something which it feels to be truth." In the
meantime, however, the youthful reader has acquired intellectual initiative.
He has learned the habit of engaging his mind in the thoughts contained by
books, and he has come to like discipline and the "exercise" of his mind.
Most of all he has learned through his freedom—from the "insensible
process" of comparing books and coming to recognize their generic formula—to exercise his own rational discretion while continuing to 'feed' an
uncontrollable passion for books. The young man no longer only finds
pleasure in "building air castles," and his plans for the future have become
less "brilliant and extravagant," tempered by a longing for truth. Only in
taking responsibility for his own reading can a clerk acquire the "genuine
passion and not an indifferent taste" so crucial to his cultivation of character.[120]

As it dispatched novels to satisfy the simultaneous demands of ever
larger numbers of members for popular fiction, the New York Mercantile
Library sought to articulate the distinctive literary value for young men of
reading as a pastime. As the managers sought to rationalize and justify the
purchase of fiction, their annual reports increasingly included fiction within
the traditional categories of literary merit, defending novel reading as a
positive good and not merely as a managerial necessity. It is important to
see, however, that the commercial imperative of making the act of reading
itself a popular "attraction" reinforced, and indeed depended on, the mechanics and expediency of imaginative engagement that are intrinsic to the
novel's literary form. Late eighteenth-century innovations in the retailing
of consumer goods transformed the market for books in part by reshaping
the representation of characters in fiction. Characters in novels took on a
new psychological depth and interiority, an "expanded inner life," as
Deirdre Shauna Lynch observes, and became "imaginative resources on
which individuals drew to make themselves into individuals."[121] Like other
objects of literary leisure such as writing, lectures, or conversation, novels
allowed a growing middle class in Europe and the United States to personalize processes of self-discipline and moral formation as exercises of taste—
to develop a newly private and affective identification with the development of one's own character within an impersonal consumer culture. The
young businessmen who ran the Mercantile Library were especially qualified to understand how the mass circulation of goods had altered the practice of reading, making the subjective, internal realization of the self within
the marketplace the modern standard of moral value.

By rationalizing how the reading pursued in one's leisure might be useful for the development of character, the annual reports came to revise the traditional conception of the ephemeral literary worth of fiction. The 1854 report, for example, assumed that fiction should necessarily be judged within a spectrum of relative value, anchored at one end by "classic English fiction" and "standard works, such as the novels of Scott, Cooper, Thackeray, Dickens, etc." It goes on to say that "In the earlier years of our association, you were accustomed to receive an annual warning against the pernicious tendency and effects of novel reading." While such caution may have been necessary at that time, the report avers that "the most careless observer cannot fail to remark a decided improvement in the works of fiction of the present, which, though they may not surpass the novels of ten or twenty years ago in literary merit, generally inculcate correct principles of conduct or enforce some great moral truth. . . . They tend to create a taste for reading, which, well-directed, and under proper cultivation, will enable us to adorn and dignify our profession, and fill with honor any position which we may be called on to assume." Explaining the supposed improvements in fiction, the managers conferred respectability on the generic literary claims of the novel: they not only disputed the supposedly pernicious tendencies of reading contemporary novels but also those "novels of ten or twenty years ago." The managers of the library in the 1820s and 1830s would have been more likely to dismiss the act of novel reading itself as pernicious, rather than holding out Cooper's works as deserving a place in the repository or as providing a benchmark for appraising newer literary work. The managers increasingly came to describe novels as pedagogic agents that had the potential to "inculcate" principles and "enforce" truth, to "create a taste for reading." Where novels were once seen as stimulating distraction, sparking unwieldy impulses in the reader, they now offered a conditional means by which one could become properly 'cultivated' and 'well-directed' toward the "standard works" of Scott, Dickens, and other works of unsurpassed "literary merit."[122]

The necessity of balancing an older commitment to useful knowledge while still satisfying popular demand widened the New York Mercantile Library's definition of what makes knowledge "useful" for the cultivation of character. The library's circulation of fiction coincided with its rhetorical exploration of how the pastime of reading and popular tastes for literary leisure might serve a business education. Novels had the power to seduce men from their absorbing pursuit of wealth, but since they were quickly read and not for "future use," they lacked the ability to truly "engross" the reader, to the detriment of their commercial vocations. They were thus a potentially efficient type of 'rational amusement' that 'economized' the clerk's brief free time. In the unstable economic conditions of the antebellum years, the genre's mechanisms of sympathy and identification may have fostered a "knowledge of the human heart" needed to navigate business transactions still dominated by face-to-face relationships. The pervasive popularity of novels made them expedient for circulating a shared body of Victorian moral discourse and normative convention among men as well as women.[123] More importantly, novels were reading material that young men actually wanted to read, holding out incentives and rewards for mental initiative. Given unfettered "liberty of intellect," left to define and pursue their interests in the free marketplace of ideas, future merchants would internalize a capacity for discretion that presumably they would exercise in other areas of their life.[124] As it became increasingly common in the library's reports to distinguish the "classic" and "standard" works of male novelists from popular works by female writers, the library's invocation of an as yet inchoate vocabulary for the value of the modern novel as literature anticipated the emergence of a privileged and exclusive literary canon.[125] The reading tastes subsequently defined by a male-dominated academic profession would, on aesthetic grounds, recreate the dichotomy between popular taste and cultural value that earlier, in the paradigm of the repository, had been made on moral grounds.

As the library extended membership to a broader base of middle-class customers who had the time and resources requisite for building character, its institutional identity increasingly reflected norms of gentility and sociability, forms of social identity that became available with new forms of mass leisure and consumption. After the Civil War, the library had ceased to be a special library for young businessmen, but like other commercial enterprises such as the department store instead served a middle-class (and largely female) public, opening suburban branch offices and offering home delivery of books for a small charge. In their desire to please the customer, the tone of the library's managers sometimes resembled the more aggressive salesmanship of the retail sector: "Give our members what they want. Let none of them go away because they are unable to get what they want. If it is not at the moment accessible, let the member have the assurance that it shall be sent to his address within a given time, and buy it, if need be, for that purpose."[126] Young men would meanwhile undertake increasingly specialized training for their professions, perhaps becoming less open to the possibility that novels could be a source of practical knowledge and ethical reflection for their future lives. By the late nineteenth century, then, the Mercantile Library became but one of many commercial enterprises that served to define middle-class identity in the metropolitan landscape, institutionalizing gendered patterns of propriety within an emerging culture of consumption. At the same time, the confluence and mutual revision of pedagogical and commercial values may have had profound and lasting consequences for the practice of reading and the study of literature within the modern disciplines and institutions of liberal arts education.

The New York Mercantile Library's shrewd awareness of fiction's market value led its managers to explore with new sophistication the question of how individuals navigate the real-world experience—the book of life—through the act of reading. Their revision of the novel's literary status depended on the distinctive pedagogical value of leisure for young men's lives, a style of literacy that was defined against the exertion and the isolation that reformers like Charles Jewett associated with study. Any knowledge that became an "employment" for its own sake—the overly directed labor of dilettantes and academics, for example—entirely lost its usefulness for cultivating business ethics. To have moral efficacy in building the capital of character, knowledge had to be popular and engaging, a pastime and not another form of work or study. The commercial policies of the New York Mercantile Library therefore point us to some fundamental norms of response and valuation that animated popular "pastimes" not only within this institution for reading but also within the larger market for middle-class recreation in the mid-nineteenth century. Like the radio melodramas or the Book-of-the-Month Club in the twentieth century, the New York Mercantile Library contributed new institutional proprieties to the subjective experience of market culture, helping to make styles of literacy integral to the way we experience public life in the democratic marketplace.[127] Within a larger economic environment that continues to be corrosive of its values, a viable civic culture in the United States emerged historically from pragmatic efforts to engage and mobilize local communities of readers in literary leisure.

As its policies evolved over several decades, and as it assumed multiple functions in the intellectual and social lives of clerks, the New York Mercantile Library did create a "market" for culture, as the *New York Times* put it in 1853, but it did so by redefining what culture meant for young businessmen. Through strategies more diffuse and complex than centralizing the stores of "the wise men of Gotham," it forged a middle path between the stark alternatives of pale-faced, bespectacled elitism and plebian egalitarianism. With its move to the Astor Place Opera House in 1855 (fig. 18), the Mercantile Library became a major tourist attraction, a neoclassical symbol of public culture that was at once democratic and elitist—the epitome of a middlebrow style of literacy. What distinguished the New York Mercantile library from so many other institutions in the literary landscape was not only its size but its importance as a symbol of democratic education. As the president of the association, M. C. Borden, observed in 1870, it had become the "University of the City."[128] It was not a university, of

Figure 18   In 1855, the New York Mercantile Library occupied the old opera house at Astor Place, where the riots of 1849 had begun and from which it had never recovered. Renamed Clinton Hall, the building became a stop in any tour of civic attractions in New York City. Courtesy of the Robert N. Dennis Collection of Stereoscopic Views, Miriam & Ira D. Wallach Division of Art, Prints & Photographs, the New York Public Library, Astor, Lennox, and Tilden Foundations.

course, although mercantile libraries helped to articulate a vision of public access to higher education that guided the founding of land-grant universities. Nor was it public in the technical sense of receiving tax support. But with 11,000 subscribers and 250,000 books in circulation, and a fiftieth anniversary celebration reported in the *New York Times* that featured William Cullen Bryant and the mayor of the City, the Mercantile Library had become a civic institution. Like the Metropolitan Museum of Art, the New York Public Library, and other sites of public culture built at the turn of the twentieth century, this institution affirmed the power of liberal capitalism to bring moral progress and civilization to America.

Chapter Five
The Melancholy of White-Collar Work: Professional Ethos and the Modern Literary Sphere

The practice of character took new shape amid nineteenth-century institutions of mass culture, leisure, and education. As they came of age, middle-class men learned to invest their free time in "self-culture" and "rational amusement." They cultivated character by improving habits of reading, conversation, and writing, joining libraries and debate clubs, and devouring the lectures that a Hartford clerk, Caleb Wall, termed "pleasant mental fete." Across many spaces of middle-class leisure, literary practices were guided by the moral imperative of utility. Clerks had to not only pass time in instructive or amusing ways but to produce character, to invest in their futures. Out of the many parts they played, individuals had to build a cohesive and integral self, to become a "whole" man, as Emerson put it, who withstands the centripetal pressures of modern life only to emerge the wiser, the better. But what happened to character when young men had to earn their living rather than improve themselves in the parlor, the lecture hall, or the library? What became of moral authority when young men entered the workplace?

The business of living pulled hardest at character in the confines of the office, where diverse and improving habits of literary leisure gave way to the static routines of work. In later life, for example, Caleb Wall (1820–1898) would become a prominent journalist in Worcester, Massachusetts. But at the beginning of his career, he was employed as a low-level copyist. In 1840, he began to keep an account of his life in a simple journal that was covered in brown paper. After a brief first entry, a month transpired before he sought to "again make an attempt at scribbling in my octavo shape of a writing book. . . . Considerable time having elapsed since I have recorded anything in my record book, I have now commenced a few remarks. Indeed, where occurrences present, as they do now to me, nearly a monotony, it seems rather difficult to think of any thing worth noticing, besides what is recorded in the papers of the day."[1] From their positions as clerks, young men like Wall found nothing "worth noticing" about adult life for hours or days or for years on end.

Shaped by the monotony of clerical work, a man's place in the middle-class landscape became increasingly static and inert. In Herman Melville's story, "Bartleby, the Scrivener" (1853), the title character tirelessly copies legal briefs while sitting by a window that looks out onto a brick façade, just one of the many constricted vistas of Manhattan's Wall Street. Bartleby becomes increasingly inert and fixed in his place of work; he stops doing the copying he was hired for, ceasing to respond to the appeals of his boss and co-workers with anything but the enigmatic phrase, "I prefer not to," and then with nothing but silence. After Bartleby's employer discovers that his intransigent clerk is living in the office, he moves his firm to a new address, surrendering the space to the mysterious scrivener. "Like the last column of some ruined temple, he remained standing mute and solitary in the middle of an otherwise deserted room."[2] The mute and solitary figure may have represented Melville's own life as what Herschel Parker called a "captive clerk" at the New York State Bank from 1832 to 1834. From the ages of twelve to fourteen he copied, ran errands, and earned an annual salary of $150 while acquaintances continued to attend a nearby academy, to take vacations, and otherwise enjoy the freedoms available to families in less straitened circumstances. "These years of relentless confinement," Parker writes, "left Herman Melville with a lifelong smoldering resentment."[3]

This chapter analyzes how the changing circumstances of white-collar work helped to alter the social status and moral authority of writing in nineteenth-century America. To do so, it examines several types of writing about work, beginning with the scribbling that a frustrated Worcester clerk, Jonathan Hill, did in his unpublished journal. It devotes much of its space to a study of "Bartleby, the Scrivener," the short story that Herman Melville published in *Putnam's Magazine* in 1853, which became a major text in the formal study of American literature in the twentieth century. These writings describe the conditions of white-collar work in nineteenth-century America, and they do so in distinctively modern ways that emphasize the distance between artistic and economic ideas of value. As they portray the alienation of men in business, these texts open a historical perspective on the development of what we now call literature, in contrast to what Wall dismisses as "scribbling" or to the mechanical penmanship of a scrivener. "Bartleby, the Scrivener" is, like the diaries of Wall, Hill, and other clerks, an artifact of the new place that literary writing would come to occupy in a mass culture of print. Melville's familiar story allows us to historically situate the experience of nineteenth-century clerks in the context of the modern literary sphere—in relation to values and institutions that continue to define our own habits of reading and writing. As with speaking in the lecture hall and reading in the New York Mercantile Library, writing in the nineteenth-century office embodied moral authority in a new social form: the professional ethos of the white-collar man.

The Blank Page and the Place of Writing

Like Bartleby and Melville himself, antebellum clerks found themselves facing walls that were both literal and figurative, boundaries to advancement and fulfillment that would become endemic to the modern world of white-collar work. When Bradford Morse landed his first job in San Francisco in 1853, he was required, like many entry-level clerks, to live at the store, tending to odd jobs during the day and to security in the evening. In a letter to his father, he complained about how cut off from the world he felt as a result: "I am so placed that I cannot hear as much as if I was moving round, day follows day, my regular vocation is the Office the first thing in the morning, and the last thing at night." As Morse suggests, the rounds of adult work introduced young men to new kinds of isolation and immobility, to being "so placed" in stores and offices. He and other clerks would spend their lives trying to place themselves in business. The transience and insecurity that typified a young man's search for work gave way, if he was successful as an adult, to the security of regular employment, to wages that increased with his time at a firm, and for the lucky few perhaps even a partnership.[4] The cost of success was a singular devotion to work that perhaps more than any other trait distinguished the lives of middle-class men in nineteenth-century America. Business leads "a man out of doors, far from the company of his wife, and it engages his mind and occupies his thoughts as to frequently engross them almost entirely," a Connecticut law clerk wrote in 1820, "and then it is upon his employment that he depends almost entirely for the happiness of his life."[5] With essential manly virtues of independence, achievement, dominance, and ambition bound up with it, "A man who steered away from the middle-class world of work," one historian notes, "was avoiding a man's proper place." Given the cultural and economic pressures on finding this place, it is not surprising that 34 percent of neurasthenic cases in men from the professional classes reported in medical journals from 1870 to 1910 diagnosed overwork or mental labor as the cause.[6]

As the character of middle-class men was increasingly measured on the job, clerks found habits of writing bred at home and school contradicted by the static roles and specialized functions of clerical work. When, like Caleb Wall, they found nothing "worth noticing," clerks commented on their apparent immobility, finding the pages of their diaries as blank of prospects as their office windows. Jonathan Hill found himself situated in this way while working as a scrivener in a Worcester law office. On his birthday in 1845, he wrote:

> Since the commencement of these little sketches it has been my practice to notice the return of this day with an extended notice. But this must at this time be disposed with by mainly saying that it is the anniversary of my birthday. They come so often now in this period of my life that a homily upon each succeeding one would be but a tiresome and commonplace affair. Each year now seemingly grows shorter, although short as they are numberless little events are crowding themselves upon one. The history of a year with me is a history of some strange things. I have found but part of my life in some respects. I am not so advanced in standing in anything as I ought to [be] when it is considered how long I have been engaged in this; and then again it looks singularly strange that I should be where I am when it is considered at what point I started and what I have passed through; but there is no end to strange things; as my speaking of them thus must be.[7]

Looking over the preceding year, Hill concludes that he has "found but part of my life." He sees that he is "not so advanced in standing in anything," despite the time and effort. With age overtaking his ambitions, Hill looks at his situation with a numbed detachment, stumbling around the word "strange." What is strange for Hill is that his moral accounting—made by his daily, prolix efforts to "record" and "notice" life in his diary—should reveal merely how little he has advanced in anything. Strange, that Hill's descriptions of "where I am" should be so unresponsive to his attempts to narrate them as a fruition of the will. Strange, that "the point I started from and what I have passed through" should not be legible as a story of progress at all, but should become a repetition of incomprehensible "strange things," the stutter of the strange in "my speaking of them thus." To be the agent of one's hope, responsible for one's becoming, is in Hill's case to become accustomed to the bitter taste of futility.

Taking the blank pages of diaries as their tabula rasa, young men in nineteenth-century America came to feel acute responsibility for the fates they incurred. They associated winning and losing in market culture with habits of literacy with which they accounted for leisure and exercised their will. By furnishing Hill and other men tangible means of moral authority in a world that seemed increasingly beyond their control, literary practices transformed the practice of character into a drama of literary "interest," the history of a life. But what do these practices produce when they only make transparent how little one has moved, the emptiness of one's homilies, the impotence of the will? "Days weeks and months follow in such rapid succession that one can scarcely take note of them," Hill wrote some four years later: "For me these passages seems to leave a blank spot, I cannot show one respect in which I can look upon myself as better for having lived. 'Tis a sad consideration and one which I must endeavor to avoid for the future."[8] And yet, Hill was unable to avoid it, filling page after page of his multivolume diary with the same "sad consideration" of the same "blank spot" of his history.

What does one say about a life that is going nowhere? As Hill returned to this inert and static spot day after day, he cultivated the habit of writing for aesthetic rather than moral ends. At a historical moment when other people continued to use their diaries for spiritual examination or the correction of conduct, he writes to see what value his life might have as a *text*.

> Nothing which can be said of today to scarcely reward a passing notice. Everything is at its highest pitch of dullness. No life in anything, but all seems as inanimate as lifeless matter. For myself I have felt as much quite like dozing away all my time as anything else. All I have done that can be mentioned is the continuance of my yesterday's labors. 'Tis almost endless and quite as dull + tedious . . . My sketches I find are becoming too much in keeping with dog days— dull and trivial. Indeed the latter characteristic is no new one. I have long contemplated giving it up and should have done so long ago but for a kind of attachment to old habits. Though long ago I discovered their utter worthlessness yet I disliked to discontinue a practice of so long standing.[9]

For Hill, to write every day with the purpose of recording matter "worthy of notice" is not only to be reminded of how routine life is but to find his "sketches becoming too much in common with the dog days—dull and trivial." In this way does the moral poverty of a life that seems to be going nowhere—Hill's inability to effect a meaningful transformation in his standing in the world—become a problem of literary interest.

> Nothing that can be gleaned from my course of life now that is worthy of note unless I should fall into a strain of moralizing, which at all times dull and tiresome, I am inclined to think at this time would be insupportable. 'Tis enough for a fellow to look at his own morals without attempting to weave a web from materials furnished by our observations of others. Be this as it may, there is no danger of my being caught moralizing + upon second thought I don't perceive much necessity for an argument in support of my position.[10]

Despite the tedium of his days, however, and the absence of any "reward" for the "notice" he pays them, Hill commits himself to a moralized habit of writing that, ironically, disavows the traditional content of moral reflection, which he dismisses as "moralizing." For Hill the value of adult autonomy is measured against what he can accomplish as an author not only figuratively, in exerting control over his life, but literally, in fashioning his life as a literary object.

As young men sought to calculate their economic fates, morality itself was infantilized and feminized, equated with the predictable and redundant pieties of home and school, as if it had no relevance for the "real world" of work. The homilies one usually invokes on one's birthday "would be but a tiresome and commonplace affair," lacking literary interest for the young man accounting his prospects. Hill would not "be caught moralizing," as though the application of moral precepts is beneath adult dignity. This material may be suited to the nursery or the church or the parlor, but a man necessarily outgrows it as he cultivates a professional identity, and claims distinction within a hierarchical culture of literary skills, institutions, and values. The habit of writing supplants any felt obligations to the "moralizing" prescriptions and virtues of which, until the nineteenth century, the content of a man's character normally consisted. For Hill, no less than for the narrator of "Bartleby, the Scrivener," a professional ethos entails the sublimation of moral values in the aesthetic values of literary practice.

As ambitious clerks found but part of their lives in the world of white-collar work, they came to see the content of morals as irrelevant to their prospects for success and failure. In Hill's journal, we have no resolutions, no ritual assessment of where the birthday boy stands in relation to God and man, no resignation to providence or avowal of faith. Instead, Hill cultivates a literary interest in his own failure, conveying his boredom with his life and a melancholy inability to effect any change in it. On 10 September 1841, he writes:

> Another day as unprofitable as its predecessors has past [*sic*]. For such I must call all those whose labors have no marks of improvement. . . . How long is this state of things to continue? Am I forever to be tormented with this incubus of gloom continually weighing down upon me and preventing me from exercising this mind with any efficiency? Any other condition is to be preferred. It seems as if every day [has] brought me an additional stock of ignorance. Triste![11]

As his diary becomes a measure of how little his days profit him, of how quickly time is running out, Hill identifies the "blank spot" of his history with the poverty of his own moral and mental capacity as a writer. Straining to record any "marks of improvement," he projects the agonism of being useful, of adding up to something, onto the labor of writing. Even the mood that prevents Hill from "exercising this mind with any efficiency" invites a stylized literary despair: "Triste!" He writes again in this vein on 1 October:

> Not another day as may be seen by my date can be added to September. And where can the month have gone? I must acknowledge that I have nothing to show by way of improvement during its short life. Heigh ho! Time flies too rapidly for me to take note of its departure and is fast hurrying me beyond the scenes of youth. Thus far my life has quite too much the appearance of blankness. What can I show as the fruits of twenty-three years of my existing? Nothing! To look back upon it presents naught but a fearful scene of indecision and misspent time. Misfortune and poverty stare me in the face at every turn and keep alive these feelings and almost are quite without a remedy. I am condemned to suffer the consequences.[12]

While disavowing the content of his moral training for its banality, Hill evaluates the progress and quality of his life according to his proficiency and skill as an author. He blames the poverty of his entries on a failure of taste—on defects in his ability to discern and render the *literary* value or "worth" of his life, which indeed stare him in the face with every turn of a page. He writes on 24 November:

> 'Tis better, perhaps, having nothing to say to keep quiet, than to prattle much without knowing what to say. There is one grand difficulty with me . . . the reason why my journal is sometimes sadly neglected: that I suffer too slight a matter to deter me from writing herein. In the present instance (I am now more than a week behind) part of the time it has been unavoidably postponed. . . . 'Tis one of those habits which once contracted are difficult to dispose of.[13]

Faced with days empty of profit, Hill can either "keep quiet" or "prattle much." But perhaps the deficit of interest lies not with life itself but with the process of its writing, with the neglect of the journal and the postponement of entries. Not knowing what to say, Hill struggles heroically to maintain the discipline of literary practice, even as he wonders whether it produces anything more than prattle. Hill writes the following day:

> About the same may be said of today as was said of yesterday, no more important that I <u>recollect</u>. If I fail so miserably I can only charge it upon a bad memory and I had almost said neglected habits. And since I have no more worth noting I will stop where I am and commence without further ceremony upon another the next day. I don't much

relish the shortness of the transcript, but brevity generally presides
with greater grace than some of her more cherished associates.[14]

Hill insists on writing about the "appearance of blankness" in his life as a
reflexive habit of aesthetic taste—in order to cultivate a moral authority
he identifies not with the repetition of commonplaces from the school-
room and the nursery but with the "interest" of his "sketches." In 1845 he
writes:

> Everything seems perfectly lifeless—as if they had been drugged into
> a quiescent state. There were many interesting things which might
> have been portrayed in my yesterday's account of "doings" + which
> I had commenced. But being broken off in the midst of my recital
> when I came to resume it, I found all my descriptive powers "stepped
> out," and my inclination to do the thing departed. Hence the fault of
> the proceedings or rather of their mood! 'Tis enough to make the
> proceedings bear their own fault without the additional one of my de-
> scription.[15]

With practice of his "descriptive powers," Hill has learned to blur the line
between subjective and objective reality. Should one "blame" the interest
of experience on the intrinsic value of external proceedings, or on the mood
in which one renders them? Like the narrators of Melville's story,
"Bartleby, the Scrivener," or Hawthorne's *The Blithedale Romance,* Hill
self-consciously raises such questions to advertise the literary ambition of
his writing. Like them, and not unlike the modern discipline of literary criticism more generally, he transposes the moral accounting of conduct and
virtues to the crafting of a literary sensibility, to the duty of reading and
writing in particular ways.

As this sequence of entries demonstrates, Jonathan Hill's diary locates
the obligation to build character in a solitary exercise of literary taste, in the
melancholy pleasure modern readers take from texts, in seeing themselves
on the blank spaces of the page. Most of Hill's peers would stop keeping diaries once they reached maturity, either lapsing into silence as the pressures
of work took over their lives, or exchanging the prolix and romantic prose
of their adolescent journals for one-line entries. Perhaps silence is a logical
way of responding to days devoid of interest, to jobs that by their monotony do not deserve what these clerks term "notice." Indeed, for many
adults the accounting of life has become a clerical matter of scheduling and
time management, the stuff of palm pilots, daily minders, and Franklin
Planners, which keep us on track without measuring where we are going or
why. As Hill's inventory of blank days makes clear, dwelling on the routine

blankness of life makes the "incubus of gloom" only harder to shake, returning him to the same strange place in his journal. Hill's determination to assess his experience with such critical acuteness produces the "sad consideration" of stasis, creating a more interior, psychological self in the literary performance of melancholy.

In modern market culture the mass of men, as Thoreau famously observed in *Walden*, lead lives of quiet desperation. When young men defined moral autonomy in terms of winning a place in an office and patiently working their way up the ladder of success, they often found their lives emptied of the promise they seemed to possess when fate remained uncertain. The development of character was, as we have seen, identified with a literary landscape in which young men, flush with the romance of youth, cultivated the interest or worth of their lives as they were socialized into middle-class norms of propriety. When clerks assumed their adult duties and responsibilities in the white-collar workplace, they began to find that moral aspiration— that vague, utopian promise Emerson makes that "the soul becomes" —was incompatible with the treadmill of work that passes for success among middle-class men. As we saw in the story "Imaginary Conversations" in chapter 1, the man of forty has given up the "indefinite longings of youth," and resigned himself to "his little routine of daily toil." As he warns his younger self, "The whip, the rein, and work will soon break down that proud spirit of yours, and you will trot along obediently and patiently." Having spent much of his adult life as a bank clerk, T. S. Eliot would make the routines of a white-collar worker an exemplum for the anomie of modern life in "The Love Song of J. Alfred Prufrock": "I have measured out my life with coffee spoons."

We might take Jonathan Hill and Prufrock as precursors of the conformity and alienation that, for modern sociologists, would define the condition of middle-class life in the twentieth century. C. Wright Mills's "new little man" (1951), William Whyte's "organization man" (1956), and David Riesman's "other directed man" (1961) would occupy a similar position at the crossroads of moral aspiration and economic stasis.[16] With his claim to social prestige unsettled by modern conditions of white-collar work, the man in this strange place is estranged and atomized. As Mills noted, he "seems to have no firm roots, no sure loyalties to sustain his life and give it a center" and he "is paralyzed with fear but does not know what frightens him."[17] These figures from the sociology of the modern middle class find their traditional moral commitment to character—where one's place in a vocation secures one's autonomy as a man—undermined by the bureaucratic routines of the work itself and the insecurity of the labor market. Under these circumstances, moral duties once owed to others, accounted in forms of public obligation and social credit, vanish amid the subjective vicissitudes of confidence. As Riesman puts it, morality gives way to morale.

This chapter explores the alienated place of character in the work lives of middle-class men by describing changes in the economic value and moral authority of writing. As Hill's fatalism about his birthday suggests, liberal ideology held young men captive to new forms of moral responsibility as it taught them how to move within the protean world of market culture. As they struggled within the confines of the white-collar office, Hill and many others learned to separate the economic value of writing as a clerical skill from its moral utility: to divorce the condition of character in the real world from literary habits and values bred at home and school. Hill discards the prescriptive "moralism" of his early training when he becomes an adult in part because he identifies professional mobility with more advanced kinds of literacy. He asserts his autonomy not in terms of a "strain of moralizing"—those homilies and ethical maxims he finds so commonplace and tedious—but by cultivating an aesthetic taste for the form of writing itself. Like the narrator of "Bartleby, the Scrivener," he cultivates a literary ethos that depends on mastery of advanced skills of literacy in school, which in the twentieth century would become qualifications for professional advancement. The specialized roles in which middle-class men found themselves "placed" at work demanded new strategies of narration to make their individual identities legible as a history of progress. Within the newly conventional experience of solitude and privacy that the mass culture of print made possible, character became whole through the reading and writing of literature. By practicing their skills in solitary writing and reading, young men cultivated a literary interest in the "blank spot" of their histories, adding pages to lives with no story to tell.

As antebellum clerks struggled to compose "little sketches" from their lowly ranks as scriveners, they confronted the questions that lie at the heart of Melville's story "Bartleby, the Scrivener": What is the value of literary taste within an emerging economy of white-collar work? What form would moral knowledge take among professional men, as the middle class was transformed by institutions of print culture and mass education? This chapter explores these questions by analyzing two developments in the literary landscape of nineteenth-century America. One concerns the emergence of modern aesthetic ideology, in which the "literary" acquired new cultural authority as a privileged, expert realm of moral divination. This realm was divorced from the quotidian and prosaic imperatives of work and also from the traditional Christian framework of spiritual accounting. The other development concerns changes in the way the practice of character was shaped by solitary modes of reading and writing that would, in the late nineteenth and twentieth centuries, be institutionalized in secondary and higher education. These developments worked in tandem to create the modern literary sphere.

Young men such as Hill displaced the "strange" reality of adult life in the detachment, if not self-absorption, of the literary ethos they assumed in both private and public as they wrote diaries and letters, visited libraries and attended lectures, and took up the adult roles of middle-class life. Pinched between literary ambitions and the other work they took on in banks, customhouses, and elsewhere to pay the bills, published authors in antebellum America such as Melville and Hawthorne sought in analogous ways to address the moral value of writing within a larger social topography. Like Jonathan Hill, they explored their ambivalence about their own place in the white-collar economy by turning self-consciously in their writing to the "work that brought them into being," as Nicholas Bromell puts it, "a work that was at once spiritualized and corporeal, mental and manual."[18] Melville's engagement with the blank space of the page was, as Elizabeth Renkar argues, a particularly "violent one that disfigured its surface, filling up every available white space with writing as well as cross-outs, revisions, carets, circles," a "material relation whose materiality he desired to efface."[19] As they sought to balance aesthetic and economic interests in an emerging profession of authorship, antebellum writers occupied the same space of alienation in which clerks found themselves stuck.

Like the diary of Jonathan Hill, "Bartleby, the Scrivener" explores the value of writing in relation to the practices and routines of white-collar work. Melville's story has the dilemma of how to "fill pages" as a primary thematic and narrative concern, depicting the struggle of its narrator to sketch the character of an eccentric clerk he had hired to copy legal briefs. The narrator is neither young nor a clerk, but a successful lawyer who already occupies the professional standing to which Jonathan Hill aspired. From his higher rank, however, the lawyer composes a sketch of one of his clerks that, like Hill's writing, turns from the monotony of the office to the artistic labor of writing. In this way, he makes a bid for literary success in the mass market for print that mirrors Melville's own, ultimately unsuccessful efforts to secure a place in the ranks of professional authors. "Bartleby, the Scrivener" portrays a public world where character was becoming increasingly personal and subjective, peripheral to the social and practical imperatives of clerical work, but increasingly identified with new kinds of cultural capital and professional credit. By dramatizing the alienation of literary interests from the routine and specialized skills of white-collar labor, the story illuminates a larger historical transformation in the form of moral authority.

When read against the aspirations of ordinary clerks, Melville's story offers a parable about how the practice of character would change in the nineteenth-century workplace, and a subtle critique of the role that the modern institutions and values of what we now call literature played in bringing those changes about. The literary sphere is "the subject of plural and changing cultural organization," as Richard Brodhead has noted. It determines "what forms of writing are in cultural operation at any time or place, what mechanisms of production support such forms, what publics such forms are brought to and what value they have attached to them," while also prescribing the "competencies required to produce its forms."[20] In making moral accounting a matter of literary interest, the work of writing in which these clerks and authors were engaged resulted in the gradual displacement and segregation of moral life to an autonomous realm of "culture." As the Victorian ideal of culture was institutionalized in schools and colleges in the new discipline and curriculum of vernacular literature, middle class readers and writers made room for an imaginative experience of freedom and individuality that was at odds with their social and economic circumstances. Or, as Terry Eagleton puts it, "The pill of middle-class ideology was to be sweetened by the sugar of literature."[21] As it was organized around the solitary study of printed texts, the competencies produced by a modern literary culture effected a profound, lasting reorientation in the medium of moral education, from the spoken word to the silent text, from the performance of social duties to exercises of literary taste. These changes marginalized moral education, delegating the traditional content of character to the pieties and homilies that dutiful children recite on their way to middle-class probity. But as I have argued throughout this book, new forms of mass literacy also altered the form of moral authority. As it came to define the "interest" of texts, the modern literary sphere created a place for the whole person, for individuality, for which the fragmented roles of everyday life left little room.

Situating these published and unpublished texts within a continuum in the development of authorship, this chapter explores the legacy that the literary landscape of nineteenth-century America continues to have for the world in which we now live. I turn at the close of the chapter to the discipline of literary studies, and to the criticism of J. Hillis Miller as but one recent example of writing in the twentieth-century academy. Miller misreads Melville's text, but he does so in particularly interesting ways that suggest how literary criticism wrestles with the same melancholy predicament faced by Jonathan Hill in his diary. Antebellum clerks helped create the values and practices by which scholars, including the author of this book, would come to assert their authority within a professional culture of literacy. By commenting on scribbling about literature today, then, I return to the same place where young men in the nineteenth-century found their identities in white-collar work. The blank page is the place to which we all turn in "the scriptural economy," as Michel de Certeau calls it, through which Western literacy came to constitute the modern subject.[22]

The Credit of Character, in Parts and Whole

Melville's notoriously bad handwriting kept him from getting work as a clerk in Manhattan in the 1840s, and may have been the reason he went to sea. From that experience Melville would start another kind of career as a writer, relying on his wife and sisters to copy his manuscripts.[23] When Jonathan Hill wrote in his diary, by contrast, he was apprenticed as a clerk in a major law office in Worcester, Massachusetts. He may have gotten this work, despite what he termed his "lack of a public course" of study and college education, because of his penmanship. So fine was Hill's hand that Worcester Academy, his alma mater, asked him to return to teach a class in writing for a few weeks in the autumn of 1841. But he did not stake his future on his clerical skill with a pen but rather on an ambition to become a lawyer. As we saw in chapter 1, he struggled to learn Latin because, like the college-bred snobs he was surrounded by, he associated it with the higher mental discipline of professional work, which brought greater prestige and wages than did the increasingly technical, manual work of copyists.[24]

The status of writing in antebellum America changed as white-collar work became increasingly specialized and hierarchical. Bradford Morse writes his brother Edward about how happy he is "to know you like your place so well, and that you have been so lucky to get it. You must have a great deal to do, your employers must put much confidence in you in having you write in their books. When I come home I shall find you are their right hand man."[25] As Morse's letter suggests, writing at mid century was still a privileged form of labor, a mark of an employer's "confidence." Edward's "lucky" position in a Boston office exemplified the potential of upward mobility that was associated with clerking, but which Morse seemed unable to find in his own search for work in San Francisco. A clerk's rise in the white-collar economy began, if he was lucky, with an apprenticeship. Competence at menial tasks would lead to more complicated and sensitive work in the office that required knowledge of accounting or, in Edward Morse's case, special skill with a pen. Bradford often complimented his brother for his penmanship: "I was surprised and happy to see what a fine hand you write. Yours surpasses mine, and if the others don't look out, you will be the best penman 'in the crowd.'"[26] Proficiency in clerical work brought greater responsibility and the chance to prove one's character to employers. Clerks hoped that by earning the trust of employers they might graduate from their lower rank within a competitive labor market, becoming a partner in a firm or setting up their own store or office. Facility with writing rebounded to a more general moral credit, in which diligent habits, hard work, and honesty were rewarded and where, in a perfect world, success was the measure of character. This was the traditional route to success that clerks associated with becoming the boss's "right hand man."

This lucky place in the white-collar economy lay beyond the reach of the vast majority of clerks who flooded the urban labor market. In part, the increasing demand for clerical work and the huge pool of applicants eroded an older paternalistic system under which merchants recruited sons of acquaintances within a close-knit community. As larger numbers of working-class youth joined middle-class boys in seeking clerkships, the social distance between masters and clerks widened, and the potential for upward mobility narrowed: "Masters came to view clerks more as a factor of production than as quasi-family retainers."[27] Periodicals such as *Hunt's Merchant's Monthly* repeatedly discouraged young men from leaving the farm for New York's overcrowded market for clerical work.[28] Letters and diaries attest to the difficulties clerks had not only in finding work but in keeping it and in improving their wages.[29] "The city is full of young men doing nothing," as Morse wrote his parents from San Francisco.[30] The clerk's status was eroded in particular as mass education made once-advanced skills more basic and elementary. "Since reading and writing have been brought within the reach of the multitude," John Stuart Mill observed in 1848, "the monopoly price of the lower grade of educated employments has greatly fallen, the competition for them having increased in an almost incredible degree."[31]

The horizontal expansion of literacy produced new kinds of vertical distinctions in labor by changing the economic value and social prestige of penmanship. The demand for clerical labor would expand enormously in the late nineteenth century with the new technologies of bureaucratic management and communication in the modern corporation. New instruments—the Remington typewriter; new means for the duplication and standardization of business forms and paperwork; and elaborate filing systems—all helped to institutionalize new methods of managerial efficiency that no longer relied on the individual knowledge and skills that had characterized traditional business practices in small, entrepreneurial firms.[32] With the feminization of clerical work that accompanied these changes, male clerks increasingly would find both themselves and what Friedrich Kittler terms their "prideful aesthetics" of script displaced within the new economy of secretarial work. Typewriting and shorthand became associated with the routine and unthinking habits of manual labor, a symptom of the broader devaluation of all kinds of manual work brought about by industrialization (fig. 19).[33]

"Bartleby, the Scrivener" reflects these broad changes in the status of

Figure 19   George Borgfeldt & Co., New York, 1902. With the entry of women into the workforce and the growth of bureaucracy in both government and the private sector, clerical work would decline in status and cease to offer much possibility for advancement into the managerial or professional ranks. As they found themselves surrounded by new technologies of information management and data storage such as the vertical file and the typewriter, clerks would be valued for their mechanical efficiency in routine tasks rather than for the traits of character or future potential. Courtesy of the Byron Collection, 93.1.1.1852 © Museum of the City of New York.

clerical work. The title character writes "silently, palely, mechanically" when first hired, epitomizing the technical and functional nature of his scrivening.[34] No reflection or interpretation is required, since the particular words of legal briefs and contracts have already been settled as a function of stipulating the nature of economic relationships and the legal obligations that codify them. To write in this narrow sense is merely to duplicate a set of "common usages," as the narrator puts it, and to facilitate the transparency of economic transactions. He notes that an "indispensable part of the scrivener's business is to verify the accuracy of his copy, word by word": one clerk enlists another's assistance to ensure the agreement of his writing with an already established usage. "They assist each other in this examination, one reading from the copy, the other holding the original" (20). This model of writing subordinates the expressive potential of writing to the mechanical reproduction of standardized legal forms. To make contracts in

THE MODEL COLLEGE,

No. 71 Main Street, Rochester, N. Y.,

FOR THE

MERCANTILE EDUCATION OF YOUNG LADIES AND GENTLEMEN.

DEVELOPING A

NEW MODE OF INSTRUCTION, COMBINING THEORY AND PRACTICE, BY MEANS OF CERTAIN COUNTING ROOM AND BANKING ARRANGEMENTS,
APPROVED PRACTICAL FORMS, ROUTINE OF BUSINESS, &c., DESCRIBED AND ILLUSTRATED:

BY G. W. EASTMAN,

(Author of "Fulton & Eastman's Book-keeping and Penmanship," and President of Rochester Commercial College.)

This Institution was Established in 1842.

The NEW SYSTEM of MERCANTILE INSTRUCTION,

Combining Theory and Practice,

was introduced in September last, and its practicability is now thoroughly demonstrated. To appreciate fully this

NOVEL, ORIGINAL & PRE-EMINENT

mode of Mercantile Education, the operations of pupils during business hours, must be witnessed.

The success it has already attained, warrants the belief that a visit to our rooms will be sufficient to satisfy any one of the

SUPERIORITY OF THIS SYSTEM

over all others ever devised or introduced, as it places the pupil at once in

ACTUAL BUSINESS,

and makes him PRACTICALLY acquainted with EVERY VARIETY OF ACCOUNTS,

NOTICE.

I wish it distinctly understood, that I have NO INTEREST in a Commercial College at Oswego, N. Y., or at St. Louis, Mo.; nor have I any connection whatever with any other College—all representations to the contrary notwithstanding.

I devote my attention exclusively to the interests of this College—the ONLY one in the world where

Theory and Practice are Combined.

The merit of this system, as

AUTHOR AND DISCOVERER,

is SECURED TO ME BY LAW, and cannot be subsidized by others.

G. W. EASTMAN,
President.

Rochester, N. Y., July, 1859.

An estimate of the character of this Institution hitherto may be had by reference to the following list of Graduates, mostly on the Full Course, and filling highly honorable and lucrative situations in this city:

E. P. GOULD, Book-keeper, Farmers and Mech. Bank
W. R. SEWARD, Cashier, do. do.
L. W. CLARKE, Cashier, Monroe County Bank.
T. W. WHITTLESEY, Teller, do.
F. D. W. CLARK, Book-keeper, do.
W. G. JONES, Assistant-Teller, do.
J. H. HARRIS, Book-keeper, Powers' Bank.
W. H. WARD, Banker.
C. P. DEWEY, Editor Daily American.
GEO. S. HARRIS, Treasurer, Rochester Savings Bank.
JAS. McGIVERN, Cor. & Ship. Clerk, Ellwanger & Barry.
HENRY BELDEN, Book-keeper, N. Y. Central R. R.
EDWARD HARRIS, firm Ives & Co.
H. B. HOOKER, Book-keeper, Farley, Hooker & Co.
E. P. STARR, Shipping Clerk, Forsyth & Co.
GEO. PUTNAM, Book-keeper, Putnam's Mills.
C. G. REED, Reporter Daily Union and Adv. Office.
D. J. HALSTED, Book-keeper, do.
B. SEARLS, Architect.
L. KELLY, Book-keeper, Daily American Office.
W. H. CUMINGS, Freight Agent, N. Y. Central R. R.
M. R. COOK, Wholesale Grocer.
G. VAN VOORHIS, Attorney-at-Law.
I. S. FULTON, Book-keeper, U. S. Collector's Office.
J. B. ROCHESTER, Banker.
H. S. ALLIS, Postmaster.
W. W. BARKER, Nurseryman.
A. KARNES, City Treasurer.
J. M. BARDWELL, Recording Clk., County Clk's Office.
J. M. PITKIN, firm Brown & Pitkin.
E. G. BOOTH, Book-keeper, E. B. Booth.
C. W. SEELYE, Nurseryman.
SQUIRE BURTIS, Book-keeper.

J. P. DABNEY, As't and Book-keeper, Novelty Works.
H. F. ATKINSON, Cashier, Commercial Bank.
H. R. OSBURN, Assistant-Teller, do.
R. W. OSBURN, Dis. Clerk, do.
E. M. HART, Teller, Flour City Bank.
J. DOOLITTLE, Ass't-Teller, do.
DARIUS COLE, Book-keeper, Rochester Savings Bank.
H. HOOKER, Proprietor Commercial Nurseries.
F. W. GLENN, Book-keeper, do.
JAS. M. DEMAREST, Book-keeper, Slauson & Cook.
C. C. STEELE, firm Steele, Avery & Co.
J. S. MUNDERBACK, Prop'r National Trans. Co.
GEO. A. ADAMS, Stationer.
J. FROST, firm A. Frost & Co., Nurserymen.
H. C. FROST, Cor. and Shipping Clerk for do.
EDWARD FROST, General Agent for do.
C. B. HOUSTON, Book-keeper for do.
S. B. DEWEY, Importer of Crockery.
J. WARNER, Architect.
M. McFALLIN, Canal Contractor.
A. BRENNAN, Dry Goods Merchant.
B. BRENNAN, do. do.
C. G. FOWLER, Book-keeper, Leighton & Co.
J. B. HILL, Hardware Merchant.
F. C. STANTON, Jeweler.
JOHN BOARDMAN, firm Boardman & Son.
M. C. MORDOFF, Book-keeper, Robinson & Co.
M. DAILY, Clerk Canal Collector.
E. BARROW, Bookseller.
B. S. POTTER, Lumber Merchant.
C. J. HILL, Merchant Miller.
C. B. HATCH, firm J. W. Hatch & Co.
A. J. HATCH, Book-keeper do.

H. OOTHOUT, Book-keeper, Oothout & Burtis.
W. S. ELY, Book-keeper, Ely's Mill.
J. C. BURNS, Teller, Union Bank.
M. E. GLEN, Teller, Eagle Bank.
THOS. HARRIS, Ward's Insurance Office.
A. G. MOODY, Book-keeper, Dewey & Monroe.
C. H. STILLWELL, Jeweler.
M. G. SEELEY, firm Hoyt & Seeley.
L. PICARD, Book-keeper, J. Picard & Co.
F. C. WHITTLESEY, firm Whittlesey & Milliman.
H. E. WHITTLESEY, Book-keeper for do.
H. E. SMITH, Hardware Merchant.
R. W. MARVIN, Book-keeper, Ellwanger & Barry.
WM. M. GEDDES, Cashier, Wanisby Brothers.
R. P. SHORCRAFT, Book-keeper, J. O. Howe & Co.
O. B. WARREN, Book-keeper, J. M. French & Co.
H. R. BACON, Book-keeper, H. L. Smith.
W. H. SHELLEY, Agent United States Express Co.
F. SMITH, firm Smith & Perkins.
G. N. HAWLEY, Teller, Monroe County Savings Bank.
H. GOULD, Book-keeper, G. Gould & Co.
H. A. WARREN, Book-keeper, I. Mock.
C. R. CHAPIN, firm Wm. Kidd & Co.
T. H. McKENNA, Book-keeper, Roe & Storms.
E. M. SMITH, firm J. H. Ward & Co.
P. RILEY, Shoe Dealer.
N. C. BARDSTREET, firm G. Gould & Co.
E. R. ALLIS, Draper.
F. AYRES, Clerk Post-office.
B. McCULLOCK, Book-keeper, Hoyt & Co.
H. F. VAN DAKE, Wholesale Shoe Dealer.
T. TONE, Assistant-Teller, Powers' Banking Office.
And many others too numerous to mention.

Entered according to Act of Congress, in the year 1858, by G. W. EASTMAN, in the Clerk's Office for the District Court of the Northern District of New York.

Figure 20 An 1859 circular for George Eastman's commercial college in Rochester, New York (established in 1842) advertises "mercantile education of young ladies and gentlemen." Clerical labor become increasingly specialized, requiring skills in accounting and rapid business writing. Courtesy of the American Antiquarian Society.

the increasingly impersonal business world of nineteenth-century America required complete trust in the legal apparatus, and so the narrator's reputation is his major asset: "All who know me, consider me an eminently safe man."[35] In this context, the writing of documents was a technical exercise, the primary vocational skill taught to boys in academies and business colleges in the nineteenth century (fig. 20). Like the "word by word" accuracy entailed by legal copying, the model scripts youths imitated in penmanship copybooks promoted legibility, discipline, and exact conformity to a uniform "mercantile running hand" designed for speed and efficiency.[36] It was precisely the "mechanical" nature of penmanship in this context that secured the safety of legal transactions against fraud. The functional nature of this writing reinforced the caste distinction that Melville's narrator makes between the "duties of a mere copyist" and "strictly professional affairs, such as the original drawing up of legal documents" (16).

The writing done in offices in mid-nineteenth century America was caught between an older moral value, as a prized habit of character, and a newer economic value as a technical skill. To become "the best penman in the crowd" could mean resigning oneself to the narrowed opportunity for professional advancement, accepting a static place as the "right hand man" of your employer. To become dependable for the efficiency of one's writing is to assume a repetitive, mechanical function in the information economy. Morse's phrase gives an entirely literal meaning to Jonathan Hill's recognition that, as a clerk copying briefs in a law office, he had found but "part" of his life. Like most adult men entering the workforce, he finds his labor alienated from him, that mere part of himself for which he gets paid. He also finds that his potential for character and capacity as a "whole person"—his moral aspiration—has become a merely literary conceit, an exercise of imagination without practical benefit to improving his standing in the labor market.

The rationalization of white-collar work left less and less room for traditional forms of moral credit, as the New York clerk Charles Rogers also discovered. In February 1864 Rogers was offered a raise if he promised to stay at that rate for a year. "This I refused to do and for so refusing was put on my old salary until the end of the year. I believe that I have made a fool of myself in this arrangement. If I had less scruples about breaking my engagement with a man who I knew would break his with me at any time I might have been getting $500."[37] If Rogers thought that honesty would earn his employer's esteem, he found instead that his prospects depended entirely on supply and demand. What he learned was that character is not rewarded with better positions and higher wages, but instead makes him a "fool." To concern oneself with "scruples" is a long-term investment that never pays in a business world of short-term interests. Success was not a matter of trust, loyalty, or the traditional virtues of character, but of guile and self-interest in the marketplace. Instead of demonstrating his value as a *person,* Rogers's scruples ended up confirming how replaceable he was as a *part* in the machinery of commerce.

As their parts in the office were circumscribed by clerical functions, local forms of moral credit on which a young man's reputation had depended gave way to market-driven considerations, impersonal ways of judging the social world. The handwritten letter of recommendation, for example, was instrumental in setting Ben Franklin up in the printing business in eighteenth-century Philadelphia. Such letters were a valuable form of credit by which a merchant assessed the character of a potential employee or customer. Already in the 1850s, such letters had become so common—so conventional and predictable with the extension of literacy—as to become meaningless in the accounting of trust. Morse wrote to his father with exasperation that the family's personal connections had not landed him a job: "as regards the sympathy shown . . . I had any quantity shown me, and there was not a businessman in town, and I know quite a few, but offered me any recommendations, enough to send one to Congress or the state prison, just as you choose."[38] The personal regard and "sympathy" of older men in business was, Morse found, of little use in landing a place with a firm. Like the arbitrary use and exaggerated claims of the letter of recommendation, sympathy would become a matter of merely personal interest, without utility as a path to employment, without authority for accounting a man's value in the workplace.

In the late nineteenth-century world of business, moral judgments rooted in local social networks and personal acquaintance would give way to new kinds of professional certification. Getting a job in a business often depends today on credentials earned from institutions of higher education, a college or business school degree. Beginning in the 1830s, information about character was compiled in credit reports by the Mercantile Agency, R. G. Dun, and other agencies. Researched and written from firsthand observation but filed anonymously, these reports rendered moral knowledge transparent in commercial forms of public credit, according to rationalized norms for the evaluation of risk.[39] They standardized the term "character" as an abstract category of moral judgment, of the sort repeated in the register that the New York publishing firm Hunt Merriam & Co. in 1851 kept on its clients: "excellent businessman honorable and prudent"; "good character & habits, prudent and safe for engagements"; "has been with D. P. Smith & Co. and Hadden Taylor & Co who speak well of him as a young man of character & habit"; "he is a prudent good businessmen good character & habit attentive to business."[40] Knowledge of character became trustworthy in modern business to the degree it became impersonal and "objective," certified by the bureaucratic research of credit agencies, for example, or by professional degrees such as the master's degree in business administration.

Whether hiring employees, choosing careers, or selecting marriage partners, however, Americans in the mid-nineteenth century continued to rely on less formal methods of moral accounting. These methods required ongoing, accurate analysis of physical and social cues. From the appearance of faces and the shapes of heads, for example, one gathered the evidence necessary to make reliable judgments about future habits and conduct.[41] In 1838, for example, the Boston clerk Bradley Cumings hired the phrenologist Lorenzo Fowler to write a report on his character: "temperament principally nervous indicating more activity than strength of mind and body. . . . He should do well in calculations, be a ready accountant if his attention is turned in that channel."[42] By testing his aptitude, Cumings presumably sought to manage his life more efficiently, to arrive more quickly at the vocation suited to his temperament. Like guides to conduct and etiquette, no less than didactic fiction and literary biography, the popular sciences of phrenology and physiognomy provided ordinary people with knowledge and skills they needed to interpret the urban social world and to locate their place within it.

As they used advertisements to hire from the anonymous labor pool, employers in the 1850s relied on their own capacity to judge the moral character of potential employees. In "Bartleby, the Scrivener," the lawyer hires a new clerk without references or other forms of credit: no record of past experience, no letter of reference or personal recommendation. "After a few words touching his qualifications, I engaged him, glad to have among my corps of copyists a man of so singularly sedate an aspect, which I thought might operate beneficially upon the flighty temper of Turkey, and the fiery one of Nippers" (19). From Bartleby's particular features—"motionless, neat, respectable, and forlorn"—the narrator makes a generalized assertion about his character, as "a man of so singularly sedate an aspect." Like phrenology and physiognomy, the lawyer's management system relies on inferring moral traits from "aspect" and using them for summary judgments, as with the "flighty temper of Turkey" or the "fiery one of Nippers." Bartleby is hired less for his qualifications than for the temperament that the lawyer can read in the clerk's appearance, for a type of character that "might operate beneficially" on the others in the office.

At the outset, Melville's story specifies the otherwise informal process of moral divination that took place in the antebellum workplace. The lawyer describes his office as an ecology, an organic community made from the informal knowledge and social relationships people acquire from working together. He employs three clerks, for example, who have given one another nicknames "mutually conferred upon each other" and "deemed expressive of their respective persons or characters" (15). The use of nicknames among co-workers assumes that their "respective persons or characters" are transparent and legible—easily apprehended in distinctive traits and codified by names that are "expressive." The narrator carefully designates the functions of the third employee, Ginger Nut—"student at law, errand boy, cleaner and sweeper"—only to focus on the way his co-workers have affectionately revised the boy's name to reflect the service he provides them. Turkey and Nippers sent him "very frequently for that peculiar cake—small, flat, round, and very spicy—after which he had been named by them" (18). The substitution of a cake's name for the boy's name suggests in a satirical way the manner in which workers adapt to one another as persons, and not merely as economic functions. Unlike the hierarchy of titles and credentials that structure social interaction and limit obligations in the corporate hierarchy today—staff assistant, foreman, executive secretary, vice president, director, chairman—nicknames that are "mutually given" humanize the office.

At the outset, the accounting of white-collar character is guided by two principles that continue to define the management of human resources: that the conduct of workers be predictable, and that it be coordinated. To explain the habits and personalities behind the office nicknames, the lawyer describes his clerks' physical appearance. Turkey "was a short, pursy Englishman," Nippers "was a whiskered, sallow, and, upon the whole, rather piratical young man" (15, 16). He also attends to the habitual behavior of his employees, features and habits that become evident from continuous observation. Of Turkey, the narrator writes: "In the morning, one might say, his face was of a fine florid hue, but after twelve o'clock, meridian— his dinner hour—it blazed like a grate full of Christmas coals; and continued blazing—but, as it were, with a gradual wane—till 6 o'clock, P.M. or thereabouts, after which I saw no more of the proprietor of the face, which gaining its meridian with the sun, seemed to set with it, to rise, culminate, and decline the following day, with the like regularity and undiminished glory" (15). The narrator correlates this routine transformation of Turkey's "red and radiant countenance" to "blazonry" with a daily shift in personality. The man changes from the "quickest, steadiest creature," the "blandest and most reverential of men in the morning," to a man of "strange, inflamed, flighty recklessness of activity," "indecorous," "noisy," "impatient," and "insolent" (15, 16). Through close description of his clerks' expressions and actions, the narrator defines character according to patterns of behavior.

At the beginning of "Bartleby, the Scrivener," then, the lawyer's moral and economic interests in his workers coincide. His management of the office depends not on a reduction of a clerk's character—one that, in Marxist terms, alienates the worker from his full humanity—but rather on rationalizing and coordinating their behavior as persons. The exhaustive inventory of Turkey's behavior allows the narrator to be flexible in his regard of his contribution to the office. Because Turkey "all the time before the twelve o'clock meridian, was the quickest, steadiest creature too, accomplishing a great deal of work in a style not easy to be matched—for these reasons, I was willing to overlook his eccentricities" (15). As negative traits are divided and isolated from positive ones, the narrator engages in a cost-benefit assessment that splits the difference. As with Turkey's "flighty temper," he assesses character in order to absolve an employee of responsibility for his defects as a worker, to make these failings constituent of his nature. With such a handicap, in other words, it is a wonder the clerk can manage ever to be a steady worker.

> It was fortunate for me that, owing to its particular cause—indigestion—the irritability and consequent nervousness of Nippers, were mainly observable in the morning, while in the afternoon he was comparatively mild. So that Turkey's paroxysms only coming on about twelve o'clock, I never had to do with their eccentricities at one time. Their fits relieved each other like guards. When Nippers' was on, Turkey's was off; and *vice versa*. This was a good natural arrangement under the circumstances. (18)

If Tucker, Nippers, and Ginger Nut mutually understand and adapt to one another informally and perhaps unconsciously, the articulation of their patterned behavior is an explicit objective within their employer's creation of an efficient and productive *social* enterprise. The law office's "good natural arrangement" requires that the workers delegate moral omniscience to their boss, that they act their parts habitually and automatically so they can be coordinated within the collective enterprise.[43] Efficiency requires the manager to balance productive hours with unproductive hours, to value the work of his clerks in the larger context of who they are.

We might read Melville's story as generations of scholars have, as a parable about the corrosive effects that the new economic order had on traditional moral obligations. Organic, traditional forms of community give way, in such a view, to the anonymity and anomie that social theorists have associated with the triumph of impersonal market relations and the ethos of capitalist rationality. As the detailed physical descriptions of Nippers, Turkey, and Ginger Nut attest, however, market culture encourages new kinds of social interest and obligation by bringing strangers into close *psychological* proximity with each other in the workplace. In the absence of the paternalistic sanctions with which masters had traditionally controlled apprentices, the lawyer must develop pragmatic strategies of sympathy, benevolence, and detachment toward his clerks' behavior. The narrator notices the "scrape of [Turkey's] pen blending with the crisp particles in his mouth" and his "boxing his papers about in an indecorous manner, very sad to behold in an elderly man like him" (15); he hears Nipper's teeth "audibly grind together over mistakes committed in copying," as well as "unnecessary maledictions, hissed, rather than spoken" (16). If only such employees exercised rational competence! Like it or not, the lawyer attends to all the unpleasant tics and habits to which one might prefer to remain oblivious, suppressing his personal reactions to this claustrophobic intimacy. To find just what "arrangement" of the workers is good or natural requires the lawyer to make such close observation of human nature a practical resource for the management of the office

Unlike the annual reports of the New York Mercantile Library, however, "Bartleby, the Scrivener" is not a case study in management. Nor does it offer guidance on how to become "whole" in the context of everyday life, as Emerson's lectures do. Instead, the story is about how a lawyer turns from a customary role and interest in his white-collar work in order to pursue a literary career. If it begins in clerical work, Melville's story devotes itself to exploring the very different prestige and utility that writing would come to have in the mass culture of print. By showing how moral knowledge circulates in a small antebellum office, Melville highlights the new meaning and form it was gradually assuming in the expert writing and reading of literature. In the rest of "Bartleby, the Scrivener," the economic interest in character and the moral obligations that support it are undone by the narrator's own literary performance.

To start with, the introduction of the new hire entirely disrupts the "good natural arrangement" of the lawyer's office. The narrator notes that his office is divided by "ground glass folding doors" into two parts: one occupied solely by himself and another occupied by his scriveners, who remain within view. Under these circumstances, he finds himself continually distracted by his scriveners. "Amid the stillness of my chambers, Nippers would sometimes impatiently rise from his seat, and stooping over his table, spread his arms wide apart, seize the whole desk, and move it, and jerk it, with a grim, grinding motion on the floor"(18). The lawyer installs Bartleby on his side of the office, "so as to have this quiet man within easy call, in case any trifling thing was to be done," bringing him physically closer to the narrator but out of eyesight: "Still further to a satisfactory arrangement, I procured a high green folding screen, which might entirely isolate Bartleby from my sight, though not remove him from my voice. And thus, in a manner, privacy and society were conjoined" (19). At the very least, the new clerk's placement suggests the lawyer's trust in Bartleby's "sedate aspect": from a quick visual impression (one reiterated by adjectives such as "motionless" and "cadaverous"), the narrator concludes that the new guy can be depended on without constant supervision. Bartleby's character permits a greater proximity without the loss of "privacy" he suffers with the "flighty" and "fiery" temperaments the other clerks bring as their baggage. The arrangement of the office places Bartleby, then, so he can be used "for any trifling thing" on any "trivial occasion," without the narrator having to take an interest in him as a whole person.

The placement of Bartleby in the story is figurative, then, as well as literal: it allows the lawyer to exercise a literary interest in character, an interest that defies the customary norms of moral accounting on which the management of the office has depended. Writing in the first person, the lawyer brings to this literary work realistic details that seem at first to draw on his real world experience as a manager, a consequence of the proximity and duration of his observation of clerks. Unlike the other workers, however, Bartleby is first described in a present-tense portrait: "I can see that figure now—pallidly neat, pitiably respectable, incurably forlorn! It was Bartleby" (19). At this moment, the lawyer emphasizes not his objectivity as a manager of human nature but his subjectivity as a narrator, stressing the importance that personal memory and feeling will have for the story. While his description of the other clerks analyzes social types and patterns of behavior, the lawyer suspends time with a snapshot of Bartleby, marshalling adjectives in the service of sentimental exclamation: "incurably forlorn!" Instead of summarizing the clerk's character in a few traits or temperaments, the lawyer dwells on particular moments from their encounters, like his first impression: "In answer to my advertisement, a motionless young man one morning stood upon my office threshold, the door being open, for it was summer." Throughout the story, the inability to account for Bartleby according to managerial norms will lead the lawyer to greater degrees of speculation and self-absorption—to the performance of a literary ethos. As the story proceeds, the inscrutable clerk will present a growing blankness that Melville's narrator will strive, with mounting frustration, to fill with writing.

The lawyer discovers from this new arrangement of his office that character has a value that is literary rather than economic, defined not by the functional value of the scrivening that Bartleby does but by the aesthetic value of his own writing. In this regard, the narrator professes his own distaste for the manual work of copying legal briefs: "I cannot credit that the mettlesome poet Byron would have contentedly sat down with Bartleby to examine a law document of, say five hundred words, closely written in a crimpy hand" (20). By referring to one of the most famous literary icons of nineteenth-century America, the narrator projects his own aspiration to artistic creativity. Byron's "mettlesome" and "sanguine" temperament would not make him fit for the "the dull, wearisome, lethargic affair" of copying, which was, as the lawyer observes of Bartleby, a "pale and mechanical" work of imitation rather than the expressive work of composition suited to the character of a poet.[44] Although the manual labor of scrivening is the primary business of his office and the basis of his legal reputation as a "safe" man, the narrator cannot "credit" its value for his own professional aspiration, for the social credit he would claim as an author.[45] Between the mechanical writing of an inert clerk named Bartleby and the literary pretensions of the lawyer who writes about him, we can see Melville's own struggle to escape the clerical work to which he would return throughout his life. Like Byron and Bartleby, the narrator and the subject of his story occupy opposite ends of a spectrum of professional authority that Melville himself would travel as he struggled to have his literary aspirations valued in the marketplace.

What finally distinguishes the lawyer's work as the narrator of "Bartleby, the Scrivener" and as a manager of an office is not the general attention to humanity each role demands, since both require that he take an active interest in character. Rather, the difference lies in the values that rationalize character as an object of professional inquiry: the literary author produces expert knowledge about "humanity" (the story's last word) that can be traded in the marketplace. If every good manager dreams of a clerk who will play his part, the good writer—at least one modeled on Byron—dreams of singularity. Onto his recalcitrant clerk the narrator projects a moral consciousness that, as the reference to Byron begins to suggest, he identifies with Romantic values of privacy and solitude. As Bartleby resists normative accounting, he presents the lawyer with an opportunity to assert his own presence on the printed page, to cultivate by writing a historically specific literary ethos. As we shall see, this interest in character results from aesthetic rather than economic considerations, and represents the lawyer's own professional aspiration to become an author. From this new place in the hierarchy of white-collar work, the lawyer's professional authority depends not on managing human nature in the workplace but on exercising his increasingly subjective preoccupation with the aesthetic value of experience.

The performance of character in the mid-nineteenth century, for an author no less than a manager, entailed a process of moral divination, the ongoing effort to acquire reliable knowledge about others and oneself, to make one's actions and words creditable to the social world. As the mechanical facility for writing and other kinds of basic literacy became more common, members of an educated middle class invested their expertise in reading and writing with new kinds of social authority. Trapped in their diminished place in the white-collar hierarchy, the clerks in the lawyer's office are precluded from acquiring or using this authority for themselves, absorbed as they are in the increasingly mechanical duties of scrivening. With their temperaments as unbalanced as their habits of work, Turkey or Nippers will never—as a far as their boss can see—put in a full day of scrivening. With his paternal indulgence, they will always play the same roles in the office, having found but "part" of their lives, as Jonathan Hill lamented on his birthday. By contrast, the narrator and aspiring members of a professional middle class could supervise others and take a seemingly objective view of human nature because they had acquired skills of advanced literacy—the ability to not only read fiction and poetry but to write it. They learned to compose their own characters as readers and writers, acquiring a self-conscious literary taste for life within the new institutions and technologies of mass culture.

As young men shared tastes for popular fiction, attended lectures, and engaged in other forms of leisure and entertainment, forms of mass media and consumption became a preferred mode of experience. As Richard Brodhead notes, "The form of mass entertainment new in America around 1850 held its audience in the position of audience by seeming to embody consumable 'life.'"[46] Institutions of mass culture commodified virtual or imaginative experience, substituting for actual life not only various kinds of visual and aural spectacle but also habits of reading and writing. In Hawthorne's *The Blithedale Romance,* the poet-narrator Coverdale describes this position as that "quality of the intellect and heart, that impelled me (against my will, and to the detriment of my comfort) to live in other lives."[47] Although Melville's narrator is disconcerted when he eventually finds that Bartleby is living in his office, he would, like increasing numbers of people in nineteenth-century America, take living in other lives for granted, a form of moral recreation and rational amusement afforded by their cultivation of literary taste.

While Jonathan Hill sits at his desk in a law office in Worcester, it is precisely the void of such experience—the absence of an oddball such as Bartleby—that makes his occupation as a clerk so profoundly alienating. Hill writes on 30 December 1845, just before New Year's Eve:

> I am dry as ever as to matter of relation. Nothing seems to favor me in this way + I am left without a bone to pick upon. One would suppose that a place the size of this would be the scene of some events to attract notice + furnish food for comment. So I suppose it is. I suppose there are a thousand little specimens of the freaks of poor human nature occurring every day which might afford instructive lessons to us if we would receive them, and the reflections drawn from such

sources would form a useful textbook for everyday: he who shuts himself from the world knows nothing of it. A man of books is to be pitied truly. I mean a man of nothing but books. He finds in his library beautiful theories of life and codes of morality + goodness, and as he goes out into the world he is sadly disappointed to find nothing of them there. He has learned the theory but cannot find the practice + application. The world to him is a sad place at the best. He has not learned how to live in it. He could abide in it if things were as they <u>should</u> be but not as they <u>are</u>. Better far, with a proper design of firmness of mind and eye, to live <u>in</u> the world and learn to receive everything as it is.[48]

A man whose movements are constricted to study can know nothing of real life; he knows nothing but books, trading in beautiful theories that are at odds with the "practice and application" of morality in the crucible of experience. From the perspective of the idealist who uses books to "shut himself from the world," things "as they are" assume a melancholy blankness: a sadness, because they do not conform to the interests and values that books have taught him. Like Melville's narrator, Hill would prefer instead to record the lessons of life, taking a positivist measure of its "thousands little specimens" from the "freaks of poor human nature." Anticipating the predilections of Emile Zola and other social realists later in the nineteenth century, Hill defines his own literary authority in terms of professional objectivity, an objectivity undistorted by the prescriptions of moralists: "To receive everything as it is" from "a proper firmness of mind and eye" that will furnish a "useful textbook for everyday." Hill imagines that his mundane experience might afford access to moral authority that the closed world of books precludes, and he assiduously seeks to find topics worthy of "notice." Because of the particular meaning he attaches to writing—because of his immersion in the hierarchical values of the literary sphere—this clerk would find himself in this same sad place, staring at the blank page of his journal "without a bone to pick upon."

Professional Authorship and the Literary Sphere

Jonathan Hill begins the first volume of his diary with an elaborate introduction in which, like Melville's narrator, he asserts his identification with the profession of authorship. Although he notes that "Prefaces and Introductions are generally dull and tiresome things," he nevertheless proceeds to write one. Under a separate heading, Hill places eight pages "prefacing" the chronological entries of his diary. By doing so, Hill observes, he intends to make a few remarks, that when during some leisure moment in after life, should my life be spared, I shall cast my eye over them, I can trace with some tolerable degree of accuracy the motives which prompted me to the performance of the task. And in so doing I shall endeavor to lay out my plan in a few words in relation to the matter with which I intend to fill the following pages, the benefits resulting from the performance of the duty, and also with a few suggestions relating to the style in which such a work should be written and of style generally.[49]

More than most nineteenth-century clerks, Hill sought to turn his life into a literary text. He writes with the detached, objective perspective of an author, rather than in the confessional or occasional mode of the spiritual autobiography or traditional commonplace book. Like so many clerks, Hill makes his daily observations "for future use," as a habit of "duty." He defines the value of this work according to self-conscious literary criteria. He identifies his future self—the moral Other for whom, as whom, young men keep diaries—with the specific image of a reader, confronting a "kind of book," a text with pages that have been filled according to an aesthetic design, having "motives," a "plan" of "matter," stated "benefits," and "suggestions relative to style." Setting forward his design at the outset, Hill seeks to distinguish himself "in this bookmaking age" from the "dry and uninteresting" prefaces of published writers: "half the authors have no design in view further than to be accounted authors by the world upon which they dare not trust themselves."[50] The "performance of the duty" of writing for Hill is about becoming an author. Hill identifies with the "literary" ends of writing, which he self-consciously distinguishes from the traditional moral utility of diary-writing in accounting for character.

Nowhere do Hill's ambitions become more obvious than in the constant invocation of an abstract criteria of literary worth as he evaluates the matter of his "book." "My situation and employment," as Hill's preface points out, "partake of monotony, which as far as form is concerned cannot well be obviated by any change in the use of words."[51] No "use of words" can, it seems, alter his constricted and dull place in the real world of work that he continually laments. And yet, it is precisely within the stylized "use of words" where Hill invests moral aspiration, as though to exemplify "as far as form is concerned" an advanced proficiency for literary taste that distinguishes the professional ethos of character. Like other habits of literary practice, the value of writing for Hill and other clerks can and must be rationalized in economic terms, according to the methodical habits of timekeeping that, as we have seen, became the primary locus of moral accounting for middle-class men. They build character precisely by measuring out their lives in coffee spoons. "Journalizing in a careful and critical manner" requires an investment of "only one hour of each day," which on subsequent reading "will repay twofold an hour's toil." On the other hand, it is what Hill terms a "careful and critical manner" rather than the mechanical "performance of the duty" that matters most. The particular method or style of writing makes the journal "an object well worth the attention of every young man who wishes to acquit himself in the manner of public appearance, in a manner that shall be creditable to him and pleasing to those around him."[52]

For ambitious clerks such as Jonathan Hill, no less than the narrator of "Bartleby, the Scrivener" and Melville himself, character came to be credited as a professional ethos, the cohesive and interior persona of an author who finds his place in books. For middle-class clerks no less than for Melville's narrator, literary subjectivity furnished an alternative moral identity, distinct from the roles they played in white-collar work. If Hill repeatedly describes journal writing as a "performance of duty," he sees this as a *professional* duty, rationalized according to the hierarchical values of literary study. Writing must be valued as a professional kind of labor, which is compensated for its diligence but, unlike manual labor, produces abstract satisfaction in the process or "method" of the work. From this perspective writing is not merely a clerical skill but a calling. It offers the moral satisfaction of higher, mental work, the "interest" of an advanced exercise of literary taste. What separates professional from manual labor is, in large part, this moralized claim to the authority of learning. Its value lies not in the products of work but in the process of work, in the exertion and moral discipline that follow from a student's expertise in the reading and writing of texts.

Jonathan Hill claims not merely a moral identity with writing but, like Melville's narrator, a professional authority defined by the particular values and skills of the modern literary sphere. The rise of what we now call literature depended on the development of a profession of authorship and a mass market for printed goods. Both Melville and Jonathan Hill were writing at a historical moment when improvements in printing technology and innovations in the distribution and sale of books had made possible the diversification and specialization of writing within the marketplace. Melville's story was first published in *Putnam's Monthly,* one of several mass circulation periodicals that, like *Harper's Monthly* and the *Atlantic Monthly,* packaged and marketed a self-consciously "literary" brand of fiction to middle-class readers. As one of Melville's first magazine stories, the design and style of "Bartleby, the Scrivener" represented a concerted effort to reach this mass market of readers, at a point when his career as a novelist seemed to have foundered.[53] By the second half of the nineteenth century, Hawthorne and other American writers would be promoted as artists, sold to an expanding school market for literary study. Harper and Brothers would issue "libraries" of "standard works of literature," bound in gilt and leather for the parlor or the "five-foot shelf," where middle-class families could worship at the secular shrine of an emerging canon of national literature. The codification of modern literature culminated at the turn of the century in the gradual inclusion of formal literary study in the curricula of high schools, colleges, and universities.[54]

In this context, professional writers in the mid-nineteenth century had to sell their moral creditability in the print marketplace: the quality of writing was indexed to the talent, skill, and character of its author. Like Henry Patterson in his criticism of Charles Dickens, antebellum periodicals judged the literary merits of Melville's work against his public reputation. "Herman Melville has achieved a name in the production of tales of fiction," the *New York Dispatch* noted; the *New Bedford Mercury* observed that "The author of Typee and Omoo, is so well known to the public, that something good is expected by it, when his name appears on the title page of a book— not only expected, but in the case of the present work, the *Piazza Tales*, is realized," and urged "those who delight in romance . . . who love strong and picturesque sentences, and the thoughtful truths of a writer" to buy it. Reviews of "Bartleby, the Scrivener" repeatedly linked its aesthetic merit to Melville's success as a writer. Describing Melville's "last appearance as an author, in *Pierre or the Ambiguities* . . . unfortunate," the *Southern Literary Message* declared that "he 'turns up' once more in *Piazza Tales* with much of his former freshness and vivacity."[55] In the public eye Melville came back to life by producing a tale "based on living characters," as though the fate of his career were mirrored by his "freshness and vivacity" on the page. "'Bartleby, the Scrivener' is a portrait from life and is one of the best bits of writing that ever came from the author's pen . . . [*The Piazza Tales*] will command a large sale, and add to the high reputation of the author."[56] With the emergence of the literary sphere, as this notice suggests, publishers and readers identified a writer's talent for composing portraits with their professional identity. Large sales of a book become a moral credit to character, a measure of an author's critical reputation in the marketplace.

Like Jonathan Hill, the narrator of "Bartleby, the Scrivener" seeks to cultivate his professional credit as an author in the mass culture of print. Melville's story begins with the narrator proposing to write about "an interesting and somewhat singular set of men, of whom yet nothing that I know of has ever yet been written—I mean the law-copyists or scriveners" (13). "Bartleby, the Scrivener" alludes to the centrality of the genre of biography in the nineteenth-century print market while also offering a subtle parody of its didactic purpose.[57] As in Freeman Hunt's *Lives of American Merchants* and similar works, an individual life derives its biographical interest from vocational identity, from the degree to which it speaks for a "singular set of men." This set of men are worth writing about, the narrator implies, because their niche in the labor market corresponds to a "singular" character shared by an entire set of persons engaged in this work that are designated "law-copyists or scriveners." The readers who first encountered the story in *Putnam's* thus might have expected to read about a representative man, an exemplar of civic character that might stand in for the "histories" or "biographies of all other scriveners." The narrator "could relate divers histories, at which good-natured gentlemen might smile, and sentimental souls might weep": part of the literary value of such histories, as in Hunt's work, was to offer examples of moral conduct in economic life in the process of creating icons of mercantile character from a bygone era.[58] Because he "believes that no materials exist for a full and adequate biography of this man," the narrator presumes the reader's trust in his credibility in speaking to the stranger's character from personal experience. "What my own astonished eyes saw of Bartleby, *that* is all I know of him . . . " (13).

After the title character's entrance into the workplace, Melville's story dramatizes the divergence in a particularly literary interest in character from the values and practices that made character both meaningful and manageable in social life. Bartleby's first refusal of a request from his boss, for example, brings an unprecedented disruption of the story's narrative flow, forcing the narrator to reflect self-consciously on his own authority:

> I sat awhile in perfect silence, rallying my stunned faculties. Immediately it occurred to me that my ears had deceived me, or Bartleby had entirely misunderstood my meaning. I repeated my request in the clearest tone I could assume. But in quite as clear a one came the previous reply, "I would prefer not to."
>
> "Prefer not to," echoed I, rising in high excitement, and crossing the room with a stride. "What do you mean? Are you moon-struck? I want you to help me compare this sheet here—take it," and I thrust it towards him.
>
> "I would prefer not to," said he.
>
> I looked at him steadfastly. His face was leanly composed; his gray eyes dimly calm. Not a wrinkle of agitation rippled him. Had there been the least uneasiness, anger, impatience or impertinence in his manner; in other words, had there been anything ordinarily human about him, doubtless I should have violently dismissed him from the premises. But as it was, I should have as soon thought of turning my pale plaster-of-Paris bust of Cicero out of doors. I stood gazing at him awhile, as he went on with his own writing, and then reseated myself at my desk. This is very strange, thought I. What had one best

do? But my business hurried me. I concluded to forget the matter for the present, reserving it for my future leisure. (20–21)

In this encounter, Melville dramatizes the disruption that Bartleby presents to the normative accounting of character on which the management of the office depends. The "least sign of uneasiness, anger, impatience or impertinence in his manner" would at once make the employee's behavior predictable and the manager's action unequivocally certain: "I should have violently dismissed him from the premises." Here and in the rest of the story, however, physical scrutiny of Bartleby does not reveal that which is "ordinarily human." The scrivener passively undermines the paradigm of moral divination established in the first few pages of the story. Bartleby never acquires a nickname, so that the narrator can only refer to him by his given name—"It was Bartleby." Within the narrator's tale he remains titled "Bartleby, the Scrivener." Representing only singularity, the clerk's oddness defies the accounting, both economic and human, that would integrate him into the ecology of the office. Bartleby remains thoroughly associated with his narrow economic function (and a correlated failure to perform that job) because, as this scene suggests, he resists becoming legible as a whole person.

In this initial encounter and subsequent ones, the lawyer's role as a narrator of a sketch supplants his role as a manager of a social enterprise. Indeed, as the reference to his bust of Cicero suggests, the lawyer makes Bartleby into a trophy for rhetorical performance—for the performance of his own literary ethos, but one that will be achieved in the silence and solitude of the printed page rather than in the sight and sound of civic eloquence. As his tale unfolds, we follow the narrator's repeated attempts to get close enough, literally and figuratively, to read Bartleby's opaque nature: "rising excitedly," striding and thrusting, inserting the key in an office door. Ransacking his employee's desk. Bartleby is in fact utterly predictable in his actions and words—the ceaseless repetition of "I would prefer not to," the narrowed scope of movements that leave him standing mute and solitary in the abandoned office. Rather than place the clerk's behavior within the social and moral conventions of the workplace—as the refusal of an employee not only to play his part but to be "ordinarily human"—the narrator seeks to *know* him through literary devices such as present tense description, the accumulation of clues, and the heightening of suspense. Every transaction between the lawyer and the clerk ceases to be obvious for what it is—an employee's refusal to cooperate—and instead becomes meaningful for its blankness, weighted with hidden truth. Subsequent encounters with the clerk are prefaced so as to heighten the reader's expectancy: "the following little scene ensued" (24), "The next morning came," "Just then the folding doors opened" (30). With detailed attention to tones of voice and gradations of mood, the narrator stages their dialogues as "little scenes" and dramatic episodes. Like the protagonist of a mystery by Edgar Allen Poe or Arthur Conan Doyle, the lawyer brings the reader along on his subjective quest to know Bartleby.

The inability to place Bartleby within the conventional knowledge of the workplace leads to an increasingly literary preoccupation with the clerk's character. Visual scrutiny yields no insight—"I looked at him steadfastly. His face was leanly composed; his gray eyes dimly calm" (20–21)—so the narrator retreats into speculation: "I sat awhile in perfect silence, rallying my stunned faculties" (20); "I staggered to my desk, and sat there in a deep study" (25). The value of character here resides not in the static, external accounting of normative traits and physical cues—in how any person is always "representative" of others—but in an internal process of identification that develops over time. From this perspective, the story lays bare the psychological process that would come to define the interest of character in modern literature. What is true in this story depends finally on the degree to which the narrator becomes whole by trying to understand the elusive Bartleby. The narrator asserts a particular kind of literary authority that, from its genealogy in Romantic aesthetics (the figure of Byron), blurs common-sense distinctions between object and subject, real and imaginary, self and other.[59] By the end of the story, the reader knows nothing of Bartleby—the inscrutable man from a class of workers, the law scriveners—but all too much about the narrator, who, as though performing a melodrama of his own subjectivity, offers an exhausting, comic, and ultimately tragic inventory of possible responses to the clerk's blankness.

This reflexive shift in narrative interest from the scrivener to the manager—from observation of another's behavior to the subjective experience of one's own mental and emotional states—embodies a shift in the moral epistemology of character that accompanied the emergence of the modern literary sphere. If the divination of character begins in the story as a vernacular system of social credit organized around the transparency of language, it becomes a hermeneutic process, organized around the opacity of language. The story documents the narrator's effort to rally his "stunned faculties." Not unlike the diaries of clerks stunned by the blankness of their lives, it represents mental processes by using interior monologues, rhetorical questions, and repeating phrases such as "thought I." In asking questions of himself, the narrator forgoes managerial expertise—the confident demonstration of knowledge acquired from careful observation—for the sake of literary speculation:

> Nothing so aggravates an earnest person as a passive resistance. If the individual so resisted be of a not inhumane temper, and the resisting

one perfectly harmless in his passivity; then, in the better moods of the former, he will endeavor charitably to construe to his imagination what proves impossible to be solved by his judgment. Even so, for the most part, I regarded Bartleby and his ways. Poor fellow! thought I, he means no mischief; it is plain he intends no insolence; his aspect sufficiently evinces that his impulses are involuntary. He is useful to me. I can get along with him. If I turn him away, the chances are he will fall in with some less indulgent employer, and then he will be rudely treated, and perhaps driven forth miserably to starve. Yes. Here I can cheaply purchase a delicious self-approval. To befriend Bartleby; to humor him in his strange willfulness, will cost me little or nothing, while I lay up in my soul what will eventually prove a sweet morsel for my conscience. But this mood was not invariable with me. The passiveness of Bartleby sometimes irritated me. I felt strangely goaded on to encounter him in new opposition, to elicit some angry spark from him answerable to my own. (23–24)

This meditation encapsulates not only the variations of mood to which the narrator is increasingly vulnerable but also the logic of contradiction and resistance that defines his feeling. He begins by invoking the disinterested authority of generalized social knowledge, denoting himself as "an earnest person" of a "not inhumane temper," and ends up feeling "strangely goaded" into an irrational desire to provoke Bartleby. Unable to solve the dilemma by calm judgment, the narrator follows his imagination through a series of provisional "regards" ranging from charitable pity and the sensational specter of Bartleby's starvation to the self-interested calculation of a cost-free "morsel for my conscience." The narrator's ever-fluctuating moods, however, undo his every attempt to see the situation from a different angle. The lawyer's capacity for rational detachment is undermined by his confession of not merely "irritation" but also anger, that "the evil impulse in me mastered me" (24).

How does the introduction of literary speculation alter the accounting of individual identity and responsibility, when they have no social consequence? Ethical *inaction* results from an author's regard: reflection, reasoning, and moods do not help the narrator take effective social and moral action, while they invite readers' imaginative investment in the sketch. The narrator suspends his preoccupation temporarily for the sake of the impersonal exigencies of his legal work. "At length, necessities connected with my business tyrannized over all other considerations" (32): the narrator establishes a deadline of six days for Bartleby's departure, and offers money. Economic imperatives, however, prove of no avail in obviating the lawyer's "considerations" of Bartleby or in alleviating the "suffering" and "perplexity and distress of mind" (25) they bring. The narrator observes that "It

was difficult to bear in mind all the time those strange peculiarities, privileges, and unheard of exemptions, forming the tacit stipulations on
Bartleby's part under which he remained in my office" (26). In the absence
of taking "necessary" action, he details his efforts to "bear in mind" those
"tacit stipulations," returning repeatedly to the action of his own thought
and feeling. "Again I sat ruminating what I should do" (30); "Dark anticipations crowded upon me more and more . . . I resolved to gather all my
faculties together and for ever rid me of this intolerable incubus" (38). The
lawyer's "considerations" regarding his new worker are subsumed in this
introspective process of gathering "all my faculties," in the narrator's literary performance of "what my own astonished eyes saw of Bartleby" (13).

Melville's story allegorizes the impact that the modern literary sphere
had on the traditional accounting of moral life. Like the "sad considerations" of Jonathan Hill's failed sketches, the lawyer's tale bears melancholy
witness to the solitary work of reading and writing. That work was made
possible by the spread of advanced skills in literacy, the new frames of mind
promoted by Romantic aesthetic values, and the literary taste for "real" life
popularized by the mass circulation of fiction. How did these developments
alter the practice of character by which educated men cultivated a social
ethos and made a place for themselves in public life? Melville's story considers the consequences of appropriating a moral ethos as a form of literary
property, the cultural capital of educational and professional achievement
displayed on walls by diplomas or on shelves by trophies like the lawyer's
bust of Cicero. How do literary tastes serve the practice of moral authority
in the social world of the white-collar office? In posing these questions,
Melville's story offers its own ironic moral about how the professional
ethos was transformed as it was adapted to the technology of reading and
the institutions of authorship in a mass print culture. The new material
objects and social forms of modern literature relocated character from the
performance of social roles and ethical duties outside the self to the development of psychological and subjective interests inside the self.

Late in the story, the narrator contemplates firing his recalcitrant worker.
He appreciates his solitary ruminations as "theory"; in lieu of doing anything, he anticipates his own "masterly management in getting rid of
Bartleby," the "beauty of my procedure." The narrator's imaginative speculation is a kind of narrative rehearsal increasingly divorced from his legal
practice and the conventions of social knowledge on which it depends. The
narrator describes walking on Broadway, "arguing the probabilities pro and
con," "veering about," and overhearing a debate about mayoral politics.
"In my intent frame of mind, I had, as it were, imagined that all Broadway
shared in my excitement, and were debating the same question with me.
I passed on, very thankful that the uproar of the street screened my mo-

mentary absent-mindedness" (34). Here, and throughout the story, the narrator represents a "frame of mind" as crossing normative social and psychological boundaries. His private fascination with the problem of Bartleby accompanies him into the public space of Broadway, not only preventing him from attending to questions of public interest but leading him to mistake his private considerations as a matter of civic consequence. At the same time, he realizes a degree of privacy in the midst of this public world, taking refuge behind the screen of the street's anonymous "uproar." In being "absent-minded," anyone can find temporary cover from the claims and scrutiny of society. This episode speaks to the power of "fancy" to remake the places in which individuals find themselves. Solitary reading and writing allows people to connect with others imaginatively in theory, and so to "absent" themselves from civic space, through preoccupation and internal speculation.

Like his physical placement in the office, Bartleby's literary placement in the lawyer's sketch is an arrangement that "conjoins privacy and society." The screen separating the lawyer from his clerk creates a barrier in place of the transparent "frames" by which the mind negotiates theory and practice, imagination and action. When the narrator describes moving his entire office to get away from the scrivener, he refers to the screen "being folded up like a huge folio," leaving the scrivener "the motionless occupant of a naked room" (38). The screen is a figure for the printed text of the narrator's account of Bartleby, of the way that a literary voice joins self and other in the absence of physical proximity. As we have seen, the narrator projects a frame of mind at once obsessively "intent" on registering the author's own sensations and motives, and yet increasingly "absent" from the demands of the social world. Like the metaphor of voice, the metaphor of the screen describes perception in the absence of physical and social proximity. It is an emblem of being heard without being seen, and of the peculiar joining of privacy and society that becomes possible in modern literature, in the simultaneous sheltering and projection of character. It is at once impersonal, a relationship mediated by frames or screens of literary artifice, and yet strangely intimate, the new kinds of human interest and identification that the social isolation of reading and writing make possible. The screen is the "folio" on which the narrator has written his account of Bartleby, and through which he has found imagined community with so many readers, each screened by the anonymity of paper and print.

The blankness of Bartleby itself becomes a screen for the lawyer's retreat from his moral obligations and social duties in the office, a retreat that occurs through the hierarchical values and expert practices of a modern literary ethos. The narrator's professional aspiration as an author depends on various kinds of absence from the social, physical, and economic realities of his working world. The narrator's preoccupation while walking along the crowded streets of Broadway, or the psychic refuge he takes up behind the "screen" become figurative expressions of both the imaginative freedom and the melancholy solitude that the modern literary sphere makes possible. To face the page of a printed text, no less than a folding screen or the brick fronts of Wall Street, is to make individual habits of literacy our reference point for how we know the social world and take our places within it. It is also an evasion of the problems of moral divination and social commitment that the vernacular practice of character sought to address. The "folio" of the narrator's story translates his momentary absentmindedness from the hurried determinations of business into literary presence for a large, anonymous crowd of potential readers.

Since the advent of a mass print culture in the nineteenth century, the modern literary sphere has institutionalized this literary presence in solitary practices of reading and writing, forming the moral imagination of a broad middle class by training individuals in the exercise of taste. The lawyer's imagined community has, as a result, included not only the readers of *Putnam's Magazine,* where "Bartleby, the Scrivener" first appeared, but also readers in the twentieth-century university, where the story became a central text in literary criticism and in anthologies of American literature for generations of teachers and students. The story has been the topic of more than three hundred and fifty articles and books by figures ranging from Alfred Kazin, Harry Levin, and Philip Rahv to J. Hillis Miller and Gilles Deleuze.[60] What one scholar calls the "Bartleby Industry" has been largely sympathetic with the character of Bartleby, seeing him as an allegory of an artist who does not conform to social conventions.[61] For instance, a 1953 essay by Leo Marx described the tale as a story "about a particular kind of writer's relation to a particular kind of society . . . [a] commercial society, dominated by a concern with property and finance." The story is set on Wall Street, after all, and so the story becomes a parable about the "walls which hem in the meditative artist and for that matter every reflective man."[62] Through decades of scholarship, as Cornelia Vismann notes, the scrivener has been "lauded and lamented, an absolute strangeness and preferred identification object of intellectuals." Melville's story has invited such extensive critical attention because it models a psychological process of identification that would shape not only the literary practices of nineteenth-century clerks but also the literary criticism of modern scholars.[63]

If Melville's story documents the new forms that interest in character would take in the nineteenth century, an interpretation of the story by the scholar J. Hillis Miller suggests how pervasive and influential those forms would become in the twentieth century. In *Versions of Pygmalion* (1990), Miller reads Melville's tale as an allegory of the artist in market culture, as many previous critics have; but he does so in a way that is both anticipated by Melville's lawyer-narrator and paradigmatic of a critical ethos that has animated much reading and writing in the modern profession of literary studies.[64] Like Miller, literary critics have been as loathe to countenance the writing by the narrator as Byron would have been to sanction the scrivening of a legal clerk. As with the evolution of Emerson's reputation outside the lecture hall, the reception of "Bartleby, the Scrivener" attests to the particular forms that literary taste would take in a middle-class culture of meritocratic achievement and professional expertise.

As the case of "Bartleby, the Scrivener" suggests, the modern literary sphere invests the *individual* engagement with texts with powerful moral authority and social credit. Miller succinctly summarizes this power of literacy when he describes storytelling as "an ethical act involving personification for which the storyteller must be held responsible, as must reader, teacher, or critic for bringing the story to life by reading about it, talking about it, writing about it."[65] Personification describes the process of reading and writing through which characters come to life and compel our interest in and response to the stories they inhabit. As in Ovid's fable of Pygmalion, works of art seem to transcend the material artifice of their existence, influencing our thoughts and actions to the extent that they persuade us to believe in them as true. As Miller goes on to show in his analysis of "Bartleby, the Scrivener," personification is the narrator's primary method as he tries to fix the identity of an eccentric employee who resists all efforts to be understood.

In a broader sense, Miller argues that personification figures the moral obligations and social consequences entailed by the aesthetic consideration of texts. Reading has it own ethics, as Miller goes on to suggest, forged from psychological identification and *prosopeia* (the attribution of human qualities to what is not in fact alive): "All those books lining the shelves of the library do not just passively sit there. They cry out to be read. They do not cease to clamor for readers. . . . Each book, text, essay, scrap of written language, even those in languages I do not know, asks to be read. The call is directed to me personally and with equal force by each text." This insistent and incorrigible "demand" makes Miller feel that he should suspend "other responsibilities and contractual obligations, to my family, to my institution, to my students, and colleagues." It demands further that a reader betray his obligation to all other books whenever he chooses "to respond to the demand made by the book that has fallen by accident into my hands."[66] Seen from this light, every text (especially the demanding ones!) becomes a screen on which readers project abstract and personal obligations to literature, becoming present to themselves at the cost of their social roles and obligations. The ethical questions raised by reading follow from what

Miller calls its "performative force." "The event of reading, like the writing of that text in the first place, 'takes place' with all the enigmatic force in this notion of an event as something that comes out of nowhere, so to speak, occupies space, and makes that space into a place, with orienting coordinates."[67] But if the event of reading situates us within a community of discourse, it also "always exceeds what was predictable from those circumstances."

The narrator of Melville's story fails by this ethics of reading. According to Miller, the lawyer's two roles as author and manager are mutually reinforcing, rather than at odds, as I have suggested: his narrative interest in his workers is contaminated by economic self-interest. The entrance of Bartleby into the story "suspends the narrator's power over those around him, both his ability to command them through narration and his control over them as their employer." As Miller points out, Bartleby's "gift for literal remarks—'I prefer not to,' 'I know where I am'—puts a stop to further conversation or interchange of words between people." Taking the lawyer as a convenient figure for the moral failure of normative accounting of character, Miller observes that the "effect of Bartleby's words on the narrator's sense of himself is as devastating as their effect on the practice of his profession." The narrator has a "most urgent need to contain Bartleby, to reduce and encompass him, to read him"; nevertheless, the various strategies by which the narrator attempts to "account" for him, to make a "comfortable assimilation" of this otherwise ghostlike figure into a normative interpretation, "all fail." Most of the story is concerned with the narrator's various attempts to do something about Bartleby—attempts that are, in fact, "all ways of doing nothing, ways of deferring action, ways of pretending that nothing has really happened to endanger the ordinary way of doing things." The narrator's "need" to use interpretation as a means to control Bartleby, to "reassimilate" this employee's abject singularity "into the flow of reason and business," figures "an allegory of the reader's own need to dominate the story by interpreting it."[68]

As with Melville's allegorical arrangement of the office in "Bartleby, the Scrivener," Miller's ethics transpose obligations and duties owed to persons—the social accounting of character—to those one owes to oneself through the act of reading, to the autonomy and integrity of literary taste. As a result, all readers must define and assert their own characters within the psychic space in which the demands of literature "take place," as Miller puts it. Every interpretation requires another personification of our own "needs" and duties as readers, that we bring to life the dead letters on the page. Thus, every object of our reading reflects back on the situation of one's own literacy. That situation, as Miller has described it, places readers between their moral obligation as individuals—to respond to the otherness of texts—and their "need" for "comfortable assimilation," to enforce conventions of knowledge within the professional communities they inhabit. With its vague imputation of weakness and compulsion to the generic reader's "need" for control, Miller's analysis of the ethics of reading entails continual disruption of a normative disposition toward literacy, a withdrawal from the social norms of moral accounting and the obligations they entail ("to my family, to my institution, to my students, and colleagues").

This withdrawal from the social context of moral life becomes literal when Miller situates himself against the other scholarly readers of Melville's story. Despite the "remarkable" diversity and multiplicity of this secondary literature, most "claim in one way or another to have identified Bartleby. . . . They tend to exemplify that function of policing or putting things in their place which is entrusted by our society to literary studies as one realm among many of the academic forms of accounting or accounting for." Making Bartleby an example of a universal, existential type, or finding some particular historical reference or context that explains him, these readings all try "to fulfill what the narrator has tried and failed to do: to tell Bartleby's story in a way that will allow us to assimilate him and the story into the vast archives of rationalization that make up the secondary literature of our profession." This term "accounting" subtly invokes the bogeyman of economics as a paradigm of thinking that is antithetical to the moral integrity of a reading of literature that is "real" or "true": it is the mean "business" of society, after all, to rationalize, police, control, assimilate. This business, which readers in the academic profession "are institutionalized to do," finds its fate figured in the narrator's own paralysis, his own "pretending" to take action while only generating more commentary, none of which "seems to quite get to the point": "Imperiously, imperatively," the story "says, 'Read me!' On the other hand, it cannot be read . . . and the reader remains paralyzed by the text, called upon to act but unable to act." This text, it seems, makes its reader inert, but obviously not mute. By not claiming to explain or rationalize Bartleby, Miller overcomes the "paralysis" of mere "commentary" to which he consigns his peers. "My accounting succeeds where the others fail," Miller says, "by showing . . . why it is that 'accounting for' in any of its usual senses cannot work, either for the story or for the character it poses."[69] Reading that would be "real" or "true," he suggests, is a devotion of solitude: the duty one assumes toward a text by refusing to control its meaning in the social world, the respect one pays its unpredictable force by disavowing consensus about it.

What Miller offers here is itself a personification that projects his agency onto the books he reads. Books do not make demands, cry out, or call upon us. In fact, they do just lie there on the shelves of libraries. The caprice of what we read and why, the neglect of social duties for the sake of being

absorbed with books, the lawless disruption of predictable contexts of social knowledge by the supposed universal "force" by which books demand
our individual response: Miller pretends that this all pertains to books as
objects rather than to practices and motives that create the "event" of reading in particular historical places. By personifying books, Miller represents his
own acts of reading as a deferential response to an abstract obligation that can
only be ethical in a figurative sense, because it is entirely divorced from the
social settings in which moral actions and obligations take place. Books never
come from nowhere. The spaces they take up in the actual world—social,
mental, emotional, moral, professional—are spaces that readers have designed for them in institutions and practices of literacy. Books do not fall
into one's hands by accident, especially when written by Melville and other
authors who, in the twentieth century, became central to the canon of
American literature. They are assigned to students, debated by critics, sold
in stores, and placed on library shelves and in course curriculums, and in
other ways have their value as cultural capital already accounted.

As I have argued throughout this book, moral authority became identified with the performance of a literary ethos across the stages of middle-
class life, at leisure and work. Amateurs like Jonathan Hill, authors like
Herman Melville, Melville's fictional narrator, and the many critics who
have commented on him have all tried through the work of writing to locate character in the pages of texts. In so doing, they have sought in diverse
ways to claim autonomy and integrity as individuals through the exercise of
literary taste. If Melville treats his narrator with ambivalence, as a figure of
satire and melodrama, Miller underscores the subtle and profound consequences that reading can have as a preoccupation. "Any reader who takes
reading at all seriously will have felt the force of this responsibility," he
writes, and indeed, the moral significance of reading is a function of the relative rareness with which we take our obligation to read "seriously":

> What happens when I read, when I *really* read, which does not hap-
> pen all that often? What happens is something always fortuitous and
> unpredictable, something surprising, however many times the book
> in question has been read before, even by me. One way to define this
> unexpected quality of true acts of reading is to say that they never cor-
> respond exactly to what other readers tell me I am going to find when
> I read that book, however learned, expert, and authoritative those
> previous readers have been. Another way to describe what is unpre-
> dictable about a genuine act of reading is to say that reading is always
> the disconfirmation or modification of presupposed literary theory
> rather than its confirmation. . . . A book is a dangerous object, and
> perhaps all books should have warning labels.[70]

The imperative of what happens in reading is categorical, "always fortu-itous and unpredictable." The moral good to which reading aspires here is the complete originality of response. When acts of reading are "true" or "real," they defy all predictability and become agents of radical disorder, re-sisting the controls and intentions of readers and authors alike. The vio-lence to which Miller alludes is the very real destruction of our once reliable commitment to social conventions, the disordering of the normative values that make knowledge real and true. Guided by this Romantic interest in au-thenticity, aesthetic experience is a means of self-realization that transforms how readers place themselves in the social world and respond to its de-mands. When it is "genuine," an otherwise passive and inert act of reading becomes an "event," even a dangerous weapon, in the heroic struggle to liberate the mind from all forms of social prescription. In this sense, Miller's sense of his duty to texts exemplifies a tendency of modern literary criticism to sublimate the historical deportment of individuals in civic life to the pro-motion of academic literary studies "as a particular ethos or style of life," as Ian Hunter notes. From the formalist preoccupations of the New Criticism to more recent trends in literary theory and cultural studies, the ethics of reading has been identified with a universal "subject" modeled on the pro-fessional critic.[71]

Regardless of the compelling merits of Miller's particular insights, his own critical style makes explicit key assumptions about the cognitive nature of moral agency that have implicitly defined modern literary values both in-side and outside of the academy. For Miller no less than the colleagues from whom he would set himself apart, "genuine" acts of reading provide exis-tential occasions for individuals to assert their moral autonomy from the control and conformity exacted by all forms of social membership (within a community of scholars, no less than an economic community of the white-collar office). In making these claims for the moral authority of his own professional mode of literacy Miller values disorder rather than the unity of the text, and emphasizes the radical instability of language rather than its rhetorical efficacy in furnishing us with reliable knowledge about other people. In Miller's view, we exercise moral obligations through individual acts of reading and interpretation. As Thomas Strychaz points out, "Liter-ary critics may lay claim to being professionals" even when they disclaim, as most critics have, "allegiance to stable, determinate truths," because their elaboration of skepticism perpetuates "the legitimacy and continuity of professional discourse itself."[72] Put another way, critics often assume that we read in the face of melancholy, driven by a profound sense of the ineffi-cacy of language as a performative utterance. The methods of reading and writing that teachers and critics arbitrate are means of acquiring and acting on symbolic moral authority—convictions about the social world and our relation to it that come from the experience of literature. Through acts of reading individuals presumably acquire "liberty of intellect," that sovereign autonomy of consciousness, by which people become moral agents in market culture. Books have become agents of freedom in liberal culture by seeming to make the comprehension and expression of "true" individualism possible.

The literary landscape in which clerks found their place was transformed in the late nineteenth century by new institutions and practices of advanced literacy. These changes included the proliferation of colleges, public libraries, and public school systems; the rise of the modern research university and specialized disciplines of academic inquiry; the emergence of English (and eventually American) "literature" and its standardization as a 'canon' within secondary and higher education; and a shift in basic literacy instruction, from an antebellum system organized around recitation and rote memorization to a national curriculum that, by 1920, codified English as a sequence of reading and grammar skills that emphasized the decoding and analysis of texts-as-objects—moving authority, as one historian has put it, from the "teacher to the text."[73] These changes effected a reorientation of the relationship between forms of knowledge and moral authority, contributing to the emergence of what Michael Halloran and Gregory Clark have termed a "professional culture of literacy" that identified the rational, autonomous individual as the "locus of a new public morality of expertise." This expertise was located in hierarchical and institutional values of advanced literacy. Although scholars often speak of professionals in economic terms, as enforcing monopolies of knowledge so as to command higher prices for their services and goods, professional authority is also defined as status based on the possession of "symbolic capital," which is sanctioned and protected in schools and universities. Within the professional culture of literacy, moral authority is a commodity, to which we gain privileged access through our expertise as readers and writers, our individual competence in protocols of silent, solitary reading and writing. As Miller's reading of "Bartleby, the Scrivener" attests, moral knowledge came to be practiced as an ethical obligation to texts, assumed in the 'method' and 'manner' by which we 'fill' blank pages before us.

The form that moral authority assumed in professional culture depended on a transposition in the meaning and practice of rhetoric: both a decline in the social prestige traditionally accorded to spoken eloquence in the learned professions, and the emergence of a new rhetoric of professional credit organized by the new institutions and practices of an autonomous literary sphere. In eighteenth-century instruction in academies and colleges, rhetoric included reading texts aloud because it was assumed that students would employ various kinds of oral performance as they entered the traditional professions. "To reserve a written or printed text for a single, private reader," as Michael Halloran notes, "was a considerable extravagance, so texts were commonly shared by the expedient of reading aloud," and writing was a way to script oral performance. In addition to learning the theory of rhetoric, eighteenth-century college students wrote 'compositions' meant to exhibit the range of techniques of rhetorical invention and persuasion. These compositions were heavily indebted to the imitation of neoclassical models. To some degree, one learned to compose to further one's facility with Latin, rather than to develop a special skill in the writing of English vernacular prose, which until the "new rhetoric" of the eighteenth century was held to be an inferior medium of literary invention. The nineteenth century brought a new emphasis on belles-lettres writing—poetry, fiction, drama, and essay—which had been less prominent in the classical curriculum and had been the province of college literary clubs and societies. The emergence of a new middle class and professional culture altered the student population, placing new importance on the social and economic value of writing. Especially important for the transformation of rhetoric was the flourishing of Romantic ideology, whose concept of taste turned "standards of rhetorical judgment from a complex domain combining the moral, the aesthetic, and the pragmatic to a more purely aesthetic one."[74]

For Melville's narrator and for modern teachers and scholars, moral life became a professional exercise of literary taste. Like clerks seeking meaning in profitless days, they realized the credit of character in the "interest" and the "notice" they took of others and themselves through specialized, 'expert' skills of reading and writing. If they find a mere "part" of themselves in their clerical employment, bored clerks claim their wholeness as persons through an imaginative projection onto the blank pages of their journals, through their identification with professional norms of authorship. As it was institutionalized throughout lower and higher education in new curriculums for composition and literature, the modern literary sphere allowed middle-class people to locate a moral authority that was distinct from their place in the world of adult work. It allowed individuals to claim an omniscient and autonomous consciousness as a prerogative of their training in the hierarchical values of literary practice. In the modern Western world, professional elites now recognize in this modern form of literary consciousness the expression of a fully realized individuality. We make the will transparent not by the performance of social duties or the assumption of moral obligations but by turning our faces to the pages of books.

The place of writing to which Jonathan Hill and Caleb Wall, like Herman Melville and J. Hillis Miller, turned was made possible by new literary norms of professional credit that accompanied a mass culture of print. The potential for authorship became quotidian and ubiquitous as a standardized habit of mass literacy. For this reason writing became a medium in which to reconstitute hierarchies of cultural deference according to a seemingly democratic and efficient order of educational steps. The "literary" acquired its modern meaning, as Clifford Siskin argues, from the new role that mass literacy played within an evolving professional economy of white collar work. This economy was characterized by "hierarchical specialization—a dividing up of knowledge and taste . . . figured and valorized as depth." As Siskin notes:

> Literature assumed a key role in the new organizations of knowledge and of labor as a specialization, but one that all of the others had in common—the prerequisite for entering them as autonomous professional fields. 'Men are men before they are lawyers,' wrote [John Stuart] Mill, who found humanity in Literature (through Wordsworth) rather than Latin. Literature's power as well as the sense that it is powerlessly detached from the real world lie in this classificatory ambiguity, for that ambiguity was not, historically, a falling away from already defined alternatives—professional, amateur, discipline/avocation, real/made up—but a means of generating and empowering them.[75]

Within the new curriculums in English and American literature, college-bound and college-bred youth would, like Mill, discover humanity prior to moving on to their vocations. As Mill suggests, and as we saw with Emerson's meditation on the composure of the senses, professionalism encouraged adult men to identify moral authority with their cultivation of the "whole person." It encouraged them to do so, however, as they inhabited increasingly narrow places of expertise, while trading on ever more specialized 'parts' of themselves in the white-collar economy. The structure of curricular and admission requirements within the educational hierarchy would, indeed, make a modicum of humanist taste a prerequisite to professional advancement. As liberal education became an object of middlebrow consumption, the acquisition of character was delegated to the schools, and moral authority was naturalized as a progressive facility with solitary reading and writing.

The institutions and practices of the literary sphere that developed in the later nineteenth century constituted the moral credentials for white-collar work. After the Civil War, the capacity to write a "sketch" and the habits of literary taste supporting it would be institutionalized as a requirement for professional advancement, and in this way become a virtual prerequisite for entry into the learned professions. Harvard would, for example, come to demand a written composition as part of its undergraduate entrance examination. In 1865 it added to its catalog a requirement for "reading aloud," and in 1873 codified a place for the study of vernacular modern "literature" in the secondary schools by making it the subject for a new entrance requirement in English composition. "Each candidate will be required," the catalog stated, "to write a short English composition, correct in spelling, punctuation, grammar, and expression, the subject to be taken from such works of standard authors as shall be announced from time to time." Prior to this, the study of literature had largely involved rote memorization and recitation. At universities like Harvard and Johns Hopkins, new requirements "institutionalized the study of standard authors and set in motion a process which eventually forced English to consolidate its position within the schools."[76] These changes ushered in normative standards and objects of literary taste defined according to epistemological and rhetorical values of silent, solitary reading. Colleges in the twentieth century would, following the U.S. Army's pioneering use of intelligence tests, make performance on standardized tests a crucial measure of one's capacity to succeed. Modern certification as a professional depended, finally, on endurance of a lengthy course of study in institutions of secondary, collegiate, and graduate education that all required expertise with what professional scholars now call "texts."[77]

Membership in the professional cultural elite is sanctioned by the ability to climb the meritocratic ladder of educational achievement—every stage of which demands ever more dexterous manipulations in the reading and composition of texts. As many scholars have noted, the comprehensive reform of education—from the grading of classes and the organization of urban school districts by centralized bureaucracies to the differentiation of skills along a hierarchy—adopted values of rationalization and efficiency that were congenial to, if not explicitly designed for, the production of workers for an industrial and corporate economy. As James Hosic stated in his *Report on the Reorganization of English in Secondary Schools* (1917): "The first step towards efficiency in the use of language is the cultivation of earnestness and sincerity; the second is the development of accuracy and correctness; the third is the arousing of individuality and artistic consciousness."[78] As Hosic describes it, the modern educational system institutionalizes development as a climb up the ladder of meritocracy: from childlike sincerity, to clerical accuracy, to the creativity and singularity of the truly successful. There is room for *individuals* only at the top, among an elite that understands its educational and social privileges as the rational outcome of an orderly progress through "steps" in the use of language, the achievement of character. In the modern economy of literacy, a person's place in white-collar work is rationalized through the differentiation and ranking of literacy skills, and for the most successful is consummated in the fully realized "consciousness" of the learned professional. As Hosic suggests, professional elites understood an autonomy of mind as the expression of a fully realized individuality, a prerogative of those trained in the university.

More than fifty years before Hosic's report, Jonathan Hill's diary rehearsed the same liberal narrative of progress when he identified his own moral realization with his itinerary as a student in the landscape of literacy. The greatest benefit from keeping a journal, as he wrote in his "Introduction," "sufficient to compensate all labor that may be expended in the performance of the task," was the "the reminiscences which it naturally furnishes us in after life." The labor of writing is repaid by the literary interest it affords in retrospect, by enabling one to experience one's life as a text.

> It is seldom that we meet with a man whose life has so completely blended with adversity, that he has not passed through some pleasant scenes, particularly in his earlier days. What pleasurable exertions must he experience in after years, in looking over the records of bye-gone days! How easily his mind reverts to the least of childhood scenes. Every sport, every scene of youthful enjoyments, every object of past time with which he was conversant, comes up before him. The playground upon which he had so often sported & his companions who there mingled their shouts with his—the favorite old elm under whose spreading branches he has so often gambolled "at close of day,"—the gurgling rivulet . . . [on] whose rippled surface he has launched his tiny sails—all, are before him in the far stretching vista of bye-gone days. There, too, he sees the old schoolhouse upon whose hacked and whittled tables he has so often lounged and conned [*sic*] his daily tasks + the village pedagogue, that paragon of wisdom and excellence—he sees the venerable seminary standing in all its pristine beauty around whose grounds cluster so many delightful associations—whose halls have rung so oft with his merry shouts—his "alma mater"—his Professional School—all are there—all come up in such rapid successions, each event calling to his recollection the thousand little incidents till the whole of his youth presents itself so vividly to his mind that he half fancies that the season is now passing.[79]

Hill composes a student's life that, as with Hosic's steps, narrates moral progress across a landscape of literacy. Hill sketches a linear movement that begins with a child's "past time" and proceeds through the "tasks" of the school, graduating to emotionally charged associations of the "alma mater," and culminating with a "Professional School." This moral progress is consummated by the achieved skill as a writer by which Hill recovers this past and makes it so vividly present as a text, in the credit he has earned by mastering skills of reading and writing. Only by a literary progress to adulthood, it seems, could Hill and these other clerks reap the emotional reward of reliving the past, experiencing life through the "pleasurable exertions" of reading.

To make life "legible" as an object of literary interest requires that one cultivate a critical style as a reader and writer, achieving an advanced proficiency in literacy that is at once the thematic object and moralized end of successive "scenes" in Hill's education. In the "vista of bye-gone days," the "whole of his youth" becomes a sequential progress through stages of literacy that stands for the mature satisfaction of a realized life. A young man achieves a moral identity as a student by learning to render his life as a literary object; he acquires the capacity to "experience in after years" that life aesthetically, *as a reader*. If Hill seems to defer the aesthetic pleasure to "after life," it is because the aesthetic has become divorced from the quotidian present of white-collar work. It can only be valued when one's time is no longer compelled by work, and when one has already fulfilled one's amorphous promise as a student. However much boys detested the drill of education while it was happening, days of youthful study become, when recalled from the rote drill of white-collar work, a scene of pastoral nostalgia. As Hill writes on 9 October 1841: "I employed myself in looking over the papers of school days: and many a pleasing reminiscences did they call to mind. I know of nothing more pleasant than to look over these little momentos of those happy days and we half fancy that we are again passing those scenes, which have passed to be present no more forever!"[80] With its durability and fragility vested in tokens of an irrecoverable past, memory ceases to exist independently from habits of reading and writing—indeed, from the scenes at school that make happiness present in retrospect.

Like clerks seeking meaning in profitless days, modern students would apprehend character through the "interest" and "notice" they took in texts as they moved their way up the educational ladder. Among the professional middle class, the credit of character is earned as a literary ethos, that moral authority that Hosic placed at the apex of the educational hierarchy as the "arousing of individuality and artistic consciousness." Hill identifies the moral 'credit' of character with a professional ethos, achieved through the specialized labor of writing and the hierarchical values of study, where the duty one performs is to one's own amorphous, unrealized potential: a duty to one's achievement in school. And so do clerks exercise literary taste to place themselves somewhere else, away from the strange monotony and stasis of their economic and social lives. Unlike the clerk in a dead-end job who has resigned himself to being a cog in the machine, to using a mere part of his potential, the student retains hope for his future. If the student's achievement can be measured according to standardized norms of value, its interest transcends the forms of social and economic credit a clerk might earn. Hill's emotional and professional identification with the student allows him to retain faith in his wholeness, to take symbolic credit for his individuality by reading and writing from the ever-receding vistas of his future promise.

Epilogue
Debris from the Business of Living

I have known the sadness of pencils,
Neat in their boxes, dolor of pad and paper-weight,
All the misery of manila folders and mucilage,
Desolation in immaculate public places,
Lonely reception room, lavatory, switchboard,
The unalterable pathos of basin and pitcher,
Ritual of multigraph, paper-clip, and comma,
Endless duplication of lives and objects.
And I have seen dust from the walls of institutions,
Finer than flour, alive, more dangerous than silica,
Sift, almost invisible, through long afternoons of tedium,
Dropping a fine film on nails and delicate eyebrows,
Glazing the pale hair, the duplicate grey standard faces.
                Theodore Roethke, "Dolor" (1943)[1]

In the twenty-first century, we remain creatures of habits that developed in the nineteenth century. We move amid the physical ruins from the past, but also among ghosts, the duplicate gray faces that men so often wear as they stare out the windows of coffee shops and offices (fig. 21). Habits of thought have become common, as standard as pencils and chalk, as crowded as city streets. Yet however familiar the paths we see before us— the inexorable rounds of classrooms and wash basins and jobs—they become, on reflection, as interior and personal as feelings that only individuals can know. Amid the debris of everyday life, public spaces take on the private features of desolation and aspiration, and common prospects become personal fates.

In following a few clerks through the urban world of nineteenth-century America, this book has moved from humble artifacts of mass literacy to the advanced methods of professional inquiry, from persons to institutions. In

Figure 21   A coffee shop at Astor Place, New York City, 2002. In the distraction of young men, self-absorbed in the midst of the bustling public life of the marketplace before them, we see white-collar ghosts of Jonathan Hill's melancholy, Bartleby's silence. Photograph by Laura Davis.

doing so, it has suggested some of the ways in which individuality came to be produced within the modern landscape of literacy. Through particular kinds of reading and writing, individuals learned to become their true selves in the pages of texts. The diffusion of literary taste made possible the complex subjectivity and self-absorption that, no less than autonomy and self-assertion, would inflect the ways in which modern men declared their independence. In the school, the home, the lecture hall, the library, the office, young men navigated the impersonal world of market culture, trading in forms of public and private identity that a growing percentage of the educated population would embrace as part of an homogenous style of living. In diverse sites of family and leisure, education and work, moral authority was personalized as the autonomous achievement of individuals and standardized as the cultural capital of a professional middle class.

Literary practices and institutions altered the scale and scope of our moral vocabulary, locating character in the stories one tells about the self, about how "the soul becomes," as Emerson put it. In the midst of modern circumstances of uncertainty and mobility, divining one's future became as inevitable as a chance encounter with a book. In 1885, for example, a Pittsburgh banker named Thomas Mellon (1813–1908), the father of financier

Andrew Mellon, wrote about coming across Benjamin Franklin's *Autobiography* in the 1830s:

> It was about my fourteenth year, at a neighbor's house, when plowing a field we had taken on his farm for buckwheat, that I happened upon a dilapidated copy of the autobiography of Dr. Franklin. It delighted me with a wider view of life and inspired me with new ambition—turned my thoughts into new channels. I had not before imagined any other course of life superior to farming, but the reading of Franklin's life led me to question this view. For so poor and friendless a boy to be able to become a merchant or a professional man had before seemed an impossibility; but here was Franklin, poorer than myself, who by industry, thrift and frugality had become learned and wise, and elevated to wealth and fame. The maxims of "poor Richard" exactly suited my sentiments. I read the book again and again, and wondered if I might do something in the same line by similar means. I had will and energy equal to the occasion, and could exercise the same degree of industry and perseverance, and felt no misgiving except on the score of talent. . . . After that I was more industrious when at school, and more constant than ever in reading and study during leisure hours. I regard the reading of Franklin's Autobiography as the turning point of my life.[2]

Mellon describes reading Franklin's *Autobiography* as a kind of conversion experience: the entire course of his life was changed when he "happened upon" Franklin's story. In its pages, the young Mellon found a practical guide to rising in the world, a book "exactly suited" to his sentiments, addressed to his needs and aspirations as a "poor and friendless boy." Mellon puts a premium on what Franklin's text can do for him here and now: he rereads it, identifies with it, perhaps memorizes its maxims, and uses it as a map to a "wider view of life." At least in retrospect, the rich banker found in its pages a moral justification, a mirror of the self-reliance, perseverance, and industry that made Franklin so lasting an exemplar of American manhood. In the nineteenth and twentieth centuries, the stories of businessmen such as Mellon and Andrew Carnegie, and their many fictional counterparts such as Silas Lapham and Jay Gatsby, would help to make Franklin's story into the national creed: the individual who rises to fame and fortune from obscurity, sui generis, with only the baggage of personal history and a pocketful of maxims. Mellon even erected a life-size, cast-iron statue of Ben Franklin above the entrance to his Philadelphia bank, and handed out copies of the *Autobiography* to any poor, friendless boy who came his way in need of advice.

Like the stories of nineteenth-century clerks told in this book, Mellon's account of his life suggests how modern individualism—the experience of the self as individual—emerged from objects and practices of mass literacy: stumbling across a book, seeing oneself in its pages, anticipating an unexpected fate. Whatever the chances that others had in finding some guidance within the limited horizons of everyday life, Mellon's chances as well as those of other, similarly situated young men in this book were greatly improved by access to tools of education that, in addition to all their practical benefits, were props in a democratic faith that individuals could control their own fortunes. It was through the newly common acts of reading, writing, and speaking that ordinary people came to possess a moral authority that had been the province of their social betters, to own a modern self by leaving behind the places in which they had been born. Passed hand to hand, read over and over again, even so dilapidated and promiscuous an object as Dr. Franklin's life was used by young men as part of the capital of character. Like so many American stories of success, however, Mellon's tale mystifies the conditions of social mobility in the nineteenth century, giving the messy process of finding a future the iconic simplicity of myth.

In their stories of moral life, modern scholars have placed the individual within a dense web of forces and circumstances. In *The Protestant Ethic,* Max Weber would take from Franklin's *Autobiography* some different lessons than Mellon about the business of modern life. In Franklin's example, Weber saw how religious motives became secularized with the development of modern capitalism. When Protestant asceticism was "carried out of monastic cells," we entered what Weber famously called the "iron cage" of rationality, where the "idea of duty in one's calling prowls about in our lives like the ghost of dead religious beliefs."[3] Weber's response to Franklin is ultimately a story of hope foreclosed, where individuals are held captive to alienating habits of thought and feeling, left to account for their lives amid the "sport" and "mundane passions" of American business. Weber's division between religious spirit and worldly forms of desire emerged from a long-standing and enduring tradition of cultural criticism rooted in Judeo-Christian tradition.[4] Animated by skepticism about the capacity of ordinary people to find wisdom within the profane world in which they live, this dualistic thinking was taken up with fresh vigor following the Protestant Reformation in repeated campaigns by better-educated cultural elites aimed at the "reform" of popular culture.[5] These campaigns sought to discipline, if not eliminate, the common grounds of credence by which ordinary people make meaning from what they can see, hear, and read. Following the influential scholarship of Weber and Emile Durkheim, this hostile opposition between a transcendent, ideal sphere of meaning and a utilitarian, rationalized ground of material life was developed throughout the twentieth century by a professional intelligentsia committed to a modernist epistemology in the social sciences as well as in the humanities.[6]

No less than Franklin's *Autobiography*, the books that Thomas Mellon and Max Weber wrote are both artifacts of a historical landscape of literacy. Like Melville's lawyer projecting his ambitions as an author on the blank screen of Bartleby, or J. Hillis Miller personifying the encounter with texts as an "ethics of reading," Mellon and Weber interpret Franklin's book in ways that reflect particular ways of reading and writing. Reading takes place for Mellon not as a scholarly exercise but as a momentary reprieve from the tedious work of plowing. As we have seen in the literary practices of nineteenth-century clerks, what made some knowledge "useful" for ordinary people were qualities that made it ready for appropriation by a mass audience, by people with widely diverging skills as readers and writers. Pursued as both instruction and recreation, popular reading opened new prospects to ordinary people, becoming an instrument of freedom from the constraints of material circumstance. Weber's work, by contrast, was written and debated within a professional culture of literacy that valued knowledge according to the expert methods and specialized disciplines of the modern academy. Weber quotes from Franklin's text at length "in order clearly to understand the object of the investigation," using it as a "document" that describes the spirit of capitalism "in almost classical purity." He claimed Franklin's text for the social sciences by using it as objective evidence for a positivist inquiry into the history of modern subjectivity. Both Mellon and Weber take Franklin as the representative man of market culture, but the possibilities and limits they see in his self-making reflect the different values they attach to their own styles of literacy. Franklin's art of living could be evaluated according to common sentiments, the practical aesthetics of advice and example that governed popular tastes for fiction in the New York Mercantile Library and for speaking in the lecture hall. So too, that art might reveal its truths about character to the specials skills and expert knowledge of the critic or scholar, in the competing vocabularies of history, art, or science that vie for moral authority in the modern university.[7] The meaning of a text like Franklin's depends in large part on the literary practices that one brings to it, practical means of obtaining and trusting its lessons.

By exploring the landscape of literacy in which ordinary young men came of age in the mid-nineteenth century, the preceding chapters have sought to illuminate social and material contexts of individualism that popular myths and scholarly theory have obscured. At the very least, we should take the history of moral life not from the completed tales of success that litter the landscape of modern America but from the process of shaping selves into stories. One purpose that Franklin had in publishing his autobiography was to induce "more men to spend lives fit to be written": writing on the page was the measure of living, the profit in lessons that might be reaped with the wise investment of one's days.[8] It was for this reason that Thomas Mellon sought to certify his professional success as lawyer, judge, banker, and civic leader by privately printing his own story in an edition of five hundred copies. If "an old copy of the book happen to fall into the hands of some poor little boy," Mellon hoped that, like the old copy of Franklin's book he had come across, "it would "impress on him the truth of the important rule of life which demands labor, conflict, perseverance and self-denial to produce character and accomplish purposes worth striving for."[9] When Edward Ayer, a Chicago book collector and benefactor of the Newberry Library and the Field Museum of Natural History, sent a typewritten memoir of his early days to the New York Public Library, Victor Palsits, the keeper of manuscripts, similarly declared its personal and historical value as a moral standard: "I assure you we are very glad to add it to our Manuscript division. There are a good many reminiscences of western pioneers; but there are not many of men who fought against fate with such American grit and lived to bestow upon their country in services and philanthropy what you have done. A frank record of such a struggle must be helpful to and hearten others."[10] To imagine a life as "fit to be written" is to justify success as having a story to tell, beyond the accumulation of wealth. To write one's story in the nineteenth century was to engage in a moral performance that was both personal and social, crafting a character that might be representative for others as well as one's self.

The young men in this book did not know what value their lives would have, even as they struggled to make them fit for writing. As we have seen, nineteenth-century clerks identified their moral aspirations with literary practices. From holding a pen, to gazing out windows, to quoting verse, to playing with metaphor: their stories unfold in rituals and implements of literacy, beginning with penmanship exercises and moving on to greater sophistication. In his diary, a clerk might describe books read or lectures heard; he might write an original composition, perhaps for a literary club or to test professional ambitions. The diary of future newspaper reporter Caleb Hill demonstrates this full spectrum of invention, having at one end copied, upside down, a poem titled "Descriptions of a Summer Noon" by G. Wilcox. At the other end, right side up, as its last entry, Wall's diary includes a first attempt at a literary sketch of "one of the handsomest main streets in New England," with its "curvilinear road" and "beautiful collection of specimens from the forest." "How amusing and productive of reflection it is," Wall declared, "to gaze from here upon the busy world in miniature below, perhaps imagining [him] oneself to be Jupiter looking down from Olympus, when he, according to Homer, 'With his broad eye, the subject world surveys.'"[11] As Wall described the view from his office window, he aspired to become a professional writer within a changing market for white-collar work. As they sat in their boardinghouses in solitary reveries at night, or stared around their offices in boredom during the day, young men cultivated a literary taste for their experience.

The stories of democratic character unfold as a contingent and hesitant process of self-making. One privilege of success is to choose what errors, or what Franklin's *Autobiography* called errata, to leave as lessons in the finished prose of lives "fit to be written." But handwritten manuscripts written by clerks leave more equivocal scars from the business of living. Wall, for instance, has crossed out "look down" in favor of "gaze," and substituted "oneself" for "him," in order to convey a more impersonal and literary persona. Note that Wall qualifies the purpose of his diary on its first page by striking out the word "writing": with a diary, one desires "to pass an evening in reading, [writing], meditation, or for the purpose of communicating a few of his ideas to paper."[12] Merely communicating ideas to paper does not quite count as "writing." For that term Wall reserves a special dignity, skill, talent, and social prestige belied by his diary's editing and revision—the material signs of manual labor that are effaced in print. As they sought to reproduce norms of literary mastery in their diaries, clerks and the generations of students who followed them learned to cultivate moral authority not by performing social duties but by turning their faces to the pages of books.

Identified with solitary reading and writing, middle-class character became an object of literary imagination, a rhetorical performance that occurs on the blank stage of the text, before an audience of one. Like Caleb Wall, Jonathan Hills toys in his diary with the persona of a professional writer, escaping the dull routines of his own life in authorial omniscience. Hill becomes exasperated with the use of "I" at the beginning of every entry: "What method can be devised for getting rid of that everlasting 'Today I.' . . . But just for the sake of experiment suppose we leave this part off for a time and let the date supply its place."[13] The crossed-out words, the awkward grammar, the blots of ink, the poor spelling, the fragments of thought, indeed the use of "I": moral life became a literary performance, in which the messy business of living disappears from view. In all of these marks of correction and criticism, middle-class clerks sought to displace their routine and mechanical skill with the pen—and the blankness of prospects that all manual labor represented to them—with demonstrations of their potential for higher work of the head. With a self-conscious, impersonal concern for method, what Hill calls the changing "use of words" "as far as form is concerned," clerks transformed older habits of moral accounting into disciplines of reading and writing—the duty owed to the text of experience. This was moral authority both abstracted from everyday life and naturalized in the humble "book" of a clerk's life.

The modern history of moral life is not about how stories end, but how they evolve through the spectrum of cultural forms by which individuals imagine potential futures and possible lives. These forms are material and symbolic, the incremental and rudimentary shapes that Wall, Hill, and other clerks gave character in their scripts and sketches. They are also institutional, the "steps" of the modern educational system. The Boston clerk, Charles French, for example, would regret his decision not to stay in school. In 1856, he wrote: "I now wish that I had staid [*sic*] longer at school, for although I can read and write and spell well enough, yet in my composition and knowledge of higher branches I am not fully pasted up [*sic*] 'A willful man will have his way' and I was rather willful about going to school any longer when I was 14 years of age."[14] Each time French complained about the "interest" of his journal, he was perhaps reminded not only of the tangible things he might have learned about "composition and the higher branches," but also of some amorphous prospects that would remain forever closed: "Ah! I look back with feelings of regret to my school days . . . I am only sorry now that I did not continue at school for 3 years or more, and aimed at what I cannot now in years of study: a good education. My path is forever before me, and I must follow it."[15] The ideal of a good education would remind French of some control he had surrendered, of another path than the one "forever before me," that "I must follow"—as though by not continuing his studies, he could never be the author of his life, whatever he might still learn of composition. In institutions like the school—"immaculate public spaces," as Theodore Roethke put it, when seen through French's nostalgia and regret—the duplication of persons and objects would furnish democratic culture with powerful standards of moral authority, the path of one's own unrealized promise.

The young men in this book would achieve only modest distinction, at best. They could not claim the prerogatives of the rich and famous, to convert their success into moral examples of national character, lessons about qualities of mind or spirit that poor, friendless boys would do well to emulate. Their stories would not, like Dr. Franklin's, be read over and over outside the classroom by youth seeking to rise, or studied inside the classroom as part of a modern canon of American literature. And yet they left a paper trail of sorts, among the fragments that make up the history of ordinary lives. Caleb Wall's brother would throw a big party to honor his fifty years as a journalist in Worcester, Massachusetts; Wall gave a speech to the local dignitaries in which, as he had done in his diary fifty years earlier, he sketched the appearance of the street where he found his first job.[16] Edward Tailer's death was noticed in the *New York Times,* perhaps as much for the historical value of the diary he had kept as for being a member of an "Old New York Family": "These social chronicles contain considerable of public interest, including personal notes of Lincoln, civil war subjects, politics and a history of the city for more than sixty years." At Tailer's death, his diaries—which he had "bound yearly and retained in his library"—made news, not as a personal document but rather as a record of city life, containing newspaper clippings and sundry materials of "public interest."[17] Henry Patterson would open a hardware store in Manhattan in 1848, Patterson Brothers, and was described by R. G. Dun's credit ledger in 1864 as "highly spoken of as a man of excellt char very correct and responsible."[18] The store remained in business for more than a century—a tribute, as one descendent put it in the 1930s, to the character of its founder and a tradition of integrity carried on by later generations of young men.[19] After several years as a clerk, Benjamin Tilton also entered the fray of business in Manhattan. He survived the bankruptcy of his first firm, Tilton, Worrall & Macy, and opened Tilton Carriages. In 1870, R. G. Dun gave him a rather poor rating: "Lacks bus[iness] tact, has been assisted by his personal friends for a long time, has never succeeded w. any of his undertakings, is socially popular and tries hard to succeed, he has not much individual responsibility."[20] Evidently, Tilton's sentimental rehearsal of domestic character in his diary did not prepare him for the practical ends of business, or develop the "individual responsibility" that, in theory, remains the golden rule of liberal capitalism. And Charles French would leave in his will a "strange and unexpected" gift of $2,000 to the public schools of Lexington, Massachusetts, to be spent on silver medals for scholarships in grammar and high schools— tokens of the educational achievement that he had felt deprived of his entire life.[21]

Regardless of what happened to them in later life, nineteenth-century clerks left behind the lessons of their aspiration. Their diaries and other artifacts of moral life allow us to see the formation of democratic character as a work in progress. Young men did not simply stumble upon a future that, as Thomas Mellon portrays it, was ready for the taking by ambitious youth fulfilling their destiny. To account for their futures, clerks learned to look inward in new ways, to engage in a dialogue with their moral Other. As young men entered the strange landscape of adulthood, they projected themselves into mental and emotional horizons of their own making, through the standard objects and implements of mass literacy. Rather than submerging the self within an anonymous and abstract public sphere that emerged with print culture, the literary practices of ordinary people embodied aspiration in tangibly material forms of self-reflection and sociability, in patterns of intimacy and feeling that defy customary distinctions between the conventional and the personal. As they recorded thoughts and feelings in the private ledger of the diary, exchanged letters with family, engaged lovers and friends in conversation, or shared popular novels, young men were creating stories for their lives in market culture.

Like the hundreds of diaries that now lie in archives and historical societies across the United States, debris from the literary landscape of nineteenth-century America has washed up on the shores of the twenty-first century. A remnant of that landscape remains at Astor Place in New York City, where one can still see a piece of Clinton Hall, the impressive building the New York Mercantile Library built when it moved uptown (fig. 22). Later in the nineteenth century, after opening its entrance to the new subway system, the library would move uptown again, to Forty-Eighth Street, where it continues to cater to businessmen and women looking for a little repose in midtown Manhattan during their lunch hours. Clinton Hall was torn down to make room for new buildings, testifying to the process of creative destruction by which market culture orients us to the marketplace rather than to the library or the museum, to the future rather than to the past (fig. 23). Instead of a "People's University" dedicated to the education of businessmen, Astor Place now features a Barnes and Noble

Figure 22 A small piece of Clinton Hall remains embedded in the walls of the Astor Place subway station, New York City, 2002. Not unlike modern systems of mass transit, institutions of public culture such as the New York Mercantile Library helped people navigate the complex, anonymous landscape of urban capitalism. Photograph by Laura Davis.

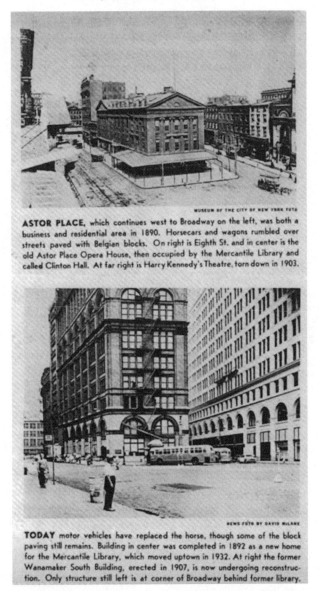

MUSEUM OF THE CITY OF NEW YORK FOTO

ASTOR PLACE, which continues west to Broadway on the left, was both a business and residential area in 1890. Horsecars and wagons rumbled over streets paved with Belgian blocks. On right is Eighth St. and in center is the old Astor Place Opera House, then occupied by the Mercantile Library and called Clinton Hall. At far right is Harry Kennedy's Theatre, torn down in 1903.

NEWS FOTO BY DAVID McLANE

TODAY motor vehicles have replaced the horse, though some of the block paving still remains. Building in center was completed in 1892 as a new home for the Mercantile Library, which moved uptown in 1932. At right the former Wanamaker South Building, erected in 1907, is now undergoing reconstruction. Only structure still left is at corner of Broadway behind former library.

Figure 23 "New York's Changing Scene," *New York Daily News*, 11 September 1955, p. 40. New York Daily News, L.P., reprinted with permission.

bookstore and a Starbucks coffee shop. These establishments continue to serve the popular taste for reading and sociability that the New York Mercantile Library had served in the same location, decades before.

Even as the physical sites of the literary landscape of the nineteenth century have given way to new spaces of commercial leisure and entertain-

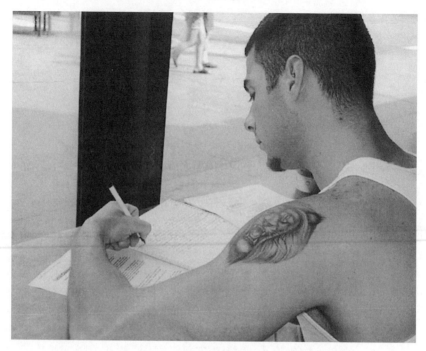

Figure 24   Marcel Luchese, a student at a community college in Brooklyn, practices business correspondence at a coffee shop at Astor Place, 2002. Photograph by Laura Davis.

ment, the literary practices of character survive as well in the skills with which ambitious young people continue to seek their places in the adult world of work. Take, for instance, a young man named Marcel Luchese who, one day in July 2002, had wound up, like so many nineteenth-century clerks, at Astor Place (fig. 24). Enrolled at a community college in Brooklyn, he had come to Manhattan to go the Public Library on Fifth Avenue, which turned out to be closed. Marcel sat at the window of Starbucks, writing a letter for a course he was taking in business communications. As he wrote in his spiral notebook, he was surrounded by other young men, sitting by themselves, reading books or newspapers. As antebellum clerks did before him, Marcel Luchese pursues economic mobility and social status by struggling with the implements and skills of literacy. At each of their "steps" up the educational ladder, students are confronted with the blank pages of paper, tests of their capacity to improve themselves. If Marcel is successful in his advance through the competitive ranks of school, he too will learn to fill the blank page with evidence of his dexterity and facility with words. Progress in the culture of literacy earns the good student the capital of character: the skills and knowledge of advanced education, but also the taste for one's own story, the ability to see vistas rather than dead ends in the path of life.

The business of living is a process of editing and revision. As a result, our modern social lessons are both singular and standard: the practical advice that Thomas Mellon stumbled upon in Benjamin Franklin's life, and the disembodied historical truths about capitalism that Max Weber took from a different edition. Their interpretations of Franklin are reverse sides of the same coin of character, like the dialogue one has with one's moral Other, or the conversation between youth and age. As we have seen, both melancholy and hope are moods of democratic philosophy, ways to account for the future from the limited horizons of the ordinary and the everyday. In a day no less than a life, antebellum clerks rationalized moral authority, finding pieces of the modern self in the different spaces of middle-class manhood and in the entries of their diaries. So too, students today move between fatalism and optimism as they confront the possibilities and limits of autonomy in their own lives, placing themselves between the lines of college-ruled paper that chart the modern course of character. Amid the dust of institutions and through long afternoons of tedium, ordinary people try to become equal to their aspirations, seeking a freedom foreclosed and foretold.

Notes

Introduction

1. Charles French, Diary, 7 May 1857–24 April 1859 (Massachusetts Historical Society), vol. 5, 290.

2. As Daniel Howe observes, "The expansion of the market economy widened the scope for personal autonomy on a scale previously unparalleled: choices of goods and services to consume, choice of occupations to follow, choice of life styles and identities." Daniel Walker Howe, *Making the American Self: Jonathan Edwards to Abraham Lincoln* (Cambridge: Harvard University Press, 1997), 116. Among the numerous studies documenting the social and cultural changes that accompanied American commercial and industrial development, see Charles Sellers, *The Market Revolution: Jacksonian America, 1815–1846* (New York: Oxford University Press, 1991); Paul Johnson, *A Shopkeeper's Millennium: Society and Revivals in Rochester, New York, 1815–1837* (New York: Hill and Wang, 1978); Alan Dawley, *Class and Community: The Industrial Revolution in Lynn* (Cambridge: Harvard University Press, 1976); Mary Ryan, *Cradle of the Middle Class: The Family in Oneida County, New York, 1790–1865* (Cambridge: Cambridge University Press, 1981). For studies in economic history that analyze the American transition to modern capitalism, see Christopher Clark, *The Roots of Rural Capitalism: Western Massachusetts, 1780–1860* (Ithaca: Cornell University Press, 1990); Winifred Barr, *From Marketplaces to a Market Economy: The Transformation of Rural Massachusetts, 1750–1850* (Chicago: University of Chicago Press, 1994); James Henretta, *The Origins of American Capitalism: Collected Essays* (Boston: Northeastern University Press, 1991); and Gordon Wood, "Inventing American Capitalism," *New York Review of Books,* 9 June 1994. For historical overviews of commercial enterprise in particular, see C. Joseph Pusateri, *A History of American Business* (Arlington Heights, Ill.: Harlan Davidson, 1988), and Stuart Bruchey, *Enterprise: The Dynamic Economy of a Free People* (Cambridge: Harvard University Press, 1990).

3. Sellers, *Market Revolution.* Also see Immanuel Wallerstein, *The Modern World System III* (New York: Academic Press, 1989), 193–256.

4. Jean-Christophe Agnew, *Worlds Apart: The Market and the Theater in Anglo-American Thought, 1550–1750* (Cambridge: Cambridge University Press, 1986), 4, 9; also see Agnew, "The Threshold of Exchange: Speculations on the Market," *Radical History Review* 21 (fall 1979): 99–118. The topic of market culture has been explored recently in Thomas Haskell and Richard Teichgraeber, eds., *The Culture of the Market: Historical Essays* (Cambridge: Cambridge University Press, 1993). Joyce Appleby explores the imagination of the market in the early United States in *Capitalism and a New Social Order: The Republican Vision of the 1790s* (New York: New York University Press, 1984). For a provocative argument about the relationship of capitalist enterprise to moral cognition, see Thomas Haskell, "Capitalism and the Origins of the Humanitarian Sensibility," parts 1 and 2, *American Historical Review* 90, no. 2 (April 1985): 339–61; no. 3 (June 1985): 547–66.

5. Warren Susman, *Culture as History: The Transformation of American Society in the Twentieth Century* (New York: Pantheon Books, 1984), 273–74.

6. As Scott Casper has noted, character increasingly referred to habitual conduct—to "habits of industry, temperance, piety," including private habits—that determined one's success or failure, a "prerequisite to becoming a self-made man or true Christian." Scott Casper, *Constructing American Lives: Biography and Culture in Nineteenth-Century America* (Chapel Hill: University of North Carolina Press, 1999), 7.

7. David Riesman, *The Lonely Crowd: A Study of the Changing American Character* (New Haven: Yale University Press, 1961).

8. As John Tosh has observed, "The idea that what a man did in his working life was an authentic expression of his individuality was one of the most characteristic—and enduring—features of middle-class masculinity." John Tosh, "What Should Historians Do with Masculinity? Reflections on Nineteenth-Century Britain," *History Workshop Journal* 38 (1994): 178–202, at 186. On the history of manhood in the nineteenth century, see Anthony Rotundo, *American Manhood: Transformations in Masculinity from the Revolution to the Modern Era* (New York: Basic Books, 1993); Mark C. Carnes and Clyde Griffen, *Meanings for Manhood: Constructions of Masculinity in Victorian America* (Chicago: University of Chicago Press, 1998). For an urban, working-class perspective on manhood and civic identity, see Amy Greenberg, *Cause for Alarm: The Volunteer Fire Department in the Nineteenth-Century City* (Princeton: Princeton University Press, 1998).

9. The lives of businessmen were among the five most popular categories of autobiographies published from the 1870s to the 1930s. Increasingly, moral character was understood as being produced in the context of work rather than genteel ease, as when three-fourths of the five hundred businessmen interviewed for an 1883 survey attributed their success to the habits of labor they had learned in childhood. These habits gave them the self-reliance and perseverance necessary to succeed as an individual in adult life. Diane Bjorklund, *Interpreting the Self: Two Hundred Years of American Autobiography* (Chicago: University of Chicago Press, 1998), 68, 79. Also see John Cawelti, *Apostles of the Self-Made Man: Changing Concepts of Success in America* (Chicago: University of Chicago Press, 1965). By 1874, this story was already so familiar that William Dean Howells opened his novel, *The Rise of Silas Lapham,* with scenes in which a journalist renders the character of a successful paint merchant in what had already become perfunctory clichés of self-making. From the 1870s through the end of the century, hundreds of success manuals were published in which character became the fundamental key to worldly success. In these books, as one historian notes, character became "a powerful and propitious tool of action," a "badge of spiritual membership in the large and amorphous mainstream known as the American middle class." Judy Hilkey, *Character Is Capital: Success Manuals and Manhood in Gilded Age America* (Chapel Hill: University of North Carolina Press, 1997), 127.

10. Max Weber, *The Protestant Ethic and the Spirit of Capitalism,* trans. by Talcott Parsons (New York: Scribner's, 1958 [1903]), 180–81. "One of the fundamental elements of the spirit of modern capitalism, and not only of that but of all modern culture, rational conduct on the basis of the idea of the calling, was born . . . from the spirit of Christian asceticism" (180).

11. Ibid., 182.

12. A mass middle class looked to consumption as a major means of social differentiation. See Richard Bushman, *The Refinement of America: Persons, Homes, Cities* (New York: Knopf, 1993). Also see Stuart Blumin, *The Emergence of the Middle Class: Social Experience in the American City, 1760–1900* (New York: Cambridge University Press, 1989), and Stephanie Coontz, *The Social Origins of Private Life: A History of American Families, 1600–1900* (New York: Verso, 1988).

13. Joyce Appleby, "New Cultural Heroes in the Early National Period," in *The Culture of the Market: Historical Essays,* ed. Thomas Haskell and Richard Teichgraeber (Cambridge: Cambridge University Press, 1994), 170.

14. Male rites of passage typically entail claims to social status and differ from female rites in the competitive and public form they take. According to anthropologist Michelle Rosaldo: "For a boy to become an adult, he must prove himself—his masculinity—among his peers.

And although all boys may succeed in reaching manhood, cultures treat this development as something that each individual has achieved." Quoted in Tosh, "Masculinity," 184.

15. For the history of the social meanings and material practices of handwriting, see Tamara Plakins Thornton, *Handwriting in America: A Cultural History* (New Haven: Yale University Press, 1996). Also see Ray Nash, *American Penmanship, 1800–1850* (Worcester, Mass.: American Antiquarian Society, 1969).

16. William James, "Talk to Teachers on Psychology and to Students on Some of Life's Ideals," in *William James: Writings 1878–1899* (New York: Library of America, 1992), 753. James elaborates on these assumptions when he discusses character in relation to biological habits of thought in "Brute and Human Intellect": With a twenty-year old woman, "her character is, in fact, finished in all respects. How inferior to her is a boy of twenty in all these respects. His character is still gelatinous, uncertain what shape to assume, 'trying it on' in every direction . . . a being of no definite contour. But this absence of prompt tendency in his brain to set into particular modes is the very condition that insures that it shall ultimately become so much more efficient than the women's. The very lack of preappointed trains of thought is the very condition by which general principles and heads of classification are formed; and the masculine brain deals with new and complex matter indirectly by means of induction, in a manner which the feminine method of direct intuition, admirably and rapidly as it performs within its limits, can vainly hope to cope with" (ibid., 949). Biological differences of sex and age determine the degree to which a young person can actively shape his or her own character. Because their habits of rational and abstract thought remain unformed, young men can deal with "new and complex matter" more efficiently than young women. A young man of twenty can meet the exigencies of adult experience by cultivating character because his habits are not yet fixed; a woman must, presumably, be protected from experience because she can develop no new habits to help her deal with the complexity and change that adult autonomy brings. The masculine tendency to rational and abstract thinking is an advantage in a brain whose limits have not been fixed within "preappointed trains of thought." For an analysis of the gendering of reason in Western philosophy, see Genevieve Lloyd, *The Man of Reason: "Male" and "Female" in Western Philosophy* (Minneapolis: University of Minnesota Press, 1984).

17. David Shields has recently asked, "Can literary history be written without a chronology of classics, without fixing upon master texts, and without depending upon a rhetoric of revisionism or a vision of a new canon?" David S. Shields, *Civil Tongues and Polite Letters in British America* (Chapel Hill: University of North Carolina Press, 1997). As a work of literary history, this book seeks to describe the category of the "literary" as it was constituted within a particular social and historical context, in relation to objects and practices—such as conversation, letter writing, oratory, diaries, and the like—that in our time have been largely displaced, at least in institutional settings, by the expert reading of master texts.

18. Martha Nussbaum, *Love's Knowledge: Essays on Philosophy and Literature* (New York: Oxford University Press, 1990).

19. Burton Bledstein, *The Culture of Professionalism: The Middle Class and the Development of Higher Education in America* (New York: W. W. Norton, 1976), 27.

20. Since the nineteenth century, middlebrow culture has redefined the very meaning of literary taste for market culture. It challenged, as Janice Radway notes, the "double discourse of value that has served to ground the humanism of modern Western thought for some two hundred years or more," a discourse that distinguishes fixed, universal, and transcendent values" from "economic, materially determined values." Janice Radway, *A Feeling for Books: The Book-of-the-Month Club, Literary Taste, and Middle-Class Desire* (Chapel Hill: University of North Carolina Press, 1997), 152.

21. Brian Roberts, *American Alchemy: The California Gold Rush and Middle-Class Culture* (Chapel Hill: University of North Carolina Press, 2000), 33. On work and middle-class identity, also see Stuart Blumin, *Emergence of the Middle Class*, and Bledstein, *Culture of Professionalism*.

22. For social and cultural histories of the nineteenth-century middle class, see Ryan,

Cradle of the Middle Class; Karen Haltunnen, *Confidence Men and Painted Women: A Study of Middle-Class Culture in America, 1830–1870* (New Haven: Yale University Press, 1982). Also see Burton Bledstein and Robert D. Johnson, *The Middling Sorts: Explorations in the History of the American Middle Class* (New York: Routledge, 2001), and Sven Beckert, *The Monied Metropolis: New York City and the Consolidation of the American Bourgeoisie, 1850–1896* (New York: Cambridge University Press, 2001).

23. John Guillory, *Cultural Capital: The Problem of Literary Canon Formation* (Chicago: University of Chicago Press, 1993), xi.

24. Jean Bethke Elshtain, "Political Theory and Moral Responsibility," in *In Face of the Facts: Moral Inquiry in American Scholarship,* ed. Richard Wightman Fox and Robert B. Westbrook (Cambridge: Cambridge University Press, 1998), 54. Elshtain argues for the need for moral inquiry to move from "narratives of closure" where "everything is known in advance, all the categories are specified, and all the possibilities are laid out," to "narratives of possibility" that can help us see everyday life itself as a rich, interesting work in process.

25. Over the nineteenth century, the values of national manhood taught white men "to internalize and balance incompatible and even antagonistic claims as an expression of their 'own' personal civic responsibility," as Dana Nelson argues. "The precondition for the white man's authorization as a civic manager would be his ability to model the ideal of national unity in his own person: to train his own self-difference into a rationally ordered singularity. In this way, the new fraternal modeling of white manhood would accumulate imperatives for self-management and self-regimentation." As Nelson points out, "White manhood's identification with national unity has worked historically to restrict others from achieving full entitlement in the United States." Dana D. Nelson, *National Manhood: Capitalist Citizenship and the Imagined Fraternity of White Men* (Durham, N.C.: Duke University Press, 1998), 12, 11, 27. For other work on civic identity from the perspectives of race, class, and gender, see Bruce Burgett, *Sentimental Bodies: Sex, Gender, and Citizenship in the Early Republic* (Princeton: Princeton University Press, 1998); Russ Castronovo, *Necro Citizenship: Death, Eroticism, and the Public Sphere in the Nineteenth-Century United States* (Durham, N.C.: Duke University Press, 2001); Lauren Berlant, *The Queen of America Goes to Washington City: Essays on Sex and Citizenship* (Durham, N.C.: Duke University Press, 1997). On the development of popular ideals of democracy and America's self-image, see Andrew Burstein, *Sentimental Democracy: The Evolution of America's Romantic Self-Image* (New York: Hill and Wang, 1999).

26. As Richard Sennett has recently asked: "How do we decide what is of lasting value in ourselves in a society which is impatient, which focuses on the immediate moment?" Amid economic circumstances hostile to the continuity of identity, "How do we create long-term purposes and durable social relations in a short-term society?" In cultivating character, individuals strive to develop a moral identity that makes sense cumulatively of one's experience, as the result of one's own actions and commitments. As Sennett puts it, "Character depends on connections to the world—the ethical value we place on our own desires and our relations with others." Character allows people to make sense of their lives as a story, and to feel that no matter how low their social standing, they are the authors of their lives. And, in cultivating character, people strive to convey this identity to others, to be recognized by their neighbors as exemplary or distinctive in some way according to commonly shared social values. Richard Sennett, *The Corrosion of Character: The Personal Consequences of Work in the New Capitalism* (New York: W. W. Norton, 1998), 10.

27. Stanley Cavell, *This New and Yet Unapproachable America: Lectures after Emerson after Wittgenstein* (Albuquerque, N.M.: Living Batch Press, 1989), 108–9. The political implications of Cavell's thinking about Thoreau are developed in relation to a democratic tradition of cultivation in Brian Walker, "Thoreau's Alternative Economy: Work, Liberty, and Democratic Cultivation," *American Political Science Review* 92, no. 4 (December 1998): 1–12.

28. Ralph Waldo Emerson, "Self-Reliance," in *Essays and Lectures* (New York: Library of America, 1983), 271.

Chapter One

1. E. E. Belding, Diary, 31 May 1834 (Winterthur Library).

2. Joseph Kett, *Rites of Passage: Adolescence in America, 1790 to the Present* (New York: Basic Books, 1977), 31. Also see Harvey Graff, *Conflicting Paths: Growing Up in America* (Cambridge: Harvard University Press, 1995).

3. Enos White, Diary and Account Book, 26 November 1821 (Winterthur Library), 1. He moves back to his father's house on the next entry on the same page, dated 22 May 1822. On page two, he dates his leaving again on 24 March 1823.

4. William Hoffman, Diary, 1847–1850 (New-York Historical Society), 107.

5. Ibid., 217.

6. Ibid., 104.

7. Cited in Lucia McMahon, "While Our Souls Together Blend: Narrating a Romantic Readershp in the Early Republic," in *An Emotional History of the United States,* ed. Peter Stearns and Jan Lewis (New York: New York University Press, 1998), 74.

8. Laurel Thatcher Ulrich, *A Mid-Wife's Tale: The Life of Martha Ballard, Based on Her Diary, 1785–1812* (New York: Knopf, 1990), 9. Scholarly interest in the historical value of diaries typically has depended on the celebrity of their authors. Since the development in the 1960s of social and cultural history "from the bottom up," however, scholars such as Ulrich have used diaries in sophisticated ways to gain access to the psychology or mentalité of individuals who were, until recently, lost from the public record. For historical overviews of the diary as a literary genre, see Steven Kagle, *Early Nineteenth-Century American Diary Literature* (Boston: Twayne, 1986). Literary scholars typically have been interested in diaries for what they tell us about the aesthetic, intellectual, or biographical concerns that informed the writer's published work. See for instance Lawrence Rosenwald, *Emerson and the Art of the Diary* (New York: Oxford University Press, 1989). Recent scholarship on women's literary culture has helped us to appreciate diaries as "private writing," which ordinary people used in complex ways when other formal avenues of publication and authorship were unavailable. See Elizabeth Hampsten, *Read This Only to Yourself: The Private Writings of Midwestern Women, 1880–1910* (Bloomington: Indiana University Press, 1982); Suzanne L. Bunkers and Cynthia A. Huff, eds., *Inscribing the Daily: Critical Essays on Women's Diaries* (Amherst: University of Massachusetts Press, 1996). On the commonplace tradition and its relation to female literary culture in late eighteenth-century America, see Catherine La Courreye Blecki and Karin A. Wulf, eds., *Milcah Martha Moore's Book: A Commonplace Book from Revolutionary America* (University Park: Pennsylvania State University Press, 1997). For an imaginative analysis of the relation of the commonplace tradition to the "cultural pedagogies" of gender and class in nineteenth-century America, see Susan Miller, *Assuming the Positions: Cultural Pedagogy and the Politics of Commonplace Writing* (Pittsburgh, Penn.: University of Pittsburgh Press, 1998).

9. For example, see Toby Ditz, "Shipwrecked; or, Masculinity Imperiled: Mercantile Representations of Failure and the Gendered Self in Eighteenth-Century Philadelphia," *Journal of American History* 81 (June 1994): 51–80.

10. Michel Foucault, *Technologies of the Self: A Seminar with Michel Foucault,* ed. Luther Martin, Huck Gutman, and Patrick Hutton (Amherst: University of Massachusetts Press, 1988), 18.

11. For recent scholarship on the role of the diary in modern individualism, exploring its relationship to autobiography and the discipline of the modern "subject," see Felicity Nussbaum, *The Autobiographical Subject: Gender and Ideology in Eighteenth-Century England* (Baltimore: Johns Hopkins University Press, 1989); Stuart Sherman, *Telling Time: Clocks, Diaries, and English Diurnal Form, 1660–1785* (Chicago: University of Chicago Press, 1996). Susan Imbarrato contrasts the prevalence of the seventeenth-century journal with the eighteenth-century American autobiography to argue for the transition from self-examination to self-expression, for the emergence of a new cultural authority of individual subjectivity. See Susan Clair Imbarrato, *Declarations of Independency in Eighteenth-Century American Auto-*

biography (Knoxville: University of Tennessee Press, 1998). For broader perspectives on the development of Western models of individual identity, see Roy Porter, ed., *Rewriting the Self: Histories from the Renaissance to the Present* (New York: Routledge, 1997).

12. John Locke, *An Essay Concerning Human Understanding,* ed. Peter H. Nidditch (Oxford: Clarendon, 1975 [1690]), 104. As Tamara Thornton points out, the central metaphor in Locke's educational philosophy, the tabula rasa, drew upon his practical experience as a tutor of handwriting. Tamara Plakins Thornton, *Handwriting in America* (New Haven: Yale University Press, 1996), 1.

13. J. A. Simpson and E. S. C. Weiner, eds., *Oxford English Dictionary,* vol. 3, 2d ed. (Oxford: Clarendon, 1989), 31. Liberal theorists drew on the pedagogical tradition of civic humanism to make their argument about the qualities that were requisite to the citizens of a modern, free state. See Daniel Walker Howe, *Making the American Self* (Cambridge: Harvard University Press, 1997).

14. In his *Rhetoric* Aristotle attributes persuasive power to the attributes of speakers rather than to the content of what they say (logos), or the emotions they inspire in their audience (pathos). "[There is persuasion] through character whenever the speech is spoken in such a way as to make the speaker worthy of credence." Aristotle, *On Rhetoric: A Theory of Civic Discourse,* translated by George Kennedy (New York: Oxford University Press, 1991), 38.

15. John Stuart Mill, *On Liberty* (London: J. W. Parker, 1859), 108. Cited in the Oxford English Dictionary.

16. In this sense, character represents an achievement of individuality that has been a recurrent concern of Western philosophers ranging from Socrates, Pascal, and Kierkegaard to Emerson, Thoreau, Dewey, and Foucault. "To create a self is to succeed in becoming someone, in becoming a character," as Alexander Nehemas puts it. It is to acquire "a set of features and a mode of life that set one apart from the rest of the world and make one memorable not only for what one did or said but for whom one was." Alexander Nehemas, *The Art of Living: Socratic Reflections from Plato to Foucault* (Berkeley: University of California Press, 1998), 5. For a psychoanalytical approach to "characterology" that focuses on creativity, see Elisabeth Young-Bruehl, *Creative Characters* (New York: Routledge, 1991). One of the problems with the concept of character historically is that it has fallen between competing paradigms of ethical philosophy and moral education. For a definition and analysis of the concept within the philosophical tradition, see Joel Kupperman, *Character* (New York: Oxford University Press, 1991). For one of the more sophisticated histories of the concept of character in relation to the shifting disciplines of knowledge, see Richard McKeon, "Character and the Arts and Disciplines," *Ethics* 78, no. 2 (January 1968): 109–23. For a consideration of the relation between ethics and pragmatism in twentieth-century philosophy, see Richard Shusterman, *Practicing Philosophy: Pragmatism and the Philosophical Life* (New York: Routledge, 1997).

17. The fundamental attribute of a liberally educated person from which most if not all of the subsequent theories arise is the "ideal of the wholeness of the individual." Sheldon Rothblatt, "The Limbs of Osiris: Liberal Education in the English-Speaking World," in *The European and American University since 1800: Historical and Sociological Essays,* ed. Sheldon Rothblatt and Bjorn Wittrock (Cambridge: Cambridge University Press, 1993), 19–73, at 22. On the liberal arts tradition, see Bruce Kimball, *Orators and Philosophers: A History of the Idea of Liberal Education* (New York: Columbia Teachers College Press, 1986).

18. Ian Hunter, *Rethinking the School: Subjectivity, Bureaucracy, Criticism* (New York: St. Martin's, 1994), 55; Stephen Greenblatt, *Renaissance Self-Fashioning from More to Shakespeare* (Chicago: University of Chicago Press, 1980), 1, 2. Mary Kelley demonstrates how learned women gained access to this power of self-fashioning through various literate practices in nineteenth-century America. Mary Kelley, "Reading Women/Women Reading: The Making of Learned Women in Antebellum America," *Journal of American History* 83 (September 1996): 401–28.

19. John Locke, "Some Thoughts Concerning Reading and Study for a Gentleman" (1703), in *The Educational Writings of John Locke,* ed. James Axtell (London: Cambridge University Press, 1968), 397.

20. Cited in George Washington's *Rules of Civility and Decent Behavior in Company and Conversation*, ed. Charles Moore (Boston: Houghton Mifflin, 1926): "These maxims were so fully exemplified in George Washington's life that biographers have regarded them as formative influences in the development of his character" (ix).

21. Howe, *Making the American Self,* 116.

22. See Charles Taylor, *Sources of the Self: The Making of Modern Identity* (Cambridge: Harvard University Press, 1989).

23. Hunter, *Rethinking the School,* 55, 57, 55.

24. Ibid., 56. Christian pastoral education "did not consist in the transmission of ideas or values whose material determination and true content lay elsewhere, in an economy that required docile workers, or in a psychology undergoing social repression. It instead consisted in the transmission of an ensemble of ethical techniques and practices."

25. For an outstanding assessment of the concept of character in the intellectual history of liberalism, see Stefan Collini, "The Idea of Character in Victorian Political Thought," *Transactions of the Royal Historical Society,* 5th ser., 35 (London, 1985): 29–50. See also Collini's *Public Moralists: Political Thought and Intellectual Life in Britain, 1850–1930* (Oxford: Clarendon, 1991). For useful accounts of the term in the transatlantic, intellectual context of cultural reform, see Joan Shelley Rubin, *The Making of Middlebrow Culture* (Chapel Hill: University of North Carolina Press, 1992). On the "Victorian connection" that linked cultural reformers across the Atlantic, see David D. Hall, "The Victorian Connection," in *Victorian America,* ed. Daniel Walker Howe (Philadelphia: University of Pennsylvania Press, 1976), 81–94. Other useful discussions of character include Scott Casper, *Constructing American Lives: Biography and Culture in Nineteenth-Century America* (Chapel Hill: University of North Carolina Press, 1999); and David MacLeod, *Building Character in the American Boy: The Boy Scouts, YMCA, and Their Forerunners* (Madison: University of Wisconsin Press, 1983).

26. Collini, *Public Moralists,* 112.

27. William Alcott, *The Young Man's Guide,* 16th ed. (Boston: T. R. Marvin, 1846), 33.

28. See Horace Mann's reports to the Massachusetts Board of Education, in Lawrence Cremin, ed., *The Republic and the School: The Education of Free Men* (New York: Teachers College, Columbia University, 1957). "Public school systems existed to shape behavior and attitudes, alleviate social problems, and reinforce a social structure under stress. In this context, the character of pupils remained a far greater concern than their minds." Michael Katz, "The Origins of Public Education: A Reassessment," in *The Social History of American Education,* ed. B. Edward McClellan and William J. Reese (Urbana: University of Illinois Press, 1988), 109.

29. Henry Anstince, stationer and account book manufacturer, New York, 1849 (American Antiquarian Society).

30. James Cunningham, Journal, 1849 (American Antiquarian Society).

31. See for instance the subtitle of Amos Armsby's Pocket Diary for 1853: *For registering events of past or present occurrence, for the use of manufacturers, merchants, housekeepers, mechanics and Professional Men.* Published annually by Denston and Company, Cambridgeport, Massachusetts, 1853. Also see *Diary and Memorandum Book for 1865, containing a blank space for Every Day in the Year, Cash Account, Bills Payable and Receivable, and Memoranda.* Published annually for The Trade, 1865. (American Antiquarian Society).

32. "The business world had long defined handwriting as an exclusively male activity," Thornton notes, and the "mercantile hand was restricted to and expressive of an exclusively masculine domain" (Thornton, *Handwriting in America,* 70).

33. Larzer Ziff, "Upon What Pretext: The Book and Literary History," *Proceedings of the American Antiquarian Society* 95 (1985): 297–316. As David Hall has emphasized, "We inherit and transmit anew a stock of assumptions about the act of reading, assumptions that intervene between us and the words that we encounter." David D. Hall, "The Old and the New: Literacy and Reading in Eighteenth-Century America," Speaker Series 14, ed. Lillian Bridwell-Bowles (Minneapolis: Center for Interdisciplinary Studies of Writing and Composition, University of Minnesota, 1999), 10.

34. Foucault, *Technologies of the Self*, 43. Also see Foucault, *The Care of the Self*, trans. Robert Hurley (New York: Random House, 1986).

35. Jeffrey Minson, *Question of Conduct: Sexual Harassment, Citizenship, Government* (New York: St. Martin's, 1993), 21.

36. "A relation developed between writing and vigilance. Attention was paid to nuances of life, mood, and reading, and the experience of oneself was intensified and widened by virtue of this act of writing." Foucault, *Technologies of the Self*, 27.

37. For this reason, Epictetus defined the primary task of philosophy as control over one's thoughts: "We ought not to accept a mental representation unsubjected to examination." This is not a generalized meditation on truth or a specialized investigation of reality but rather an ongoing attention that one brings to one's experience, which takes the form of a continual screening and monitoring of representations. "To keep constant watch over one's representations," as Foucault notes, "is not to try and decipher a meaning hidden beneath the visible . . . it is to assess the relationship between oneself and that which is represented, so as to accept in the relation to the self only that which can depend on the subject's free and rational choice." Foucault, *Technologies of the Self*, 58, 65.

38. Mariana Valverde, *Diseases of the Will: Alcohol and the Dilemmas of Freedom* (New York: Cambridge University Press, 1998), 136, 140.

39. Quintillian quoted in Jocelyn Penny, *Wax Tablets of the Mind* (New York: Routledge, 1997), 178–79.

40. Quoted in Miller, *Assuming the Positions*, 23.

41. "Every Latin-literate individual started to compose a commonplace-book as soon as he could read and write reasonably accurately. It was formative and it was programmatic. It shaped the way he thought and determined the way he handled language." Ann Moss, *Printed Commonplace-Books and the Structuring of Renaissance Thought* (Oxford: Clarendon, 1996), viii.

42. John Locke, *A New Method of Making Common-Place Books* (London: Greenwood, 1706). On the survival of the commonplace book in early modern pedagogy, see Moss, *Commonplace-Books*, and Miller, *Assuming the Positions*.

43. Moss, *Commonplace-Books*, vi.

44. John Locke, *Some Thoughts Concerning Education and Of the Conduct of the Understanding*, ed. Ruth Grant and Nathan Tarcov (Indianapolis, Ind.: Hackett Publishing, 1996), 121.

45. George Jaques, Diary and Memorandum, doc. 372, diary 1/folder 1 (Winterthur Library).

46. Gerald Graff, *Professing Literature: An Institutional History* (Chicago: University of Chicago Press, 1987), 29.

47. I thank Tom Clayton for deciphering Jaques's writing here, and for pointing out the inconsistency of Greek characters in his transliteration of English words. Personal correspondence, October 4, 2002.

48. Academies offered very different educations to men and women; women were generally not expected to learn any foreign language but French. See Miller, *Assuming the Positions*, 56. Women's colleges founded after the Civil War adopted the classical curriculum—at the same moment when men's colleges were abandoning it—to challenge the "assumption that women were incapable of rigorous intellectual tasks." Graff, *Professing Literature*, 37.

49. For a thorough consideration of the historical function of the classical curriculum and the institutional production of cultural capital, see John Guillory, *Cultural Capital: The Problem of Literary Canon Formation* (Chicago: Chicago University Press, 1993).

50. J[onathan] Henry Hill, Diary, vol. 1, 1841 (American Antiquarian Society), 78.

51. The narrator first alludes to the bust to explain his not firing Bartleby at the first sign of his disobedience: "Had there been any thing ordinarily human about him, doubtless I should have violently dismissed him from the premises. But as it was, I should have as soon thought of turning my pale plaster-of-paris bust of Cicero out of doors." The analogy redefines Bartleby's non-ordinary quality as a nonhuman, static object. This suggests that Bartleby

might become a possession that the narrator prizes because of some special opportunity it offers him to identify with a sensibility outside of the ordinarily human. The plaster-of-Paris bust is a small, kitsch-like version of the nineteenth-century neoclassical figures that transformed individual American statesmen into timeless exemplars of a heroic, republican dignity. Like the busts the Fowlers displayed in their phrenological cabinet, or the banal, predictable portraits of great men, these objects were not prized for artistic quality, as realistic depictions of individual personality and personal appearance. Rather, they were valued for the idealized traits and "representative" types of character they made available for identification and emulation. The bust of Cicero thus represents an ideal aspiration to a civic prominence that Melville's narrator associates with rhetorical skill and ambition. Herman Melville, "Bartleby, the Scrivener," in *The Piazza Tales and Other Prose Pieces, 1839–1860* (Chicago: Northwestern University Press and the Newberry Library, 1987), 21.

52. Hill Diary, vol. 1, 64.

53. On 9 September 1841, Hill writes in vol. 1 of his diary: "I have but little worth recording today, scarcely enough to pay for writing a day. My reading has been confined to a very few pages and that few yielding but little profit. It seems almost useless for me to attempt studying anything. I know what is to become of me. I can do nothing and am almost discouraged. Classics go tremendous hard + why I know not. The case is soon to have an issue. Things look dark and ominous indeed." The next day, he wrote: "I had flattered myself that my every recitation would be a good one. But having discovered to the contrary no I had half finished it, I thrust it aside in disgust half resolving never to touch a book in that language. How long is this state of things to continue?" Hill Diary, 56, 57.

54. Bradley Cumings, Diary, 1836, 13.

55. Benjamin Tilton, Diary, 1841 (New York Mercantile Library), 1.

56. Hoffman Diary (1848), 81–82, 65–67.

57. Ibid., 77, 78, 80.

58. And yet, for Hoffman, no less than for the thousands of other readers of the *American Phrenological Journal*, this search for "improvement" and "advancement" manifests itself in the pursuit of economic mobility while also transcending it. Mental cultivation draws his attention from any present work in which he is engaged to some future moment when the present labor of reading will offer some tangible return as one's future character, which for men required a resolute and confident identification with, and devotion to, a particular vocation, or what would come to be called a "career." On the concept of a career, see Burton Bledstein, *The Culture of Professionalism: The Middle Class and the Development of Higher Education in America* (New York: Norton, 1976).

59. James L. Whittier, Diary, 1830–1831 (American Antiquarian Society).

60. According to the precepts of neoclassical rhetoric, the student who had obediently copied and saved this capital of culture would have acquired the means for asserting his own authority in civic discourse, as an orator or writer. This hoarding of culture and the facility with references is modeled finally on the relationship of teachers and students: the student "earns" his later capacity to speak or write with authority through the deference and obedience with which he responds to teachers. To appear learned is to demonstrate through quotation the quality and extent of one's "memory," the range of one's references.

61. Brian Stock, *Augustine the Reader: Meditation, Self-Knowledge, and the Ethics of Interpretation* (Cambridge: Harvard University Press, 1996).

62. Ian Watt, *The Rise of the Novel: Studies in Defoe, Richardson, and Fielding* (London: Chatto & Windus, 1957), 75. Watt cites Perry Miller and Thomas Johnson's observation that in New England, "almost every literate Puritan kept some sort of journal." Watt argues that Puritanism internalized the conscience, bringing "about a fundamental and in a sense democratic orientation in the social and literary outlook of its adherents, an orientation which was described by Milton in Paradise Lost: "To know / that which before us lies in daily life / is the prime wisdom (VIII 192–94)." On the popular culture of Puritan religious practice, see David D. Hall, *Worlds of Wonder, Days of Judgment: Popular Religious Belief in Early New England* (New York: Knopf, 1989); on the relationship of Protestant piety to Romantic habits

of feeling, see Colin Campbell, *The Romantic Ethic and the Spirit of Modern Consumerism* (Oxford: Basil Blackwell, 1987).

63. Hill Diary, vol. 3 (1845), 14.

64. Jacqueline S. Reinier, *From Virtue to Character: American Childhood, 1775–1850* (New York: Twayne, 1996), 89. On the Protestant orientation of educational institutions and their relation to moral education, see Carl Kaestle, *Pillars of the Republic: Common Schools and American Society, 1780–1860* (New York: Hill and Wang, 1983). For an overview of the familial and educational institutions that were assuming new importance in nineteenth-century moral education, see Edward B. McClellan, *Moral Education in America: Schools and the Shaping of Character from Colonial Times to the Present* (New York: Columbia Teachers College Press, 1999).

65. "Diary kept by an unknown student, 1833–1834," in the Manuscript and Rare Book Division, New York Public Library, Diaries, Box 2. Also see "Journal of a young religious zealot, 1853," in the Manuscript and Rare Book Division, New York Public Library, Diaries, Box 3.

66. Tilton Diary, 12–13.

67. Hill Diary, vol. 1, 15.

68. Cited in Graff, *Conflicting Paths,* 46. As Drake suggests, mothers were, by the nineteenth century, assuming the central role in a benevolent inculcation of domestic and Christian duty: "This she never did by protracted lectures, nor force and punishment, but mixed them up with our daily chores."

69. Albert Lane Norris, Diary, 30 April 1858, vol. 3, 33 (Winterthur Library), doc. 633.

70. Ibid., 7–8.

71. Hoffman Diary, 17 March 1848.

72. Ibid., 6 March 1848.

73. "For a few sabbaths past I have felt almost a horror upon the bare mention of church going. I know not why it is + if I cannot account for it seems to be my duty to rid myself of this feeling and I will endeavor to [do so] for the future." Hill Diary, 9 October 1841.

74. James B. Blake, Diary, 1851 (American Antiquarian Society); also see entry for 7 January 1851. Blake was elected mayor largely because of his work at the Worcester gasworks and for trying to improve air quality. He was fatally injured during an explosion at the gasworks in 1865. For biographical information, see *A Memorial of James Barnard Blake* (Worcester, 1871), at the American Antiquarian Society.

75. We might also think of this use of the diary as a practice of "visual piety." Mass production of images and new visual technologies encouraged Protestants to use the imagination as a vehicle for religious experience. See David Morgan, *Protestants and Pictures: Religion, Visual Culture, and the Age of American Mass Production* (New York: Oxford University Press, 1999), 269, 99–137.

76. Norris Diary, 31 December 1858, vol. 3, 24.

77. Blake Diary, 8 March 1851. Blake alludes to "copious" discourse, which was a prominent concern in works of Renaissance rhetoric such as Erasmus's *De Copia.*

78. Hill Diary, vol. 1, 15.

79. Like Jonathan Hill, Blake had received an academy education and was a Unitarian, and was inclined to value religion primarily as a form of moral improvement. Blake's use of Sunday and his observation about "professional Christians" reflected mid-nineteenth-century campaigns for cultural reform waged around the Sabbath. See Alexis McCrossen, *Holy Day, Holiday: A History of the American Sunday* (Ithaca: Cornell University Press, 2000).

80. Norbert Elias, "Time and Timing," in *On Civilization, Power, and Knowledge: Selected Writings,* ed. Stephen Mennell and Johan Goudsblom (Chicago: University of Chicago Press, 1998), 258.

81. In Roman antiquity, *liberales* meant both political freedom and the possession of wealth affording time for study. See Kimball, *Orators and Philosophers,* 7.

82. Mary Poovey, *A History of the Modern Fact: Problems of Knowledge in the Sciences of Wealth and Society* (Chicago: University of Chicago Press, 1998), 56, 64, 38. Standardization

of bookkeeping practices imposed norms on "what had been a loose and class-specific set of rules governing the use of place into a generally adoptable and more easily enforced set of regulations governing writing," subordinating the status and personality of the writer to the abstract imperative of accounting, the temporal and spatial "rule" imposed by the form of the diary. In this way, "the precision of arithmetic replaced the eloquence of speech as the instrument that produced both truth and virtue" (Poovey, 37, 55).

83. Benjamin Franklin, *The Autobiography* (New York: Library of America, 1990), 85.

84. White Diary, 1 December 1841, doc. 746, 94.

85. Hoffman Diary, 1.

86. Ibid., 81–82.

87. Edward Tailer, Diary, 8 June 1850.

88. Peter Von Geist, "Imaginary Conversations," *Knickerbocker Magazine* 24, no. 6 (December 1843): 535.

89. Timothy Shay Arthur, *Advice to Young Men on Their Duties and Conduct in Life* (Boston: Phillips Sampson & Co, 1855 [1847]), 20, 21.

90. William James, *The Principles of Psychology*, 2 vols. (1890), 1:127; quoted in Collini, "'Character' in Victorian Political Thought," 35.

91. Kett, *Pursuit of Knowledge*, 107.

92. Arthur, *Advice to Young Men*, 21.

93. Hill Diary, vol. 2 (19 November 1845): 159, 160.

94. Howe, *Making the American Self*, 12.

95. Howe, *Making the American Self*, 125. The political dimensions of these changes are addressed in Robert Wiebe, *Self-Rule: A Cultural History of American Democracy* (Chicago: University of Chicago Press, 1995); a useful discussion of the nineteenth-century work ethic remains Daniel T. Rodgers, *The Work Ethic in Industrial America, 1850–1920* (Chicago: University of Chicago Press, 1974).

96. Franklin, *Autobiography*, 14, 16. Franklin invokes penmanship as a metaphor for the process of acquiring virtue: "As those who aim at perfect Writing by imitating the engraved Copies, tho' they never reach the wish'd for Excellence of those Copies, their Hand is mended by the Endeavour, and is tolerable while it continues fair & legible" (87). For studies of Franklin in the context of early national print culture, see Larzer Ziff, *Writing in the New Nation: Prose, Print, and Politics in the Early United States* (New Haven: Yale University Press, 1991); Michael Warner, *The Letters of the Republic: Publication and the Public Sphere in Eighteenth-Century America* (Cambridge: Harvard University Press, 1990).

97. Ibid., 68.

98. For a summary and bibliography of this conduct literature, see Sarah Newton, *Learning to Behave: A Guide to American Conduct Books before 1900* (Westport, Conn.: Greenwood, 1994). On the spread of gentility in the nineteenth century, see Richard Bushman, *The Refinement of America: Persons, Houses, Cities* (New York: Knopf, 1992), and John Kasson, *Rudeness and Civility: Manners in Nineteenth-Century America* (New York: Hill and Wang, 1990).

99. John Grigg, *The American Chesterfield* (Philadelphia: Grigg and Elliot, 1833 [1828]).

100. Alcott, *Young Man's Guide*, 29. Frank Ferguson, *The Young Man* (Nashua, New Hampshire, 1848) 14–15. The basis for moral character is, Ferguson writes, "virtuous principle, or a deep, fixed, sense of moral obligation, sustained and invigorated by the love and fear of God . . . integrity truth benevolence justice are not with him words without meaning; he knows and feels their sacred import, and aims . . . to exemplify the virtues they express" (13).

101. On the problem of duplicity for middle-class formation, see Karen Haltunnen, *Confidence Men and Painted Women: A Study of Middle-Class Culture in America, 1830–1870* (New Haven: Yale University Press, 1982).

102. Richard Wightman Fox, *Trials of Intimacy: Love and Loss in the Beecher–Tilton Scandal* (Chicago: University of Chicago Press, 1999), 214.

103. N. Beekley, Diary, 1859 (American Antiquarian Society).

104. White Diary, 94.

105. Cumings Diary.

106. Hill Diary, 40.

107. Charles Rogers, Diary (New York Public Library), 35, 46, 39.

108. Dana D. Nelson, *National Manhood: Capitalist Citizenship and the Imagined Fraternity of White Men* (Durham, N.C.: Duke University Press, 1998), 12.

Chapter Two

1. Henry Patterson, Diary, vol. 3, 1842 (New-York Historical Society), 101, 95.

2. Only strangers to the shipboard world can adequately appreciate the particular literary novelty of this experience. "With regard to the work that men are put, it is a matter which probably would not be understood by one who has not been to sea," Dana notes, and it is his and Ishmael's status as outsiders that allows them to take such detailed interest in the routine business of ships—their close description of the work to which other men are put becomes their own particular *literary* work while at sea. Richard Henry Dana, *Two Years Before the Mast* (New York: Macmillan, 1916 [1840]), 16.

3. *Mercantile Library Reporter* 2, no. 3 (Boston, 1855), 54.

4. Jerome Paine Bates, *The Imperial Highway; or, the Road to Fortune and Happiness, with Biographies of Self-Made Men, Their Business Traits, Qualities, and Habits* (Chicago: G. W. Borland, 1883).

5. Richard Wightman Fox, *Trials of Intimacy: Love and Loss in the Beecher-Tilton Scandal* (Chicago: University of Chicago Press, 1999), 253–54.

6. Michael S. Halloran, "From Rhetoric to Composition: the Teaching of Writing in America to 1900," in *A Short History of Writing Instruction: From Ancient Greece to Twentieth-Century America,* ed. James J. Murphy (Davis, Calif.: Hermagoras Press, 1990), 170.

7. Richard Hewlett, Commonplace Book 1767 (Winterthur Library).

8. On elite literary culture in early America, see David S. Shields, *Civil Tongues and Polite Letters in British America* (Chapel Hill, N.C.: University of North Carolina Press, 1997).

9. On the history of composition, see Halloran, "From Rhetoric to Composition"; Lucille Schultz, *The Young Composers: Composition's Beginnings in Nineteenth-Century Schools* (Carbondale: Southern Illinois University Press, 1999). Miles Myers describes instruction in basic literacy from 1776 to 1860 as "signature and recording literacy," a period differentiated from the preceding one of "oral literacy" primarily by the creation of schools to teach elementary writing skills. "The purpose of the schools," he notes, "was to teach students to sign their names, to make lists, to record information, to copy word lists, to read a few essential words, to read a few things aloud from memory, to have some awareness of how devotional books were organized, to know some religious passages 'by heart,' to know how to write a few numbers, to be able to arrange numbers in inventory columns, and, possibly, to be able to do a few, simple arithmetic calculations." Miles Myers, *Changing Our Minds: Negotiating English and Literacy* (Urbana, Ill.: National Council of Teachers of English, 1996), 49. Also see Lawrence Cremin, *American Education: The National Experience, 1783–1876* (New York: Harper and Row, 1980).

10. Quoted in Schultz, *Young Composers,* 61.

11. Cremin, *American Education,* 88.

12. For a summary of the nineteenth-century culture of childhood and the pedagogical values that underlay them, see Jacqueline S. Reinier, *From Virtue to Character: American Childhood, 1775–1850* (New York: Twayne, 1996).

13. William Alcott, *The Young Man's Guide,* 16th ed., revised and enlarged (Boston: T. R. Marvin, 1846 [1833]), 226. Alcott's book was among the most popular conduct-of-life books published in the antebellum years, and had been published in eighteen editions by 1864. See Cremin, *American Education,* 259.

14. Hannah ("Anna") Gale, Diary (Gale Family Papers, American Antiquarian Society), 2, 27.

15. Ibid., 130–31.

16. Richard H. Brodhead, *Cultures of Letters: Scenes of Reading and Writing in Nineteenth-Century America* (Chicago: University of Chicago Press, 1993); Nancy Armstrong, *Desire and Domestic Fiction: A Political History of the Novel* (New York: Oxford University Press, 1987); David A. Miller, *The Novel and the Police* (Berkeley: University of California Press, 1988).

17. For a history of the changes in postal costs and services that facilitated the great rise in letter writing at mid century, see Richard Johns, *Spreading the News: The American Postal System from Franklin to Morse* (Cambridge: Harvard University Press, 1995).

18. Bradford Morse, Letters, 31 August 1854 (Morse Family Papers, American Antiquarian Society). Further references to this collection will be indicated in the text.

19. Joan Hedrick, *Harriet Beecher Stowe: A Life* (New York: Oxford University Press, 1994), 80. Hedrick emphasizes the importance of the letter in accommodating families to new environments and argues more generally that "the domestic production of literature" in the middle-class parlor from the 1830s through the 1850s "began to serve some of the same functions as the voluntary societies that proliferated at the same time" (77)—adjustment to change, the imaginative sustenance of familial intimacy and social community. The new affective and social importance of the letter in circumstances of geographic mobility and dispersal also contributed to the development of a form of writing, a literary realism founded in the evocation of quotidian details of domestic scenes and the transmission of local and regional cultures. "As letter writing increasingly bore the burden of painting pictures of those who were absent, it became more novelistic and more firmly established within the domain of parlor literature" (79).

20. While Morse kept mention of his difficulties in finding work from his mother, his cousin (who also lived in San Francisco) would write of him: "Bradford is very ambitious—to be idle here where all are so full of life and activity was very annoying to him." Morse Family Papers, 29 December 1853.

21. Patricia Crain discusses the feminization of basic literacy instruction in her analysis of "maternal narratives" of the alphabet in *The Story of A: The Alphabeticization of America from the* New England Primer *to* The Scarlet Letter (Stanford: Stanford University Press, 2000).

22. Morse Letters, 15 June 1854.

23. E. B. Howe, Papers, letter of 23 June 1872 (Bancroft Library, UC Berkeley).

24. On the significance of the mother's voice within the "discourse network" of the early nineteenth century, see Friedrich A. Kittler, *Discourse Networks, 1800–1900,* trans. Michael Meteer with Chris Cullens (Stanford: Stanford University Press, 1990). The oral method of teaching reading was dominant until 1880, when a new emphasis on silent reading began to take hold. See Ada Hyatt, *The Place of Oral Reading in the School Program: Its History and Development from 1880 to 1941* (New York: Columbia Teachers College Press, 1943).

25. Ronald Zboray and Mary Zboray, "Books, Reading, and the World of Goods in Antebellum New England," *American Quarterly* 48, no. 4 (December 1996): 603. "Despite the rapid commercialization that characterized antebellum publishing and book selling, these people charged their literary possessions with meaning in ways that countered the natural depersonalizing effects of mass production."

26. For a study of the everyday context of reading in relation to family and natural cycles, religious and political commitments, and ephemeral events and encounters, see Ronald J. Zboray and Mary Zboray, "Reading and Everyday Life in Antebellum Boston: The Diary of Daniel F. and Mary D. Child," *Libraries and Culture* 23, no. 3 (summer 1997): 285–323. The Childs kept a diary in common, which they used primarily to inventory their reading and other forms of recreation. Although it was devoted to family activities and events, and written by both husband and wife, Daniel Child appears to have been the primary author. After his wife's death, he compiled a meticulous index for the many volumes. See the Daniel and Mary Child Diary, manuscript collection, Massachusetts Historical Society.

27. See Michel de Certeau, "Reading as Poaching," in *The Practice of Everyday Life,* trans. by Steven Rendall (Berkeley: University of California, 1984).

28. As the countless books recommending "the best usage" in speaking and writing attest,

the spread of literacy in the Anglophone world coincided with an unprecedented standardization of English in both Britain and the United States. See Richard Bailey, *Nineteenth-Century English* (Ann Arbor: University of Michigan Press, 1996).

29. Myers, *Changing Our Minds,* 49.

30. Lawrence Levine, *Highbrow/Lowbrow: The Emergence of Cultural Hierarchy in America* (Cambridge: Harvard University Press, 1988).

31. Morse Letters, 15 February 1854.

32. Henry Patterson, Diary, vol. 4 (1843), 65; 2 (1838), 134; 4 (1843), 65; 2 (1838), 134.

33. Ibid., vol. 3 (1841), 2; 2 (1842), 181; 2 (1838), 132, 133.

34. Ibid., 3 (1842), 70, 21, 61.

35. Ibid., 3 (1842), 65, 124, 83; 2 (1839), 200.

36. Patterson, 4 (1843), 45; 3 (1841), 28; 3 (1842), 114.

37. Ibid., 3 (1842), 186; 3 (1842), 58.

38. Ibid., 2 (1837), 78, 198, 209; 4 (1843), 126, 109.

39. Ibid., 3 (1842), 59.

40. See Iver Bernstein, *The New York City Draft Riots: Their Significance for American Society and Politics in the Age of the Civil War* (New York: Oxford University Press, 1990); Daniel Walker Howe, *The Political Culture of the American Whigs* (Chicago: University of Chicago Press, 1979).

41. Patterson Diary, 3 (1841), 37; 3 (1842), 48; 3 (1842), 59; 3 (1842), 119.

42. Ibid., 4 (1843), 67; 3 (1842), 177.

43. Nina Baym, *Novels, Readers, and Reviewers: Responses to Fiction in Antebellum America* (Ithaca: Cornell University Press, 1984), 74, 175. For a related discussion of "moral reading" in the context of nineteenth-century fiction, see Jane P. Tompkins, *Sensational Designs: The Cultural Work of American Fiction, 1790–1860* (New York: Oxford University Press, 1985). For an interpretation of classic nineteenth-century literary works about faith in the "truth-telling power of language," see Janet Gabler-Hover, *Truth in American Fiction: The Legacy of Rhetorical Idealism* (Athens: University of Georgia Press, 1990).

44. Patterson Diary, 3 (1841), 15; 3 (1842), 178; 4 (1843), 57.

45. Ibid., 4 (1843), 116; 3 (1842), 177.

46. Ibid., 3 (1842), 124; 4 (1843), 43; 3 (1842), 74.

47. *Mercantile Library Reporter* 2, no. 1 (1855): 4; "Punctuation," *Mercantile Library Reporter* 1, no. 5 (1855): 73.

48. F. W. Poole, "Hiawatha," *Mercantile Library Reporter* 2, no. 3 (1856): 47.

49. Carol Gilligan, *In a Different Voice: Psychological Theory and Women's Development* (Cambridge: Harvard University Press, 1982).

50. See G. J. Barker-Benfield, *The Culture of Sensibility: Sex and Society in Eighteenth-Century Britain* (Chicago: University of Chicago Press, 1992).

51. See James Raven, *Judging New Wealth: Popular Publishing and Responses to Commerce in England, 1750–1800* (Oxford: Oxford University Press, 1992).

52. Richard Bushman, *The Refinement of America: Persons, Houses, Cities* (New York: Knopf, 1992).

53. Alcott, *Young Man's Guide,* 203, 247, 259, 250.

54. Bradley Cumings, Diary (Massachusetts Historical Society), 1.

55. See Karen Haltunnen, *Confidence Men and Painted Ladies: A Study of Middle-Class Culture in America, 1830–1870* (New Haven: Yale University Press, 1982); John Kasson, *Rudeness and Civility: Manners in Nineteenth-Century Urban America* (New York: Hill and Wang, 1990).

56. Patterson Diary, 3 (1841): 165, 22–24, 165, 47.

57. Ibid., 150, 45.

58. Ibid., 75.

59. George Noyes, "Good Conversation and Prose Writing," *Mercantile Library Reporter*

2, no. 4 (1856): 69–70. The musicality of the voice so frequently alluded to in discussions of oratory suggests that the ultimate freedom a speaker can achieve in language is a metaphoric freedom of spirit from words, as with the "thrilling" charge of Emerson's voice described by James Russell Lowell in chapter 3. Also note the extensive attention that was given to Henry Ward Beecher's voice in nineteenth-century reviews: "His voice now suddenly loses the heavy, nasal peculiarity before mentioned, and rises into a rich, sonorous melody, perfectly audible in every part of the hall." "Henry Ward Beecher and His Lecture," *Mercantile Library Reporter* 2, no. 4 (1855): 57.

60. Noyes, "Good Conversation," 70.

61. Ibid.

62. Conversation was a central practice in the eighteenth-century literary culture of the American colonies. See Shields, *Civil Tongues and Polite Letters*. For an excellent study of the centrality of conversation to nineteenth-century American literature and culture, see Peter Gibian, *Oliver Wendell Holmes and the Culture of Conversation* (New York: Cambridge University Press, 2001).

63. Noyes, "Good Conversation," 70.

64. Patterson Diary, 4 (1843), 89.

65. In *Le genre des genres littéraires français: La conversation* (New York: Oxford University Press, 1992), Marc Fumaroli has traced the continuities between classical models of eloquence with a peculiarly French tradition of conversation that reached its apotheosis in the salon of the seventeenth and eighteenth centuries. An enigmatic combination of wit, intelligence, character, and disposition, "spirit" *(esprit)* depended to a large extent on a wide range of reading, on familiarity with modes of erudition that applied as much to the literary art of writing as to the conversational art of speaking. "L'art de bien parler et de se persuader réciproquement fait appel à une foule de genres litteraires: récits, anecdotes, portraits, maximes, traits d'esprit, réflexions, mais aussi poèmes de forme fixe plus ou moins impromptus, ornements naturels de la galanterie" (13). Esprit was the quality by which individuals spontaneously exercised their minds in relation to others, using knowledge to reciprocally engage one's peers in the "common cause" of civic leisure. Without it, discussion became banal and artificial, an ossified collection of formulaic received ideas.

As perfected by Cicero, eloquence was a public form of discourse, the conquest of an audience. As extended by Montaigne, Voltaire, Descartes, and Madame de Staël, the humanist tradition of conversation was private and contemplative discourse among peers who were also friends, among individuals cooperating for their mutual enlightenment on topics of general human interest, in language that was simple and natural. Despite the difference of contexts, both forms of discourse were governed by the same rules of clarity and both sought to reveal wisdom amid the *lieux communs,* the "commonplaces" of knowledge circulated and shared in by all. While providing a provisional respite from public life, the salon provided a venue for the exercise of civic leisure that de-emphasized promotion of one's wit, intelligence, and eloquence: "La conversation ainsi entendue devient un grand apprentissage réciproque de l'humanité, où chacun apprend à dompter son amour propre, et à tenir sa partie dans le respect des règles communes du jeu" (16). By respecting the "common rules of the game" of conversation, individuals tamed the self-esteem that expressed itself through purely spontaneous speech.

66. Patterson Diary, 3 (1842), 70; 3 (1841), 29; 3 (1841), 41; 3 (1842), 62, 75.

67. On the rhetoric and politics of sentimentality, see Shirley Samuels, *The Culture of Sentiment: Race, Gender, and Sentimentality in Nineteenth-Century America* (New York: Oxford University Press, 1992); Tompkins, *Sensational Designs;* Mary Chapman and Glenn Hendler, eds., *Sentimental Men: Masculinity and the Politics of Affect in American Culture* (Berkeley: University of California Press, 1999); Bruce Burgett, *Sentimental Bodies: Sex, Gender, and Citizenship in the Early Republic* (Princeton: Princeton University Press, 1998); Glenn Hendler, *Public Sentiments: Structures of Feeling in Nineteenth-Century American Literature* (Chapel Hill: University of North Carolina Press, 2001). Also see Thomas Augst, "Frederick Doug-

lass, Between Speech and Print," in *Professing Rhetoric,* ed. Frederick Antczak, Cinda Coggins, and Geoffrey D. Klinger (Mahwah, N.J.: Lawrence Erlbaum, 2001), 53–62.

68. Patterson Diary, 3 (1842), 113, 72.

69. Noyes, "Good Conversation," 70.

70. Ibid., 69.

71. Patterson Diary, 4 (1843), 62, 39.

72. Ibid., 3 (1842), 158.

73. N. Beekley, Diary, 1849 (American Antiquarian Society), 16.

74. George Watson Cole, Diary, vols. 1 and 3 (George Watson Cole Papers, American Antiquarian Society). Cole's peripatetic career was typical of the mobility and uncertainty that typified a clerk's career throughout the nineteenth century. He taught Latin at an academy, clerked in a legal office, and then was among the first generation of students to enroll in Melvil Dewey's new school of library science at Columbia.

75. James F. Fiske, Diary, 1857–1860, vol. 1 (American Antiquarian Society).

76. Edward Tailer, Diary, 9 July 1852 (New-York Historical Society).

77. Fox, *Trials of Intimacy,* 71. Elizabeth Tilton wrote of receiving letters from her husband, "I read every word eagerly; drop instantly whatever I am doing when the postman comes, and give myself up utterly, body and soul, locking the doors to prevent intruders, just as we are wont to do after an absence" (220). "Each spouse reflected frequently on the paradox that they seemed to love one another better during his long winter lecture tours in the West. . . . As the months of separation lengthened, each writer voiced the thrill of anticipated reunion" (215). Beecher claimed that he was incapable of even talking directly about sexual intercourse, "such loathsome and odious stuff, that I don't talk about. . . . Such language is simply impossible to me." Quoted in Fox, *Trials of Intimacy,* 116.

78. Patricia Cline Cohen, *The Murder of Helen Jewett: The Life and Death of a Prostitute in Nineteenth-Century New York* (New York: Knopf, 1998), 150.

79. Beekley Diary, 28 August 1850.

80. Quoted in Lucia McMahon, "While Our Souls Together Blend: Narrating a Romantic Readership in the Early Republic," in *An Emotional History of the United States,* ed. Peter Stearns and Jan Lewis (New York: New York University Press, 1998), 74.

81. Karen Lystra, *Searching the Heart: Women, Men, and Romantic Love in Nineteenth-Century America* (New York: Oxford University Press, 1989), 18.

82. Edward E. Ayer, "Reminiscences from Edward Ayer's First Trip from Home in 1860," in manuscript autobiography of Edward Ayer, 1919 (New York Public Library, manuscript and rare books collection). Ayer writes of the "first real lesson I got on the trip was about 5 or 6 days out." He'd been referring repeatedly to what his parents did, and "one of the boys ahead hollered back, 'Ed, come on up here; I want to find out how your Father or Mother did this.' The cure was instantaneous and permanent."

83. Ellen Rothman, *Hands and Hearts: A History of Courtship in America* (Cambridge: Harvard University Press, 1987), 107.

84. Lucia McMahon offers a detailed portrait of the role of "Romantic readership" in the courtship of Rachel van Dyke and Ebenezer Grovesner in the early nineteenth century, in "While Our Souls Together Blend," 66–90.

85. Benjamin Tilton, Diary (New York Mercantile Library), 41, 43.

86. "Henry Ward Beecher and His Lecture," *Mercantile Library Reporter* 1, no. 4 (1855): 57.

87. Tilton Diary, 43.

88. Ibid., 6.

89. Tilton Diary, 37, 42, 40.

90. For recent analyses of heteronormative ideology and its historical and social role in the formation of civic life and the politicizing of privacy, see Michael Warner and Lauren Berlant, "Sex in Public," in *Intimacy,* ed. Lauren Berlant (Chicago: University of Chicago Press, 2000).

91. Tilton Diary, 2, 7, 8.

92. Patterson Diary, 4 (1842), 142.

93. Lucia McMahon, "While Our Souls Together Blend: Narrating a Romantic Readership in the Early Republic," 74, 82.

94. Patterson Diary, 4 (1842), 119.

95. Fox, *Trials of Intimacy,* 253–54.

96. Richard Sennett, *The Fall of Public Man* (New York: Knopf, 1977).

97. Arthur J. Breton, *A Guide to Manuscript Collections of the New-York Historical Society,* vol. 1 (Westport, Conn.: Greenwood Press, 1972), 440.

98. On the role of gender in letter writing, see Nan Johnson, "Dear Millie: Letter Writing and Gender in Postbellum America," *Nineteenth-Century Prose* 27, no. 2 (fall 2000): 22–46.

99. On the literacy practices of women's clubs, see Anne Ruggles Gere, *Intimate Practices: Literacy and Cultural Work in U.S. Women's Clubs, 1880–1920* (Urbana: University of Illinois Press, 1997); on women's reading groups, also see Elizabeth Long, "Textual Interpretation as Collective Action," in *The Ethnography of Reading,* ed. Jonathan Boyarin (Berkeley: University of California Press, 1993).

Chapter Three

1. Benjamin Tilton, 1842 (New York Mercantile Library), 10–11.

2. Ibid., 12–13.

3. At the end of *The Protestant Ethic and the Spirit of Capitalism,* Max Weber used a similar image of captivity to suggest how the secularization of the Protestant idea of the calling had trapped modern man in a "disenchanted" world.

4. Pierre Hadot, *Philosophy as a Way of Life: Spiritual Exercises from Socrates to Foucault,* ed. Arnold Davidson, trans. Michael Chase (Oxford: Blackwell, 1995), 83, 103. Also see Hadot, "Forms of Life and Forms of Discourse in Ancient Philosophy," trans. Arnold Davidson and Paula Wissing, *Critical Inquiry* 16 (spring 1990): 483–505. For a useful commentary on the "poetics of philosophy" in the work of Stanley Cavell, John Dewey, and Michel Foucault, see Richard Shusterman, *Practicing Philosophy: Pragmatism and the Philosophical Life* (New York: Routledge, 1997).

5. Hadot, *Philosophy as a Way of Life,* 102. The ancient schools differed as much in their emotional and affective strategies as in their particular values: where the Stoics emphasized the "mobilization of energy and consent to destiny," or the Epicurians taught students the *techné* of relaxation and detachment, the Platonists sought to develop "mental concentration and renunciation of the sensible world" (101).

6. Stanley Cavell, *This New and Yet Unapproachable America: Lectures after Emerson after Wittgenstein* (Albuquerque, N.M.: Living Batch Press, 1989), 109, 108, 10.

7. Peter Gibian, *Oliver Wendell Holmes and the Culture of Conversation* (New York: Cambridge University Press, 2001), 16. For concise overviews of the lecture system in the nineteenth century, see Donald Scott, "Print and the Public Lecture System, 1840–1860," *Printing and Society in Early America,* ed. William L. Joyce et al. (Worcester, Mass.: American Antiquarian Society, 1983); Donald Scott, "The Profession that Vanished: Public Lecturing in Mid-Nineteenth-Century America," *Professions and Professional Ideologies in America,* ed. Gerald Geison (Chapel Hill: University of North Carolina Press, 1987).

8. Quoted in Gibian, *Oliver Wendell Holmes,* 16.

9. In particular, see Mary Kupiec Cayton, "The Making of an American Prophet: Emerson, His Audiences, and the Rise of the Culture Industry in Nineteenth-Century America," in *Ralph Waldo Emerson: A Collection of Critical Essays,* ed. Lawrence Buell (Englewood Cliffs, N.J.: Prentice-Hall, 1993), 77–100.

10. Tilton Diary, 10–11.

11. Henry W. Bellows, *The Ledger and the Lexicon: or, Business and Literature in Account with American Education* (Cambridge, Mass., 1853), 15.

12. See Thomas Augst, "The Commerce of Thought: Professional Authority and Business Ethics in Nineteenth-Century America," *Prospects* 27 (2002): 49–76.

13. Sacvan Bercovitch, "Emerson, Individualism, and the Ambiguities of Dissent," in *Ralph Waldo Emerson: A Collection of Critical Essays,* ed. Lawrence Buell, 122. Also see Christopher Newfield, *The Emerson Effect: Individualism and Submission in America* (Chicago: University of Chicago Press, 1996).

14. Cayton, "Making of an American Prophet," 98. Also see Cayton, *Emerson's Emergence: Self and Society in the Transformation of New England, 1800–1845* (Chapel Hill: University of North Carolina Press, 1989). For more general considerations of Emerson's lecturing within the fuller context of his literary career, see Herbert Wichelns, "Ralph Waldo Emerson," in *A History and Criticism of American Public Addresses,* ed. William Brigance, vol. 2 (New York: McGraw-Hill, 1943); David Robinson, *Apostle of Culture. Emerson as Preacher and Lecturer* (Philadelphia: University of Pennsylvania Press, 1982); and Cayton, *Emerson's Emergence.* For other studies of Emerson's work in the context of nineteenth-century rhetoric and oratory, see Dorothy Broaddus, *Genteel Rhetoric: Writing High Culture in Nineteenth-Century Boston* (Charleston: University of South Carolina Press, 1999); James Warren, *Culture of Eloquence: Oratory and Reform in Antebellum America* (University Park: Pennsylvania State University Press, 1999).

15. Richard Teichgraeber, *Sublime Thoughts/Penny Wisdom: Situating Emerson and Thoreau in the American Market* (Chicago: University of Chicago Press, 1995), 42.

16. Stanley Cavell, "The Philosopher in American Life," in his *In Quest of the Ordinary: Lines of Skepticism and Romanticism* (Chicago: University of Chicago Press, 1988).

17. Cornel West, *The American Evasion of Philosophy: A Genealogy of Pragmatism* (Madison: University of Wisconsin Press, 1989), 212. For a succinct discussion of Emerson scholarship from the perspective of "antifoundationalism" and its bearing on the ideology of American liberalism, see Newfield, *The Emerson Effect,* 153–73. Emerson's "epistemological radicalism" consists of a rejection of conformity that "entails not so much changing what the facts are but changing our understanding of what a fact is" (154).

18. Teichgraeber, *Sublime Thoughts,* 38. "Where most have seen the immediate cultural impact of the market to be the fostering of a more empirical, rationally ordered style of thinking, Emerson was determined to show that it was actually encouraging a different and far more significant transformation—one that was releasing a creative energy he assumed to be bottled up in every person" (39). For a compelling, nuanced account of Emerson's concept of individualism (one that draws expansively from throughout his career), see George Kateb, *Emerson and Self-Reliance* (Thousand Oaks, Calif.: Sage, 1995).

19. Emerson, "Wealth," *Essays and Lectures* (New York: Viking, 1983), 989. Further page references to this essay will be indicated in the text.

20. Emerson is not saying here that only some people can do something, but rather emphasizing the obligation to discern one's intrinsic talent. As he suggested in a later essay, the essential equivalence of these talents as gifts to which nature has disposed us effaces a meaningful distinction between mental and physical labor: "Men are made each with some triumphant superiority, which, through some adaptation of fingers, or ear, or eye, or ciphering, or pugilistic or musical or literary craft, enriches the community with some new art . . . " "Success," *Society and Solitude* (Boston, 1870) 253.

21. Ralph Waldo Emerson, "Character," *Lectures and Biographical Sketches,* vol. 10 (Boston, 1883), 103.

22. Tilton Diary, 67–68.

23. I take this phrase from a study of the construction of knowledge in seventeenth-century science: Steven Shapin, *A Social History of Truth: Civility and Science in Seventeenth-Century England* (Chicago: University of Chicago Press, 1994).

24. Scott, "The Profession that Vanished," 21. The popular lecture validated the importance of liberal knowledge that did not have instrumental value, seeking to "foster deeper understanding of human nature and mankind and, either explicitly or implicitly, to deepen the audience's awareness of American character and custom." Scott suggests that the typical lecture was governed by "an interpretive imperative": "The good lecture had to be grounded in something concrete. . . . It was the connection of the specific topic or theme with some more

comprehensive view that rendered thought and knowledge ultimately 'useful,' at once 'practical' and 'ennobling,' to use terms frequently used in praise of lectures. . . . They focused on something familiar and of obvious concern—an institution like matrimony, a quality like beauty or character, a theme like success or progress," and drew "upon a broad array of concrete references and allusions taken from literature and history, the experiences of everyday life, and some of the most startling facts of the day" (Scott, "The Profession that Vanished," 25).

25. Ibid., 26, 27.

26. Cavell, "Thinking of Emerson," 196.

27. Maurice Gonnaud, *An Uneasy Solitude: Individual and Society in the Work of Ralph Waldo Emerson* (Princeton: Princeton University Press, 1987), 387.

28. Robert E. Burkholder and Joel Myerson, *Emerson: An Annotated Secondary Bibliography* (Pittsburgh: University of Pennsylvania Press, 1985); Robert E. Burkholder and Joel Myerson, *Ralph Waldo Emerson, An Annotated Bibliography of Criticism, 1980–1991* (Westport, Conn.: Greenwood, 1994). This paucity of attention has only begun to be rectified in the recent efforts of Richard Teichgraeber and George Kateb among others to show that Emerson's thinking about the institutions and ethics of liberal capitalism was more nuanced and consistent than criticism over the last four decades has supposed. For a consideration of the ethical dimensions of Emerson's earlier work, see Gustaaf Van Cromphout, *Emerson's Ethics* (Columbia: University of Missouri Press, 1999); on his later work, see David M. Robinson, *Emerson and the Conduct of Life: Pragmatism and Ethical Purpose in the Later Work* (New York: Cambridge University Press, 1993).

29. Cited in Charles Mitchell, *Individualism and Its Discontents: Appropriations of Emerson, 1880–1950* (Amherst: University of Massachusetts Press, 1997), 51, 48. Brooks's dislike for Emerson is an indication of the degree to which Emerson had been thoroughly claimed by the Genteel literary critics, and been installed in the academy as a fixture of American culture—a place, Brooks noted, "where ideals are cherished precisely because they are ineffectual." Modern critics such as Brooks, Waldo Frank, and T. S. Eliot were seeking to release American literature from the influence of the Genteel tradition, which in many ways had claimed Emerson as its patron saint. As Frank observed in *Our America*, Emerson "ruled supreme in thoughtful circles. His philosophy supplied the norm for our poetry and fiction, his manner became the manners of the cultured" (53–54). In their pioneering efforts to develop a new kind of cultural criticism and a new role for public intellectuals and journalists in small magazines and venues outside the university, these modern critics rebelled against the aesthetic and humanist values of the academy by challenging the iconic status that Emerson had achieved in the Genteel tradition.

30. Joseph Kett, *The Pursuit of Knowledge under Difficulties: From Self-Improvement to Adult Education in America, 1750–1990* (Stanford: Stanford University Press, 1994), 55.

31. Cayton, "Making of an American Prophet," 614, 618. This interpretation is most persuasive in relation to the frankly provincial life of commercial boomtowns such as Cincinnati and St. Louis. The rapid and haphazard process of urban growth made such towns particularly dependent on 'ready-made' cultural products, which, like clothing, furnishings, and food, also came by way of a regional commercial infrastructure. For a related interpretation of the pressures exerted on Emerson's thinking by the commercial lecture circuit, see Frederick Antczak, *Thought and Character: The Rhetoric of Democratic Education* (Ames: Iowa State University Press, 1985).

32. Kett, *Pursuit of Knowledge*, 42.

33. For T. S. McMillan, the silent, solitary and difficult process of reading is an antidote to a legacy of "consumptive readings" of Emerson that occurred among new thought and self-help gurus since his death. See T. S. McMillan, *Our Preposterous Use of Literature: Emerson and the Nature of Reading* (Urbana: University of Illinois Press, 2000).

34. Cayton, "Making of an American Prophet," 98, 100.

35. Teichgraeber, *Sublime Thoughts*, 40, 42.

36. Michael Halloran, "Rhetoric in the American College Curriculum: The Decline of

Public Discourse," *Pre/Text* 3 (1982): 247; Peter Gibian, "Walt Whitman, Edward Everett, and the Culture of Oratory," *Intellectual History Newsletter* 16 (1994): 19. On the "oratorical culture" of antebellum America, see Peter Gibian, *Oliver Wendell Holmes;* Gerald Graff, *Professing Literature, An Institutional History* (Chicago: University of Chicago Press, 1987); Kenneth Cmiel, *Democratic Eloquence: The Fight over Popular Speech in Nineteenth-Century America* (Berkeley: University of California Press, 1990); Nancy Ruttenberg, *Democratic Personality: Popular Voice and the Trial of American Authorship* (Stanford: Stanford University Press, 1998). On the history and theory of eloquence in eighteenth-century America, see Sandra Gustafson, *Eloquence Is Power: Oratory and Performance in Early America* (Chapel Hill: University of North Carolina Press, 2000); Jay Fliegelman, *Declaring Independence: Jefferson, Natural Language, and the Culture of Performance* (Stanford: Stanford University Press, 1993). On the symbolic importance of voice in American literature, see Christopher Looby, *Voicing America: Language, Literary Form, and the Origins of the United States* (Chicago: University of Chicago Press, 1996); and Allesandro Portelli, *The Text and the Voice: Writing, Speaking, and Democracy in American Literature* (New York: Columbia University Press, 1994).

F. O. Mathiessen emphasized the importance of oratory to Emerson, Melville, and Whitman. Emerson "believed that the orator could speak both most directly and most deeply to men, breaking down their reserves, tugging them through the barriers of themselves, bringing to articulation their own confused thoughts, flooding them with sudden surprise that the moment of their life was so rich." Americans subscribed to the ancient ideal of the orator calling men out of the wilderness: "A man speaking to men first unlocked their primitive awareness of themselves; through eloquence, the hearer loses sense of dualism, and enters immediately into universal truth." F. O. Mathiessen, *American Renaissance: Art and Expression in the Age of Emerson and Whitman* (New York: Oxford University Press, 1941), 17, 18. As Lawrence Buell notes, a "myth of eloquence" attended the oratorical reputations of Daniel Webster and Edward Everett, in which "oratorical power seemed to take on a life of its own, detach itself from the context of real politik that allowed it to flourish, and loom up as the autonomous expression of some hypostasized Nature or inherent quality of character." Buell argues that the mid-nineteenth century marked a "turning point in the disengagement, within the field of oratory, of the dimensions of aesthetics and advocacy, in keeping with the growing autonomy of the aesthetic domain." Lawrence Buell, *New England Literary Culture: From Revolution through Renaissance* (New York: Cambridge University Press, 1986), 150, 151.

37. Peter Gibian, "Walt Whitman, Edward Everett, and the Culture of Oratory," 21.

38. Henry Patterson, Diary, vol. 3, 1842 (New-York Historical Society), 58, 51.

39. Ibid., 46.

40. Ibid., 43, 78; 3 (1842), 169.

41. Cited in Buell, *New England Literary Culture*, 146–47.

42. Patterson Diary, 3 (1842), 62; 4 (1843), 109.

43. For anthologies of contemporary reviews, see Milton R. Konvitz, ed., *The Recognition of Ralph Waldo Emerson: Selected Criticism since 1837* (Ann Arbor: University of Michigan Press, 1972); Joel Myerson, ed., *Emerson and Thoreau: The Contemporary Reviews* (Cambridge: Cambridge University Press, 1992).

44. Margaret Fuller, "Emerson's Essays" (1844), in Konvitz, *Recognition of Ralph Waldo Emerson*, 22.

45. Theodore Parker, "The Writings of Ralph Waldo Emerson," in Konvitz, 37; John Morley, "Emerson," in Konvitz, 76.

46. Amos Bronson Alcott, *Ralph Waldo Emerson: An Estimate of His Character and Genius, in Prose and Verse* (Boston: A. Williams and Company, 1882) 11, 10.

47. James Russell Lowell, "Emerson the Lecturer," *Books and Libraries* (Boston, 1888), 28, 34, 30.

48. Ibid., 27.

49. Ibid.

50. Ibid., 34.

51. Bronson Alcott refers to him as a "rhapsodist"; John Albee noted in 1903 that "The enchantment of his voice and presence moved nearly all auditors to a state of exaltation like fine music, and like the effects of music it was a mood hard to retain." John Albee, *Remembrances of Emerson* (London: Gay & Bird, 1903), 13–14.

52. Lowell, "Emerson the Lecturer," 28.

53. Ibid., 34–35.

54. Ralph Waldo Emerson, "Montaigne; or, the Skeptic," in *Essays and* Lectures (New York: Viking, 1983), 700.

55. For an analysis of the rhetoric of conversation in the salon, see Marc Fumaroli, *Le genre des genres littéraires français: la conversation* (Oxford: Oxford University Press, 1992).

56. Ralph Waldo Emerson, "Books," in *Society and Solitude* (Boston, 1870), 170.

57. Lowell, "Emerson the Lecturer," 30.

58. Fuller, "Emerson's Essays," 23.

59. Writing about his first encounter with Emerson's work in his *Remembrances of Emerson,* John Albee described coming across a copy of *Representative Men* (1850) in a bookstore. "I opened the volume at the beginning, 'Uses of Great Men,' and read a few pages, becoming more and more agitated, until I could read no more. It was as if I had looked into a mirror for the first time. I turned around, fearful lest someone had observed what had happened to me; for a complete revelation was opened in those few pages, and I was no longer the same being that had entered the store." This book in particular he described as "the talisman to all its fellows. The first work we read with an ardent mental awakening teaches us how to read, and gives to us a power of divination in the choice of reading" (15–16). As Albee points out, this experience is best understood as a rite of passage, a threshold to adult consciousness through which one must pass to acquire what might be called a philosophical agency: "It pertains to an inward crisis of life when it is passing from childhood to consciousness, and therefore difficult to be communicated or understood unless already experienced" (122).

60. Buell, *New England Literary Culture,* 141.

61. Fuller, "Emerson's Essays," 23.

62. Hadot, *Philosophy as a Way of Life,* 18.

63. Emerson, "Eloquence," in *Society and Solitude,* 68.

64. Ibid., 69.

65. Ibid., 71.

66. Emerson, "Behavior," *Essays and Lectures,* 1042.

67. George Kateb, *Emerson and Self-Reliance.*

68. Lowell, "Emerson the Lecturer," 29.

69. Tilton Diary, 15, 32.

70. Ibid., 32.

71. "Boston Notions," *American Phrenological Journal* 15, no. 2 (February 1852): 44.

72. Parker, "Writings of Emerson," 36, 37.

73. Quoted in O. B. Frothingham, "Emerson the Seer," in Konvitz, 51.

74. Walt Whitman, "Emerson," in *Specimen Days,* excerpted in Konvitz, 65.

75. Fuller, "Emerson's Essays," 23.

Chapter Four

1. *New York Times,* 18 April 1853, 490.

2. See Benedict Anderson, *Imagined Communities* (New York: Verso, 1991), 36, 34.

3. Ronald J. Zboray, *A Fictive People: Antebellum Economic Development and the American Reading Public* (New York: Oxford University Press, 1993), 178, 190–91; Richard D. Brown, *Knowledge Is Power: The Diffusion of Information in Early America, 1700–1865* (New York: Oxford University Press, 1989), 286.

4. See Steven Mailloux, *Interpretive Conventions: The Reader in the Study of American Fiction* (Ithaca: Cornell University Press, 1982); Jane Tompkins, *Sensational Designs: The Cultural Work of American Fiction, 1790–1860* (New York: Oxford University Press, 1985);

Cathy Davidson, *Revolution and the Word: The Rise of the Novel in America* (New York: Oxford University Press, 1986); Michael Denning, *Mechanics Accents: Dime Novels and Working-Class Culture in America* (London: Verso, 1987); Janice Radway, *Reading the Romance: Women, Patriarchy, and Popular Literature* (Chapel Hill: University of North Carolina Press, 1987). For a useful array of sociohistorical perspectives on the history of reading, see William J. Gilmore-Lehne, *Reading Becomes a Necessity of Life: Material and Cultural Life in Rural New England, 1780–1835* (Knoxville: University of Tennessee Press, 1989); Cathy Davidson, ed., *Reading in America: Literature and Social History* (Baltimore, Md.: Johns Hopkins University Press, 1986); for a concise overview of theoretical perspectives and historical scholarship on reading in America, see Carl F. Kaestle et al., eds., *Literacy in the United States: Readers and Reading since 1880* (New Haven: Yale University Press 1991).

5. Historical accounts of the mercantile libraries include F. B. Perkins, "Mercantile Libraries," in *Public Libraries in the United States of America: Their History, Condition, and Management, Part I*, a special report of the Department of the Interior, Bureau of Education (Washington, D.C., 1876), 378–385; Jesse H. Shera, *Foundations of the Public Library: A Social History of the Public Library Movement in New England from 1629 to 1855* (Chicago: University of Chicago Press, 1949), 71 72; Sidney Ditzion, "Mechanics and Mercantile Libraries," *Library Quarterly* 10 (April 1940): 218–19; Anthony Thomas Kruzas, *Business and Industrial Libraries in the United States, 1820–1940* (New York: Special Libraries Association, 1968), 22. For a survey of twenty-four of these institutions see William Boyd Jr.'s dissertation, "Books for Young Businessmen: Mercantile Libraries in the United States, 1820–1865" (University of Indiana, 1975). For a survey of the many kinds of libraries in early America, see Haynes McMullen, *The Library in America before 1876* (Westport, Conn.: Greenwood Press, 2000).

6. Peter Hall sketches "the reorientation of the Old Standing Order . . . from an elite with public responsibilities to a group whose influence was mediated through private institutions," which included colleges, museums, libraries, hospitals, and other benevolent institutions. Peter Dobkin Hall, *The Organization of American Culture, 1700–1900: Private Institutions, Elites, and the Origins of American Nationality* (New York: New York University Press, 1984), 109–10. For a broad interpretation of the library's historical role as an agency of culture, see Thomas Augst, "American Libraries and Agencies of Culture," in *Libraries as Agencies of Culture*, ed. Thomas Augst and Wayne Wiegand (Madison: University of Wisconsin Press, 2002), 5–22.

7. New York Mercantile Library Association *Annual Report* (hereafter NYMLAAR) 6 (1827), 31; 29 (1850), 22. (No report was issued for 1826). On the centrality of the parlor for middle-class reading, see Louise Stevenson, *The Victorian Homefront: American Thought and Culture, 1860–1880* (Boston: Twayne, 1991).

8. "The New York Mercantile Library," *Scribner's* 1, no. 4 (February 1871): 358. The managers no doubt recognized the utility of employing women to impart a more refined atmosphere: "The good order and quiet which always prevail in the reading room are no doubt attributable to the frequent visits of the gentler sex, as well as to the fact that it is a woman who is charged with enforcement of the rules. The most boisterous and incorrigible of young bloods would immediately stop talking and take his feet off the table, if the request came from the lips of a good-looking superintendent in petticoats."

9. Anthony Rotundo, *American Manhood: Transformations in Masculinity from the Revolution to the Modern Era* (New York: Basic Books, 1993), 69. "Debating replaced the physical skills and primal aggression of boyhood with the abstract skills and verbal aggression that were needed for middle-class work." Men in the marketplace continued to "engage in endless small competitions—for business, for advancement, or in the playful, competitive testing of wits that formed the cornerstone of male sociability" (204).

10. "New York Mercantile Library," *Scribner's*, 358.

11. Scholars have built upon Foucault's work in analyzing the dynamics of governmentality under modern liberalism. See Nikolas S. Rose, *Powers of Freedom: Reframing Political Thought* (Cambridge: Cambridge University Press, 1999); Graham Burchell, Colin Gordon,

and Peter Miller, eds., *The Foucault Effect: Studies in Governmentality* (London: Harvester Wheatsheaf, 1991).

12. See David Henkin, *City Reading: Written Words and Public Spaces in Antebellum New York* (New York: Columbia University Press, 1998).

13. Perkins, "Mercantile Libraries," 380, 378.

14. Ibid., 380, 382, 383.

15. Building on Jesse Shera's seminal work, scholars of library history have tended to reinforce Perkins's verdict, by viewing mercantile libraries as a "transitional form" in a historical evolution that culminates with the public library. As Shera observed, "these specialized types" of libraries embodied the diversity of interests that, when added together, "composed a totality of forces that converged to bring tax support for a truly public library service." Other scholars see the demise of mercantile libraries resulting from their competition with public libraries, their institutional and financial weakness, and ultimately from their general inability to represent the changing educational interests of "the public." Shera, *Foundations of the Public Library,* 71–72; Ditzion, "Mechanics and Mercantile Libraries," 218–19. As Perkins pointed out, converting such libraries into municipal, tax-supported institutions identified "the ownership of, responsibility for, and interest in the library, not with any one class, no matter how intelligent and respectable, but with the whole community" (383). In becoming interchangeable with prisons, poorhouses, and other agencies of government dedicated to serving the "whole community," public libraries would have the advantage of being planned and administered by an entrenched bureaucracy, by professionals such as Perkins, who claimed to serve the interests of all classes while purporting to have no particular interests of their own.

16. Boyd, "Books for Young Businessmen," 81; Shera, *Foundations of the Public Library,* 57–65. By acquiring "privileges of unified action" that were equally available to church congregations and turnpike companies, for example, libraries functioned like other private corporations created to serve "public" functions—some of which would later be taken over by government agencies. On the use of corporate charters for philanthropy, see Hall, *Organization of American Culture.*

17. A legal contract joined the Mercantile Association and Clinton Hall, guaranteeing the association the right to use rooms owned by Clinton Hall so long as it met the stated purpose of providing a library, reading room, and lecture hall. See "This Agreement . . . " and "An Act to Incorporate the Clinton Hall Association," reprinted in the New York Mercantile Library Association's *Annual Report* 17 (1838), 124–28.

18. NYMLAAR 3 (1823), 18–19; 14 (1835), 84; 29 (1850), 10; 22 (1843), 7.

19. NYMLAAR 6 (1827), 34; 39 (1860), 38; 14 (1835), 90. For an inventory of art objects in the New York library, see NYMLAAR 35 (1856), 55–58. The St. Louis Mercantile Library published a separate guide to its art collection. Saint Louis Mercantile Library Association, *A Guide to the Sculpture, Paintings, Coins and Other Objects of Art* (St. Louis, 1862).

20. NYMLAAR 38 (1859), 30–31, 23. Often the reports would translate such specific analysis of lecture popularity into general policy pronouncements: "The public taste, proverbially fickle and always yielding to the influence of novelty, has become estranged from this once popular and interesting means of instruction;" "nowadays, lectures are oftener a source of loss than of profit." Ibid., 27 (1848), 17; 42 (1863), 22.

21. Ibid., 30 (1851), 10.

22. NYMLAAR 33 (1854), 9, 12, 16; 49 (1870), 17; *Scribner's,* "New York Mercantile Library," 358. Also see O. C. Gardiner, "Public Libraries of New York City," in *Public Libraries in the United States* (Washington D.C., 1876), 931. Gardiner attributed the New York Mercantile Library's eminence partly to its refinement of library technology, noting that the managers had "sought to prove what is best in the daily record of deliveries, in classifying and arranging books upon the shelves, and the selection of books with special reference to the future needs of the library." By 1876 it been displaced from first place as a circulating library by the Boston Public and the Chicago Public Libraries. See "General Statistics of All Public Libraries," in *Public Libraries in the United States,* 1010.

23. NYMLAAR 1 (1821), 3, 4; 13 (1834), 77.

24. NYMLAAR 2 (1822), 9. As the St. Louis library noted, "The press, unfortunately, teems with works of a superficial and worthless character, and the libraries of the world are loaded with literary lumber." St. Louis Mercantile Library Association, *Annual Report* 3 (1849), 17.

25. NYMLAAR 13 (1834), 87–88. The paradigm of the culture repository was consistent with the moralistic condemnation of fiction prevalent in Federalist literary culture. See Lawrence Buell, *New England Literary Culture from Revolution through Renaissance* (New York: Cambridge University Press, 1986); Davidson, *Revolution and the Word*.

26. NYMLAAR 2 (1822), 9; 13 (1834), 87–88; 6 (1827), 32; 27 (1848), 13; 10 (1831), 55.

27. St Louis Mercantile Library Association, *Annual Report* 6 (1852), 28.

28. NYMLAAR 2 (1822), 9; 1 (1821), 4; 15 (1836): 76.

29. NYMLAAR 10 (1831), 55; 23 (1844), 9; 27 (1848), 13; 42 (1863), 17. "Our members decreasing in number week after week, our shelves remaining unexplored, our library rapidly becoming devoid of general interest," the 1859 report described the "gloomy prospects" of the association as a consequence of not catering to popular taste, or "general interest," in book purchases. Ibid., 38 (1859), 29–30.

30. See "New York Mercantile Library," *Scribner's;* Boyd, "Libraries for Young Businessmen." Although Boyd does not analyze borrowing, annual reports occasionally break down circulation into particular categories. Fiction is usually double, and sometimes triple, the next closest category, history and biography.

31. NYMLAAR 32 (1853), 11; 38 (1859), 14; 49 (1870), 22.

32. NYMLAAR 49 (1870), 22; 32 (1853), 11; 38 (1859), 14.

33. "New York Mercantile Library," *Scribner's,* 363.

34. NYMLAAR 38 (1859), 14.

35. Ibid., 26 (1847), 14; 31 (1852), 14; 42 (1863), 17; 49 (1870), 22.

36. Ibid., 49 (1870), 19.

37. See "Annual Meeting," NYMLAAR 49 (1870), 39. Mercantile libraries had differing policies on full membership (which included the right to vote and run for office) and subscribing membership (which included only the right to use the library and reading room and to borrow books). In New York, women were admitted in small numbers in the 1850s as subscribing members, but by the 1890s constituted a majority of full members. See NYMLA, *Address to the Clerks of the City of New York* (New York, 1858); NYMLA, *Constitution, By-Laws and Regulations* (New York, 1840). By 1862 the Mercantile Library Company of Philadelphia allowed "any person over fifteen years of age" to become a full member through the payment of $10 for a share of company stock—a financial threshold that would have excluded many of more modest means. In that year, the library listed over 200 single women and 15 married women out of 2,120 stockholders, and 80 single women and 10 married women out of 520 subscribers. Mercantile Library Company of Philadelphia, *Constitution and Bylaws* (Philadelphia, 1862).

38. See "Annual Meeting," NYMLAAR 49 (1870), 39; "New York Mercantile Library," *Scribner's,* 361. As Scribner's also noted, the definition of a clerk had itself been stretched to "include nearly everyone who lives on a salary."

39. NYMLAAR 38 (1859), 14.

40. Boston Mercantile Library, *Annual Report* 34 (1854), 5, 10–11, 13. This pattern of specialization in "general interest" literature as a response to the public libraries is consistent with other circulating libraries, in which fiction constituted half of the collections from 1820 to 1850, and an even higher percentage after 1850. By the Civil War, these small and short-lived libraries invested three to four times of their resources in fiction as did contemporary public and other private institutions, which understocked contemporary fiction as they made nonfiction works more available to the reading public. David Kaiser, *A Book for a Sixpence: The Circulating Library in America* (Pittsburgh, Penn.: Beta Phi Mu, 1980), 67, 86, 103.

41. Boston Mercantile Library, *Annual Report* 34 (1854), 22.

42. Ibid., 35 (1855), 33. Even when they should have recognized the weakness of their management, the managers of the New York Mercantile Library never undercut their own authority in this way.

43. On the early history of social libraries in general, see Shera, *Foundations of the Public Library*, 76–77; Kaiser, *Circulating Library;* and McMullen, *The Library in America before 1876.*

44. NYMLAAR 38 (1859), 14.

45. NYMLAAR 32 (1853), 13. The report for 1849 noted with certainty that 43 out of 400 closed accounts had joined the gold rush to California, and presumed that "many others went the same direction, as they cannot be found" (NYMLAAR 29 [1850], 13).

46. Ibid., 39 (1860), 9–10.

47. Benjamin Tilton, Diary, August 1841-July 1844 (New York Mercantile Library, New York City), 13–14.

48. Ibid., 1–2.

49. Ibid., 4.

50. Ibid., 5.

51. Henry A. Patterson, Diary, 10 October 1838, vol. 2 (New-York Historical Society), 174. Also see entry for 19 December 1838, 186.

52. Patterson Diary, vol. 2, 192; vol. 3, 47.

53. For members' sense of ownership of the library, also see Patterson Diary for 9 January 1839, vol. 2, 192; 15 January 1842, vol. 3, 47.

54. NYMLAAR 26 (1847), 4.

55. Mercantile Library Company of Philadelphia, *Annual Report* 20 (1843), 11.

56. See Patricia Cline Cohen, *The Murder of Helen Jewett: The Life and Death of a Prostitute in Nineteenth-Century New York* (New York: Alfred A. Knopf, 1998); Timothy J. Gilfoyle, *City of Eros: New York City, Prostitution, and the Commercialization of Sex, 1790–1920* (New York: W. W. Norton, 1992).

57. See, for example, Freeman Hunt, *Lives of American Merchants* (New York, 1858); T. S. Arthur, *True Riches: or Wealth Without Wings* (Boston: L. P. Crown, 1852). This literature on "mercantile character" that proliferated before the Civil War has been interpreted in terms of status anxiety, as part of a campaign waged by traditional elites to secure social influence as their cultural authority was being eroded by mass electoral participation and a new breed of professional politician. Tied to a system of mercantile apprenticeship that depended on personal connections and paternalistic stewardship, these values were increasingly anachronistic to the conditions of modern capitalism. According to Richard Hofstadter, "the old mercantile ideal" promoted a traditional morality of sobriety, thrift, and improvement in an essentially nostalgic and anachronistic bid to have merchants respected as gentlemen. See Allan Stanley Horlick, *Country Boys and Merchant Princes: The Social Control of Young Men in New York* (Lewisburg, Penn.: Bucknell University Press, 1975); Richard Hofstadter, *Anti-Intellectualism in American Life* (New York: Knopf, 1963). For other studies of the changing role of traditional elites in the urban landscape, see Barbara Solomon, *Ancestors and Immigrants: A Changing New England Tradition* (Cambridge: Harvard University Press, 1956); Amy Bridges, *A City in the Republic: Antebellum New York and the Origins of Machine Politics* (New York: Cambridge University Press, 1984).

58. Stuart Blumin, *The Emergence of the Middle Class: Social Experience in the American City, 1760–1900* (New York: Cambridge University Press, 1989), 121.

59. Richard Lathers, in NYMLAAR 41 (1862), 43.

60. Edwin T. Freedley, *A Practical Treatise on Business* (Philadelphia, 1852), 1.

61. Henry W. Bellows, *The Ledger and the Lexicon: or, Business and Literature in Account with American Education* (Cambridge, Mass., 1853), 5.

62. Ibid., 10–12.

63. Rush Welter, *The Mind of America* (New York: Columbia University Press, 1975), 129; Marvin Myers, *The Jacksonian Persuasion* (New York: Columbia University Press, 1959).

64. Leonard Neufeldt, *The Economist* (New York: Oxford University Press, 1989), 31. Neufeldt suggests that in this period "the richest register of lexical and semantic shifts [were] linked to economic developments."

65. Sigmund Diamond, *The Reputation of the American Businessman* (New York: Harper Colophon Books, 1966), 178–79. On the "folklore of success," see John G. Cawelti, *Apostles of the Self-Made Man: Changing Concepts of Success in America* (Chicago: University of Chicago Press, 1965); Irvin G. Wiley, *The Self-Made Man in America: The Myth of Rags to Riches* (New Brunswick, N.J.: Rutgers University Press, 1954). For more recent studies of the ideology of success in the context of changing cultural narratives about failure, see Scott Sandage, "Deadbeats, Drunkards, and Dreamers: A Cultural History of Failure in America, 1819–1893" (Ph.D. diss., Rutgers University, 1995); in the context of the changing law of bankruptcy, see Edward Balleisen, *Bankruptcy and Commercial Society in Antebellum America* (Chapel Hill: University of North Carolina Press, 2001). On the representation of business and failure, also see Toby Ditz, "Shipwrecked; or, Masculinity Imperiled: Mercantile Representations of Failure and the Gendered Self in Eighteenth-Century Philadelphia," *Journal of American History* 81 (June 1994): 51–80; Tim Ruppel, "Gender Training: Male Ambitions, Domestic Duties, and Failure in the Magazine Fiction of T. S. Arthur," *Prospects* 24 (1999): 311–337.

66. Diamond, *American Businessman,* 247.

67. Hofstadter, *Anti-Intellectualism,* 238. "Since the development of industrialism after the Civil War, the estrangement between men of business and men of letters has been both profound and continuous; and since the rise of Progressivism and the New Deal, the tension between businessmen and liberal intellectuals in the social sciences has also been acute. . . . The values of business and intellect are seen as eternal and inevitably at odds" (234).

68. Bellows, *Ledger and Lexicon,* 5, 6, 5.

69. On the representation of business as mental work, see Thomas Augst, "The Commerce of Thought: Literacy, Professional Ideology, and the Representation of Business in Nineteenth-Century America," *Prospects* 27 (2002): 49–76.

70. Bellows, *Ledger and Lexicon,* 15.

71. Henry Bellows, "Edward Alford and His Playfellows," *Knickerbocker* magazine (March 1842), 220.

72. NYMLAAR 10 (1831), 54.

73. NYMLAAR 1 (1821), 6. The president of the Mercantile Library Company of Philadelphia similarly used the threat of members' future regret to influence the actions of their present 'selves': "You have the facilities, and your period of life furnishes the time for mental cultivation. Hereafter, with the cares and duties of middle or advanced age pressing on you, if you have been indifferent to your early advantages, you will discover that neglected means of improvement never return, but that regretful memory will recall precious hours of leisure misapplied." Mercantile Library Company of Philadelphia, *Annual Report* 23 (1846), 9. Also see NYMLAAR 11 (1832), 64.

74. NYMLAAR 17 (1838), 7.

75. Ibid., 10 (1831), 54; 15 (1836), 112.

76. "Mercantile Associations," (Boston) *Mercantile Library Reporter* 1, no. 4 (February 1855): 50. Some of the libraries sponsored courses in languages, accounting, and mathematics, along with occasional courses in gymnastics and horsemanship, although they rarely attracted more than a few dozen students. The New York library stressed that its classes were a "means of obtaining information at a rate of cost much less than is attainable through any other channel." *Address to the Clerks of the City of New York* (New York, 1858), 5. The library also sold copies of James Kent's *Course of Reading* (New York, 1840), which was designed to provide members with a sort of liberal arts curriculum of ancient and modern European literature, American history, travel works, and a small diet of prose fiction that included Cooper, Irving, and Brockden Brown with some eighteenth-century British novels.

77. NYMLAAR 17 (1838), 8.

78. Ibid., 17 (1838), 7; 14 (1835), 88. The progress of the mercantile libraries could be

proudly pointed to, as in St. Louis, as evidence that "thought, feeling and desire are not wholly absorbed in grasping for, or in contemplation of, 'the almighty dollar,' but that in the hot scramble for wealth, the claims of the moral and intellectual faculties have received some attention, and prove most conclusively that amidst all that anxiety, competition, and bustle of business . . . we have found the time and the means to cherish and uphold this noble institution." The "noble institution" becomes testimony to the clerks' feat of retaining intellectual and moral faculties, of not having their time and means (and autonomy) completely usurped by the frenzied demands of business life. St. Louis 6 (1852), 11. "The spirited competition of our age and country has engendered an excited feeling, an energetic action in all conditions of society." The democratic advance of knowledge and virtue among an educated electorate similarly assumed that the books and the system of reading would provide a tempering antidote to this "excited feeling," which was as potentially volatile and dangerous for society as a whole as for individuals. Mercantile Library Company of Philadelphia, *Annual Report* 23 (1846), 11.

79. NYMLAAR 14 (1835), 88; "Mercantile Character," (Boston) *Mercantile Library Reporter* 2, no. 2 (January 1856), 34, 35.

80. NYMLAAR 17 (1838), 7.

81. NYMLAAR 13 (1834), 54; see "Report of the Young Men's Philosophical Society," *Mercantile Library Reporter* 1, no. 2 (1854), 25–27; "Why Do Men Carry Canes?," ibid., no. 3 (1855), 36; "The Advantages of a College Education," ibid., no. 6 (1855), 83.

82. NYMLAAR 17 (1838), 8; 18 (1839), 19; 17 (1838), 8.

83. NYMLAAR 15 (1836), 117; Mercantile Library Company of Philadelphia, *Annual Report* 23 (1846), 10.

84. NYMLAAR 15 (1836), 117.

85. NYMLAAR 32 (1853), 13.

86. NYMLAAR 11 (1832), 80; 18 (1839), 17.

87. NYMLAAR 34 (1855), 36; 35 (1856), 45.

88. William Anderson Scott, "Some Hints on the Moral Influence of the Commercial Spirit of the Age," in *Trade and Letters: Their Journeyings Round the World* (New York, 1856).

89. NYMLAAR 17 (1837), 5. The nostalgic attachment to the institution could be based on the shared sense of having experienced an emotional engagement with reading that was both distinctive and unique because it was "privileged" within the walls of the mercantile library and its particular 'influence.' Those who are older "have felt its refining influence," the Philadelphia library noted, and could look back on the "pleasure of the evenings, redeemed from the waste of time which they have passed within its walls. The recollections of those evenings are fraught with emotions of the happiest kind. Whether a merchant or clerk, if the pulse of honor has been quickened by the pages of Beauty and Truth, then and there perused, or the intellect expanded under the magic spell of some master mind, or the heart melted beneath the sweet images of the Poet; no one, who has been thus moved, thus instructed, and thus delighted, will ever think with indifference, of this laudable institution." Of course, the pleasure and delight described here pertains more to the individual experience of reading than to any distinctive qualities of membership in the library association. Mercantile Library Company of Philadelphia, *Annual Report* 17 (1840), 11.

90. Patterson Diary, 15 January 1842, vol. 2, 44. The electoral contests between "*belligerent* parties" mounted smear campaigns in the local media. In an oration John Ghourlie pleaded with the association to suppress their "turbulent party spirit": "Gentlemen, I entreat you not to alarm the public by bringing before them, through the newspapers, discussion . . . [which] should remain entirely private. The practice of publishing attacks and recriminations, the one against the other" could only engender "unnecessary alarm of the public mind" and "acrimonious feelings among the members." John Ghourlie, *An Address, Delivered before the Mercantile Library Association* (New York, 1839), 15–16.

91. Mercantile Library Association of Boston, *Annual Report* 34 (1854), 5.

92. "New York Mercantile Library," *Scribner's*, 365–66.

93. There is evidence of a serious rift between younger members and those committed to an older, Federalist model of the literary club in Boston, where in 1855 the slate of candidates

chosen by the official nominating committee was defeated. "This change in the management of affairs is the result of a secret organization, which has been in operation among the younger members for some time previous to the election." Boston Mercantile Library, *Annual Report* 34 (1854), 37.

94. "New York Mercantile Library," *Scribner's*, 365, 366; also see reference to vote fraud in NYMLAAR 37 (1858), 24.

95. Charles C. Jewett, "Report of the Assistant Secretary, Relating to the Library," *Third Annual Report of the Smithsonian Institution* (Washington, D. C., 1849), 39.

96. See Wayne Wiegand, "Research Libraries, the Ideology of Reading, and Scholarly Communication, 1876–1900," in *Libraries and Scholarly Communication in the United States: The Historical Dimension*, ed. John Cole and Phyllis Dain (New York: Greenwood Press, 1990)

97. Robert Gross, "Much Instruction from Little Reading: Books and Libraries in Thoreau's Concord," *Proceedings of the American Antiquarian Society* 97, part I (1987): 182. After Massachusetts provided tax support for libraries in 1851, the new Concord Town Library went about "consolidating the world of Victorian culture," as Robert Gross has shown, by purchasing 'serious' genres of history, biography, and travels, as well as the complete works and "standard" sets of "the great works of antiquity, the classical writers of seventeenth- and eighteenth-century England, even the newly canonized English and American 'men' of letters' of the day" (180). Gross's analysis of the history of three libraries in Concord offers a microcosm of ideological and institutional factors that shaped the fate of circulating libraries in nineteenth-century America.

98. Mercantile Library Company of Philadelphia, *Annual Report* 20 (1843), 11. The Boston Mercantile Library described its establishment of a course of lectures as affording "healthy incitements to study." Boston Mercantile Library Association, *Annual Report* 36 (1856), 49.

99. NYMLAAR 14 (1835), 91.

100. NYMLAAR 25 (1846), 14; 27 (1848), 21. The Boston Mercantile Library Association held weekly exercises in composition, declamation, and debate.

101. NYMLAAR 17 (1838), 14; most of the mercantile libraries depended heavily on income from their public lecture courses. For general discussion of the commercialization of the lecture in the nineteenth century, see Donald Scott, "The Popular Lecture and the Creation of a Public in Mid-Nineteenth-Century America," *Journal of American History* 66, no. 4 (March 1980); Scott, "Print and the Public Lecture System, 1840–1860," in *Printing and Society in Early America*, ed. William L. Joyce et al. (Worcester, Mass.: American Antiquarian Society, 1983).

102. Patterson Diary, 1832–1848.

103. NYMLAAR 14 (1835), 90.

104. NYMLAAR 17 (1838), 14.

105. NYMLAAR 28 (1849), 9; 22 (1843), 17–18.

106. NYMLAAR 17 (1838), 6.

107. NYMLAAR 19 (1840), 15.

108. NYMLAAR 25 (1846), 14; 27 (1848), 21–22.

109. NYMLAAR 8 (1829), 50; 10 (1831), 54; 19 (1840), 14.

110. "New York Mercantile Library," *Scribner's*, 363; NYMLAAR 42 (1863), 17. The annual report of the Boston Mercantile Library made the same point: "Experience has shown that the first demand for ephemeral works is frequently greater than for those of more permanent interest. This demand probably arises from the fact that many members purchase the latter class for their own libraries; and, not deeming the former class worth the outlay, and wishing only for a hasty perusal, apply to the library for them." BMLA 34 (1854), 22.

111. NYMLAAR 33 (1854), 15.

112. NYMLAAR 11 (1832), 64; 17 (1838), 6. For an overview of the contemporary understanding of the genre of the novel, see Nina Baym, *Novels, Readers, and Reviewers: Responses to Fiction in Antebellum America* (Ithaca: Cornell University Press, 1984), which

emphasizes the centrality of plot in the genre's appeal; Baym suggests that whether a novel had an "absorbing" or "enchanting" "interest" depended on whether it had the "vigor" and "energy" supplied by a well-constructed story line.

113. NYMLAAR 13 (1834), 77; 32 (1853), 11.

114. NYMLAAR 42 (1863), 17; 39 (1860), 9; 38 (1859), 15. "The distinguishing feature of our Library," one report claimed in 1870, "was that it had been uniformly more liberal than any other in supplying its readers with the fresh and the new." NYMLAAR 49 (1870), 22.

115. NYMLAAR 38 (1859), 14; 33 (1854), 15. On the other hand one could argue that making readers wait for weeks is an unreasonable claim on their patience when they have paid for the library's services: "It is a disappointment to a member to find the book out that he most desires. A second unsuccessful application makes the matter worse. When it is repeated for several weeks as is frequently the case and still the book cannot be had, the disappointment becomes a serious grievance and the chances are about even that the member will close his account or fail to renew it when it expires. There can be no doubt but that we lose very many members in just this way." NYMLAAR 49 (1870), 32.

116. Gerald Graff, *Professing Literature: An Institutional History* (Chicago: University of Chicago Press, 1987), 45.

117. NYMLAAR 12 (1834), 77.

118. On this ideology of literacy, see Lee Soltow and Edward Stevens, *The Rise of Literacy and the Common School in the United States: A Socioeconomic Analysis to 1870* (Chicago: University of Chicago Press, 1979); Carl F. Kaestle, *Pillars of the Republic: Common Schools and American Society, 1780–1860* (New York: Hill and Wang, 1983).

119. B. F., "Novel Reading," (Boston) *Mercantile Library Reporter* 1 (November 1854): 8–9.

120. Ibid., 9.

121. Deirdre Shauna Lynch, *The Economy of Character: Novels, Market Culture, and the Business of Inner Meaning* (Chicago: University of Chicago Press, 1998), 126.

122. NYMLAAR 33 (1854), 15.

123. Zboray's analysis of the borrowing habits of a brother and sister stresses the commonalities of reading tastes among young men and women. See *A Fictive People*.

124. As the century progressed, the obedience of readers to cultural authority would be exacted through a variety of formal channels. On the reading 'advisors' that proliferated with the print market by the 1850s, see Louise Stevenson's *Victorian Homefront*. On the emergence of "culture" in the publishing industry with Charles Eliot Norton's "Five Foot Shelf of Books" and the like, see Joan Shelley Rubin, *The Making of Middlebrow Culture* (Chapel Hill: University of North Carolina Press, 1992). It would become an explicit goal of the public libraries for professional librarians to serve as gatekeepers or stewards to guide their young, infantilized readers through this dangerous terrain both through regulation and censorship of book collections. See Dee Garrison, "Immoral Fiction in the Late Victorian Library," in *Victorian America,* ed. Daniel Walker Howe (Philadelphia: University of Pennsylvania Press, 1976). "More cheap and trashy literature is thrown off by the American press and consumed by the American mind . . . To prevent the evils which flow from such promiscuous and desultory reading, and to cultivate a taste for something more substantial," were the stated ends of the establishment of the Public School Library Society of St. Louis. "Circular," *Catalogue of Books for the St. Louis Public Schools* (St. Louis, 1865).

125. NYMLAAR 33 (1854), 15. The 1870 report explicitly excludes "that class" of writing by women while referring to Twain's *Innocents Abroad* and other "standard works." For a case study of the politics of canon formation and literary valuation in the nineteenth century, see Richard Brodhead, *The School of Hawthorne* (New York: Oxford University Press, 1986). Lawrence Levine's *Highbrow/Lowbrow* (Cambridge: Harvard University Press, 1988) documents the emergence of 'cultural hierarchy' by the end of the century.

126. NYMLAAR 49 (1870), 32. On the dominance of women in the mercantile library by the 1890s, see the membership ledgers, New York Mercantile Library, New York City.

127. See Lawrence Levine, "The Folklore of Industrial Society: Popular Culture and Its Audiences," *American Historical Review* 97, no. 5 (December 1992): 1369–99; Rubin, *The Making of Middlebrow Culture;* Radway, *A Feeling For Books.*

128. Cited in "Mercantile Library," *New York Times,* 10 November 1870, p. 5.

Chapter Five

1. Caleb A. Wall, Diary, August 1840 (American Antiquarian Society), 12.

2. Herman Melville, "Bartleby, the Scrivener: A Story of Wall Street," in *The Piazza Tales and Other Prose Pieces, 1839–1860* (Evanston and Chicago: Northwestern University Press and The Newberry Library, 1987), 33. Originally published in November and December of 1853 in *Putnam's Magazine.* All further page references to the story will be indicated in the text. As the narrator of Melville's story describes the view from his office: "In that direction my windows commanded an unobstructed view of a lofty brick wall, black by age and everlasting shade" (14). For an analysis of the thematics of urban space in Melville's corpus, see Wyn Kelley, *Melville's City: Literary and Urban Form in Nineteenth-Century New York* (Cambridge: Cambridge University Press, 1996). Gillian Brown interprets the story in relation to agoraphobia in *Domestic Individualism: Imagining Self in Nineteenth-Century America* (Berkeley: University of California Press, 1990).

3. Hershel Parker, *Herman Melville: A Biography,* vol. 1, 1819–1851 (Baltimore: Johns Hopkins University Press, 1996), 97.

4. When his brother Edward landed a "situation" as "Chief Clerk" in "one of the largest houses in Boston," Morse wrote: "You must be a good boy, and do all they tell you to, for I hope you will remain with them a number of years." Bradford Morse, Letters, 12 June 1853 (American Antiquarian Society).

5. Cited in Anthony Rotundo, *American Manhood: Transformations in Masculinity from the Revolution to the Modern Era* (New York: Basic Books, 1993), 113. As Rotundo notes, "Years of immersion in boy and youth cultures accustomed men to enjoy the ceaseless competitive striving, the uncertain fortunes, and assertions of self that were typical of their work world" (190). Also see Daniel T. Rodgers, *The Work Ethic in Industrial America, 1850–1920* (Chicago: University of Chicago Press, 1978).

6. Rotundo, *American Manhood,* 190, 189.

7. Jonathan Henry Hill, Diary, vol. 2, July 1845 (American Antiquarian Society), 40–41.

8. Ibid., 26 June 1845, 1.

9. Hill Diary, vol. 1 (20 August 1841), 58–59.

10. Ibid., 21 August 1841, 59–60.

11. Ibid., 10 September 1841, 57.

12. Ibid., 1 October 1841, 77.

13. Ibid., 24 November 1841, 166.

14. Ibid., 25 November 1841, 167.

15. Hill Diary, vol. 2 (5 July 1845), 11.

16. C. Wright Mills, *White Collar* (New York: Oxford University Press, 1951); William Whyte, *The Organization Man* (New York: Simon and Schuster, 1956); David Riesman, *The Lonely Crowd: A Study of the Changing American Character* (New Haven: Yale University Press, 1961).

17. Mills, *White Collar,* xxi.

18. Nicholas Bromell, *By the Sweat of the Brow: Literature and Labor in Antebellum America* (Chicago: University of Chicago Press, 1993), 11. For studies of authorship in relation to Melville and other nineteenth-century writers, also see Michael Newberry, *Figuring Authorship in Antebellum America* (Stanford: Stanford University Press, 1997); Michael Gilmore, *American Romanticism and the Marketplace* (Chicago: University of Chicago Press, 1985). On the representation of white-collar work in later American fiction, see Christopher P. Wilson, *White Collar Fictions: Class and Social Representation in American Literature, 1885–1925* (Athens: University of Georgia Press, 1992).

19. Elizabeth Renkar, *Strike through the Mask: Herman Melville and the Scene of Writing* (Baltimore: Johns Hopkins University Press, 1996), xix. "Indeed, writing was a struggle for Melville: his handwriting was illegible; he found spelling impossible; and, among other physical ailments, he suffered from eye, back, and head trouble that made the activity painful."

20. Richard H. Brodhead, *Cultures of Letters: Scenes of Reading and Writing in Nineteenth-Century America* (Chicago: University of Chicago Press, 1993), 113.

21. Terry Eagleton, *Literary Theory: An Introduction* (Minneapolis: University of Minnesota Press, 1984), 26. The rise of "literature" in the late nineteenth century, Eagleton argues, was "concomitant with an historic shift in the very meaning of the term moral. Morality is no longer to be grasped as a formulated code or explicit ethical system: it is rather a sensitive preoccupation with the whole quality of life itself, with the oblique, nuanced particulars of human experience" (27). On the development of the Victorian concept of "culture," see Raymond Williams, *Society and Culture, 1750–1950* (New York: Harper and Row, 1958).

22. "In front of his blank page, every child is already put in the position of the industrialist, the urban planner, or the Cartesian philosopher—the position of having to manage a space that is his own and distinct from all others and in which he can exercise his will." Michel de Certeau, *The Practice of Everyday Life,* translated by Steven Rendall (Berkeley: University of California, 1984), 134.

23. Renkar, *Strike through the Mask,* 18.

24. See Hill Diary, entries for August and September, 1841.

25. Morse Letters, 15 October 1853.

26. Ibid., 28 April 1854.

27. "A complaint literature sprang up in Britain, accusing the masters of paying substandard wages, firing established clerks and replacing them with youths, treating clerks as labor to be hired at the lowest price rather than as employees whose responsibilities, skills and loyalty merited their employers' trust and friendship. The result of this, clerks complained, was that they could not maintain middle-class norms of respectability in terms of standards of dress and marriage." Paul Attewell, "The Clerk Deskilled: A Study in False Nostalgia," *Journal of Historical Sociology* 2, no. 4 (December 1989): 370. For a general history of clerical work in nineteenth-century Britain, see Gregory Anderson, *Victorian Clerks* (Manchester: Manchester University Press, 1976). On clerical work in the United States, see Allan Stanley Horlick, *Country Boys and Merchant Princes: The Social Control of Young Men in New York* (Lewisburg, Penn.: Bucknell University Press, 1975).

28. Horlick, *Country Boys and Merchant Princes,* 165.

29. Ibid.

30. Morse Letters, 29 April 1854.

31. Quoted in Attewell, "The Clerk Deskilled," 371.

32. JoAnne Yates, *Control through Communication: The Rise of System in American Management* (Baltimore: Johns Hopkins University Press, 1989). For innovations in corporate management, see Alfred Chandler, *The Visible Hand: The Managerial Revolution in American Business* (Cambridge: Harvard University Press, 1977). On the meaning and practice of white-collar work in the development of a bureaucratic ethos of a "new" managerial middle class, distinguished from the entrepreneurial values of an "old" middle class, see Oliver Zunz, *Making America Corporate, 1870–1920* (Chicago: University of Chicago Press, 1990).

33. Friedrich A. Kittler, *Gramophone, Film, Typewriter,* trans. by Geoffrey Winthrop-Young and Michael Wutz (Stanford: Stanford university Press, 1999), 193, 194. The entrance of women into the clerical workforce was facilitated by the invention of the typewriter, which allowed them to bypass an educational regimen from which they had been excluded and to dominate a labor market that was entirely reorganized around the mechanization of writing. "Ironically enough, the clerks, office helpers, and poet-apprentices of the nineteenth century, who were exclusively male, had invested so much pride in their laboriously trained handwriting" that they overlooked the skill of typewriting for several years when women were entering the field. For the millions of female secretaries who emerged from the working and middle class, "it was precisely their marginal position in the power system of script that forced women

to develop their manual dexterity, which surpassed the prideful aesthetics of male secretaries." On the feminization of penmanship as a secretarial skill through the development of shorthand in the late nineteenth century, see Tamara Plakins Thornton, *Handwriting in America: A Cultural History* (New Haven: Yale University Press, 1996).

34. "Palely" also suggests that Bartleby does not press too hard, as though he lacks some degree of will: he makes little 'impression' because he does not put the weight of moral character into his work, or indeed is devoid of such character.

35. Economic growth in nineteenth-century America depended on the development of abstract forms of property; the fungibility of wealth in the form of various legal documents facilitates the transfer of wealth. As the narrator notes, he is "one of those unambitious lawyers who never addresses a jury, or in any way draws down public applause," but rather in the safe, "cool tranquility of a snug retreat," does a "snug business among rich men's bonds and mortgages and title-deeds" (14). Lawyers of this self-effacing sort were essential middlemen in the transfer of capital, and their fundamental task was, as the narrator's language suggests, to secure these transactions against error and fraud by making exact copies of these documents.

36. After the Civil War, this regimen of writing instruction was institutionalized in the public schools. The Boston School Committee insisted that "every pupil must sit in the right position," write "the same copy at the same time," and that teachers "require an exact copy of a copy." Cited in Thornton, *Handwriting in America*, 56.

37. Charles Rogers, Diary (New York Public Library), 28.

38. Morse Letters, 15 January 1854.

39. On the history of credit reporting, see James D. Norris, *R. G. Dun & Co., 1841–1900: The Development of Credit Reporting in the Nineteenth Century* (Westport, Conn.: Greenwood Press, 1978). On credit reporting as "bureaucratic narrative," see Scott Sandage, "Deadbeats, Drunkards, and Dreamers: A Cultural History of Failure in America, 1819–1893" (Ph.D. diss., Rutgers University, 1995).

40. Hunt Merriam & Co., Order book with memoranda, 1851 (New York Public Library, manuscript division). The process of moral divination would be further rationalized to take advantage of new communications technology. See *The Telegraphic Cypher, for the exclusive use of the Mercantile Agency* (New York: Dun, Barlow & Company, 1875).

41. For a social history of phrenology, see Roger Cooter, *The Cultural Meaning of Popular Science: Phrenology and the Organization of Consent in Nineteenth-Century Britain* (Cambridge: Cambridge University Press, 1984).

42. "Phrenological Sketch of the Character of Mr. Cumings given by L. N. Fowler Dec 8th 1838" (Massachusetts Historical Society).

43. In exchange for his obedience, each worker has implicitly delegated responsibility for both assessing and managing his whole person in a way that serves the economic interest of the firm (which coincides with the worker's interest in keeping a job). The manager assumes the obligation to explain and mitigate all those actions that the worker is unconscious of and cannot control, in effect serving as an omniscient ego or monitor, obliged for the most part to suffer the spectacle of human indignity with silent tolerance. In reading character in the interest of the firm, the narrator has an economic incentive to engage in scrutiny that would be embarrassing, invasive, humiliating, and uncomfortable under any other circumstances. This incentive affords the narrator a detachment from mere prejudice, which the workers do not have with one another. Disgusted with Turkey's appearance, the narrator says, "I had much ado to keep him being a reproach to me." This "ado" consists mainly of the elaborate justification of his value as a worker.

44. By refusing to engage in the social project of securing the accuracy of scrivening, which makes writing an economic object of "common" circulation, the artist literally stands for solitude, for the Romantic autonomy required for writing to give unique expression to individual genius.

45. Some scholarship has argued that Melville modeled his narrator on Washington Irving, who in "The Sketchbook" created an influential model of literary composition, which as the title implies remained within the belletristic tradition of portraiture and the picturesque.

See Martin Leonard Pops, *The Melville Archetype* (Kent, Ohio: Kent State University Press, 1970); R. Bruce Bickley, *The Method of Melville's Short Fiction* (Durham, N.C.: Duke University Press, 1975). Irving's biographies cast a long shadow over the proliferation of the genre in nineteenth-century America, as a successful author generally did over the literary sphere. Scott Casper, *Constructing American Lives: Biography and Culture in Nineteenth-Century America* (Chapel Hill: University of North Carolina Press, 1999).

46. Brodhead, *Cultures of Letters*, 61, 62. For a study of the cultural impact of the print medium, see Isabelle Lehuu, *Carnival on the Page: Popular Print Media in Antebellum America* (Chapel Hill: University of North Carolina, 2000).

47. Quoted in ibid., 61.

48. Hill Diary, vol. 2 (30 December 1845), 13–14.

49. Ibid., vol. 1, 1.

50. Ibid.

51. Ibid.

52. Ibid., 6, 5.

53. Bickley, *Method of Melville's Short Fiction*.

54. For discussion of these developments see Richard H. Brodhead, *The School of Hawthorne* (New York: Oxford University Press, 1986); Jeffrey D. Groves, "Judging Literary Books by Their Covers: House Styles, Ticknor and Fields, and Literary Promotion," and "Packaging Literature for High Schools: From the Riverside Literature Series to Literature and Life," in *Reading Books: Essay on the Material Text and Literature in America,* ed. Michele Moylan and Lane Stiles (Amherst: University of Massachusetts Press, 1996).

55. Reprinted in M. Thomas Inge, *Bartleby the Inscrutable: A Collection of Commentary on Herman Melville's Tale "Bartleby, the Scrivener"* (Hamden, Conn.: Archon Books, 1979), 44, 39, 38. The *New York Daily News* took the publication of the *Piazza Tales* as an occasion to provide a lengthy overview of Melville's career that attributed his vicissitudes in the court of public opinion to the fact that any performer is burdened by the history of his previous productions: "A precisely similar gauge operates upon the public judgment respecting all achievements of the human mind. The orator, the advocate, the poet, the artist, the dramatist, the actor, is constantly, and we think, quite unreasonably, expected to surpass himself; and if he does not, the world says he is declining, when a more philosophical examination of his efforts would prove the reverse. Intellect is not always revealed in a succession of surprises, but rather by its permanent and steady blaze." Ibid., 34.

56. *The Criterion,* in Inge, *Bartleby the Inscrutable,* 37; *Berkshire County Eagle,* ibid., 36.

57. On the genre of biography, see Casper, *Constructing American Lives.*

58. A 'good-natured smile' of recognition, the pleasing familiarity of old ways and habits: our affective response to the stories of their lives validates the didactic importance of the values their example might impart.

59. On the transition between "flat" and "round" characters in British fiction from the eighteenth to the early nineteenth centuries, see Deirdre Shauna Lynch, *The Economy of Character: Novels, Market Culture, and the Business of Inner Meaning* (Chicago: University of Chicago Press, 1998).

60. For a comprehensive annotated bibliography of interpretations of the story through 1979, see Inge, *Bartleby the Inscrutable.*

61. For a critique of this simple conflict, see Cornelia Vismann, "Cancels: On the Making of Law in Chanceries," *Law and Critique* 7, no. 2 (1996): 131–51. Melville's story is framed, as Vismann puts it, between the "poles of economy and equity, administration and humanity, vanity and pit, the machinery of law and the charity." At once inviting and resisting the divination of readers no less than co-workers, Bartleby becomes the blankness that puts the economic and literary framing of character in acute relief, and pushes these poles to their simplistic, alienating extremes. From the economic accounting of character at the outset—with its elaborate praise of John Jacob Astor—to its stylized, impotent lament, "Ah, humanity," Melville's story trades in the dualisms on which the modern accounting of moral life depends.

62. Leo Marx, "Melville's Parable of the Walls," in Inge, *Bartleby the Inscrutable,* 85–86.

For a useful summary and critique of the "Bartleby industry," see Dan McCall, *The Silence of Bartleby* (Ithaca: Cornell University Press, 1989); Lea Bertani Vozar Newman, *A Reader's Guide to the Short Stories of Herman Melville* (Boston: G. K. Hall, 1986).

63. Vismann, "Cancels," 142. Gilles Deleuze describes the psychological process of identification as "a complex operation that passes through all of the adventures of resemblance, and that always risks falling into neurosis or turning into narcissism." Gilles Deleuze, "Bartleby; or, The Formula," *Essays Critical and Clinical,* trans. Daniel W. Smith and Michael A. Greco (Minneapolis: University of Minnesota Press, 1997), 76.

64. J. Hillis Miller, *Versions of Pygmalion* (Cambridge: Harvard University Press, 1990).

65. Ibid., ix.

66. Ibid., 18.

67. Ibid., 22. This "event" of reading entails a psychic orientation, a composing of one's senses that renders the potential disorder of words and the nowhere of space into one's literary sense of a particular place, situated in relation to "certain historical, personal, institutional, and political circumstances" in which it takes place—the context of normative expectations and conventions that render such "events" predictable or makes them reliable sources of social knowledge.

68. Ibid., 154, 160, 164, 162.

69. Miller, 173, 177, 175, 174. Like Bartleby himself, this reading "is the otherness that all along haunts or inhabits life from the inside," that "can by no method . . . be accounted for, narrated, rationalized, or in any other way reassimilated into ordinary life, though it is a permanent part of ordinary life" (172).

70. Ibid., 20.

71. Ian Hunter, "Literary Theory in Civil Life," *South Atlantic Quarterly* 95, no. 4 (fall 1996): 1099.

72. Thomas Strychaz, *Modernism, Mass Culture, and Professionalism* (Cambridge: Cambridge University Press, 1991), 24, 23.

73. Miles Myers, *Changing Our Minds: Negotiating English and Literacy* (Urbana, Ill.: National Council of Teachers of English, 1996), 80. Challenges to recitation literacy occurred first at the top of the educational hierarchy, and moved down from there, as "English and its collection of interests in English literature, language, and composition became a nationally recognized subject," certified as one of the primary subjects in secondary schools by the National Education Association's Committee of Ten. In 1892, the committee, under the leadership of Charles Eliot, defined the purpose of English as learning to express oneself clearly and learning to understand others, while placing "emphasis in secondary education on college preparation, not education for all students" (77).

74. Michael Halloran, "From Rhetoric to Composition: The Teaching of Writing in America to 1900," in *A Short History of Writing Instruction: From Ancient Greece to Twentieth-Century America,* ed. James J. Murphy (Davis, Calif.: Hermagoras Press, 1990), 153, 161, 163. Halloran suggests that one of the major consequences of the revolution in rhetoric that occurred in the late eighteenth century was a displacement of the rhetorical virtue of eloquence—a virtue of the person who invents a text, in speaking or writing—to a belletristic model of literary taste, a virtue associated with the capacity to read and appreciate texts. "Belletristic rhetoric thus set the stage for the elevation of interpretation and reading over invention and writing that would characterize the discipline of English studies" (163). Halloran understands the transformation of writing as a loss of "the larger purpose of social leadership through discourse that had been both central to and explicit in neo-classical rhetoric" (177).

75. Clifford Siskin, *Literature and Social Change in Britain, 1700–1830* (Baltimore: Johns Hopkins University Press, 1998), 6–7.

76. Arthur Appleby, *Tradition and Reform in the Teaching of English: A History* (Urbana, Ill.: National Council of Teachers of English, 1974), 30.

77. On the role of standardized tests in class formation, see Nicholas Lemann, *The Big Test: The Secret History of the American Meritocracy* (New York: Farrar, Straus, and Giroux, 1999).

78. Cited in Myers, *Changing Our Minds,* 85. On the origins and impact of educational systems, see Carl Kaestle and Maris A. Vinovskis, *Education and Social Change in Nineteenth-Century Massachusetts* (Cambridge: Cambridge University Press, 1980); Michael Katz, "The Origins of Public Education: A Reassessment," in *The Social History of American Education,* ed. B. Edward McClellan and William J. Reese (Urbana: University of Illinois Press, 1988). For an overview of educational history, see H. Warren Button and Eugene Provenzo, *History of Education and Culture in America* (Englewood Cliffs, N.J.: Prentice-Hall, 1989). Two collections that analyze the legacy and cultural politics of liberal education in the contemporary United States are: Darryl J. Gless and Barbara Herrnstein Smith, *The Politics of Liberal Education* (Durham, N.C.: Duke University Press, 1992), and Wlad Godsich, *The Culture of Literacy* (Cambridge: Harvard University Press, 1994). For a recent analysis of the place of the university, see Bill Readings, *The University in Ruins* (Cambridge: Harvard University Press, 1996).

79. Hill Diary, 5–6.

80. Hill Diary, 87. As Hill suggests a few pages later, it also requires one to privilege an ascetic solitude as morally superior (because more authentic and transparent) to all forms of sociability. "For the faithful and persevering student the freaks and frivolities of the gay and fashionable have but few charms. If but little trained in the habits and customs of such society he unavoidably commits some blunders and then being taken up and subjected to the railing criticism of those who have taken more pains to cultivate the graces of a genteel bow or scrape than any thing of an intellectual character, he becomes at once disgusted and as soon yields every claim to their attentions. By steps he departs from their society and becomes a being devoted to seclusion" (91).

Epilogue

1. "Dolor," copyright 1943 by Modern Poetry Association, Inc., from *The Collected Poems of Theodore Roethke.* Used by permission of Doubleday, a division of Random House.

2. Thomas Mellon, *Thomas Mellon and His Times,* ed. Marie Briscoe (Pittsburgh, Penn.: University of Pittsburgh Press, 1994), 32–33.

3. Max Weber, *The Protestant Ethic and the Spirit of Capitalism,* trans. Talcott Parsons (New York: Charles Scribner's Sons, 1958), 181, 182.

4. See Christine McDannell, *Material Christianity* (New Haven: Yale University Press, 1996).

5. For an excellent summary of these developments in Europe, see Peter Burke, *Popular Culture in Early Modern Europe* (New York: Oxford University Press, 1980).

6. See David Hollinger, "The Knower and the Artificer," *Modernist Impulses in the Human Sciences, 1870–1930,* ed. Dorothy Ross (Baltimore: Johns Hopkins University Press, 1994). On the rhetorical nature of disciplinary inquiry in the social sciences, see John S. Nelson, Alan McGill, Donald McCloskey, eds., *The Rhetoric of the Human Sciences: Language and Argument in Scholarship and Public Affairs* (Madison: University of Wisconsin Press, 1987).

7. Weber, *The Protestant Ethic,* 48. With the decline of religious instruction in the modern academy, contests for moral authority would be played out as questions of discipline and methodology in scholarly inquiry. See Julie Reuben, *The Making of the Modern University: Intellectual Transformation and the Marginalization of Morality* (Chicago: University of Chicago Press, 1996).

8. The words appear in a letter from Benjamin Vaughn in 1783, which Franklin published as part of his text. Benjamin Franklin, *The Autobiography* (New York: Library of America, 1990), 73.

9. Mellon, *Life and Times,* 5.

10. Letter from Victor Palsits, 30 January 1919, filed with Reminiscences of Edward Ayer's First Trip from Home in 1860 (Manuscript and Rare Book Division, New York Public Library). Evidently, Ayer did not think the librarian had properly recognized its worth, be-

cause he wrote again to Palsits: "I really wish that you would read it over carefully. It shows what a young man between the ages of 18 and 22 had to go through fifty to sixty years ago." See the letter from Ayer to Palsits, dated 3 February 1919, also filed with Reminiscences of Edward Ayer's First Trip from Home in 1860.

11. Caleb Wall, Diary, 1840 (American Antiquarian Society), 36, 37, 40.

12. Wall Diary, 1.

13. Jonathan Henry Hill, Diary, 18 September 1841 (American Antiquarian Society), 65.

14. Charles French, Diary, vol. 4 (Massachusetts Historical Society), 256.

15. Ibid., vol. 5, 162.

16. Proceedings of the Semi-Centennial Anniversary of the Connection of Caleb Arnold Wall (of the *Worcester Spy*) with the *Worcester Country Press,* May 18, 1887 (Worcester, Mass.: Daniel Seagrave, 1887), 6–7.

17. "Edward N. Tailer Dead," *New York Times,* 16 February 1917, 11. Also see *New York Times,* 6 March 1917, 11.

18. Entry for 7 March 1864, R. G. Dun Credit ledgers, New York City, vol. 316 (Cambridge, Mass.: Baker Library, Harvard Business School), 78.

19. Annie Patterson, "A Brief Sketch of the Life of Henry Patterson," 1939 (New-York Historical Society), 4.

20. R. G. Dun Credit Ledgers, New York City, vol. 13, 156.

21. Fred S. Piper, "Charles Edward French the Founder of the Scolarship Medals for Lexington Public Schools," 1908 (Massachusetts Historical Society).

Selected Bibliography

Manuscripts
American Antiquarian Society, Worcester, Massachusetts
   Amos Armsby Diary, 1853
   N. Beekley Diary, 1849
   Arthur Bennett Diary, 1844–1846
   Blackstone Literary Society, Papers, 1814–1916
   James B. Blake Diary, 1851
   George Watson Cole Papers, 1851–1939
   James Henry Cunningham Journal, 1849
   James F. Fiske Diaries, 1857–1860
   Hannah ("Anna") Gale Diary, Gale Family Papers, 1828–1854
   J.[onathan] Henry Hill Papers, 1841–1884
   Bradford Morse Letters, Morse Family Papers, ca. 1819–ca. 1886
   John Frederick Schroeder Diary, 1848–1851
   Caleb A. Wall Diary, 1840–1841, in Wall Family Papers, 1833–1899
   James L. Whittier Diary, 1830–1831
Baker Library, Harvard Business School
   R. G. Dun Credit Ledgers, New York City
Bancroft Library, University of California, Berkeley
   Edward B. Howe, Letters
Massachusetts Historical Society
   William G. Brooks Papers, 1838–1900
   Daniel F. Child Papers, 1829–1876
   Bradley N. Cumings Journal, 1828–1847
   Charles E. French Papers, 1837–1904
   Mercantile Elocution Class Records, 1835–1836
   "Phrenological Sketch of the Character of Mr. Cumings given by L. N. Fowler Dec 8th
      1838"
The New-York Historical Society
   William Hoffman Diary, 1847–1850
   Henry A. Patterson Diary, 1832–1848
   Edward Tailer Diary, 1850
New York Mercantile Library
   Benjamin Tilton Diary, 1841–1842
New York Public Library, Astor, Lennox, and Tilden Foundations
   Edward Everett Ayer, Autobiographical Narrative

"Diary kept by an unknown student 1833–1834," in Diaries, 1833–1834

Hunt Merriam & Co., Order Book with Memorandum, 1851

Charles E. Rogers Diary, 1864–1865

Joseph Downs Collection of Manuscripts and Printed Ephemera, Winterthur Library, Winterthur, Delaware

E. E. Belding Travel Diary, 1834

Nicholas Cheesbrough Diary, 1836–1838

Maria Fifield Diary, 1858–1862

Richard Hewlett Commonplace Book, 1767

George Jaques Diary, 1840–1851

William Kirkbride Diary, 1868–1869

Albert Lane Norris Journal, 1857–1862

Charles Stone, Tramp Diary, 1871

Hiram Taylor Diary and Account Book, 1828–1855

Enos White Diary and Account Book, 1821–1851

Primary Sources

Albee, John. *Remembrances of Emerson.* London: Gay & Bird, 1903.

Alcott, Amos Bronson. *Ralph Waldo Emerson: An Estimate of His Character and Genius, in Prose and Verse.* Boston: A. Williams and Company, 1882.

Alcott, William. *The Young Man's Guide,* 16th ed., revised and enlarged. Boston: T.R. Marvin, 1846 [1833].

American Phrenological Journal, 1840–1860.

Arthur, Timothy Shay. *Advice to Young Men on Their Duties and Conduct in Life.* Boston: Phillips, Sampson and Company, 1855 [1847].

———. *True Riches: or Wealth Without Wings.* Boston: L. P. Crown, 1852.

Bates, Jerome Paine. *The Imperial Highway; or, The Road to Fortune and Happiness, With Biographies of Self-Made Men, Their Business Traits, Qualities, and Habits.* Chicago: G.W. Borland, 1883.

Bellows, Henry W. "Edward Alford and His Playfellows." *Knickerbocker,* March 1842.

———. *The Ledger and the Lexicon: or, Business and Literature in Account with American Education.* Cambridge, Mass., 1853.

Boston Mercantile Library Association. *Annual Report.* 1830–1860.

Dana, Richard Henry. *Two Years Before the Mast: A Personal Narrative of Life at Sea.* New York: Macmillan, 1916 [1840].

Emerson, Ralph Waldo. *Essays and Lectures.* Boston: Houghton, Mifflin Co., 1870.

———. *Society and Solitude.* Boston, 1870.

———. *Lectures and Biographical Sketches* 10. Boston, 1883.

———. *Essays and Lectures.* New York: Viking Press, 1983.

Ferguson, Frank. *The Young Man.* Nashua, New Hampshire, 1848.

Fowler, Orson S. *Self-Culture, and Perfection of Character.* New York, 1856.

Franklin, Benjamin. *The Autobiography.* New York: Library of America, 1990.

Freedley, Edwin T. *A Practical Treatise on Business.* Philadelphia, 1852.

Gardiner, O. C. "Public Libraries of New York City," in *Public Libraries in the United States of America: Their History, Condition, and Management, Part I.* Special Report of the Department of the Interior, Bureau of Education. Washington, D.C., 1876.

Geist, Peter Von. "Imaginary Conversations." *Knickerbocker* 24, no. 6 (December 1843).

Ghourlie, John. *An Address, Delivered Before the Mercantile Library Association.* New York, 1839.

Grigg, John. *The American Chesterfield.* Philadelphia: Grigg and Elliot, 1833 [1828].

Hunt, Freeman. *Lives of American Merchants.* New York, 1858.

James, William. *Writings, 1878–1899.* New York: Library of America, 1992.

Jewett, Charles C. "Report of the Assistant Secretary, Relating to the Library," *Third Annual Report of the Smithsonian Institution.* Washington, D.C., 1849.

Konvitz, Milton, ed. *The Recognition of Ralph Waldo Emerson: Selected Criticism since 1837.* Ann Arbor: University of Michigan Press, 1972.

Locke, John. *An Essay Concerning Human Understanding.* Edited by Peter H. Nidditch. Oxford: Clarendon Press, 1975 [1690].

———. *Some Thoughts Concerning Education* and *Of the Conduct of the Understanding.* Edited by Ruth Grant and Nathan Tarcov. Indianapolis, Ind.: Hackett Publishing, 1996.

———. *A New Method of Making Common-Place Books.* London: Greenwood, 1706.

Lowell, James Russell. "Emerson the Lecturer." In *Books and Libraries.* Boston, 1888.

Mellon, Thomas. *Thomas Mellon and His Times.* Pittsburgh, Penn.: University of Pittsburgh Press, 1994.

Melville, Herman. *The Piazza Tales and Other Prose Pieces, 1839–1860.* Evanston, Ill.: Northwestern University Press; Chicago: Newberry Library, 1987.

Mercantile Library Association, Boston. *Mercantile Library Reporter,* 1854–1857.

"Mercantile Library." *New York Times.* 10 November 1870.

Mercantile Library Company of Philadelphia. *Constitution and Bylaws.* 1862.

———. Annual Reports, 1838–1870.

Mill, John Stuart. *On Liberty.* London: J. W. Parker, 1859.

Moore, Charles, ed. *George Washington's Rules of Civility and Decent Behaviour in Company and Conversation.* Boston: Houghton Mifflin Company, 1926.

New York Mercantile Library. *Address to the Clerks of the City of New York.* New York, 1858.

———. Annual Reports, 1820–1880.

———. *Constitution, By-Laws and Regulations.* New York, 1840.

"The New York Mercantile Library," *Scribner's Monthly* 1, no. 4 (February 1871).

Noyes, George. "Good Conversation and Prose Writing." *Mercantile Library Reporter* 2, no. 4 (1856): 69–70.

Perkins, F. B. "Mercantile Libraries," in *Public Libraries in the United States of America: Their History, Condition, and Management, Part I.* Special Report of the Department of the Interior, Bureau of Education. Washington, D.C., 1876.

Pomeroy, J. W. *The Young Merchant.* Boston, 1840.

Poole, F. W. "Hiawatha." *Mercantile Library Reporter* 2, no. 3 (1856): 47.

Saint Louis Mercantile Library Association. *Annual Report,* 1850–1865.

———. *A Guide to the Sculpture, Paintings, Coins and Other Objects of Art.* St. Louis, 1862.

Scott, William Anderson. "Some Hints on the Moral Influence of the Commercial Spirit of the Age." In *Trade and Letters: Their Journeyings Round the World.* New York, 1856.

Sparks, Jared. *The Life of George Washington.* Boston: F. Andrews, 1844 [1839].

Weber, Max. *The Protestant Ethic and the Spirit of Capitalism.* New York: Scribner, 1958 [1904].

Index

Academy of Fine Arts (New York), 89
accounting: diaries as, 49–55; double-entry bookkeeping, 49, 278n.82; in literary criticism, 245
accuracy, 49, 50, 221, 223
acquisition of wealth: character associated with, 7, 181; Emerson on, 124, 126, 127; European criticism of American obsession with, 182; as sport, 6; stereotype of the nouveau riche merchant, 93
adult education: at lectures, 5, 118; at mercantile libraries, 118, 187–88, 294n.76; at New York Mercantile Library, 5, 162–63, 166, 294n.76; useful knowledge sought in, 133; venues for, 5, 118
advertisements for jobs, 225
Advice to Young Men (Arthur), 53–54
Agnew, Jean-Christophe, 4
Albee, John, 289nn. 51, 59
Alcott, Bronson, 28, 68, 137–38, 289n.51
Alcott, Louisa May, 172
Alcott, William, 28, 57, 69, 93–94, 280n.13
Alger, Horatio, 5
alienation, 215–16, 217, 223, 227
almanacs, 49
American Chesterfield, The (Grigg), 57
American Notes (Dickens), 87, 89–90
American Phrenological Journal, 39, 153, 155, 277n.58
Amos Armsby's Pocket Diary, 275n.31
ancient languages, 35–38, 186, 276n.48
Anderson, Benedict, 160
animated conversation, 97–100
Anstince, Henry, 30
anthologies, 34
Appleby, Joyce, 7
Aristotle, 9, 25, 26, 34, 274n.14
Armstrong, Nancy, 71
Arthur, T. S., 53–54, 178, 183, 293n.57

aspiration: becoming equal to, 55–61; in diaries, 20
Astor, John Jacob, 181
Astor Library (New York), 158, 173, 192
Astor Place (New York): New York Mercantile Library relocates to, 158–60, 162, 193, 204, *205;* remains of, 264–65, *264, 265*
Atlantic Monthly, 234
Attewell, Paul, 299n.27
Augustine, St., 41
Autobiography (Franklin): on a book that would function like an almanac, 49–50; on "errata," 25, 261; list of virtues in, 43; Mellon on, 256–58, 259, 260, 267; on printing and character, 25; purpose of, 260; on self-creation, 10, 12; Weber on, 6, 258, 259, 267; on writing and advancement, 56–57, 279n.96
Ayer, Edward E., 105–6, 260, 284n.82, 303n.10

Baker, Mary, 108
Ballard, Martha, 22
bankruptcy, 59, 120
Barker-Benfield, G. J., 93
"Bartleby, the Scrivener": Bartleby's first refusal of a request, 236–37; Bartleby's placement in, 228–29, 241; blank wall in, 208, 298n.2; bust of Cicero in, 38, 236, 237, 240, 276n.51; good natural arrangement of office in, 226–28; Jonathan Hill compared with narrator of, 212, 214, 216, 217, 232, 234, 235, 240; hiring of Bartleby, 225; how to "fill pages" as primary theme of, 217; identifying Bartleby, 245; Irving as model for narrator in, 300n.45; in literary criticism, 242; mass audience sought for, 234–35; Miller's reading of, 242–48; monotony of clerical work

Rogers, Charles, 59, 60, 223–24
Romanticism: on authenticity, 247; "Bartleby, the Scrivener" and aesthetics of, 238, 240; and domestic intimacy, 65, 106, 111; and liberal Protestantism, 104; on privacy and solitude, 151, 230; self-expression in, 71, 136; on spiritual power of reading and writing, 65; and transformation of rhetoric, 249
Rosaldo, Michelle, 270n.14
rote memorization, 248
Rothman, Ellen, 106
Rotundo, Anthony, 178–79, 290n.9, 298n.5
Rousseau, Jean Jacques, 42, 68
Rowlandson, Mary, 42
Rush, Benjamin, 57

St. Louis Mercantile Library, 170, 291n.19, 292n.24, 294n.78
salary, 6, 52, 59
San Francisco Mercantile Library Association, 188
San Francisco Post Office, *77*
Say, J. B., 87
schools. *See* education
Scott, Donald, 129, 130, 286n.24
Scott, Walter, 202
Scott, William, 188
Scottish Enlightenment, 56
Scribner's Monthly (magazine), 167, *168, 169,* 172, 173, 198, *199*
Second Reform Bill (Britain), 28
self: classical philosophy as liberation of, 116; literature in fashioning sense of, 14; self-examination, 41–48, 51, 55; self-expression, 70–71, 110; self-interest, 224; self-organizing personality, 63, 65; self-reliance, 4, 17, 130, 257; technologies of, 33, 58, 118, 159, 185, 195. *See also* individualism; self-control; self-culture; self-realization
self-control: clerks needing, 120; conversation as bringing about, 103; formal education associated with, 185; in genteel character, 178; good penmanship acquired through, 8; as middle-class Protestant virtue, 4, 27; Washington on, 26
self-culture: Channing on duty to, 4; clerks pursuing, 39, 207; in mercantile libraries, 163; in middle-class hegemony, 6; as a product, 133
self-examination, 41–48, 51, 55
self-expression, 70–71, 110
self-improvement: American devotion to, 11; books for, 192; calendar for measuring, 51; conduct books on, 57; in leisure activity, 84; mercantile libraries for, 163; as moral obligation, 59; secular model of, 56; voluntary associations devoted to, 5; writing and, 56–57, 71

self-interest, 224
self-made man, 5, 7, 15, *64*
self-organizing personality, 63, 65
self-realization: aesthetic experience as means of, 247; American project of, 17; in Christian pastoral guidance, 27; in clerks' diaries, 22, 60; conduct books on, 57; liberal ideology on, 58; Mill on, 28; as psychological rather than social, 112; and self-expression, 71; sentimental domesticity as, 111
self-reliance, 4, 17, 130, 257
"Self-Reliance" (Emerson), 17, 121, 147
Seneca, 34
Sennett, Richard, 112, 272n.26
sensibility, culture of, 93
separate spheres, 3, 66, 73, 79, 106
sermons, 81, 85, 86, 118, 135
Sewall, Samuel, 42
Shera, Jesse, 291n.15
Shields, David, 271n.17
shorthand, 220
shrewdness, 124–25, 126, 143, 147
silent reading: as academic paradigm of literary value, 81–82, 145; comprehension versus quick appraisal of, 92; conversation as more natural than, 99; as discipline of bourgeois subjectivity, 71; eloquence contrasted with, 119; Emerson's lectures contrasted with, 133, 134, 138; mass print culture and, 242; moral authority and, 248, 250; moral education affected by, 218; practice of character affected by, 216–17, 218; as self-conscious, 151; sites of training in, 130
Silliman, Benjamin, 135
Siskin, Clifford, 250
"Sketchbook, The" (Irving), 300n.45
"sketches," 250
Smiles, Samuel, 15
Smithsonian Institution Library, 191, 192
socialization: conversation as socializing men into intimacy, 102–4; disciplinary intimacy, 71; in domestic intimacy, 65; gendered socialization in morality, 92; into literacy, 79–93; mercantile libraries socializing young men, 163, 179
social libraries, 165, 715
social realists, 232
social status: character associated with pursuit of, 7; classical curriculum imparting, 37; education conferring, 13; middle class young men competing for, 5. *See also* class
Society and Solitude (Emerson), 143
solitary reading. *See* silent reading
Some Thoughts Concerning Education (Locke), 26
Sparks, Jared, 26
speaking: Golden Age of Oratory, 134; modern critics seeing as inferior to writing,

melancholy of, 207–54; predictability and coordination in, 226; rationalization of, 223–24; specialization of, 14, 219. *See also* businessmen

Whitman, Walt, 87, 144, 155

Whittier, James, 40

Whyte, William, 215

Wilcox, G., 260

Willis, N. P., 91

Winthrop, John, 42

wisdom, 117, 149

women: conversation of, 100–102; feminization of clerical work, 220, *221,* 299n.33; gendered socialization in morality, 92; middle-class aspirations becoming charge of, 113; as New York Mercantile Library attendants, 162, 290n.8; as New York Mercantile Library members, 113, 161, 173, 203, 292n.37; novels by, 203, 297n.125. *See also* mothers

women's clubs, 113

women's colleges, 276n.48

work: character associated with, 270n.9; independence as bound up with, 209; independence from wage system sought, 6; moral authority as located apart from place of adult, 249, 252; overwork, 209. *See also* white-collar work

Works and Days (Hesiod), 144

writing: changing status in nineteenth century, 219–20; complex subjectivity acquired by,

12, 59–60; composition, 68, 74, 251; compositions, 72, 249, 251; compulsory education in, 5; conversation contrasted with, 100; for declaring independence, 7–8, 9, 12; devotional, 27, 45–47; diversification and specialization in, 234; improvements in implements of, 66, 68; as initiation into manhood, 7–10, 12; intellectual authority attributed to, 137; as male virtue in humanist tradition, 35; in moral education, 35; moral responsibility associated with, 21–22; new centrality of, 30–31; pen and paper as tools of advancement, 10; and power to control one's identity, 26; professional authorship, 232–54; as self-expression, 70–71; and self-improvement, 56–57, 71; sites of learning of, 32; in spiritual development, 42; taught in common schools, 32; as technical skill, 32; as technology of self, 33. *See also* diaries; letters; literature; penmanship

Young Man, The (Ferguson), 57, 279n.100

Young Man's Guide, The (Alcott), 28, 57, 69, 93–94, 280n.13

Zboray, Mary, 81, 281n.25

Zboray, Ronald J., 81, 281n.25, 297n.123

Ziff, Larzer, 32

Zola, Emile, 232